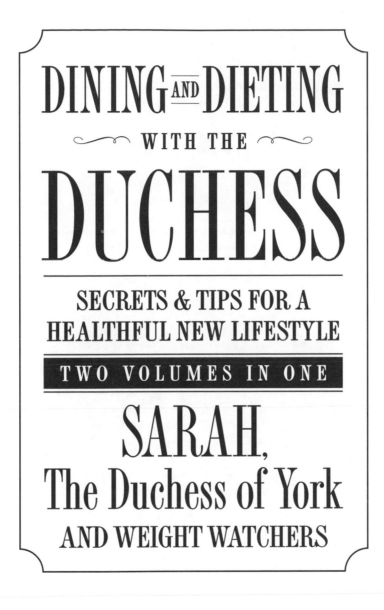

DINING AND DIETING
WITH THE
DUCHESS

SECRETS & TIPS FOR A HEALTHFUL NEW LIFESTYLE

TWO VOLUMES IN ONE

SARAH,
The Duchess of York
AND WEIGHT WATCHERS

BARNES
& NOBLE
BOOKS
NEW YORK

Dining with The Duchess

Also by Sarah, The Duchess of York

What I Know Now: Simple Lessons Learned the Hard Way

Energy Breakthrough: Jump-start Your Weight Loss and Feel Great

Reinventing Yourself with The Duchess of York:
Inspiring Stories and Strategies for Changing Your Weight and Your Life

Win the Weight Game: Successful Strategies for Living Well

Dieting with The Duchess: Secrets and Sensible Advice for a Great Body

Dining with The Duchess: Making Everyday Meals a Special Occasion

My Story

The Palace of Westminster

Victoria and Albert: Life at Osborne House

Travels with Queen Victoria

Also by Weight Watchers

Weight Watchers Greatest Hits

Weight Watchers Cook It Quick

Weight Watchers Take-Out Tonight

Weight Watchers Simply Delicious

Great Cooking Every Day

New Complete Cookbook

Simply the Best Italian

Simply the Best: 250 Prizewinning Family Recipes

Stop Stuffing Yourself: 7 Steps to Conquering Overeating

The Fit Factor

. . . and many more

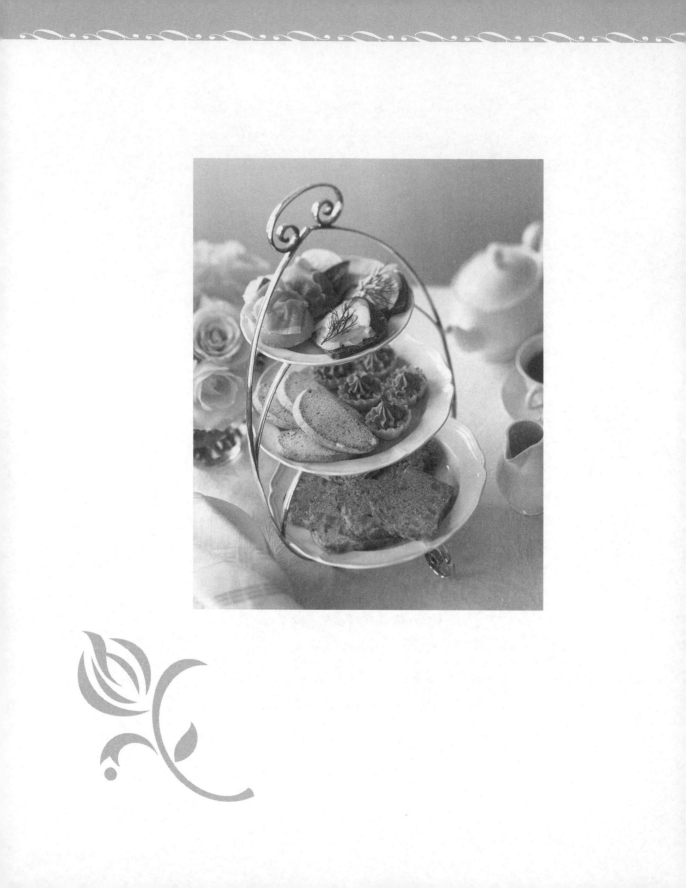

Dining with The Duchess

MAKING EVERYDAY MEALS
A SPECIAL OCCASION

◆

Sarah, The Duchess of York
and
Weight Watchers

Weight Watchers Publishing Group
Editorial Director: Nancy Gagliardi
Senior Editor: Martha Schueneman
Associate Editor: Christine Senft, M.S.
Recipe Developers: Regina Ragone, M.S., R.D., Maureen Luchejko,
Barry Bluestein, and Kevin Morrissey
Nutrition Consultant: Mindy Hermann, M.B.A., R.D.
Photographer: Rita Maas
Food Stylist: Mariann Sauvion
Prop Stylist: Valorie Fisher

Contents

Contents
9

Recipes not included.

Contents
11

Introduction

By now, the world over has heard my story: When it was first announced that I would be marrying Prince Andrew, the British press greeted me with open arms, calling me "Great Fun Fergie, a breath of fresh air." Yet the moment I began gaining weight, that very same press turned on me, calling me "Fat Fergie" which gave way to "Fat and Appalling Fergie" and ultimately, "The Duchess of Pork."

While I can laugh at those names today, it is no surprise that at the time I felt humiliated, alone, defeated. When my life was out of control, so was my weight. At times, I felt as if I was on a downward spiral, spinning faster and faster.

I have since learned that those dismal feelings I had were not unlike the emotions experienced by almost everyone who has done battle with his or her weight. Losing weight and trying to maintain a fit body and healthy lifestyle truly is one of life's great challenges. Yet I have also learned that rock bottom can be a powerful place from where to restart one's life. There's no place to go but up.

In the past year, I have learned a tremendous amount about eating the right foods, exercising and banishing bad habits. I have learned these lessons from women who have refused to become victims: my old friends, my new friends at Weight Watchers, and health and fitness experts I have met in my travels. Happily, I can call on these people when I need them most. They are my support network.

At the first thought of doing a cookbook, I was skeptical, to say the least. First of all, I very rarely cook, given my hectic schedule. When I was a single working girl living in London, I tended to live on student staples like baked beans on toast or whatever I could find in the fridge. Once I was married, I was unable to cook for myself and my husband because our apartment at Buckingham Palace did not have a kitchen.

Today, I am lucky enough to employ a cook who knows my likes and dislikes. Yet, in the past year, I have given her a whole new list of favorite foods because my tastes and habits have changed.

Now, instead of simply giving in to my penchant for sausage rolls and mayonnaise, I seek out food that is good for my body. My cook and I discuss menus together, and then she creates in the kitchen. Given my mad travel schedule, I need to know that there is somewhere, a home base, where I can go and refuel my body as well as my soul.

This collection of delicious and healthy recipes masterfully blends the tastes of the old Sarah with the knowledge of the new Sarah. I have based the menus on favorite dishes from my childhood, my travels and some memorable meals I have shared with my family and friends.

Nowadays, food is not the enemy. I am not fearful of every forkful. Rather, I now use food as a way to control my life. I recognize that fresh, wholesome foods will keep me steady and energized. I still enjoy my ham sandwiches, but now I know I can have a little and still maintain control.

I know now that if I can control my weight and food intake, it changes my mood for the day.

It is comforting to know that you can rearrange your thinking and readjust your habits, that you can change. I am happy to say that I have changed. Rock bottom seems like a long time ago. Nowadays, I rather like the view from up here.

SARAH, THE DUCHESS OF YORK

A Weekend Lunch with Friends

Perhaps one of the greatest challenges I have encountered while trying to lose weight and start a healthier lifestyle is to change my old habits. In the past, when things were going badly or I hit a rough patch, my natural inclination was to eat. My weaknesses are French breads with butter, croissants, sausage rolls (sausages wrapped in buttery puff pastry) and egg and mayonnaise sandwiches, which I think are just delicious. These foods are still my triggers, but I have worked hard at trying to keep my food goblins at bay. I've also worked hard at changing the habits I've developed over a lifetime, and I know how truly difficult that can be. But the results are well worth the sacrifice. Now I am learning that I can be around food and not feel literally consumed by it.

Serves 4

Classic Bloody Marys

Genoa Canapés

Classic Vegetable Frittata

Baked Chicken with Wine

Light Cheese Popovers

Ginger Pears

Mulled Peaches

Classic Bloody Marys

Makes 4 servings

One 32-ounce bottle (4 cups) tomato juice

1 cup vodka

¼ cup fresh lemon juice

2 teaspoons Worcestershire sauce

2 teaspoons prepared horseradish

½ teaspoon celery salt

½ teaspoon hot red pepper sauce

Freshly ground pepper, to taste

4 celery stalks, with leaves

In a large pitcher, mix the tomato juice, vodka, lemon juice, Worcestershire sauce, horseradish, celery salt, pepper sauce and ground pepper. Pour into tall glasses over ice; garnish with the celery stalks.

Per serving: 186 CALORIES, 1 G TOTAL FAT, 0 G SATURATED FAT, 1 MG CHOLESTEROL, 1,188 MG SODIUM, 13 G TOTAL CARBOHYDRATE, 2 G DIETARY FIBER, 2 G PROTEIN, 42 MG CALCIUM.

POINTS PER SERVING: 3

Tip

To make a Classic Virgin Mary, omit the vodka; you'll save almost 130 calories and 2 **POINTS**. If you're concerned about your salt intake, use low-sodium tomato juice.

Genoa Canapés

Makes 4 servings

12 slices light rye cocktail bread (3″ squares), halved diagonally
1 tablespoon Dijon mustard
6 paper-thin slices Genoa salami, cut in half

Spread the bread with the mustard. Fold a piece of salami over the bread.

Per serving: 112 CALORIES, 6 G TOTAL FAT, 2 G SATURATED FAT, 13 MG CHOLESTEROL,
381 MG SODIUM, 12 G TOTAL CARBOHYDRATE, 0 G DIETARY FIBER, 5 G PROTEIN,
27 MG CALCIUM.

POINTS PER SERVING: 3

Tip

For a change of pace, try smoked trout or salmon instead of the salami; use prepared horseradish or dill butter in place of the mustard.

Classic Vegetable Frittata

Makes 4 servings

4 eggs

1 cup fat-free egg substitute

½ teaspoon salt

¼ teaspoon freshly ground pepper

¼ teaspoon dried oregano, crumbled

1 teaspoon olive oil

2 onions, chopped

1 red bell pepper, seeded and chopped

1 cup sliced mushrooms

Half 10-ounce bag triple-washed spinach,
rinsed (do not dry) and chopped

1. In a medium bowl, lightly beat the eggs; whisk in the egg substitute, salt, pepper and oregano.
2. In a medium nonstick skillet, heat the oil. Sauté the onions, bell pepper and mushrooms until the onions are golden brown, about 8 minutes. Reduce the heat to low; add the spinach and cook, stirring frequently, until it wilts, about 4 minutes. Stir in the egg mixture; cook, covered, until the eggs are set, 10–13 minutes. Invert the frittata onto a plate and cut into quarters. Serve hot or at room temperature.

Per serving: 164 CALORIES, 7 G TOTAL FAT, 2 G SATURATED FAT, 212 MG CHOLESTEROL, 462 MG SODIUM, 12 G TOTAL CARBOHYDRATE, 3 G DIETARY FIBER, 15 G PROTEIN, 102 MG CALCIUM.

POINTS PER SERVING: 3

Tip

To get that wonderful brown top, preheat the broiler when you add the eggs to the vegetables; cook the frittata on the stove 9–10 minutes, then uncover the skillet and run under the broiler for a minute or so. If your skillet doesn't have an ovenproof handle, wrap the handle in a few layers of foil.

Baked Chicken with Wine

Makes 4 servings

2 tablespoons fresh lemon juice
1 teaspoon minced thyme
½ teaspoon minced rosemary
½ teaspoon salt
½ teaspoon coarsely ground pepper
Four 4-ounce skinless boneless chicken breasts
½ cup dry white wine

1. Preheat the oven to 425° F; spray a 7 x 11" baking dish with nonstick cooking spray. In a small bowl, mix the lemon juice, thyme, rosemary, salt and pepper.
2. Rub the lemon mixture onto each breast. Place the chicken in the baking dish; pour in the wine. Bake, basting occasionally with the pan juices, until browned and cooked through, about 20 minutes. Serve, drizzled with any pan juices.

Per serving: 147 CALORIES, 3 G TOTAL FAT, 1 G SATURATED FAT, 72 MG CHOLESTEROL, 313 MG SODIUM, 2 G TOTAL CARBOHYDRATE, 0 G DIETARY FIBER, 26 G PROTEIN, 20 MG CALCIUM.

POINTS PER SERVING: 3

Tip

Speedy and simple, this family favorite is delicious teamed with Parsley Rice (page 49). Serve with a light Chardonnay or Sauvignon Blanc.

Light Cheese Popovers

Makes 4 servings

⅔ cup skim milk

½ cup + 2 tablespoons all-purpose flour

2 teaspoons olive oil

¼ teaspoon salt

¼ teaspoon freshly ground pepper

Pinch cayenne pepper

2 eggs, beaten

⅓ cup shredded extra-sharp cheddar cheese

2 tablespoons grated Parmesan cheese

1. Preheat the oven to 450° F; spray a shiny aluminum 12-cup muffin tin with nonstick cooking spray.
2. In a medium bowl, whisk the milk, flour, oil, salt, pepper and cayenne; whisk in the eggs.
3. Spoon about 1 tablespoon of batter into each muffin cup; sprinkle with the cheddar and Parmesan, then top with the remaining batter. Bake 15 minutes; reduce the oven temperature to 350° F and bake until the tops of the popovers are golden brown, about 15 minutes longer. Serve warm.

Per serving: 203 CALORIES, 10 G TOTAL FAT, 4 G SATURATED FAT, 120 MG CHOLESTEROL, 301 MG SODIUM, 18 G TOTAL CARBOHYDRATE, 1 G DIETARY FIBER, 10 G PROTEIN, 179 MG CALCIUM.

POINTS PER SERVING: 5

Tip

Be sure to use a shiny muffin tin, since a dark tin may cause the popovers to burn. Be liberal with the cayenne if you prefer spicy foods.

Ginger Pears

Makes 4 servings

4 pears, cored and halved
1 tablespoon minced crystallized ginger
1 tablespoon ginger marmalade

Cut a thin slice from the skin side of the pears so they lie flat; place in a shallow 1-quart microwavable dish. Fill the cavities of the pears with the ginger and marmalade; sprinkle with 2 tablespoons water. Cover the dish with wax paper and microwave on High 3 minutes, then baste the pears with the pan juices; microwave on High until tender, 1 minute longer. Serve, drizzled with the pan juices.

Per serving: 118 Calories, 1 g Total Fat, 0 g Saturated Fat, 0 mg Cholesterol, 5 mg Sodium, 30 g Total Carbohydrate, 4 g Dietary Fiber, 1 g Protein, 28 mg Calcium.

POINTS PER SERVING: 2

Tip

Ginger marmalade imparts a tangy, sophisticated flavor. It is available in most specialty shops and better supermarkets.

Mulled Peaches

Makes 4 servings

2 cups fruity red wine
¼ cup sugar
1 cinnamon stick, cracked
1 teaspoon allspice berries
3–4 whole cloves
4 peaches, halved and pitted
1 orange, sliced

1. In a medium saucepan, combine the wine, sugar, cinnamon, allspice and cloves, stirring until the sugar dissolves; bring to a boil. Reduce the heat and add the peaches and orange; simmer, spooning the cooking liquid over the fruit, until tender, 15–20 minutes.
2. Transfer the fruit to dessert bowls; discard the spices. Pour the mulled wine over the fruit.

Per serving: 186 Calories, 0 g Total Fat, 0 g Saturated Fat, 0 mg Cholesterol, 6 mg Sodium, 28 g Total Carbohydrate, 3 g Dietary Fiber, 1 g Protein, 27 mg Calcium.

POINTS PER SERVING: 3

Tip

Merlot, Gamay Beaujolais or Sauternes (if you prefer white wine) would be a good choice in wine. Nectarines or fresh plums can be used in place of the peaches. If you like, spoon on a dollop of nonfat whipped dairy topping.

Writer's Respite

From an early age, I have always enjoyed reading—poetry and prose—and writing. The latter is one medium where I can channel my thoughts and imagination. I love creating with words on a page; then, of course, I have a sense of achievement when a book has come off press.

When I was single, I worked in publishing. Once I was married, it seemed only natural that I gravitate back to writing: The first work I assembled was *The Palace of Westminster*, a coffee-table book on the history of this great palace, with lots of up-to-date photographs. Then I cowrote *Victoria and Albert: Life at Osborne House*, a book filled with wonderful photographs that showcased the royal couple's life. The following book, *Travels with Queen Victoria*, was a high point in my publishing career; it truly was a labor of love as I retraced the Queen's travels at the end of the nineteenth century. I tried to recapture the sights and sounds she experienced so the reader could as well.

Today, writing is something I love. It's hard work and hardly for the meek. But I always discover something new about myself when I'm working on a new project.

Serves 4

Ginger-Carrot Soup

Spinach Salad with Tangy Orange Dressing

Crusty Bread*

Vanilla-Poached Fruit

Pot of Tea*

Ginger-Carrot Soup

Makes 4 servings

3 carrots, scrubbed and thinly sliced
2 cups chicken broth
2 teaspoons minced peeled gingerroot
2 garlic cloves, minced
¼ teaspoon freshly ground pepper
¼ teaspoon ground allspice
1 cup low-fat (1%) milk

In a large saucepan or Dutch oven, combine the carrots, broth, gingerroot, garlic, pepper and allspice; bring to a boil. Reduce the heat and simmer until the carrots are tender, about 10 minutes. Transfer to a blender; add the milk and puree. Return to the saucepan and cook, stirring, until heated through, 2–3 minutes; do not let the soup boil.

Per serving: 69 Calories, 2 g Total Fat, 1 g Saturated Fat, 12 mg Cholesterol, 545 mg Sodium, 10 g Total Carbohydrate, 2 g Dietary Fiber, 4 g Protein, 94 mg Calcium.

POINTS PER SERVING: 1

Tip

Be careful peeling gingerroot—its knobs are prime slipping areas for knives and vegetable peelers.

Spinach Salad
with Tangy Orange Dressing

Makes 4 servings

2 tablespoons orange juice

4 teaspoons balsamic vinegar

1 tablespoon sugar

1 tablespoon olive oil

¼ teaspoon salt

¼ teaspoon freshly ground pepper

One 10-ounce bag triple-washed spinach, rinsed and
torn into bite-size pieces

2 cups sliced mushrooms

3 slices bacon, crisp-cooked and crumbled

1 red onion, thinly sliced

1. In a small bowl, whisk the orange juice, vinegar, sugar, oil, salt and pepper.
2. In a large salad bowl, mix the spinach, mushrooms, bacon and onion. Drizzle
   with the dressing; toss to coat.

Per serving: 114 Calories, 6 g Total Fat, 1 g Saturated Fat, 4 mg Cholesterol,
269 mg Sodium, 12 g Total Carbohydrate, 3 g Dietary Fiber, 5 g Protein,
82 mg Calcium.

POINTS PER SERVING: 2

Tip

For tangy lemon or lime dressing, substitute lemon or lime juice for the o.j.
and cut the vinegar to 2 teaspoons; add more vinegar to taste.

Vanilla-Poached Fruit

Makes 4 servings

1 lemon
¼ cup sugar
One 2″ length vanilla bean, split
2 pears, peeled, cored and cut into wedges
2 Granny Smith apples, peeled, cored and cut into wedges
¼ cup dried cranberries or raisins

1. With a zester or vegetable peeler, remove the zest from the lemon in long strips; place in a medium saucepan. Squeeze the lemon juice into the saucepan. Add the sugar, vanilla bean and 1 cup water, stirring until the sugar dissolves; bring to a boil. Reduce the heat and simmer 5 minutes.
2. Add the pears, apples and cranberries to the poaching liquid; simmer, spooning the poaching liquid over the fruit, until tender, about 10 minutes longer.
3. With a slotted spoon, transfer the fruit to a medium bowl; discard the vanilla bean. Simmer the liquid, stirring occasionally, until thick and syrupy, about 5 minutes; pour over the fruit.

Per serving: 140 CALORIES, 0 G TOTAL FAT, 0 G SATURATED FAT, 0 MG CHOLESTEROL, 3 MG SODIUM, 37 G TOTAL CARBOHYDRATE, 3 G DIETARY FIBER, 1 G PROTEIN, 12 MG CALCIUM.

POINTS PER SERVING: 2

Tip

This is every bit as delicious cold. Refrigerate any leftovers to enjoy for breakfast with vanilla nonfat yogurt.

A Highlands Picnic

When things get particularly trying or my schedule is hectic (which is always!), I would eat to soothe my frazzled soul but seldom to satisfy my hunger. To offset this, I have found what I call my "tonics." My children, obviously, are my number one tonic. Spending time with them always helps me put things in perspective. Skiing and riding are tonics for my body; painting and writing, tonics for my soul.

Nature also is a tonic, particularly the mountains. Balmoral, the castle in the Scottish Highlands which is the Royal Family's summer home, was the perfect retreat. I will always treasure the time I spent there, walking in the rolling hills or sitting on the banks of the River Dee. The Highlands are an idyllic sanctuary. I love immersing myself in the total sense of isolation. Moving the body and the mind, I have found, are critical for happiness, as well as good health. My trainer and friend Josh Saltzman has been a great encouragement and has reiterated my theory, "Free your mind, and the weight will follow."

Serves 4

Easy Cream of Tomato Soup

Mediterranean Tuna Salad

Mesquite Chicken Salad

Honey-Orange Biscotti

Fuji and Granny Smith Apples*

Easy Cream of Tomato Soup

Makes 4 servings

2 cups skim milk

1 tablespoon all-purpose flour

¾ teaspoon salt

4 tomatoes, coarsely chopped

¼ onion, coarsely chopped

1 tablespoon coarsely chopped parsley

1 teaspoon sugar

¼ teaspoon freshly ground pepper

2 teaspoons Worcestershire sauce (optional)

1. In a medium saucepan over low heat, combine the milk, flour and ½ teaspoon of the salt; cook, stirring almost constantly, until thickened, about 5 minutes.

2. Meanwhile, in a blender or food processor, combine the tomatoes, onion, parsley, sugar, pepper, Worcestershire sauce (if using) and the remaining ¼ teaspoon of salt; puree. Place a large sieve over the saucepan; slowly pour the pureed tomatoes into the milk mixture, pressing with a wooden spoon. Cook, stirring constantly, until heated through, 2–3 minutes; do not let the soup boil.

Per serving: 83 Calories, 1 g Total Fat, 0 g Saturated Fat, 2 mg Cholesterol, 475 mg Sodium, 15 g Total Carbohydrate, 2 g Dietary Fiber, 6 g Protein, 164 mg Calcium.

POINTS PER SERVING: 1

Tip

For a main-dish soup, toss in some diced ham; serve with Spicy Polenta (page 56) or Herbed Parmesan Biscuits (page 181) on the side. Pressing the tomatoes through a sieve strains the peels and seeds, yielding a smooth, creamy texture.

Mediterranean Tuna Salad

Makes 4 servings

1 cup orzo

Two 6-ounce cans solid white water-packed tuna,
drained and flaked

1 celery stalk, minced

¼ cup minced flat-leaf parsley

3 scallions, sliced

2 tablespoons fresh lemon juice

¼ teaspoon salt

¼ teaspoon coarsely ground pepper

8 green-leaf lettuce leaves

1. Cook the orzo according to package directions; drain and place in a serving bowl. Stir in the tuna, celery, parsley, scallions, lemon juice, salt and pepper. Refrigerate, covered, until the flavors are blended, at least 2 hours.
2. Divide the lettuce among 4 salad plates; top with the salad.

Per serving: 316 CALORIES, 2 G TOTAL FAT, 0 G SATURATED FAT, 26 MG CHOLESTEROL, 436 MG SODIUM, 44 G TOTAL CARBOHYDRATE, 2 G DIETARY FIBER, 29 G PROTEIN, 34 MG CALCIUM.

POINTS PER SERVING: 6

Tip

If you like, serve this classic summertime salad in the classic warm-weather way: stuffed into scooped-out tomatoes.

Mesquite Chicken Salad

Makes 4 servings

2 tablespoons fresh lemon juice

1 tablespoon olive oil

¼ teaspoon freshly ground pepper

¼ teaspoon mustard powder

Pinch salt

One 8-ounce package skinless mesquite-flavored cooked
chicken breasts, diced

12 cherry tomatoes, halved

1 yellow bell pepper, seeded and diced

1 red onion, diced

8 radicchio leaves

1. In a small bowl, whisk the lemon juice, oil, pepper, mustard powder and salt.
2. In a large bowl, mix the chicken, tomatoes, bell pepper and onion. Drizzle with the dressing; toss to coat. Refrigerate, covered, until the flavors are blended, at least 2 hours.
3. Divide the radicchio among 4 salad plates; top with the salad.

Per serving: 129 CALORIES, 4 G TOTAL FAT, 1 G SATURATED FAT, 25 MG CHOLESTEROL, 241 MG SODIUM, 12 G TOTAL CARBOHYDRATE, 2 G DIETARY FIBER, 13 G PROTEIN, 23 MG CALCIUM.

POINTS PER SERVING: 3

Tip

If your supermarket's refrigerator poultry case doesn't have mesquite-flavor chicken breasts, check the deli counter for mesquite-smoked turkey breast. If you run out of luck in both places, stir in ½–1 teaspoon mesquite-flavored liquid smoke with the other dressing ingredients.

Honey-Orange Biscotti

Makes 42 servings

3 cups all-purpose flour

1 tablespoon cinnamon

1 teaspoon baking soda

¾ teaspoon baking powder

½ teaspoon ground allspice

¼ teaspoon salt

½ cup golden raisins

½ cup finely chopped dried apricots

2 teaspoons grated orange zest

½ cup sugar

½ cup honey

2 egg whites

1 egg

1. Adjust the racks to divide the oven into thirds. Preheat the oven to 325° F; spray 2 large nonstick baking sheets with nonstick cooking spray.
2. In a large bowl, combine the flour, cinnamon, baking soda, baking powder, allspice and salt; stir in the raisins, apricots and orange zest. In a medium bowl, whisk the sugar, honey, egg whites, egg and 2 tablespoons water. Add to the dry ingredients, stirring until combined.
3. On a lightly floured surface, divide the dough into fourths and form each into a 15" log. Place 2 logs on each baking sheet, with space in between. Bake, reversing the baking sheets once, until golden brown and firm to the touch, about 25 minutes. Reduce the oven temperature to 250° F.
4. While the logs are hot, transfer to a cutting board. With a serrated knife, cut on the diagonal into ⅜" slices, making 84 biscotti. Place the slices upright on the baking sheets, 1" apart. Bake the biscotti until the cut sides feel just dry to

the touch, 15–20 minutes (the biscotti will crisp and dry completely upon cooling). Cool completely on wire racks. Store in an airtight container.

Per serving: 70 CALORIES, 0 G TOTAL FAT, 0 G SATURATED FAT, 5 MG CHOLESTEROL, 57 MG SODIUM, 16 G TOTAL CARBOHYDRATE , 1 G DIETARY FIBER, 1 G PROTEIN, 15 MG CALCIUM.

POINTS PER SERVING: 1

--- *Tip* ---

Most ovens have "hot spots," so it's important to reverse the baking sheets so that the biscotti cook evenly. Give each sheet a half-turn, and switch them top-to-bottom as well.

After-Workout Reviver

I won't lie and tell you I am mad about exercise. While I do enjoy activities like riding and skiing, working out at the local gym can be, at times, impossible. But over the years, I have learned that my body needs to move about. Fit body, fit mind is how I see it.

I now know what works for me. For instance, I know that exercising first thing in the morning invigorates me and sets me straight for the day ahead.

When I am home, I work out at least three times a week with my personal trainer, Josh, at a health club. If I am going out to dinner in the evening or want to allow myself a pudding or treat, I often spend an extra 30 minutes on the exercise bike. When I am away on business trips, I rarely have a moment to exercise—a fact I am fully aware of. When I can, I do climb the steps (it drives my security men mad!) or step up on a piece of furniture (a footstool does the trick) in my hotel room so I can keep on working.

Serves 4

Red Snapper Primavera

Lemon Capellini

Fresh Mesclun* with Basic Vinaigrette

Red Snapper Primavera

Makes 4 servings

Four 6-ounce red snapper fillets
½ teaspoon salt
¼ teaspoon freshly ground pepper
1 red bell pepper, seeded and thinly sliced
1 medium yellow squash, julienned
½ small leek, cleaned and julienned
1 carrot, julienned
¼ cup dry white wine
4 teaspoons fresh lemon juice

1. Preheat the oven to 425° F; lightly spray four 12 x 18″ sheets of foil with non-stick cooking spray. Place a fillet in the center of each sheet; season with the salt and pepper. Top with the vegetables; sprinkle with the wine and lemon juice. Make packets by bringing the sides of the foil up to meet in the center and folding over the edges, then folding the edges of the ends together. Allowing room for the packets to expand, crimp the edges together.

2. Bake the packets until the fish is opaque, about 10 minutes; open the packets carefully when testing for doneness, as steam will escape. Serve, drizzled with any juices that collect in the packets.

Per serving: 189 CALORIES, 3 G TOTAL FAT, 0 G SATURATED FAT, 52 MG CHOLESTEROL, 378 MG SODIUM, 7 G TOTAL CARBOHYDRATE, 2 G DIETARY FIBER, 30 G PROTEIN, 76 MG CALCIUM.

POINTS PER SERVING: 4

Tip

Use this technique, known as *en papillote*, with different ingredients—try salmon instead of the snapper, or snow peas instead of the peppers.

Lemon Capellini

Makes 4 servings

6 ounces capellini
2 teaspoons olive oil
1–2 garlic cloves, minced
¼ cup minced parsley
2 tablespoons fresh lemon juice
¼ teaspoon salt
Freshly ground pepper, to taste

1. Cook the capellini according to package directions; drain.
2. Meanwhile, in a large nonstick skillet over medium-low heat, heat the oil. Sauté the garlic until it turns a rich, nutty brown, 2–3 minutes (take care to keep the heat fairly low so the garlic doesn't scorch). Add the capellini, parsley, lemon juice and salt; toss to coat. Serve, sprinkled with the pepper.

Per serving: 183 CALORIES, 3 G TOTAL FAT, 0 G SATURATED FAT, 0 MG CHOLESTEROL, 140 MG SODIUM, 33 G TOTAL CARBOHYDRATE, 1 G DIETARY FIBER, 6 G PROTEIN, 16 MG CALCIUM.

POINTS PER SERVING: 4

Tip

Fine angel-hair pasta complements the delicate lemon flavor of this dish. If you're looking for an extra kick, sprinkle on a few chopped anchovies (a little-known source of heart-healthy Omega-3 fatty acids) before serving.

Basic Vinaigrette

Makes 6 servings

2 tablespoons extra virgin olive oil
2 tablespoons red-wine vinegar
2 teaspoons balsamic vinegar
½ teaspoon Dijon mustard
Pinch salt

In a small bowl, whisk all the ingredients with 1 tablespoon water.

Per serving: 42 Calories, 5 g Total Fat, 1 g Saturated Fat, 0 mg Cholesterol, 24 mg Sodium, 1 g Total Carbohydrate, 0 g Dietary Fiber, 0 g Protein, 1 mg Calcium.

POINTS PER SERVING: 1

Tip

This dressing keeps in the refrigerator for about a week. If you'll be serving it right away, mix it in the salad bowl and add the greens to it; if you'll be keeping it awhile, shake it in a small jar.

Quick and Easy Family Dinner

I write a syndicated column that appears in newspapers across the country. Each week, I write about the subjects that are closest to my heart: children and helping the less fortunate children round the world, my travels and the challenges I face living the life of a working mother while trying to stay healthy.

Even though things often feel quite hectic, now that I am at a healthy weight, I've found that I am becoming more confident. The more I can control my weight, the more I can control my life and the more I can get out there with confidence and do what needs to be done.

Serves 4

Steak Frites

Corn Salsa

Cucumber Relish

Minted Zucchini

Frozen Yogurt Sundaes

Steak Frites

Makes 4 servings

2 large baking potatoes, scrubbed and cut into ¼″ sticks

2 egg whites

½ teaspoon salt

½ teaspoon freshly ground pepper

3 shallots, minced

4 garlic cloves, minced

One 1-pound lean boneless sirloin steak (1″ thick)

¼ cup steak sauce

1. Preheat the oven to 425° F; spray a nonstick baking sheet with nonstick cooking spray. In a large bowl, combine the potatoes, egg whites, salt and ¼ teaspoon of the pepper; toss to coat. Transfer to the baking sheet. Bake until the potatoes are barely tender, about 15 minutes. Remove the potatoes from the oven and increase the oven temperature to broil.

2. Spray the broiler rack with nonstick cooking spray. In a small bowl, mix the shallots, garlic and the remaining ¼ teaspoon of pepper. Place the steak on the rack; brush on one side with half the steak sauce. Broil 4″ from heat 4 minutes; turn over and brush with the remaining steak sauce. With a fork, press the shallot mixture into the steak; broil until cooked through, about 3 minutes longer. Let the steak stand 10 minutes before slicing.

3. While the steak stands, return the potatoes to the broiler; broil until crispy, about 10 minutes.

Per serving: 374 Calories, 8 g Total Fat, 3 g Saturated Fat, 57 mg Cholesterol, 578 mg Sodium, 44 g Total Carbohydrate, 4 g Dietary Fiber, 32 g Protein, 29 mg Calcium.

POINTS PER SERVING: 7

Continued on next page.

Tip

This is classic French bistro fare. If you can't find shallots, substitute a small onion. If you prefer to grill the steak, don't let the fries sit between baking and broiling—just increase the oven temperature.

Corn Salsa

Makes 4 servings

1½ cups fresh or thawed frozen corn kernels

1 tomato, chopped

1 onion, chopped

1 tablespoon chopped cilantro

1 tablespoon fresh lime juice

½ teaspoon salt

In a medium bowl, combine all the ingredients. Refrigerate, covered, until the flavors are blended, at least 1 hour.

Per serving: 70 Calories, 0 g Total Fat, 0 g Saturated Fat, 0 mg Cholesterol, 274 mg Sodium, 17 g Total Carbohydrate, 2 g Dietary Fiber, 2 g Protein, 13 mg Calcium.

POINTS PER SERVING: 1

Tip

This colorful salsa is a tasty accompaniment for most simple main dishes; try it with grilled burgers, poultry, pork or fish. Turn it into a hearty salad by stirring in some black beans.

Cucumber Relish

Makes 4 servings

2 cucumbers, peeled, seeded and diced

2 tomatoes, seeded and diced

¾ cup plain nonfat yogurt

6 scallions, sliced

1 pickled jalapeño pepper, drained, seeded and minced,
with 1 tablespoon liquid

½ teaspoon dried oregano leaves

In a medium bowl, combine all the ingredients. Refrigerate, covered, until the flavors are blended, at least 1 hour.

Per serving: 56 Calories, 0 g Total Fat, 0 g Saturated Fat, 1 mg Cholesterol, 119 mg Sodium, 10 g Total Carbohydrate, 2 g Dietary Fiber, 4 g Protein, 114 mg Calcium.

POINTS PER SERVING: 1

Tip

Serve this cool yet zippy condiment with Baby Lamp Chops (page 167). Or try it instead of salsa with baked tortilla chips.

Minted Zucchini

Makes 4 servings

4 teaspoons olive oil
4 medium zucchini, thinly sliced
3 tablespoons finely chopped mint
1 garlic clove, crushed
½ teaspoon salt
¼ teaspoon freshly ground pepper

In a large nonstick skillet, heat 2 teaspoons of the oil. Sauté the zucchini until golden brown, 7–8 minutes (depending on the size of your skillet, you may have to do this in batches). Transfer to a bowl. Add the mint, garlic, salt, pepper and the remaining 2 teaspoons of oil; toss to combine. Refrigerate, covered, until the flavors are blended, about 2 hours.

Per serving: 60 CALORIES, 5 G TOTAL FAT, 1 G SATURATED FAT, 0 MG CHOLESTEROL, 278 MG SODIUM, 4 G TOTAL CARBOHYDRATE, 1 G DIETARY FIBER, 2 G PROTEIN, 25 MG CALCIUM.

POINTS PER SERVING: 1

Tip

To make the most of all your garden's bounty, toss in a few chopped tomatoes when adding the remaining ingredients to the zucchini.

Frozen Yogurt Sundaes

Makes 4 servings

¼ cup walnuts, coarsely chopped (optional)

¼ cup semisweet chocolate chips

1 tablespoon smooth peanut butter

1 tablespoon skim milk

One 16-ounce container nonfat sugar-free frozen yogurt
(chocolate, vanilla or coffee)

1. If you are using the walnuts, toast them to boost their flavor: Line a microwavable plate with a paper towel; place the walnuts in a single layer on the plate. Microwave on High until fragrant, 1–2 minutes.

2. In a 2-cup microwavable bowl, mix the chocolate chips, peanut butter and milk; microwave on Medium (50% power), stirring once, until the chocolate is melted and smooth, 1–2 minutes. Stir in the walnuts.

3. Serve the frozen yogurt, topped with the chocolate sauce.

Per serving (with walnuts): 198 CALORIES, 9 G TOTAL FAT, 2 G SATURATED FAT,
0 MG CHOLESTEROL, 101 MG SODIUM, 24 G TOTAL CARBOHYDRATE, 2 G DIETARY FIBER,
9 G PROTEIN, 161 MG CALCIUM.

POINTS PER SERVING: 4

Tip

If you decide not to use the nuts, you'll save 1 **POINT**. And don't get complacent about label-reading when it comes to frozen desserts. Many of these so-called "healthy" or "low-fat" products still pack significant amounts of calories and, yes, even fat. Check the label: a 4-ounce serving that provides 100–150 calories and 2–3 grams of fat is a good baseline.

Sunday Night Supper

Sunday tends to be my favorite day. It is the one day of the week when I can spend the most time with my children, which makes it a very special time. We play games, go riding, or swimming in the summer and for long, long walks. We also make great use of the trampoline in the garden. That trampoline has saved my sanity on more than one occasion! We also just talk and enjoy each other's company, without the office calling me. Dinner is an early, informal event where we can all talk together.

Serves 4

Cider Pork Chops

Ginger Pear and Apple Sauce

Stuffed Sweet Dumpling Squash

Parsley Rice

Angel Food Cake with Lemon Curd

Cider Pork Chops

Makes 4 servings

3 tablespoons all-purpose flour
½ teaspoon freshly ground pepper
¼ teaspoon salt
Four 4-ounce lean boneless center-cut pork loin chops
2 teaspoons vegetable oil
½ cup apple cider
1 tablespoon cider vinegar
1 teaspoon grated lemon zest

1. In a gallon-size sealable plastic bag, combine the flour, ¼ teaspoon of the pepper and the salt; one at a time, add the pork chops and shake to coat.
2. In a large nonstick skillet, heat the oil. Sauté the pork until lightly browned, 1–2 minutes on each side. Reduce the heat and add the cider; simmer, covered, until the pork is cooked through and tender, 15–20 minutes. With a slotted spatula, transfer the pork to a platter; keep warm.
3. Add the vinegar and lemon zest to the pan juices; bring to a boil. Cook, stirring occasionally, until slightly thickened, about 5 minutes; season with the remaining ¼ teaspoon of pepper. Spoon the sauce over the pork.

Per serving: 231 CALORIES, 10 G TOTAL FAT, 3 G SATURATED FAT, 73 MG CHOLESTEROL, 188 MG SODIUM, 8 G TOTAL CARBOHYDRATE, 0 G DIETARY FIBER, 22 G PROTEIN, 10 MG CALCIUM.

POINTS PER SERVING: 5

Tip

The zest of the lemon is the peel without any of the pith (white membrane). To remove the zest from the lemon, use a zester or the fine side of a vegetable grater.

Ginger Pear and Apple Sauce

Makes 4 servings

2 teaspoons vegetable oil

2 shallots, minced

2 teaspoons grated peeled gingerroot

Pinch ground allspice

Pinch salt

Pinch freshly ground pepper

3 pears, peeled, cored and chopped

1 McIntosh apple, peeled, cored and chopped

½ cup apple juice

¼ cup dry white wine

¼ teaspoon grated lemon zest

In a medium nonstick saucepan, heat the oil. Sauté the shallots, gingerroot, allspice, salt and pepper until the shallots are softened, about 3 minutes. Stir in the pears, apple, apple juice, wine and lemon zest; cook, stirring gently, until the fruit is very tender, about 15 minutes.

Per serving: 101 Calories, 2 g Total Fat, 0 g Saturated Fat, 0 mg Cholesterol, 36 mg Sodium, 19 g Total Carbohydrate, 3 g Dietary Fiber, 0 g Protein, 11 mg Calcium.

POINTS PER SERVING: 2

Tip

Use the ripest pears you can find. Bartletts, Anjous or Boscs will do the trick. McIntosh apples cook down considerably; peeling them eliminates the unpleasant texture. Spoon a pool of this spicy sauce alongside a favorite pork or chicken dish.

Stuffed Sweet Dumpling Squash

Makes 4 servings

Two 1-pound sweet dumpling squash, halved and seeded
2 teaspoons reduced-calorie margarine
1 large onion, diced
2 apples, peeled, cored and diced
1 celery stalk, diced
¼ cup golden raisins

1. Preheat the oven to 350° F. Place the squash, cut-side down, in a 9 x 13" baking dish. Cover with foil and bake 10 minutes.
2. Meanwhile, in a medium nonstick skillet, melt the margarine. Sauté the onion until softened, about 3 minutes. Stir in the apples, celery and raisins; cook, stirring frequently, until the apples are soft, 5–6 minutes. Divide the filling among the squash. Re-cover with the foil and bake until the squash is soft and the filling is lightly browned, about 40 minutes.

Per serving: 140 CALORIES, 1 G TOTAL FAT, 0 G SATURATED FAT, 0 MG CHOLESTEROL, 43 MG SODIUM, 34 G TOTAL CARBOHYDRATE, 8 G DIETARY FIBER, 2 G PROTEIN, 76 MG CALCIUM.

POINTS PER SERVING: 1

Tip

Sweet dumpling squash is rather squat; it has green skin with white stripes. The common acorn, or the less well-known delicata squash (it's shaped somewhat like a cucumber, with green-and-beige striped skin) can be used instead of the sweet dumpling, if you like. Whichever you choose, be sure to select a squash that feels heavy for its size.

Parsley Rice

Makes 4 servings

1 cup long-grain white rice
1 teaspoon vegetable oil
½ celery stalk, minced
1 garlic clove, minced
½ cup minced flat-leaf parsley
¼ teaspoon dried thyme leaves, crumbled

1. Cook the rice according to package directions.
2. In a medium nonstick skillet, heat the oil. Sauté the celery and garlic until they just begin to soften, 1–2 minutes. Stir in the parsley and thyme; cook, stirring constantly, until the vegetables are softened, about 2 minutes longer. Add to the rice; toss to combine.

Per serving: 184 CALORIES, 2 G TOTAL FAT, 0 G SATURATED FAT, 0 MG CHOLESTEROL, 11 MG SODIUM, 38 G TOTAL CARBOHYDRATE, 1 G DIETARY FIBER, 4 G PROTEIN, 28 MG CALCIUM.

POINTS PER SERVING: 4

Tip

If you're looking to boost this recipe's nutrient content, stir in 1 cup chopped spinach when you add the parsley and thyme.

Angel Food Cake with Lemon Curd

Makes 16 servings

Lemon Curd

¾ cup granulated sugar

2 tablespoons cornstarch

1 tablespoon grated lemon zest

½ cup lemon juice

2 tablespoons reduced-calorie margarine

2 egg yolks

Cake

1½ cups cake flour

1½ cups granulated sugar

12 egg whites, at room temperature

1½ teaspoons cream of tartar

½ teaspoon salt

2 teaspoons vanilla extract

Confectioners' sugar, for dusting

1. To prepare the lemon curd, in a medium nonstick saucepan, mix the sugar, cornstarch and lemon zest; whisk in the lemon juice, margarine and ½ cup water, stirring until the sugar dissolves. Bring to a boil; cook, stirring constantly, until the mixture thickens slightly, about 1 minute.

2. In a small bowl, lightly beat the egg yolks. Slowly whisk ¼ cup of the lemon mixture into the egg yolks, then slowly pour the egg-yolk mixture into the lemon mixture, whisking quickly and constantly. Reduce the heat to low and cook 1 minute longer; do not let the mixture boil. Transfer the lemon curd to a bowl; refrigerate, covered, until chilled, at least 3 hours.

3. To make the cake, preheat the oven to 375° F. In a sifter or large strainer, combine the flour and ¾ cup of the granulated sugar; sift into a small bowl.

4. In a very large bowl, with an electric mixer on high speed, beat the egg whites, cream of tartar and salt until soft peaks form; add the vanilla. With the mixer at high speed, sprinkle in the remaining ¾ cup sugar, 2 tablespoons at a time, until the sugar completely dissolves and whites stand in stiff peaks. With a rubber spatula, fold the flour mixture into the egg whites just until the flour mixture disappears.

5. Pour the batter into an ungreased 10″ tube pan. Bake until the cake springs back when lightly touched, 35–40 minutes. Invert the cake in the pan onto funnel or bottle; cool completely in the pan.

6. To serve, with a metal spatula, carefully loosen the cake from pan; place on a cake plate, bottom-side up. With a long serrated knife, carefully cut the cake crosswise in half. Spread the cake with the lemon curd, letting some flow down the sides of the cake. Replace the top of the cake. Sprinkle with the confectioners' sugar. Serve at once.

Per serving: 181 CALORIES, 1 G TOTAL FAT, 0 G SATURATED FAT, 27 MG CHOLESTEROL, 126 MG SODIUM, 38 G TOTAL CARBOHYDRATE, 0 G DIETARY FIBER, 4 G PROTEIN, 8 MG CALCIUM.

POINTS PER SERVING: 4

Tip

This lightened version of lemon curd helps to make an impressive dessert; if you're pressed for time, use a store-bought cake. Angel food cake is delicate, so be sure to use a serrated knife with a long blade for easier slicing. Don't be tempted to use egg substitute instead of egg whites—it doesn't whip up.

A Tuscan Dinner

The time of the year that I insist is mine and mine alone is when my children are on summer school holiday. Summer holiday is when we reconnect as a family and I reconnect to myself.

I have just spent the summer in Tuscany with the girls. It truly is one of the most beautiful parts of the world. The small country towns have names I have long recognized on bottles of delicious wines.

A glass of fine wine is something I enjoy with my meal. I have learned that I can have a glass of wine with dinner or a wonderful dessert. But I must tally up everything, and I must watch portions. I now realize overeating is only a symptom of suppressed feelings. When I was at my highest weight, I believe I had truly lost control of my life. I would reach out for food instead of delving deeply into my feelings. Now I know not to go on with life mindlessly; I try to be mindful of every moment—with my children and with myself.

Serves 4

Crock of Italian Olives*

Warm White Bean Salad

Lemon Chicken

Steamed Broccoli*

Spicy Polenta

Bittersweet Fruit

Warm White Bean Salad

Makes 4 servings

4 teaspoons olive oil

4 plum tomatoes, seeded and chopped

1 onion, minced

2 tablespoons minced fresh sage, or 1 teaspoon dried

1 garlic clove, minced

¼ teaspoon salt

¼ teaspoon freshly ground pepper

One 16-ounce can cannellini beans, rinsed and drained

In a medium nonstick skillet, heat the oil. Sauté the tomatoes, onion, sage, garlic, salt and pepper until the sauce thickens, about 5 minutes. Stir in the beans.

Per serving: 138 CALORIES, 5 G TOTAL FAT, 1 G SATURATED FAT, 0 MG CHOLESTEROL, 264 MG SODIUM, 18 G TOTAL CARBOHYDRATE, 6 G DIETARY FIBER, 6 G PROTEIN, 40 MG CALCIUM.

POINTS PER SERVING: 2

Tip

This salad makes an ideal stuffing for peppers: Halve and seed 4 red bell peppers, then bake at 425° F until tender, about 30 minutes; drain any liquid from the peppers before stuffing them.

Lemon Chicken

Makes 4 servings

1 tablespoon all-purpose flour
¼ teaspoon salt
¼ teaspoon freshly ground pepper
Four 4-ounce skinless boneless chicken breasts, pounded into ¼″ scallops
2 teaspoons olive oil
½ cup chicken broth
2 tablespoons fresh lemon juice
1 tablespoon chopped flat-leaf parsley
1 tablespoon capers, rinsed and drained
Lemon slices, to garnish

1. On a sheet of wax paper, combine the flour, salt and pepper. Coat one side of each chicken scallop with the flour mixture.
2. In a medium nonstick skillet, heat the oil. Add the chicken, floured-side down; cook until lightly browned and cooked through, about 1 minute on each side. Transfer to a plate.
3. In the skillet, mix the broth, lemon juice, parsley and capers; bring to a boil. Cook until the liquid is reduced to about ⅓ cup, about 2 minutes. Return the chicken and any accumulated juices to the skillet; cook until just heated through, 1–2 minutes. Serve, garnished with the lemon slices.

Per serving: 167 CALORIES, 5 G TOTAL FAT, 1 G SATURATED FAT, 71 MG CHOLESTEROL, 365 MG SODIUM, 2 G TOTAL CARBOHYDRATE, 0 G DIETARY FIBER, 26 G PROTEIN, 16 MG CALCIUM.

POINTS PER SERVING: 4

Tip

This recipe also works with veal or turkey scallops in place of the chicken. To keep raw meat from spattering all over your kitchen when you pound the scallops, place the chicken breasts between sheets of wax paper; if you don't have a meat mallet, use a small skillet.

Spicy Polenta

Makes 4 servings

1 teaspoon salt
1 cup cornmeal
½ teaspoon crushed red pepper flakes, or to taste

1. Spray an 8 x 4″ loaf pan with nonstick cooking spray.
2. In a large heavy saucepan, bring 3 cups water and the salt to a boil. Reduce the heat and gradually add the cornmeal in a slow, thin stream, whisking constantly to prevent lumps from forming. Cook, stirring frequently, until thickened, 5–10 minutes. Stir in the pepper flakes. Spread the polenta into the pan, smoothing the top. Refrigerate, covered, until firm, at least 30 minutes.
3. Preheat the oven to 350° F; lightly spray a baking sheet with nonstick cooking spray. Invert the loaf pan to release the polenta, then cut into 1″ slices; place on the baking sheet. Bake until the edges are golden brown, about 30 minutes.

Per serving: 158 CALORIES, 1 G TOTAL FAT, 0 G SATURATED FAT, 0 MG CHOLESTEROL, 552 MG SODIUM, 33 G TOTAL CARBOHYDRATE, 2 G DIETARY FIBER, 4 G PROTEIN, 7 MG CALCIUM.

POINTS PER SERVING: 3

Tip

To make this an entrée, stir in ½ cup grated Parmesan cheese with the pepper. Serve with a zesty ratatouille to round out the meal.

Bittersweet Fruit

Makes 4 servings

1 blood orange, peeled and thinly sliced
1 navel orange, peeled and thinly sliced
1 cup honeydew melon chunks
¼ cup Italian bitters

1. Arrange the oranges on a platter.
2. In a small bowl, combine the melon and bitters; spoon over the oranges. Refrigerate, covered, until chilled, at least 30 minutes.

Per serving: 99 Calories, 0 g Total Fat, 0 g Saturated Fat, 0 mg Cholesterol, 1 mg Sodium, 19 g Total Carbohydrate, 2 g Dietary Fiber, 1 g Protein, 32 mg Calcium.

POINTS PER SERVING: 2

Tip

Italian bitters, such as Campari®, are available in most liquor stores. For a refreshing apéritif, serve a dash of bitters in sparkling mineral water with a twist of lemon (bitters have a reputation as an excellent digestive). If blood oranges aren't available, tangerines will do the trick.

A Working Mother's Lunch

Sooner or later, every working mother realizes the importance of having a solid support system in place.

As a young working girl, living in Clapham and before my engagement to Prince Andrew, I subsisted on black coffee and ill-balanced meals. As a result, I became a weak, jittery wreck, completely wired. I used to feel faint in the middle of the day through lack of food.

I was always dieting, at least when I wasn't bingeing.

Thankfully, I have since learned the importance of finding time to eat three balanced meals each day. I have also learned that the road to happiness is not paved with a thin body, and no one need struggle alone when it comes to weight. Now, I turn to my old friends and new Weight Watchers friends to provide support when I need it.

Serves 4

Gorgonzola and Pear Pizza
Arugula and Watercress Salad
Fresh Tangerines*

Gorgonzola and Pear Pizza

Makes 4 servings

½ pound prepared pizza dough
1 teaspoon extra virgin olive oil
1 large pear, thinly sliced
⅓ cup crumbled Gorgonzola cheese

1. Spray the grill rack with nonstick cooking spray; preheat the grill.
2. On a lightly floured surface, divide the dough into fourths; roll out each into rounds ⅛″ thick. Carefully place the dough directly onto the grill rack; brush the tops with the oil. Grill until the dough bubbles on the top and begins to char on the bottom, about 2 minutes; turn over. Divide the pear and cheese over the crusts; cover the grill or tent with foil and grill until the cheese melts and crust is crisp, 3–5 minutes.

Per serving: 282 CALORIES, 6 G TOTAL FAT, 2 G SATURATED FAT, 8 MG CHOLESTEROL, 423 MG SODIUM, 49 G TOTAL CARBOHYDRATE, 4 G DIETARY FIBER, 8 G PROTEIN, 74 MG CALCIUM.

POINTS PER SERVING: 5

Tip

If you find whole-wheat pizza dough (which gives a crisper crust than white-flour dough), it is ideal with these toppings. Ask for it at your local pizzeria or bakery.

Arugula and Watercress Salad

Makes 4 servings

1½ teaspoons Dijon mustard
1 garlic clove, minced
1½ tablespoons honey
1 tablespoon champagne vinegar
1 bunch watercress, cleaned and coarsely chopped
1 small bunch arugula (about ¼ pound), cleaned and coarsely chopped
1 carrot, shredded

1. In a small bowl, mix the mustard and garlic; whisk in the honey and vinegar.
2. In a large salad bowl, combine the watercress, arugula and carrot. Drizzle with the dressing; toss to coat.

Per serving: 46 CALORIES, 0 G TOTAL FAT, 0 G SATURATED FAT, 0 MG CHOLESTEROL, 37 MG SODIUM, 10 G TOTAL CARBOHYDRATE, 1 G DIETARY FIBER, 2 G PROTEIN, 88 MG CALCIUM.

POINTS PER SERVING: 1

Tip

Remove all of the thick, woody stems when cleaning fresh watercress.

Supper After a Horseback Ride

From an early age, I have loved riding horses. When we moved to Dummer Down, a dairy farm Dads inherited, I was in heaven. Located in the depths of the English countryside in Hampshire, England, Dummer was *real* country: acres of rolling pasture, fields filled with corn, oats and barley, an apple orchard. And the stables: My most vivid memories of Dummer somehow all lead back to riding my treasured horses.

Throughout my childhood, I had a succession of extraordinary horses and ponies who were faithful and always pushed themselves for me. When I was about nine years of age, Herbert, my chestnut pony, was my trusty friend. I remember once he stood stock-still when I got my foot caught in the stirrup. Most little ponies would have run away, but not Herbert.

As an adult, I certainly have been to my fair share of events. However, the most grueling test of my riding ability was the Qatar Horse Marathon on the Arabian Peninsula. The event is commonly known as "Desert Storm," and for good reason: you ride your horse across 26 miles of barren desert. The horse that carried me through was Gal, an Akhal-Teke, a Russian breed that was once favored by the likes of Alexander the Great. Desert Storm truly was a formidable task, but it did show me I can do whatever I put my mind to.

Serves 8

Sun-Dried Tomato and Smoked Mozzarella Crostini
Fennel and Blood Orange Salad with Sweet Onions
Classic Roast Beef with Wild Mushrooms
Haricots Verts
Braised Leeks
Basil-Rice Pilaf
Strawberries in Champagne

Sun-Dried Tomato and
Smoked Mozzarella Crostini

Makes 8 servings

16 sun-dried tomatoes (not oil-packed)
2 plum tomatoes, chopped
2 tablespoons low-sodium tomato juice
4 teaspoons olive oil
2 garlic cloves, minced
Sixteen ½″ slices crusty Italian bread, toasted
⅔ cup shredded smoked mozzarella cheese
½ teaspoon dried thyme leaves, crumbled
½ teaspoon dried oregano, crumbled

1. Line the broiler pan with foil, shiny-side up; preheat the broiler.
2. In a food processor or blender, combine the sun-dried tomatoes, plum tomatoes, tomato juice, oil and garlic; puree. Spread about 1 teaspoon of the tomato mixture on each slice of toast, then sprinkle with the mozzarella, thyme and oregano. Broil 1 minute, until the cheese is melted and bubbling. Serve at once.

Per serving: 133 Calories, 5 g Total Fat, 2 g Saturated Fat, 7 mg Cholesterol, 317 mg Sodium, 18 g Total Carbohydrate, 2 g Dietary Fiber, 7 g Protein, 102 mg Calcium.

POINTS PER SERVING: 3

Tip

If you're not a fan of smoked flavors, just use the plain mozzarella—but do make the effort to find fresh, sold in balls in some supermarkets, gourmet stores and Italian delis. Smoked mozzarella is seldom available in any but the whole-milk version. Using skim-milk mozzarella will save you 1 *POINT*.

A Working Mother's Lunch

GORGONZOLA AND PEAR PIZZA

Supper After a Horseback Ride

CLASSIC ROAST BEEF WITH WILD MUSHROOMS

A Perfect Picnic

SPINACH CHICKEN SALAD, TOMATO PARMESAN TOASTS

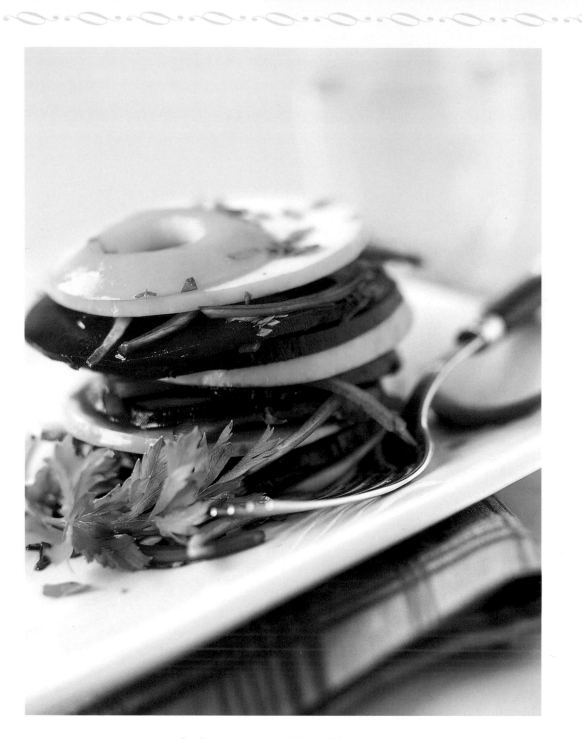

A Girlfriends' Get-Together

BEET AND APPLE "NAPOLEON"

An American Barbecue

BARBECUE BEEF SANDWICH, RAINBOW COLE SLAW,
ROASTED CORN ON THE COB WITH CILANTRO BUTTER, ICED TEA

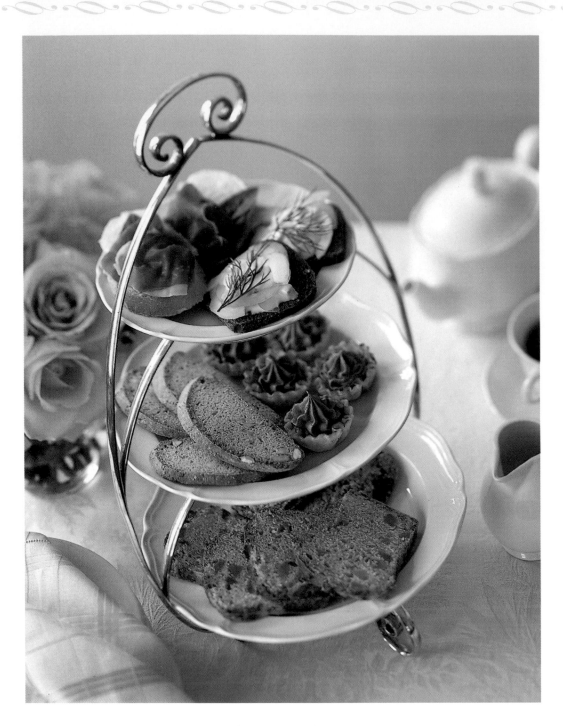

Afternoon Tea

Top: OPEN-FACE HAM SANDWICHES AND CUCUMBER SANDWICHES

Middle: ALMOND BISCOTTI AND CHOCOLATE MOUSSE TARTLETS

Bottom: PEAR-PORT QUICK BREAD AND BLACKBERRY SCONES

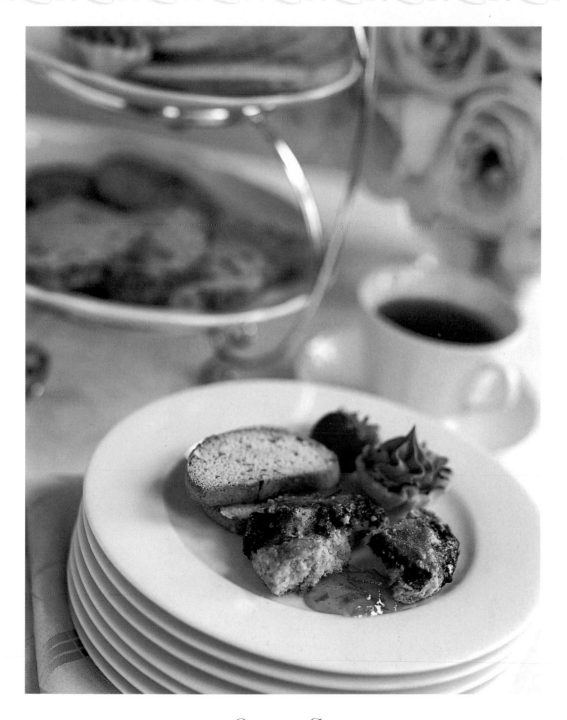

Afternoon Tea

ALMOND BISCOTTI, BLACKBERRY SCONES,
CHOCOLATE MOUSSE TARTLET

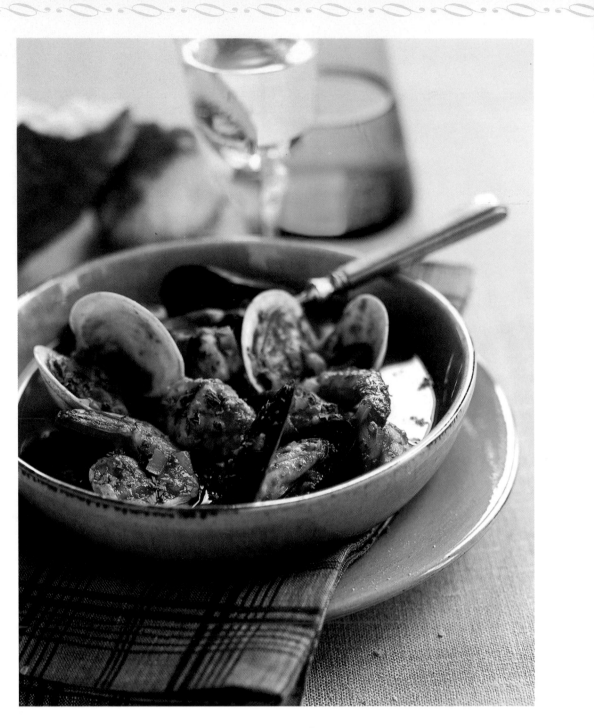

A Provençal Feast

MEDITERRANEAN FISHERMAN'S STEW, CRUSTY BAGUETTE

Fennel and Blood Orange Salad with Sweet Onions

Makes 8 servings

¼ cup red-wine vinegar

¼ cup orange juice

4 teaspoons sugar

4 teaspoons olive oil

1 teaspoon Dijon mustard

¼ teaspoon salt

Freshly ground pepper, to taste

2 large fennel bulbs

4 large blood oranges, peeled and cut into ¼" slices

2 sweet onions, cut into ⅛" slices and separated into rings

1. In a small bowl, whisk the vinegar, orange juice, sugar, oil, mustard, salt and pepper.
2. Cut the feathery tops and stems from the fennel bulb and discard. Trim any yellow or bruised outer leaves, then cut the bulb in half through the stem end. Cut out the tough core; place the halves, cut-side down, on a cutting board. With a sharp knife, cut the fennel crosswise into paper-thin slices. Divide the slices among 8 salad plates; top with the orange slices and onion rings. Drizzle with the dressing.

Per serving: 130 Calories, 3 g Total Fat, 0 g Saturated Fat, 0 mg Cholesterol, 126 mg Sodium, 26 g Total Carbohydrate, 2 g Dietary Fiber, 3 g Protein, 119 mg Calcium.

POINTS PER SERVING: 2

Tip

Feel free to substitute navel oranges or tangerines for the blood oranges.

Classic Roast Beef with Wild Mushrooms

Makes 8 servings

One 2-pound eye round beef roast
½ teaspoon salt
½ teaspoon freshly ground pepper
2 teaspoons olive oil
1 onion, diced
1 cup chopped shiitake mushrooms
1 cup chopped cremini mushrooms
½ cup chopped porcini mushrooms
1 garlic clove, minced
¼ cup red wine
1 tablespoon minced parsley
½ teaspoon dried thyme leaves, crumbled

1. Preheat the oven to 325° F; spray a rack with nonstick cooking spray and place in a large roasting pan. Season the beef with the salt and pepper; place on the rack. Roast until the beef reaches an internal temperature of 145–150° F, about 1 hour. Transfer to a cutting board and let stand 10–15 minutes.
2. Meanwhile, in a medium nonstick skillet, heat the oil. Sauté the onion until softened, about 3 minutes. Add all three kinds of mushrooms and the garlic; sauté, stirring constantly, 5 minutes longer. Stir in the wine, parsley and thyme; cook, stirring constantly, until the mushrooms are soft, 5–6 minutes. Slice the beef and serve with the mushrooms on the side.

Per serving: 171 Calories, 5 g Total Fat, 2 g Saturated Fat, 59 mg Cholesterol, 188 mg Sodium, 3 g Total Carbohydrate, 1 g Dietary Fiber, 25 g Protein, 14 mg Calcium.

POINTS PER SERVING: 4

Tip

If there are any leftovers, slice up the cold roast for next-day sandwiches. Top with a bit of the remaining mushrooms and a dollop of zesty horseradish for a satisfying lunch. If you have trouble finding fresh porcinis, use dried: Soak ¼ cup in hot water until pliable, about 20 minutes. Add the mushrooms and the soaking liquid with the wine and herbs; there's no need to strain them.

Haricots Verts

Makes 8 servings

2 teaspoons olive oil
4 garlic cloves, minced
4 cups fresh haricots verts
¼ teaspoon salt

In a medium nonstick skillet, heat the oil. Sauté the garlic until golden brown, 1–2 minutes. Stir in the haricots, salt and 3 tablespoons water; cook, covered, until the haricots are tender, about 2 minutes.

Per serving: 48 CALORIES, 1 G TOTAL FAT, 0 G SATURATED FAT, 0 MG CHOLESTEROL, 41 MG SODIUM, 9 G TOTAL CARBOHYDRATE, 2 G DIETARY FIBER, 2 G PROTEIN, 37 MG CALCIUM.

POINTS PER SERVING: 1

Tip

The slender French green beans called haricots verts (pronounced *ah-ree-co vair*) are a delicacy. If they are unavailable at your market, use the smallest fresh green beans you can find; increase the cooking time to about 5 minutes.

Braised Leeks

Makes 8 servings

8 medium leeks, halved lengthwise and cleaned

½ cup chicken broth

¼ cup minced parsley

¼ cup white-wine vinegar

2 tablespoons olive oil

1 teaspoon minced thyme leaves

1 teaspoon grated orange zest

1 teaspoon Dijon mustard

½ teaspoon salt

¼ teaspoon freshly ground pepper

1. Preheat the oven to 350° F. In a 9 x 13″ baking dish, combine the leeks and broth. Cover with foil and bake until tender, about 25 minutes.
2. Meanwhile, in a small bowl, combine the parsley, vinegar, oil, thyme, orange zest, mustard, salt and pepper with 2 teaspoons water. Serve the leeks, drizzled with the vinaigrette.

Per serving: 93 CALORIES, 4 G TOTAL FAT, 0 G SATURATED FAT, 0 MG CHOLESTEROL, 171 MG SODIUM, 15 G TOTAL CARBOHYDRATE, 1 G DIETARY FIBER, 2 G PROTEIN, 64 MG CALCIUM.

POINTS PER SERVING: 2

Tip

Leeks, with their subtle flavor, make an excellent side dish for grilled fish or chicken, like Baked Chicken with Wine (page 20) or Citrus Red Snapper (page 87).

Basil-Rice Pilaf

Makes 8 servings

4 teaspoons olive oil

1 red bell pepper, seeded and minced

6 scallions, sliced

1½ cups regular (not converted) long-grain rice

12 large black olives, pitted and chopped

1 teaspoon salt

¼ teaspoon cayenne pepper, or to taste

½ cup chopped basil

1. In a large nonstick saucepan, heat the oil. Sauté the bell pepper and scallions until they just begin to soften, 4–5 minutes. Stir in the rice and olives; cook, stirring constantly, until the vegetables are softened and the rice becomes opaque, 2–3 minutes longer.

2. Stir in the salt, cayenne and 3 cups water; bring to a boil. Reduce the heat and simmer, covered, until the liquid is absorbed, 15–20 minutes. Fluff with a fork; re-cover and let stand 5 minutes, then stir in the basil.

Per serving: 163 CALORIES, 3 G TOTAL FAT, 0 G SATURATED FAT, 0 MG CHOLESTEROL, 328 MG SODIUM, 30 G TOTAL CARBOHYDRATE, 1 G DIETARY FIBER, 3 G PROTEIN, 26 MG CALCIUM.

POINTS PER SERVING: 3

Tip

We like the flavor of basil in this dish, but herbs like oregano or parsley or greens like spinach or watercress would be tasty as well. Take your inspiration from whatever looks best in your garden or at the farm stand.

Strawberries in Champagne

Makes 8 servings

24 small whole strawberries
4 cups champagne, chilled

Place 3 strawberries in each of 8 champagne flutes; top with the champagne.

Per serving: 103 Calories, 0 g Total Fat, 0 g Saturated Fat, 0 mg Cholesterol,
7 mg Sodium, 6 g Total Carbohydrate, 2 g Dietary Fiber, 1 g Protein,
21 mg Calcium.

POINTS PER SERVING: 2

Tip

Look for long-stemmed strawberries; leave the stems on the whole berries for easy plucking from your champagne flute.

A Casual Weeknight Supper

Without question, losing weight is *hard*. At least it has been for me. Despite all my years of losing, then more often than not, regaining the weight, I never truly understood the *how* of losing weight. I did the mad crash diets—like the one when I lived on meat and oranges so that I could lose 26 pounds to fit into my wedding gown! But now I truly understand all the hard work that goes into losing weight—and trying to keep it off.

I work every single day at staying healthy and trim. It certainly is one of the greatest challenges I have ever encountered. But now that I am a mother—a mother who wants to set a good example for her daughters—I know that living a healthy, happy life is a priority.

Serves 4

Chicken Calvados

Oven-Roasted Root Vegetables

Peppered Parsley Noodles

Parmesan-Baked Asparagus

Chicken Calvados

Makes 4 servings

½ teaspoon salt
½ teaspoon freshly ground pepper
¼ teaspoon cinnamon
¼ teaspoon ground ginger
Four 4-ounce skinless boneless chicken breasts
4 teaspoons vegetable oil
2 onions, thinly sliced
4 Golden Delicious apples, peeled, cored and thinly sliced
1 cup apple cider or apple juice
2 tablespoons Calvados (apple brandy)

1. In a small bowl, combine the salt, pepper, cinnamon and ginger. Rub into the chicken.
2. In a large nonstick skillet, heat the oil. Sauté the chicken until browned, about 3 minutes on each side. Transfer to a plate.
3. In the skillet, sauté the onions until softened, about 5 minutes. Stir in the apples and cook, turning occasionally, until golden brown and tender, 3–5 minutes. Stir in the cider; bring to a boil. Return the chicken to the skillet and cook, turning as needed, until cooked through, about 5 minutes longer. Transfer to a platter.
4. Stir the Calvados into the skillet; cook until the apples and onions are glazed and the liquid is thickened, about 3 minutes. Serve the chicken, topped with the apple mixture.

Per serving: 286 CALORIES, 6 G TOTAL FAT, 1 G SATURATED FAT, 66 MG CHOLESTEROL, 350 MG SODIUM, 28 G TOTAL CARBOHYDRATE, 3 G DIETARY FIBER, 27 G PROTEIN, 33 MG CALCIUM.

POINTS PER SERVING: 6

Continued on next page.

Tip

Calvados, a French apple brandy produced in Normandy, is distilled from cider, much in the same way that cognac and armagnac are distilled from wine. Its flavor marries well with pork dishes, too. If you prefer, use apple jack or plain brandy.

Oven-Roasted Root Vegetables

Makes 4 servings

1 tablespoon olive oil

¾ pound new potatoes, scrubbed

1 large sweet potato, peeled and cut into chunks

4 carrots, scrubbed and cut into chunks

2 parsnips, peeled and cut into chunks

2 onions, cut into chunks

½ cup chicken broth

2 garlic cloves, minced

½ teaspoon dried thyme leaves, crumbled

½ teaspoon salt

¼ teaspoon freshly ground pepper

1. Preheat the oven to 400° F. Place the oil in a large shallow roasting pan. Heat the oil in the oven until hot, about 5 minutes. Add the new potatoes, sweet potato, carrots, parsnips and onions.

2. In a small bowl, combine the broth, garlic, thyme, salt and pepper. Pour over the vegetables; toss to coat. Roast the vegetables, stirring as needed, until tender, about 45 minutes.

Per serving: 279 CALORIES, 4 G TOTAL FAT, 0 G SATURATED FAT, 0 MG CHOLESTEROL, 490 MG SODIUM, 57 G TOTAL CARBOHYDRATE, 9 G DIETARY FIBER, 6 G PROTEIN, 81 MG CALCIUM.

POINTS PER SERVING: 4

Tip

Roast vegetables are an easy accompaniment to almost any meat or poultry dish—use this combination, or whatever strikes your fancy. Just be sure they're not crowded into the pan when they're roasting.

Peppered Parsley Noodles

Makes 4 servings

1½ cups medium egg noodles
½ cup minced flat-leaf parsley
½ teaspoon cracked black pepper
¼ teaspoon salt

1. Cook the noodles according to package directions; drain, reserving ¼ cup of the cooking liquid, and place in a medium bowl.
2. Add the cooking liquid, parsley, pepper and salt to the noodles; toss to combine.

Per serving: 58 CALORIES, 1 G TOTAL FAT, 0 G SATURATED FAT, 14 MG CHOLESTEROL, 141 MG SODIUM, 11 G TOTAL CARBOHYDRATE, 0 G DIETARY FIBER, 2 G PROTEIN, 17 MG CALCIUM.

POINTS PER SERVING: 1

Tip

Of the more than 30 different kinds of parsley, the two most common are curly (the pretty sprigs of which are often used as garnishes) and the more flavorful flat-leaf (sometimes called Italian) parsley. In dishes such as this, where this herb is given a featured role, you'll want to use flat-leaf parsley.

Parmesan-Baked Asparagus

Makes 4 servings

1 pound asparagus
2 teaspoons olive oil
¼ teaspoon salt
¼ teaspoon freshly ground pepper
¼ cup grated Parmesan cheese

Preheat the oven to 425° F. Place the asparagus on a nonstick baking sheet. Drizzle with the olive oil and sprinkle with the salt and pepper; toss to coat. Bake 10 minutes, then toss again; sprinkle with the cheese and bake until the cheese melts, about 5 minutes longer.

Per serving: 67 CALORIES, 4 G TOTAL FAT, 1 G SATURATED FAT, 4 MG CHOLESTEROL, 237 MG SODIUM, 4 G TOTAL CARBOHYDRATE, 2 G DIETARY FIBER, 5 G PROTEIN, 90 MG CALCIUM.

POINTS PER SERVING: 1

Tip

We like the thinner asparagus spears—unlike their thicker counterparts, they don't need to be peeled. Whichever you use, select a bunch where all the spears are of fairly equal thickness. Baby artichokes, found in better supermarkets, are about the size of walnuts and can be eaten whole—including the leaves. They'd make a novel substitution.

Holiday Buffet

Who doesn't love the holidays? Good cheer, family, friends, great food. For the past few years, the girls and I have spent Christmas at Wood Farm, a lovely farmhouse on the Sandringham Estate where the Royal Family spends the festive season. We have a house full of decorations, and a huge tree, which all help the spirit of the holiday fill every room. We generally have a wonderful feast with everyone taking their place at the table.

The holidays can be a terror if you are trying to lose weight, with sweets and treats at every turn, ready to set you off on a binge. I try not to do that. I find Christmas to be a very quiet and relaxing time. It is a time when I can reflect on the past year's trials and tribulations, as well as its rewards. I have a good deal to be thankful for: two wonderful daughters, good health and a full life.

Serves 12

Mediterranean Tian

Provençal Beef Tenderloin

Turkey Breast with Cremini Mushrooms and Leeks

Risotto di Pavia

Venetian Radicchio

Assorted Breads*

Blueberry Zabaglione

Mediterranean Tian

Makes 12 servings

3 tablespoons olive oil

6 red bell peppers, seeded and quartered

3 medium (about 1¼-pound each) eggplants, thinly sliced

12 scallions, trimmed

¼ cup + 2 tablespoons red-wine vinegar

½ teaspoon dried oregano, crumbled

½ teaspoon dried basil, crumbled

½ teaspoon salt

Freshly ground pepper, to taste

1. Line a baking sheet with foil and spray with nonstick cooking spray; preheat the broiler. Using 1 tablespoon of the oil, brush the peppers, eggplants and scallions on both sides; place on the baking sheet. Broil until slightly charred and fork-tender, about 5 minutes on each side for the peppers, 2–3 minutes on each side for the eggplant, and 1–2 minutes on each side for the scallions. Cut the scallions into 2" lengths.

2. In a medium bowl, whisk the remaining 2 tablespoons of oil, the vinegar, oregano, basil, salt and pepper with 3 tablespoons water.

3. In two or three shallow serving dishes, alternate layers of the eggplant, peppers and scallions, drizzling a small amount of the vinaigrette over each layer. Pour the remaining dressing over the tops. Refrigerate, covered, until chilled and the flavors are blended, at least 1 hour. Serve at room temperature or slightly chilled.

Per serving: 81 Calories, 4 g Total Fat, 0 g Saturated Fat, 0 mg Cholesterol, 41 mg Sodium, 12 g Total Carbohydrate, 3 g Dietary Fiber, 2 g Protein, 62 mg Calcium.

POINTS PER SERVING: 1

Continued on next page.

A tian (pronounced *tee-yahn*) simply involves alternating layers of vegetables in a shallow dish. This surprisingly easy recipe makes an attractive, brightly colored presentation.

Provençal Beef Tenderloin

Makes 12 servings

One 3-pound beef tenderloin

¾ cup minced parsley

3 tablespoons minced rosemary

3 tablespoons Dijon mustard

6–8 garlic cloves, minced

1 tablespoon minced oregano

1 tablespoon minced thyme

1 tablespoon olive oil

1 teaspoon freshly ground pepper

1. Place the beef on a sheet of plastic wrap. In a small bowl, mix the remaining ingredients to make a paste. Rub the paste all over the beef; wrap in the plastic and refrigerate 1 hour.

2. Meanwhile, preheat the oven to 425° F. Place the beef in a 9 x 13″ baking dish or shallow roasting pan. Roast until the beef reaches an internal temperature of 145° F, about 45 minutes. Transfer to a cutting board and let stand 10 minutes before slicing.

Per serving: 198 CALORIES, 10 G TOTAL FAT, 3 G SATURATED FAT, 71 MG CHOLESTEROL, 146 MG SODIUM, 1 G TOTAL CARBOHYDRATE, 0 G DIETARY FIBER, 24 G PROTEIN, 19 MG CALCIUM.

POINTS PER SERVING: 5

Tip

Take care not to overcook the beef tenderloin. We like to test for doneness with an instant-read thermometer—it's virtually foolproof. The heat-reading element of an instant-read is halfway between the tip of the thermometer and the small indentation that's about 2″ from the tip; to get an accurate reading, make sure the thermometer is deep enough in the meat and that it's not touching bone or fat.

Turkey Breast with Cremini Mushrooms and Leeks

Makes 12 servings

2 tablespoons olive oil
3–4 leeks, cleaned and thinly sliced
1 onion, chopped
4 garlic cloves, minced
2 cups sliced cremini mushrooms
2 teaspoons minced thyme leaves
1 teaspoon salt
1 teaspoon freshly ground pepper
5 slices firm white bread, cubed
¾ cup chicken broth
½ cup flat-leaf parsley, finely chopped
One 3-pound skinless boneless turkey breast

1. Preheat the oven to 350° F. In a large nonstick skillet, heat 1 tablespoon of the oil. Sauté the leeks, onion and garlic until the leeks just begin to soften, 5–7 minutes. Transfer to a large bowl.

2. In the skillet, heat the remaining tablespoon of oil. Sauté the mushrooms with the thyme, ½ teaspoon of the salt and ½ teaspoon of the pepper until the mushrooms are browned and tender, about 10 minutes. Transfer to the bowl; stir in the bread, broth and parsley.

3. Place the turkey, skinned-side down, between two sheets of wax paper. With a meat mallet or small heavy skillet, pound the turkey so it is ½" thick. Transfer to a work surface; spread with the stuffing to within 1" of the edges. Roll up the turkey and tie with kitchen twine; place, seam-side down, on a rack in a roasting pan, then sprinkle with the remaining salt and pepper. Roast, basting occasionally with the pan juices, until the turkey is cooked through,

1¼–1½ hours. Transfer to a cutting board and let stand 10 minutes before slicing. Serve with the pan juices on the side.

Per serving: 203 Calories, 4 g Total Fat, 1 g Saturated Fat, 70 mg Cholesterol, 292 mg Sodium, 12 g Total Carbohydrate, 1 g Dietary Fiber, 30 g Protein, 56 mg Calcium.

POINTS PER SERVING: 4

Tip

Be sure to use only the white and palest-green parts of the leeks, and to wash them thoroughly to remove all traces of grit (leeks grow in sandy soil). If you like, substitute shiitake mushrooms for the cremini.

Risotto di Pavia

Makes 12 servings

12 cups vegetable or chicken broth
1 tablespoon olive oil
2 onions, chopped
4 shallots, chopped
3 cups Arborio rice
¾ cup dry sherry
3 pounds asparagus, cut into 1″ lengths
1½ cups grated Parmesan cheese
1 teaspoon freshly ground pepper

1. In a large saucepan, bring the broth to a boil. Reduce the heat and simmer.
2. In a large nonstick saucepan or Dutch oven, heat the oil. Sauté the onions and shallots until softened, 5–8 minutes. Add the rice; cook, stirring to coat, 1–2 minutes.
3. Add about 1 cup of the broth and the sherry; cook, stirring constantly, until the liquid is absorbed. Continue adding the broth, about 1 cup at a time, stirring while the broth is absorbed, until the rice is just tender; add the asparagus with the last cup of broth. The total cooking time should be about 25–30 minutes. Remove from the heat and stir in the cheese and pepper.

Per serving: 317 CALORIES, 5 G TOTAL FAT, 2 G SATURATED FAT, 8 MG CHOLESTEROL, 285 MG SODIUM, 54 G TOTAL CARBOHYDRATE, 4 G DIETARY FIBER, 11 G PROTEIN, 172 MG CALCIUM.

POINTS PER SERVING: 6

Tip

Because risotto-making is so labor intensive, even if you aren't serving 12, you might want to make a batch this large. It reheats nicely in the microwave, or, for sublime risotto pancakes, mix leftovers with just enough beaten egg to hold the risotto together without making it too moist, then fold in a bit of shredded part-skim mozzarella. Heat a teaspoon or so of oil in a nonstick skillet and drop the risotto mixture into the pan by generous tablespoonfuls, flattening the blobs with the back of the spoon. Cook until golden brown, about 5 minutes on each side.

Venetian Radicchio

Makes 12 servings

3 heads radicchio, cleaned and quartered
¼ cup + 2 tablespoons fresh lemon juice
3 tablespoons olive oil
Pinch freshly ground black pepper

1. In a large nonreactive bowl, combine all the ingredients, tossing to coat. Cover and let stand 1–4 hours, tossing occasionally.
2. Preheat the oven to 425° F. Transfer the radicchio to a baking sheet and roast until just wilted, about 3 minutes on each side. Serve, drizzled with any remaining marinade.

Per serving: 47 Calories, 3 g Total Fat, 0 g Saturated Fat, 0 mg Cholesterol, 9 mg Sodium, 4 g Total Carbohydrate, 2 g Dietary Fiber, 1 g Protein, 1 mg Calcium.

POINTS PER SERVING: 1

Tip

Fresh radicchio is plentiful in Veneto, a farmland-rich and fertile region of Italy. You've probably seen it in salad blends, but it's also delicious cooked. Besides roasting it, you can toss radicchio on the grill for a few minutes; just be careful not to char the delicate leaves.

Blueberry Zabaglione

Makes 12 servings

6 cups fat-free egg substitute

3 cups skim milk

¾ cup sugar

¼ cup cornstarch

1½ cups dry marsala wine

6 cups blueberries

1. Pour the egg substitute into a large bowl. In a large nonstick saucepan, whisk the milk, sugar and cornstarch, whisking until the sugar dissolves. Bring to a simmer over medium heat, whisking constantly, then cook, whisking constantly, until thickened, 5–6 minutes.

2. Slowly whisk the milk mixture into the egg substitute, then slowly pour back into the saucepan, whisking quickly and constantly. Reduce the heat to low and cook, whisking constantly, until hot, thick and fluffy, 7–10 minutes; do not let the mixture boil. Slowly whisk in the marsala; cook, whisking constantly, 1 minute longer. Serve the zabaglione in wine or parfait glasses, topped with the blueberries.

Per serving: 201 CALORIES, 0 G TOTAL FAT, 0 G SATURATED FAT, 1 MG CHOLESTEROL, 238 MG SODIUM, 30 G TOTAL CARBOHYDRATE, 2 G DIETARY FIBER, 15 G PROTEIN, 123 MG CALCIUM.

POINTS PER SERVING: 4

Tip

Always wash fresh fruit thoroughly to help eliminate troublesome bacteria. Cooking fruit eliminates most potential health risks, but it also lowers the nutrient levels.

Traveler's Repast

Between my charity work and my travels for Weight Watchers, I spend a good deal of my time in transit. I have visited many states in America and have countless fond memories of each one. But I do find it difficult to compare and contrast the states because each one is so individual and distinctive in its own way.

Oklahoma City does hold a special place in my heart, however: I visited the city just after the bombing in 1995 and, like the rest of the world, was devastated by what I saw. I have been back several times and recently revisited the area. Through one of my charities, Chances for Children, I was able to raise money that was donated for building a new pediatric center.

While I recognize that I am quite fortunate to be able to travel the globe, there truly is no place like home. When I do get back from a trip, I most look forward to seeing my girls and sitting down with them. Frankly, after I've been on a long trip, food is not one of my major concerns. But since a traveler's fare is often not the healthiest, I try to reinstate the healthy habits I have learned. I do look forward to a simple, home-cooked meal: some meat, ham or fish, a baked potato and a salad.

Serves 4

Citrus Red Snapper

Baked Potato*

Crunchy Fennel Salad

Pears with Peppered Goat Cheese

Pot of Herbal Tea*

Citrus Red Snapper

Makes 4 servings

2 tablespoons all-purpose flour

¾ teaspoon ground coriander

¾ teaspoon ground ginger

¼ teaspoon cayenne pepper

Four 8-ounce red snapper fillets

2 teaspoons vegetable oil

1 yellow bell pepper, seeded and sliced

3 scallions, sliced

¼ cup low-sodium chicken broth

2 tablespoons orange juice

1 tablespoon fresh lemon juice

1 tablespoon fresh lime juice

Lemon and lime slices, to garnish

1. On a sheet of wax paper, combine the flour, coriander, ginger and cayenne. Coat one side of each fillet with the flour mixture.
2. In a large nonstick skillet, heat the oil. Add the fillets, floured-side down; cook until browned on the bottom, 2–3 minutes. Transfer to a plate.
3. In the skillet, mix the bell pepper, scallions, broth, orange juice, lemon juice and lime juice; return the fish to the skillet, browned-side up. Reduce the heat and cook, covered, until the fish is just opaque and the bell pepper is softened, 3–5 minutes. With a slotted spatula, transfer the fish and vegetables to a platter. Cook the pan juices until they are reduced to about ¼ cup; pour over the fish. Serve, garnished with the lemon and lime slices.

Continued on next page.

Per serving: 279 CALORIES, 5 G TOTAL FAT, 1 G SATURATED FAT, 84 MG CHOLESTEROL, 150 MG SODIUM, 7 G TOTAL CARBOHYDRATE, 1 G DIETARY FIBER, 48 G PROTEIN, 83 MG CALCIUM.

POINTS PER SERVING: 6

Tip

Just about any firm-fleshed fish fillets will do the trick in this recipe: Try ocean perch, flounder, sea bass, cod or haddock.

Crunchy Fennel Salad

Makes 4 servings

3 tablespoons white-wine vinegar
2 tablespoons fresh lime juice
1 teaspoon sugar
2 fennel bulbs, trimmed and thinly sliced
½ red onion, thinly sliced

1. In a small bowl, mix the vinegar, lime juice and sugar, stirring until the sugar dissolves.
2. In a large bowl, combine the fennel and onion. Drizzle with the dressing; toss to coat.

Per serving: 31 Calories, 0 g Total Fat, 0 g Saturated Fat, 0 mg Cholesterol, 111 mg Sodium, 6 g Total Carbohydrate, 1 g Dietary Fiber, 2 g Protein, 57 mg Calcium.

POINTS PER SERVING: 0

Tip

With its subtle licoricelike flavor, fennel (also called anise or *finocchio*) makes a light side dish for a robust, rich entrée like beef or pork. Try it as the Italians do, sliced and unadorned, after dinner as a digestive. (See Step 2 of the Fennel and Blood Orange Salad on page 63 for fennel-trimming instructions.)

Pears with Peppered Goat Cheese

Makes 4 servings

2 large Bosc pears, halved and cored
1 teaspoon fresh lemon juice
⅓ cup crumbled peppered goat cheese

Brush the cut side of the pears with the lemon juice; place the pears on dessert plates. Sprinkle with the cheese.

Per serving: 131 Calories, 4 g Total Fat, 2 g Saturated Fat, 8 mg Cholesterol, 148 mg Sodium, 24 g Total Carbohydrate, 4 g Dietary Fiber, 3 g Protein, 74 mg Calcium.

POINTS PER SERVING: 2

Tip

Use the ripest pears you can find for this easy yet elegant dessert—their sweetness will provide the most contrast to the tangy bite of the cheese. Experiment with other cheeses; a blue like Roquefort or Gorgonzola would be good. For best flavor, let the cheese come to room temperature.

Gardener's Supper

In my life, a "day off" is almost unheard of; however, if I can catch a few hours of free time, I like to indulge my love of painting.

In a funny way, my painting has helped me on the dieting front. In searching for ways other than eating to indulge my senses, I have happily become reacquainted with my creative side. I enjoy sketching and painting, primarily watercolors.

Nature plays a tremendous role in my work: I use the garden, the mountains, the wilds of Scotland and the beautiful English countryside for inspiration. (I do understand why so many Americans have fallen in love with our English gardens: they are spectacular!)

Thanks to my new habits, I have also discovered the riches of the garden: just-picked produce like wonderfully ripe tomatoes or fresh green beans. I try to include as many fresh vegetables and fruits as possible in all my meals—but never just steamed! Pairing those treasures with small tastes of other foods with intense flavor, like prosciutto or Parmesan, truly can make a simple meal a feast.

Serves 4

Twenty-Minute Minestrone

Stuffed Baby Eggplant

Lemon Couscous

Asparagus Vinaigrette with Parmesan and Prosciutto

Raspberries with Citrus Sauce

Twenty-Minute Minestrone

Makes 4 servings

1 tablespoon olive oil

1 tomato, chopped

1 onion, chopped

1 garlic clove, minced

4 cups chicken broth

2 medium red potatoes, scrubbed and diced

½ pound green beans, cut into 1″ lengths

1 medium zucchini, chopped

1 medium yellow squash, chopped

2 cups coarsely chopped cleaned spinach

One 15-ounce can red kidney beans, rinsed and drained

2 tablespoons grated Parmesan cheese

1. In a large nonstick saucepan or Dutch oven, heat the oil. Sauté the tomato, onion and garlic until softened, about 5 minutes. Stir in the broth and potatoes; bring to a boil. Reduce the heat and simmer, partially covered, until the potatoes are almost tender, about 10 minutes.
2. Add the green beans, zucchini and yellow squash; cook until tender, about 5 minutes. Stir in the spinach and kidney beans; cook until heated through, about 3 minutes. Serve, sprinkled with the cheese.

Per serving: 254 Calories, 7 g Total Fat, 2 g Saturated Fat, 19 mg Cholesterol, 1,176 mg Sodium, 39 g Total Carbohydrate, 10 g Dietary Fiber, 12 g Protein, 127 mg Calcium.

POINTS PER SERVING: 4

When the weather starts to cool off, you can make this soup more of a hearty stew by adding small tubular pasta and winter vegetables. Serve it with a crisp Italian white wine like Pinot Grigio and crusty Italian bread.

Stuffed Baby Eggplant

Makes 4 servings

2 baby eggplants, halved lengthwise

1 teaspoon olive oil

1 onion, chopped

1 tomato, diced

1 garlic clove, minced

¼ cup + 2 tablespoons seasoned dried bread crumbs

1 egg, slightly beaten

2 tablespoons grated Parmesan cheese

6 kalamata olives, pitted and chopped

1 tablespoon pine nuts, coarsely chopped and toasted (optional)

1 tablespoon chopped basil

1 tablespoon capers, rinsed, drained and coarsely chopped

1. Preheat the oven to 400° F; spray a shallow 1-quart baking dish with non-stick cooking spray.

2. Fill a medium skillet ½″ deep with water; add the eggplant, cut-side down. Bring to a boil, then reduce the heat and simmer, covered, until the eggplant is fork-tender, about 5 minutes. Drain the eggplant on paper towels.

3. In a small nonstick skillet, heat the oil. Sauté the onion until softened, about 5 minutes. Add the tomato and garlic; cook, stirring occasionally, until the vegetables begin to soften, about 5 minutes. Remove from the heat.

4. With a spoon, carefully scoop out the pulp from each eggplant half, leaving a ¼″ shell. Coarsely chop the pulp.

5. In a medium bowl, mix the eggplant pulp with the sautéed vegetables, the bread crumbs, egg, cheese, olives, pine nuts (if using), basil and capers. Spoon the filling into the eggplant shells and place in the baking dish. Bake until the filling is hot and browned on top, about 25 minutes.

Per serving (with pine nuts): 150 CALORIES, 6 G TOTAL FAT, 1 G SATURATED FAT,
55 MG CHOLESTEROL, 444 MG SODIUM, 20 G TOTAL CARBOHYDRATE,
4 G DIETARY FIBER, 7 G PROTEIN, 76 MG CALCIUM.

POINTS PER SERVING: 3

Tip

Pine nuts, also called pignoli, really are the seeds of a pine cone. They have a mild delicate flavor and are used in many Mediterranean dishes. Pine nuts are highly perishable because of their high fat content; never buy more than you need, and keep them in the refrigerator or freezer (bring them to room temperature before using). Chopped walnuts may be substituted, if you like. Using this small an amount of nuts doesn't affect the ***POINTS*** per serving.

Lemon Couscous

Makes 4 servings

1¾ cups chicken broth

2 teaspoons grated lemon zest

2 tablespoons fresh lemon juice

1 tablespoon unsalted butter or margarine

¼ teaspoon salt

One 10-ounce box couscous

1 tablespoon chopped parsley

In a medium saucepan, combine the broth, lemon zest, lemon juice, butter and salt; bring to a boil. Stir in the couscous and parsley; cover and remove from the heat. Let stand until the liquid is absorbed, about 5 minutes. Fluff the couscous with a fork.

Per serving: 309 CALORIES, 4 G TOTAL FAT, 2 G SATURATED FAT, 16 MG CHOLESTEROL, 575 MG SODIUM, 56 G TOTAL CARBOHYDRATE, 4 G DIETARY FIBER, 10 G PROTEIN, 22 MG CALCIUM.

POINTS PER SERVING: 6

Tip

Couscous cooks in just 5 minutes, and is an excellent alternative to rice or potatoes. The variations to this dish are endless; add chopped sautéed vegetables, such as carrots and zucchini, for added flavor and a nutritional boost.

Asparagus Vinaigrette with Parmesan and Prosciutto

Makes 4 servings

1 pound asparagus

2 tablespoons fresh lemon juice

1 teaspoon Dijon mustard

¼ teaspoon sugar

¼ teaspoon salt

¼ teaspoon freshly ground pepper

1 tablespoon olive oil

2 paper-thin slices prosciutto or Parma ham (about 1 ounce), finely chopped

1 tablespoon grated Parmesan cheese

1. If the asparagus spears are more than ½″ thick, peel them. In a large skillet of boiling water, cook the asparagus until tender, about 5 minutes. Drain and rinse under cold running water; pat dry and transfer to a wide bowl or platter.
2. Meanwhile, in a small bowl, whisk the lemon juice, mustard, sugar, salt and pepper with 1 tablespoon water; slowly whisk in the oil. Drizzle the dressing over asparagus; sprinkle with the prosciutto and cheese.

Per serving: 78 Calories, 5 g Total Fat, 1 g Saturated Fat, 8 mg Cholesterol, 343 mg Sodium, 5 g Total Carbohydrate, 2 g Dietary Fiber, 5 g Protein, 41 mg Calcium.

POINTS PER SERVING: 2

Tip

This simple side dish can also double as an elegant appetizer. You can also drizzle the mild lemon-mustard vinaigrette over your favorite combination of greens, or other veggies—try steamed green beans, carrots or beets.

Raspberries with Citrus Sauce

Makes 4 servings

3 tablespoons orange juice
2 tablespoons sugar
2 tablespoons fresh lemon juice
1 tablespoon fresh lime juice
1½ teaspoons cornstarch
½ teaspoon grated orange zest
½ teaspoon grated lemon zest
½ teaspoon grated lime zest
3 cups raspberries

In a small saucepan over medium heat, whisk the orange juice, sugar, lemon juice, lime juice, cornstarch, all three kinds of zest and ⅓ cup cold water, blending until the cornstarch dissolves. Cook, stirring constantly, until thickened, about 3 minutes. Serve the berries, topped with the sauce.

Per serving: 93 Calories, 0 g Total Fat, 0 g Saturated Fat, 0 mg Cholesterol, 0 mg Sodium, 23 g Total Carbohydrate, 5 g Dietary Fiber, 1 g Protein, 38 mg Calcium.

POINTS PER SERVING: 1

Tip

If you like, substitute fresh blackberries for the raspberries. This sauce is also delicious spooned over fat-free pound cake.

A Provençal Feast

A good friend of mine has a villa in the hills of Provence; I have been a visitor there countless times. In Provence, magic comes up with the sun. The setting simply feeds the senses. Green olive trees, blue swimming pools and a virtual symphony of smells: pine, eucalyptus, wild rosemary.

I love the beauty of Provence and the heady scent of the countryside after a rainstorm. I paint a good deal when I am in the French countryside. I try to capture every image in order to create magic in my head, which hopefully flows into my brushes and my life.

Serves 6

Mediterranean Fisherman's Stew

Tarte Provençale

Crusty Baguette*

Assorted Cheese and Fruit Platter*

Mediterranean Fisherman's Stew

Makes 6 servings

One 7-ounce jar roasted red peppers, rinsed and drained

½ cup tomato sauce

2 garlic cloves, peeled

½ teaspoon dried thyme

½ teaspoon dried oregano

2 cups fish broth or clam juice

½ cup dry white wine

1 small onion, chopped

1 bay leaf

12 littleneck clams (about 1 pound), scrubbed

12 mussels (about ¾ pound), scrubbed and debearded

1 pound monkfish, cut into 2″ pieces

½ pound medium shrimp, peeled and deveined

12 kalamata olives, halved lengthwise and pitted

2 tablespoons anise-flavored liqueur

¼ teaspoon crushed red pepper flakes, or to taste

1. In a food processor or blender, combine the roasted red peppers, tomato sauce, garlic, thyme and oregano; puree.
2. Transfer the puree to a large nonreactive Dutch oven. Cook, stirring occasionally, until the flavors are blended, about 5 minutes. Stir in the broth, wine, onion, bay leaf and ½ cup water; bring to a boil. Add the clams and mussels; cook, covered, until most of the shells have opened, 6–7 minutes. Remove and discard any clams or mussels whose shells remain closed.
3. Stir in the monkfish, shrimp, olives and liqueur; cook, covered, until the monkfish is opaque and the shrimp pink, 3–4 minutes. Discard the bay leaf; sprinkle with the pepper flakes.

Per serving: 198 CALORIES, 4 G TOTAL FAT, 0 G SATURATED FAT, 95 MG CHOLESTEROL, 450 MG SODIUM, 8 G TOTAL CARBOHYDRATE, 2 G DIETARY FIBER, 26 G PROTEIN, 85 MG CALCIUM.

POINTS PER SERVING: 4

Tip

This unique seafood stew has a less pervasive tomato taste than the more common bouillabaisse; it derives its tangier Mediterranean accent from roasted red pepper and olives. The liqueur is an easy way to get the flavor of fennel without having to crush seeds. Fish broth is available frozen or in bouillon cubes; bottled clam juice may be substituted. For quicker preparation, buy debearded mussels from your fishmonger. Remember to provide bowls for clam and mussel shells.

Tarte Provençale

Makes 6 servings

1 medium (about 1¼-pound) eggplant, cut crosswise into ¼″ slices

½ teaspoon salt

¼ teaspoon freshly ground pepper

2 teaspoons olive oil

Two 14½-ounce cans diced tomatoes

1 cup sliced mushrooms

2 tablespoons chopped basil

2 tablespoons capers, rinsed and drained

1 tablespoon chopped oregano

1 tablespoon minced thyme

2 garlic cloves, minced

3 ounces Montrachet (goat cheese), cut into ¼″ slices

1. Adjust the oven rack to divide the oven in half. Spray a nonstick baking sheet with nonstick cooking spray; preheat the broiler. Place the eggplant on the baking sheet; sprinkle with ¼ teaspoon of the salt and ⅛ teaspoon of the pepper. Broil until lightly browned, about 2–3 minutes on each side. Remove the eggplant from the broiler. Reduce the oven temperature to 450° F.

2. Meanwhile, in a large nonstick skillet, heat the oil. Cook the tomatoes, mushrooms, basil, capers, oregano, thyme, garlic, the remaining ¼ teaspoon of salt and ⅛ teaspoon of pepper, stirring as needed, until thickened, 5–10 minutes. Remove from the heat.

3. Spray a 9″ flameproof pie plate with nonstick cooking spray. Spread the pie plate with one-third of the tomato sauce; top with half of the eggplant slices, overlapping as necessary; repeat the layers, pouring the last third of the tomato sauce over the eggplant. Arrange the goat cheese over the sauce. Bake until the cheese is melted and the edges of the tart are bubbling, about 10

minutes. Increase the oven temperature to broil; broil the tart 4″ from the heat until the cheese is golden brown, 1–2 minutes.

Per serving: 119 Calories, 8 g Total Fat, 3 g Saturated Fat, 11 mg Cholesterol, 527 mg Sodium, 9 g Total Carbohydrate, 2 g Dietary Fiber, 5 g Protein, 96 mg Calcium.

POINTS PER SERVING: 3

Tip

Try goat cheese flavored with dill or cracked black or red pepper for a subtly different flavor.

A Simple Pasta Dinner

I have had a good deal written about my life in the press. Yet, without doubt, the most hurtful comments have focused on my weight, the hobgoblin I have fought since my teenage years. Although I have tried countless fad diets, I calmed down during my courtship with Andrew, who took me as I was. I recall in an interview before our wedding, I dismissed my battle of the bulge: "I'm not going to get thin. I'm not going to change a lot. I'm just going to be me."

Fact was, as long as my life was in control, so was my weight. When my life was in disarray, my weight followed suit. But who can ever say their life is *always* under control?

I have learned that knowledge is just one way to take control of your life. In those bleak days, I felt a pasta dinner was the enemy that would blow me up for no less than three days. Now, I know that almost any food can be eaten when you are trying to lose weight. You just must remember portion size—and control!

Serves 4

Linguine Riviera

Roasted Pepper Salad

Fresh Fig and Pear Plate*

Linguine Riviera

Makes 4 servings

6 ounces linguine

2 teaspoons olive oil

1 onion, chopped

3 garlic cloves, minced

3 medium zucchini, quartered lengthwise and thinly sliced

2 tomatoes, seeded and diced

1 tablespoon balsamic vinegar

½ teaspoon salt

4 teaspoons grated Parmesan cheese

1. Cook the linguine according to package directions; drain.
2. In a large nonstick saucepan or Dutch oven, heat the oil. Sauté the onion and garlic until softened, about 3 minutes. Stir in the zucchini and sauté until softened, about 3 minutes.
3. Stir in the tomatoes, vinegar and salt; cook, stirring as needed, until the sauce thickens slightly, about 5 minutes. Stir in the linguine; cook, tossing constantly, until heated through, 2–3 minutes. Serve, topped with the cheese.

Per serving: 231 CALORIES, 4 G TOTAL FAT, 1 G SATURATED FAT, 1 MG CHOLESTEROL, 311 MG SODIUM, 42 G TOTAL CARBOHYDRATE, 3 G DIETARY FIBER, 8 G PROTEIN, 58 MG CALCIUM.

POINTS PER SERVING: 4

Tip

Fresh basil is a nice addition to this recipe. Add ½ cup of minced fresh leaves or 1–2 tablespoons dried when you stir in the linguine.

Roasted Pepper Salad

Makes 4 servings

2 tablespoons fresh lemon juice

4 teaspoons olive oil

1 teaspoon minced thyme

½ teaspoon salt

¼ teaspoon freshly ground pepper

1 red bell pepper

1 yellow bell pepper

1 green bell pepper

1 tablespoon chopped parsley

1. In a small bowl, whisk the lemon juice, oil, thyme, salt and ground pepper.
2. Line a baking sheet with foil; preheat the broiler. Place the bell peppers on the baking sheet; broil 4–6″ from the heat, turning frequently with tongs, until the skin is lightly charred on all sides, about 10 minutes. Transfer the peppers to a paper bag; fold the bag closed and let the peppers steam 10 minutes. Peel, seed, devein and chop the peppers, then place them in a bowl. Drizzle with the dressing; toss to coat. Serve, sprinkled with the parsley.

Per serving: 74 Calories, 5 g Total Fat, 1 g Saturated Fat, 0 mg Cholesterol, 271 mg Sodium, 8 g Total Carbohydrate, 3 g Dietary Fiber, 2 g Protein, 16 mg Calcium.

POINTS PER SERVING: 1

Tip

To make this a main dish, mix in 1 cup cooked brown rice and 1 cup diced, cooked chicken breast.

A Quiet New Year's Eve Celebration

My New Year's Eves tend to be very low-key. My most recent New Year's Eve was a quiet celebration with my daughters and the staff who look after us at Wood Farm. We played board games, and although the girls go to bed before midnight, I toast the New Year in with those who help keep my life in order.

Serves 12

Red Potatoes with Caviar and Cheese

Tricolor Salad with Gorgonzola Dressing

Lamb Chops with Mint Salsa

Orzo Pilaf

Individual Ginger-Peach Soufflés

Red Potatoes with Caviar and Cheese

Makes 12 servings

12 new red potatoes (about 1 pound), scrubbed
3 tablespoons Neufchâtel cheese
1 tablespoon low-fat (1%) buttermilk
1 teaspoon chopped dill
1 tablespoon black lumpfish caviar

1. Place the potatoes in a single layer in a shallow microwavable container; cook on High until fork-tender, about 3 minutes. Alternately, bake the potatoes at 350° F for 20 minutes.

2. Cut the potatoes in half; place, cut-side down, on a platter. With a spoon or a melon baller, make a small well in the top of each potato.

3. In a small bowl, mix the cheese and buttermilk until smooth; with a rubber spatula, fold in the dill and caviar. Dollop about ¾ teaspoon of the mixture into the well of each potato.

Per serving: 54 Calories, 1 g Total Fat, 1 g Saturated Fat, 11 mg Cholesterol, 39 mg Sodium, 10 g Total Carbohydrate, 1 g Dietary Fiber, 2 g Protein, 12 mg Calcium.

POINTS PER SERVING: 1

— *Tip* —

The caviar is readily available in the canned seafood section of the supermarket; red lumpfish caviar or salmon caviar may be substituted. Pass the filled potatoes as an hors d'oeuvre; serve with flutes of champagne.

Tricolor Salad with Gorgonzola Dressing

Makes 12 servings

1 cup crumbled Gorgonzola cheese

¼ cup + 2 tablespoons white-wine vinegar

¼ cup olive oil

3 tablespoons dry white wine

1 tablespoon Dijon mustard

½ teaspoon salt

Freshly ground pepper, to taste

3 heads radicchio, cleaned and torn into bite-size pieces

3 bunches arugula, cleaned and torn into bite-size pieces

1 head Boston or Bibb lettuce, cleaned and torn into bite-size pieces

1. In a blender or food processor, combine the cheese, vinegar, oil, wine, mustard, salt and pepper; pulse until the dressing is creamy and smooth, 4–5 times.
2. In a large salad bowl, combine the radicchio, arugula and lettuce. Drizzle with the dressing; toss to coat.

Per serving: 101 Calories, 8 g Total Fat, 3 g Saturated Fat, 8 mg Cholesterol, 208 mg Sodium, 4 g Total Carbohydrate, 1 g Dietary Fiber, 4 g Protein, 133 mg Calcium.

POINTS PER SERVING: 2

Tip

If this combination of lettuces doesn't strike your fancy, use a mixture of red leaf lettuce, green leaf lettuce and endive, or watercress, romaine and frisée, for alternatives to the three colors.

Lamb Chops with Mint Salsa

Makes 12 servings

12 plum tomatoes, chopped
2 yellow bell peppers, seeded and diced
2 onions, chopped
¼ cup + 2 tablespoons chopped mint
¼ cup fresh lime juice
2 tablespoons olive oil
3–4 garlic cloves, minced
½ teaspoon salt
½ teaspoon freshly ground pepper
¼–½ teaspoon crushed red pepper flakes
Twelve 4-ounce loin lamb chops, ¾" thick

1. In a large nonreactive bowl, mix the tomatoes, bell peppers, onions, mint, lime juice, oil, garlic, salt, pepper and pepper flakes. Let stand at room temperature until the flavors are blended, about 1 hour.
2. Spray a broiler rack with nonstick cooking spray; preheat the broiler. Broil the lamb chops, turning once, 5–6 minutes on each side. Serve with the salsa on the side.

Per serving: 245 Calories, 13 g Total Fat, 4 g Saturated Fat, 81 mg Cholesterol, 211 mg Sodium, 5 g Total Carbohydrate, 1 g Dietary Fiber, 26 g Protein, 29 mg Calcium.

POINTS PER SERVING: 6

Tip

This unusual salsa combines the coolness of mint with the heat of red pepper. Make it up to two days ahead and store it, covered, in the refrigerator.

Orzo Pilaf

Makes 12 servings

2¼ cups orzo

2 tablespoons olive oil

2 onions, chopped

2 celery stalks, chopped

3–4 garlic cloves, minced

3 cups packed chopped cleaned spinach leaves

¾ cup chicken broth

1½ tablespoons red-wine vinegar

¾ cup grated Asiago cheese

Freshly ground pepper, to taste

1. Cook the orzo according to package directions; drain.
2. Meanwhile, in a large nonstick saucepan or Dutch oven, heat the oil. Sauté the onions, celery and garlic until softened, 5–8 minutes. Stir in the spinach, about ⅓ cup of the broth and the vinegar; cook, stirring frequently, until the liquid evaporates, 3–5 minutes longer. Stir in the orzo, cheese, pepper and the remaining broth.

Per serving: 217 CALORIES, 5 G TOTAL FAT, 1 G SATURATED FAT, 5 MG CHOLESTEROL, 176 MG SODIUM, 35 G TOTAL CARBOHYDRATE, 2 G DIETARY FIBER, 8 G PROTEIN, 99 MG CALCIUM.

POINTS PER SERVING: 4

Tip

If you're in a time crunch, frozen chopped spinach works, too. Just be sure to thaw it completely and squeeze out any excess moisture.

Individual Ginger-Peach Soufflés

Makes 12 servings

12 ounces dried peaches
1 cup + 6 tablespoons sugar
1½ tablespoons all-purpose flour
3 tablespoons brandy
1 tablespoon ground ginger
12 large egg whites, at room temperature
1 tablespoon confectioners' sugar

1. In a medium saucepan, combine the peaches, 1 cup of the sugar and 2¼ cups water, stirring until the sugar dissolves; bring to a boil. Reduce the heat and simmer, covered, until the peaches are very soft, 25–30 minutes.

2. Meanwhile, spray twelve 1-cup soufflé dishes lightly with nonstick cooking spray, spreading with your fingers to coat the dishes evenly; dust each with 1 teaspoon of the remaining sugar. Preheat the oven to 375° F.

3. Transfer the peach mixture to a food processor or blender; puree (you should have 2¼ cups puree; if necessary, add sufficient boiling water to reach that volume).

4. Return the puree to the saucepan; stir in the flour and 2 tablespoons water. Cook over low heat, stirring constantly, until the mixture just begins to give off steam, about 2 minutes. Remove from the heat; stir in the brandy and ginger.

5. In 1 very large bowl or 2 large bowls, beat the egg whites until soft peaks form. Add the remaining 2 tablespoons of sugar and beat until stiff, glossy peaks form.

6. Transfer the peach puree to a very large mixing bowl. Mix in one-third of the egg whites until thoroughly incorporated; with a rubber spatula, gently fold in the remaining egg whites. Divide evenly among the soufflé dishes. With the rubber spatula, make a shallow ridge around the inside rim of each dish. Place the soufflés on a 15 x 20" baking sheet. Bake until the tops are puffed

and browned, 18–20 minutes. Put the confectioners' sugar in a small sieve and dust the soufflés as they come out of the oven. Serve at once.

Per serving: 189 CALORIES, 0 G TOTAL FAT, 0 G SATURATED FAT, 0 MG CHOLESTEROL, 57 MG SODIUM, 42 G TOTAL CARBOHYDRATE, 2 G DIETARY FIBER, 5 G PROTEIN, 11 MG CALCIUM.

POINTS PER SERVING: 3

Tip

For best results, execute Steps 1 through 4 before sitting down to dinner. If desired, the peach puree can be made up to 24 hours in advance and refrigerated. Beating this volume of egg whites will require at least a 5½-quart bowl. If you don't have two bowls that large, beat the egg whites in 2 equal batches; save your biggest bowl for Step 6. Three 1-quart soufflé dishes can be used instead of twelve 1-cup dishes; the baking time remains the same.

A Birthday Gala

Dads was always a major romantic. When I was a small child, he would flood me with birthday cards—not just from him and Mum, but also "signed" by the cat, the dog, the ponies, the house and even the car! Birthdays are still very special days—especially my children's birthdays. I always make an extra effort to be around and celebrate with them. I love to watch their faces light up with glee and excitement, which always gives me such a great sense of pride and pleasure.

Serves 10

Dilly Dip and Vegetables

Honey-Dipped Crunchy Chicken Nuggets

Celebration Birthday Cake

Sugar Cookies

Chocolate-Coconut Fruit Kebabs

Strawberry Lemonade

Dilly Dip and Vegetables

Makes 10 servings

¾ cup light sour cream

1 cucumber, peeled, seeded and finely chopped

2 tablespoons chopped dill

2 tablespoons cider vinegar

1 teaspoon sugar

1 teaspoon Dijon mustard

¼ teaspoon salt

1 head green-leaf lettuce, cleaned and separated

1 small head red cabbage

1 green bell pepper

1 red bell pepper

1 yellow bell pepper

1 orange bell pepper

2 carrots, peeled and cut into sticks

2 celery stalks, cut into sticks

1 cup cauliflower florets

1. In a medium bowl, mix the sour cream, cucumber, dill, vinegar, sugar, mustard and salt. Refrigerate, covered, until ready to use.

2. Line a flat basket or platter with the lettuce leaves. Hollow out the center of the cabbage; place it in the center of the leaves.

3. Holding each pepper upright, cut off the four sides; discard the core with the seeds and membranes. With cookie cutters, cut the peppers into shapes; thread onto bamboo skewers and arrange in the basket with the carrot sticks, celery sticks and cauliflower florets.

4. Just before serving, fill the hollowed-out cabbage with the dip.

Continued on next page.

Per serving: 66 CALORIES, 2 G TOTAL FAT, 0 G SATURATED FAT, 6 MG CHOLESTEROL, 91 MG SODIUM, 11 G TOTAL CARBOHYDRATE, 3 G DIETARY FIBER, 3 G PROTEIN, 71 MG CALCIUM.

POINTS PER SERVING: 1

─── *Tip* ───

Get out your favorite animal cookie cutters and let the kids have fun making animal shapes out of veggies. They'll never know this is good-for-you party food.

Honey-Dipped Crunchy Chicken Nuggets

Makes 10 servings

3 tablespoons honey
1 egg white, lightly beaten
2 pounds skinless boneless chicken breasts, cut into 1½″ chunks
1 cup cornflake crumbs
½ teaspoon salt
½ cup reduced-calorie mayonnaise
¼ cup Dijon mustard

1. Preheat the oven to 400° F; spray a large baking sheet with nonstick cooking spray. In a large bowl, mix 1 tablespoon of the honey and the egg white; add the chicken and stir to coat. Transfer the chicken to a colander and set over a large bowl.
2. On a sheet of wax paper, combine the cornflake crumbs and salt. One at a time, dip the chicken pieces into the crumbs, then place on the baking sheet. Spray the tops of the chicken lightly with nonstick cooking spray. Bake until the chicken is cooked through, 8–10 minutes.
3. Meanwhile, in a small bowl, mix the mayonnaise, mustard and the remaining 2 tablespoons of honey. Serve the chicken nuggets with the dipping sauce.

Per serving: 192 CALORIES, 7 G TOTAL FAT, 1 G SATURATED FAT, 55 MG CHOLESTEROL, 332 MG SODIUM, 11 G TOTAL CARBOHYDRATE, 0 G DIETARY FIBER, 21 G PROTEIN, 19 MG CALCIUM.

POINTS PER SERVING: 4

Tip

Freeze the leftovers, if there are any! Thaw them completely, then reheat at 350° F and enjoy.

Celebration Birthday Cake

Makes 12 servings

3 egg whites
2 tablespoons vegetable oil
One 18.25-ounce box reduced-fat devil's food cake mix
1¾ cups reduced-fat ready-to-serve vanilla frosting
1 cup sliced strawberries
Assorted tubes frosting gel
Assorted candy rosettes and cake decorations

1. Preheat the oven to 350° F. Spray two 9″ round pans with nonstick cooking spray. Using the egg whites, oil and 1⅓ cups water, prepare the cake mix according to package directions; transfer the batter to the pans. Bake until a tester inserted in the center of the cakes comes out clean, 25–30 minutes. Cool the cakes in the pans 5 minutes, then invert onto wire racks to cool completely.

2. To assemble the cake, place one cake layer, bottom-side up, on a cake stand or large round platter; slide strips of wax paper under the bottom of the cake. Using ½ cup of the frosting, frost the top of the layer; top with the strawberries. Place the remaining cake layer over the berries, bottom-side up. Spread the top and sides of the cake with the remaining frosting; with the frosting gel, write the message, then decorate with the rosettes and cake decorations. Gently remove the wax paper strips from under the cake. Refrigerate until ready to serve.

Per serving: 458 Calories, 11 g Total Fat, 3 g Saturated Fat, 0 mg Cholesterol, 473 mg Sodium, 86 g Total Carbohydrate, 2 g Dietary Fiber, 3 g Protein, 78 mg Calcium.

POINTS PER SERVING: 10

Tip

Frosting the layers bottom-side up ensures that the top of the cake will be flat and smooth. Buy a 16-ounce can of frosting; use the remaining ¼ cup to frost the cookies.

Sugar Cookies

Makes about 30 cookies

¾ cup all-purpose flour
½ teaspoon baking powder
¼ teaspoon salt
¼ cup + 2 tablespoons sugar
2½ tablespoons butter or margarine
2 tablespoons fat-free egg substitute
½ teaspoon vanilla extract
¼ cup reduced-fat ready-to-serve vanilla frosting
Assorted colored sugars

1. Preheat the oven to 375° F. In a small bowl, combine the flour, baking powder and salt. In a medium bowl, with an electric mixer on medium speed, beat the sugar and butter until light and fluffy. Beat in the egg substitute and vanilla; stir in the flour mixture.

2. On a lightly floured surface, turn out the dough. If necessary, knead in up to 2 tablespoons flour, 1 tablespoon at a time, to make a firm dough. Roll out to ⅛" thick. Dip 2" cookie cutters in flour; cut the dough into shapes. Transfer the cookies to a large nonstick baking sheet. Bake until the cookies are lightly golden on the bottom, 8–10 minutes. Cool completely on wire racks.

3. With a small pastry brush, brush the cookies with the frosting; if necessary, thin the frosting with a little water. Sprinkle the cookies with the colored sugars.

Per cookie: 45 CALORIES, 1 G TOTAL FAT, 1 G SATURATED FAT, 3 MG CHOLESTEROL, 49 MG SODIUM, 8 G TOTAL CARBOHYDRATE, 0 G DIETARY FIBER, 0 G PROTEIN, 1 MG CALCIUM.

POINTS PER COOKIE: 1

Tip

Bake and decorate the sugar cookies a day ahead. Place them in a single layer on a wire rack and cover loosely with plastic wrap. Cookies cut in fanciful shapes lend a festive air to a party; if you like, use 2″ alphabet cookie cutters and cut out "Happy Birthday" and your child's name.

Chocolate-Coconut Fruit Kebabs

Makes 10 servings

1 small honeydew melon, seeded and cut into chunks

1 small cantaloupe, seeded and cut into chunks

2 bananas, cut into chunks

3 cups strawberries, hulled (leave whole)

3 tablespoons maple syrup

¼ cup sweetened shredded coconut

Two 1-ounce squares semisweet chocolate, melted

On each of twenty 8″ bamboo skewers, alternately thread the honeydew, cantaloupe, bananas and strawberries. Brush the tops of the kebabs with the syrup; sprinkle with the coconut, then drizzle with the chocolate.

Per serving: 142 Calories, 3 g Total Fat, 2 g Saturated Fat, 0 mg Cholesterol, 37 mg Sodium, 31 g Total Carbohydrate, 4 g Dietary Fiber, 2 g Protein, 26 mg Calcium.

POINTS PER SERVING: 2

Tip

Here is a dessert that kids will love to put together themselves. After you peel and seed the fruit, let the kids have fun garnishing (and eating!) with the chocolate and coconut. If you don't have 2 squares of chocolate, melt ½ cup chocolate chips instead.

Strawberry Lemonade

Makes 8 servings

3 cups strawberries, halved
1½ cups sugar
1½ cups fresh lemon juice (about 8 lemons)
2 tablespoons grated lemon zest
Mint sprigs, to garnish

In a food processor or blender, puree the strawberries and sugar. Transfer to a large pitcher; blend in 2 cups cold water, the lemon juice and lemon zest. Pour into tall glasses over ice; garnish with the mint sprigs.

Per serving: 174 Calories, 0 g Total Fat, 0 g Saturated Fat, 0 mg Cholesterol, 2 mg Sodium, 46 g Total Carbohydrate, 2 g Dietary Fiber, 1 g Protein, 13 mg Calcium.

POINTS PER SERVING: 3

Tip

If you're serving more than eight, make this in two batches rather than one double batch unless you have a very large pitcher. For a sophisticated adult drink, stir in 1 cup water and 1 cup vodka instead of the 2 cups water. Using raspberries in lieu of the strawberries would be quite tasty, but you will need to strain the fruit puree through a cheesecloth-lined sieve to eliminate the seeds.

Saturday Night Supper and Videos

I love watching videos and all kinds of films. Some of my fondest memories of my life at Sunninghill Park involve being with Andrew and the girls, simply watching videos as a family.

Some favorite films that come to mind are *Braveheart* with Mel Gibson and *The Shawshank Redemption* with Morgan Freeman and Tim Robbins. *Dances with Wolves* also holds a special place in my heart. I enjoy films that are purely entertaining and fun: they allow me to escape from the realities of life for a few hours. But I also enjoy movies that revolve around stories of those who have overcome adversity and learned something about themselves or their worlds. Once you discover who you truly are and what your real needs are, then, I believe, you can live a truly happy life.

Serves 4

Tuscan Soup

Mixed Green Salad with Orange Dressing

Balsamic Strawberries

Tuscan Soup

Makes 4 servings

2 cups chicken broth

One 15-ounce can cannellini beans, rinsed and drained

One 14½-can diced tomatoes, drained

1 carrot, peeled and chopped

1 white onion, finely chopped

2 garlic cloves, minced

1 pound kale, cleaned and chopped

½ pound low-fat beef or turkey smoked sausage, chopped (optional)

½ teaspoon salt

Freshly ground pepper, to taste

4 teaspoons grated Parmesan cheese

1. In a large saucepan or Dutch oven, combine the broth, beans, tomatoes, carrot, onion and garlic; bring to a boil. Reduce the heat and simmer, covered, until the carrot is tender, about 15 minutes.
2. Stir in the kale and sausage (if using); cook until the kale is tender, about 10 minutes. Add the salt and pepper to taste. Serve, sprinkled with the cheese.

Per serving (with sausage): 247 CALORIES, 4 G TOTAL FAT, 1 G SATURATED FAT, 31 MG CHOLESTEROL, 1,579 MG SODIUM, 32 G TOTAL CARBOHYDRATE, 11 G DIETARY FIBER, 18 G PROTEIN, 193 MG CALCIUM.

POINTS PER SERVING: 3

Tip

Instead of kale, you can substitute such other greens as escarole, Bibb lettuce, Savoy cabbage or mustard greens. Similarly, great Northern, small white beans or navy beans can be used in lieu of the cannellini. Omitting the sausage will bring the *POINTS* per serving down to 2.

Mixed Green Salad with Orange Dressing

Makes 4 servings

1 tablespoon packed dark brown sugar

1 tablespoon Dijon mustard

3 tablespoons orange juice

1 tablespoon white-wine vinegar

4 cups bitter greens salad mix (escarole, romaine and arugula)

¼ cup walnuts, toasted and chopped (optional)

1. In a small bowl, mix the brown sugar and mustard thoroughly; whisk in the orange juice and vinegar.
2. In a salad bowl, combine the greens and walnuts (if using). Drizzle with the dressing; toss to coat.

Per serving (with walnuts): 79 CALORIES, 5 G TOTAL FAT, 0 G SATURATED FAT, 0 MG CHOLESTEROL, 28 MG SODIUM, 7 G TOTAL CARBOHYDRATE, 1 G DIETARY FIBER, 3 G PROTEIN, 40 MG CALCIUM.

POINTS PER SERVING: 2

Tip

For a milder-tasting salad, substitute spinach for the bitter greens. For a more pungent salad, use coarse-grain mustard and add freshly ground black pepper to taste. Toast the nuts in a small skillet, or see Step 1 in the recipe for Frozen Yogurt Sundaes (page 44). If you decide not to use them, you'll save 1 *POINT*.

A Simple Pasta Dinner

LINGUINE RIVIERA, FRESH FIG AND PEAR PLATE

A Casual Weeknight Supper

CHICKEN CALVADOS, OVEN-ROASTED ROOT VEGETABLES

A Formal Luncheon

Cocktails at Six

PARMESAN CHEESE STRAWS AND PINWHEELS,
SPICED OLIVES WITH LEMON AND FENNEL

Cocktails at Six

DUMPLINGS WITH GINGER DIPPING SAUCE,
NOT-SO-DEVILISH DEVILED EGGS, SAUCISSON EN CROÛTE

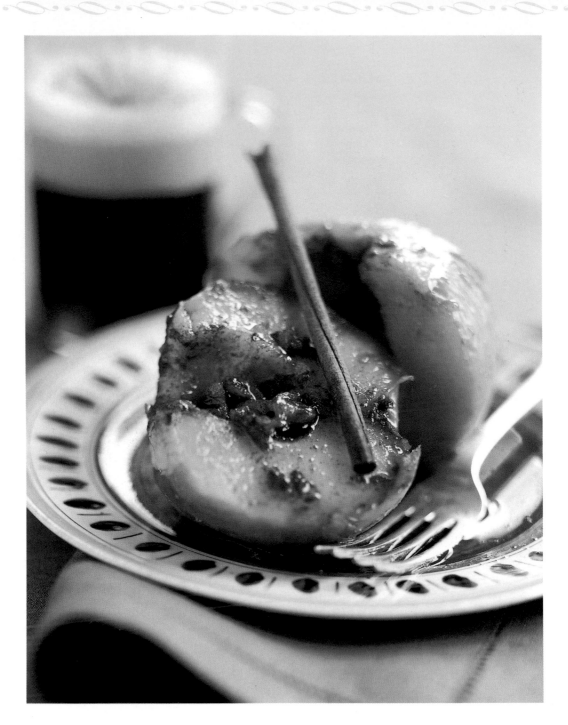

Après-Ski Lunch

CINNAMON-NUT BAKED APPLE WITH MAPLE GLAZE,
ESPRESSO WITH KAHLÚA CREAM

A Formal Luncheon

ROAST CHICKEN AND CHUTNEY TEA SANDWICH,
MINTED CARROT SALAD WITH LEMON VINAIGRETTE

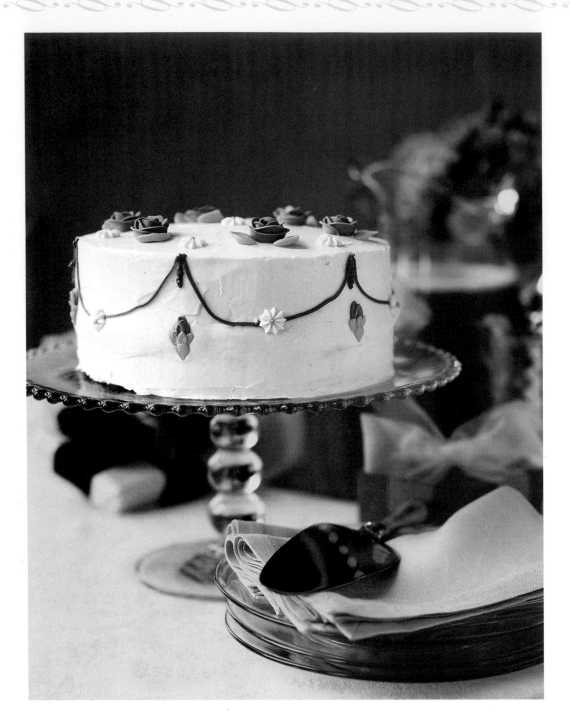

A Birthday Gala

CELEBRATION BIRTHDAY CAKE, STRAWBERRY LEMONADE

Balsamic Strawberries

Makes 4 servings

4 teaspoons sugar
1 tablespoon balsamic vinegar
4 cups strawberries, quartered
Freshly ground black pepper, to taste

In a medium bowl, mix the sugar and vinegar, stirring until the sugar dissolves. Add the strawberries and pepper; toss to coat. Let stand 20 minutes, tossing occasionally.

Per serving: 62 Calories, 1 g Total Fat, 0 g Saturated Fat, 0 mg Cholesterol, 2 mg Sodium, 15 g Total Carbohydrate, 4 g Dietary Fiber, 1 g Protein, 21 mg Calcium.

POINTS PER SERVING: 1

Tip

For a more substantial dessert, serve this with Almond Biscotti (page 194) and shaved Parmesan or a bit of Brie cheese.

Après-Ski Lunch

I have been lucky enough to ski since an early age. Two of my favorite resorts are in Switzerland, and I have been going there for so many years now that I feel like a local. I have a good many friends there, and I can relax and feel comfortable. When I have a chance, I especially enjoy skiing with Bruno, an avid skier and one of my dearest friends for years.

A lesson I learned while trying to lose weight is that exercise is crucial, but sticking to it can be a challenge. That's precisely why you must discover what it is you love to do. Skiing is a sport I truly enjoy. I feel strong yet graceful when I ski. I also love the freedom of skiing. When it is just me against the elements (and when I maneuver my way down a particularly difficult slope), I feel absolutely and totally triumphant and exhilarated. The immensity of the mountain also gives me a sense of solitude and security. My troubles—and I—feel incredibly small in such peaceful surroundings.

Serves 4

Mushroom-Caraway Soup

Crunchy Sesame Chicken Salad with Ginger Dressing

Cinnamon-Nut Baked Apples with Maple Glaze

Espresso with Kahlúa Cream

Mushroom-Caraway Soup

Makes 4 servings

1 tablespoon olive oil
One 10-ounce package mushrooms, sliced
3 scallions, sliced
4 cups chicken broth
3 medium red potatoes, scrubbed and cut into 1″ chunks
½ cup dry white wine
1 teaspoon dried thyme leaves, crumbled
1 teaspoon caraway seeds, crushed
¼ teaspoon salt
¼ cup half-and-half

1. In a large nonstick saucepan or Dutch oven, heat the oil. Sauté the mushrooms and scallions until the mushroom liquid evaporates, about 10 minutes.

2. Stir in the broth, potatoes, wine, thyme, caraway seeds and salt; bring to a boil. Reduce the heat and simmer, partially covered, until the potatoes are tender, about 20 minutes. Transfer to a blender and remove the knob in the lid; puree. Return the soup to the saucepan; bring back to a boil. Remove from the heat and stir in the half-and-half.

Per serving: 289 CALORIES, 8 G TOTAL FAT, 2 G SATURATED FAT, 24 MG CHOLESTEROL, 1,147 MG SODIUM, 44 G TOTAL CARBOHYDRATE, 5 G DIETARY FIBER, 8 G PROTEIN, 52 MG CALCIUM.

POINTS PER SERVING: 5

Tip

Just a touch of half-and-half makes a big difference in the richness of this comforting, stick-to-your-ribs soup. Removing the knob from the blender's lid lets the steam escape (if it builds up, the lid may pop off).

Crunchy Sesame Chicken Salad with Ginger Dressing

Makes 4 servings

3 tablespoons sesame seeds

½ teaspoon salt

¼ teaspoon freshly ground pepper

Four 4-ounce skinless boneless chicken breasts

1 tablespoon vegetable oil

2 tablespoons rice-wine vinegar

2 tablespoons reduced-sodium soy sauce

1 tablespoon honey

2 teaspoons grated peeled gingerroot

1 teaspoon mustard powder

1 teaspoon Asian sesame oil

¼ teaspoon crushed red pepper flakes

½ pound baby greens or mesclun

1. In a small bowl, mix the sesame seeds, salt and pepper. Place the chicken on a sheet of wax paper; sprinkle on both sides with the sesame-seed mixture.
2. In a large nonstick skillet, heat the vegetable oil. Sauté the chicken until cooked through, 4–6 minutes on each side. Transfer the chicken to a plate.
3. Meanwhile, in a small saucepan, combine the vinegar, soy sauce, honey, gingerroot, mustard, sesame oil and pepper flakes; bring just to a boil. Remove from the heat.
4. Divide the greens among 4 salad plates. Cut each chicken breast into fourths on the diagonal. Keeping the slices together, arrange the chicken over the greens. Drizzle with the dressing.

Per serving: 251 CALORIES, 11 G TOTAL FAT, 2 G SATURATED FAT, 69 MG CHOLESTEROL, 611 MG SODIUM, 9 G TOTAL CARBOHYDRATE, 2 G DIETARY FIBER, 28 G PROTEIN, 122 MG CALCIUM.

POINTS PER SERVING: 6

Tip

This main-dish salad can be served either warm or cold. Be sure to sprinkle the chicken with the sesame seeds instead of dredging it in them; otherwise, you'll use more sesame seeds than you really need.

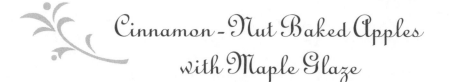

Cinnamon-Nut Baked Apples with Maple Glaze

Makes 4 servings

¼ cup packed light brown sugar

1 tablespoon chopped walnuts

½ teaspoon cinnamon

4 large baking apples (we like Rome)

1 tablespoon reduced-calorie margarine

2 tablespoons maple syrup

Cinnamon sticks, to garnish

1. Preheat the oven to 375° F; place ¼ cup water in an 8″ square baking dish.
2. In a small bowl, mix the brown sugar, walnuts and cinnamon. With a small knife, core the apples, but do not cut all the way through the bottoms; peel about ½″ of skin from the top of the apples. Place the apples in the baking dish. Fill each apple with the brown-sugar mixture; dot with the margarine, then drizzle with the maple syrup. Bake, basting the apples occasionally with the pan juices, until just tender, about 40 minutes.
3. With a slotted spoon, transfer the apples to dessert plates. Pour the pan juices over the apples. If you like, garnish each apple with a cinnamon stick.

Per serving: 223 Calories, 3 g Total Fat, 0 g Saturated Fat, 0 mg Cholesterol, 39 mg Sodium, 52 g Total Carbohydrate, 6 g Dietary Fiber, 1 g Protein, 41 mg Calcium.

POINTS PER SERVING: 4

Tip

Be sure to use baking apples for this, since they'll retain their shape and flavor. Besides Rome, look for Northern Spy, Cortland and Winesap.

Espresso with Kahlúa Cream

Makes 4 servings

½ cup skim milk
1 tablespoon sugar
3 tablespoons Kahlúa or other coffee-flavored liqueur
1½ cups brewed hot espresso
Dash ground nutmeg

1. In a small saucepan over medium heat, combine the milk and sugar, stirring until the sugar dissolves; bring just to a boil. Remove from the heat; add the liqueur, whisking vigorously until the mixture is frothy.
2. Pour the espresso into demitasse cups; spoon the milk mixture over the coffee, then sprinkle with the nutmeg. Serve at once.

Per serving: 65 CALORIES, 0 G TOTAL FAT, 0 G SATURATED FAT, 0 MG CHOLESTEROL, 19 MG SODIUM, 9 G TOTAL CARBOHYDRATE, 0 G DIETARY FIBER, 1 G PROTEIN, 40 MG CALCIUM.

POINTS PER SERVING: 1

Tip

Chocolate-flavored liqueur would be an excellent substitute for the Kahlúa. Or try this iced when the warm days of summer arrive: Combine everything in a blender with ice cubes; whirl until frothy.

An American Barbecue

I have been fortunate enough to have traveled around the world, but America has secured a special place in my travel memories. Like the Irish, the American people have always been extremely warm, kind and hospitable. I wholeheartedly embrace this American characteristic.

I admire the gutsy, positive attitude toward life so many Americans seem to possess. And for someone whose every move and action has been scrutinized (and publicized!), that particularly American trait of always seeing people for who they really are—and not being swayed by the judgment of the press and its opinion—is truly refreshing.

Serves 8

Cowboy Beans

Rainbow Cole Slaw

Roasted Corn on the Cob with Cilantro Butter

Barbecue Beef Sandwiches

Zesty Barbecue Sauce

Sandies

Iced Tea*

Cowboy Beans

Makes 8 servings

6 slices turkey bacon, diced
1 large white onion, chopped
Two 15½-ounce cans pinto beans, rinsed and drained
1 cup beer
½ cup Zesty Barbecue Sauce (page 139)
⅛ teaspoon cayenne pepper

1. In a medium nonstick saucepan, combine the bacon and onion. Cook, stirring constantly, until the onion is translucent and the bacon has just begun to brown on the edges, about 15 minutes.
2. Stir in the beans, beer, barbecue sauce and cayenne; bring to a boil. Reduce the heat and simmer, covered, until the flavors are blended, about 15 minutes. Uncover and increase the heat to medium; cook until most of the liquid is absorbed and the sauce thickens, about 5 minutes longer.

Per serving: 132 CALORIES, 2 G TOTAL FAT, 0 G SATURATED FAT, 8 MG CHOLESTEROL, 398 MG SODIUM, 20 G TOTAL CARBOHYDRATE, 4 G DIETARY FIBER, 6 G PROTEIN, 43 MG CALCIUM.

POINTS PER SERVING: 2

Tip

Don't confuse this chuck-wagon-style dish with its sugary Boston cousin; these beans are firmer and spicier. For best results, use a spicy, tangy sauce, such as the Zesty Barbecue Sauce on page 139.

Rainbow Cole Slaw

Makes 8 servings

2 tablespoons Dijon mustard

1 tablespoon fresh lemon juice

⅔ cup reduced-calorie mayonnaise

½ teaspoon sugar

¼ teaspoon salt

1 small head red cabbage, shredded

1 small head green cabbage, shredded

2 carrots, peeled and shredded

1 yellow bell pepper, seeded and thinly sliced

1 small white onion, thinly sliced

1½ teaspoons celery seeds

1. In a small bowl, whisk the mustard and lemon juice; whisk in the mayonnaise, then the sugar and salt.
2. In a large serving bowl, mix the red cabbage, green cabbage, carrots, bell pepper, onion and celery seeds. Drizzle with the dressing; toss to coat.

Per serving: 123 Calories, 7 g Total Fat, 1 g Saturated Fat, 0 mg Cholesterol, 260 mg Sodium, 13 g Total Carbohydrate, 3 g Dietary Fiber, 2 g Protein, 78 mg Calcium.

POINTS PER SERVING: 2

Tip

This colorful side dish provides a welcome antidote to a spicy barbecue dinner. The recipe lends itself to many variations: Try substituting a head of bok choy or Chinese cabbage for the red or green cabbage, or a green or red bell pepper for the yellow.

Roasted Corn on the Cob with Cilantro Butter

Makes 8 servings

2 tablespoons unsalted butter, softened
1–2 tablespoons finely chopped cilantro
8 ears corn

1. Preheat the grill, or preheat the oven to 400° F. In a small bowl, mix the butter and cilantro.
2. Gently pull back the corn husks, but don't pull them off completely; remove the silk. Smooth the husks back over the corn, then soak in cold water 10 minutes. Place the corn on the grill and cover; grill, with all the grill vents open, 20–30 minutes, or roast directly on the oven rack 20–30 minutes. Serve with the cilantro butter.

Per serving: 109 CALORIES, 4 G TOTAL FAT, 2 G SATURATED FAT, 8 MG CHOLESTEROL, 14 MG SODIUM, 19 G TOTAL CARBOHYDRATE, 2 G DIETARY FIBER, 3 G PROTEIN, 3 MG CALCIUM.

POINTS PER SERVING: 2

Tip

Corn can be grilled in advance and used for a variety of dishes, including salsas, salads, soups and chowders. Once you remove the kernels from the cob, they can be frozen.

Barbecue Beef Sandwiches

Makes 8 servings

One 3-pound beef brisket, trimmed of all excess fat
Two 12-ounce bottles beer
1 tablespoon liquid smoke
2 garlic cloves, minced
2 cups Zesty Barbecue Sauce (page 139)
8 kaiser rolls

1. Preheat the oven to 325° F; line a 10 x 15″ baking dish with foil, leaving about a 9″ overhang on each end. Place a metal rack on the foil. Place the brisket on the rack; pour the beer into the dish, around the brisket. Add the liquid smoke to the beer and scatter the garlic over the meat. Fold the foil over securely to enclose the brisket. Bake until tender, about 2 hours.

2. Shred the brisket lengthwise with the grain. In a medium saucepan, combine the shredded meat and the barbecue sauce, stirring to coat. Cook until heated through, 2–3 minutes. Divide the barbecue among the kaiser rolls.

Per serving: 483 Calories, 12 g Total Fat, 4 g Saturated Fat, 92 mg Cholesterol, 544 mg Sodium, 50 g Total Carbohydrate, 1 g Dietary Fiber, 36 g Protein, 80 mg Calcium.

POINTS PER SERVING: 10

Tip

Buy fresh beef brisket, as opposed to the corned variety. Choose the leanest possible brisket and trim any excess fat. For an even zestier sandwich, add a teaspoon liquid smoke when you combine the shredded brisket and the barbecue sauce. If you'd rather not have this as a sandwich, omitting the kaiser roll will save you 3 *POINTS*.

Zesty Barbecue Sauce

Makes 20 servings

Two 8-ounce cans tomato sauce

1 cup packed dark brown sugar

1 cup cider vinegar

2 tablespoons Worcestershire sauce

2 teaspoons chili powder

¼ teaspoon cayenne pepper

In a medium saucepan, combine all the ingredients; bring to a boil. Reduce the heat to maintain a gentle boil; cook until the sauce is thick enough to coat the back of a spoon, about 10 minutes.

Per serving (2 tablespoons): 53 CALORIES, 0 G TOTAL FAT, 0 G SATURATED FAT, 0 MG CHOLESTEROL, 134 MG SODIUM, 13 G TOTAL CARBOHYDRATE, 0 G DIETARY FIBER, 0 G PROTEIN, 12 MG CALCIUM.

POINTS PER SERVING: 1

Tip

The barbecue sauce can easily be made in advance and stored in the refrigerator for up to a week. Homemade barbecue sauces are thinner than commercially prepared varieties; if you prefer a very thick sauce, stir in 2 teaspoons cornstarch dissolved in 2 teaspoons reduced-sodium soy sauce after the mixture has cooked for the 10 minutes. Continue to cook until the mixture has been incorporated fully and the barbecue sauce is clear, about 1 minute.

Sandies

Makes about 40 cookies

⅔ cup all-purpose flour
½ cup wheat-and-barley cereal nuggets
½ teaspoon baking powder
½ cup packed dark brown sugar
¼ cup granulated sugar
¼ cup unsalted margarine or butter, melted
¼ cup fat-free egg substitute
½ teaspoon vanilla extract

1. Preheat the oven to 375° F; lightly spray 2 nonstick baking sheets with nonstick cooking spray.
2. In a food processor, combine the flour, cereal and baking powder; process until the cereal is finely ground, about 1 minute.
3. In a large mixing bowl, beat the brown sugar, granulated sugar and margarine until totally incorporated. Add the egg substitute and vanilla, beating until light and fluffy. With a wooden spoon, stir in the flour mixture. Drop the dough by the ½ tablespoon onto the baking sheets, making about 40 cookies. Bake until the edges begin to brown and cracks begin to appear on the tops of the cookies, 7–8 minutes. Cool completely on wire racks.

Per cookie: 38 CALORIES, 1 G TOTAL FAT, 0 G SATURATED FAT, 0 MG CHOLESTEROL, 9 MG SODIUM, 6 G TOTAL CARBOHYDRATE, 0 G DIETARY FIBER, 0 G PROTEIN, 6 MG CALCIUM.

POINTS PER COOKIE: 1

Tip

When ground, wheat-and-barley cereal nuggets impart the flavor and texture of nuts, with none of the fat. These sturdy cookies travel well and are ideal for barbecues and picnics. Store the sandies in cookie tins or loosely wrapped in aluminum foil for up to 5 days; they also can be frozen for up to 3 months.

An Ideal Breakfast

Since I am always running about, traveling, in business meetings or at charity engagements, I sometimes find it a struggle to ensure I have three proper meals a day. But I know that three meals are crucial to keep up my energy and help me stay trim, so that I am not bingeing the moment things get hectic.

My favorite breakfast in the world is hardly a culinary masterpiece: boiled eggs and butter on my toast "soldiers"—or pieces of toast that have been cut into strips—just as Dads used to make them.

This, however, is hardly the ideal meal on which to base one's day. Since I travel so much, I try to keep my morning meal light and refreshing. I enjoy a wonderful bowl of fresh fruit salad, whole-wheat toast and my customary cup of weak Earl Grey tea.

Serves 2

Summer Fruit Salad

Whole-Wheat Toast with Marmalade*

The Perfect Pot of Tea*

Summer Fruit Salad

Makes 4 servings

2 peaches, pitted and sliced

1 cup strawberries, hulled and halved

1 cup blueberries

1 cup honeydew chunks

1 tablespoon sugar

1½ teaspoons fresh lemon juice

One 8-ounce tub plain nonfat yogurt

1 tablespoon honey

½ teaspoon vanilla extract

1. In a large bowl, combine the fruit. Sprinkle with the sugar and lemon juice; toss to combine. Let stand at room temperature 30 minutes–1 hour, or refrigerate, covered, 1–2 days.
2. In a small bowl, mix the yogurt, honey and vanilla. Just before serving, pour over the fruit; toss to coat.

Per serving: 127 Calories, 0 g Total Fat, 0 g Saturated Fat, 1 mg Cholesterol, 51 mg Sodium, 29 g Total Carbohydrate, 3 g Dietary Fiber, 4 g Protein, 126 mg Calcium.

POINTS PER SERVING: 2

Tip

To make the perfect pot of tea, fill a teakettle with cold water; bring to a rolling boil. Meanwhile, put a little hot tap water in your teapot and swirl it gently to warm the pot. Put the loose tea in the teapot (the rule of thumb is one heaping teaspoon per person, plus one for the pot). Pour the boiling water into the teapot, then cover and let the tea steep for 5 minutes. Serve the tea with milk and lumps of sugar, if you wish.

Cocktails at Six

I enjoy devoting my time to a number of charities—particularly those that benefit the world's less fortunate children. The focus of the countless events and dinners I attend is, rightly so, to raise money for a good cause.

I love meeting new people at these events. I am always so interested in those I'm talking with that I seldom touch any of the food on my plate. I think you can always learn much from listening to and meeting new people, by hearing new views and ideas.

On the few occasions I can gather friends together, I make sure the conversation and good times are the priorities. The food must be delicious and healthy.

Serves 8–10

Parmesan Cheese Straws

Not-So-Devilish Deviled Eggs

Saucisson en Croûte

Dumplings with Ginger Dipping Sauce

Spiced Olives with Lemon and Fennel

Parmesan Cheese Straws

Makes 8 servings

½ cup grated Parmesan cheese
2 teaspoons chili powder
½ teaspoon ground cumin
Three 12 x 17″ sheets phyllo dough, at room temperature

1. Preheat the oven to 400° F; spray a large nonstick baking sheet with nonstick cooking spray.

2. In a small bowl, mix the cheese, chili powder and cumin. Place the sheets of phyllo on a work surface and cover them with a damp towel. Remove the first sheet and place it with short side toward you. Coat with nonstick cooking spray (butter-flavored is nice), then sprinkle with about 2 teaspoons of the cheese mixture; fold the phyllo in half to form a 12 x 8½″ rectangle. Spray the phyllo again and sprinkle with 2 more teaspoons of cheese mixture; fold in half again to form a 6 x 8½″ rectangle. Spray again and sprinkle with 2 more teaspoons of cheese mixture; fold in half again to form a 6 x 4¼″ rectangle. Spray again and sprinkle with just a bit of the cheese mixture; with a serrated knife, cut into 8 short strips. Transfer the strips to the baking sheet, placing them about ½″ apart. Repeat the process two more times to make 24 cheese straws. Bake until the cheese straws are crisp and golden, 8–10 minutes. Cool on wire racks.

Per serving: 47 Calories, 2 g Total Fat, 1 g Saturated Fat, 4 mg Cholesterol, 134 mg Sodium, 4 g Total Carbohydrate, 0 g Dietary Fiber, 3 g Protein, 73 mg Calcium.

POINTS PER SERVING: 1

Continued on next page.

Tip

Once you've cut the phyllo into straws, form them into different shapes. Twist some as you transfer them to the baking sheet, and roll some into pinwheels. If you're really feeling creative, experiment with bows, hearts or stars. The cheese straws may be stored in an airtight container for 1 week or in the freezer for up to 2 months.

Not-So-Devilish Deviled Eggs

Makes 8 servings

8 hard-cooked eggs, peeled and halved lengthwise
½ cup reduced-calorie mayonnaise
¼ cup low-fat (1%) creamy cottage cheese, drained
1 tablespoon curry powder
1 tablespoon Dijon mustard
Dash hot red pepper sauce
Paprika, for sprinkling
Parsley sprigs, to garnish

1. Place 4 of the eggs yolks in a food processor or blender (discard the other 4) with the mayonnaise, cottage cheese, curry, mustard and pepper sauce; process until blended and smooth.
2. Spoon the filling into a pastry bag with star tip. Pipe the filling into the egg whites, then sprinkle with the paprika. Garnish with the parsley. Refrigerate, covered, until ready to serve.

Per serving: 87 Calories, 6 g Total Fat, 1 g Saturated Fat, 97 mg Cholesterol, 231 mg Sodium, 4 g Total Carbohydrate, 0 g Dietary Fiber, 6 g Protein, 23 mg Calcium.

POINTS PER SERVING: 2

Tip

The food processor gives a very fine, smooth texture to the filling; if you prefer a slightly chunkier texture, use a fork to mash the yolks and mix in the remaining ingredients. Using half the egg yolks and creamy low-fat cottage cheese makes this all-time favorite a fairly virtuous treat. This combination makes a tasty egg salad, too.

Saucisson en Croûte

Makes 8 servings

1 tablespoon oil
One 1-pound bag sauerkraut, rinsed and drained
2 onions, thinly sliced
1 teaspoon caraway seeds
1 pound low-fat turkey kielbasa
One 10-ounce can refrigerated pizza dough
1 cup honey mustard

1. In a large nonstick skillet, heat the oil. Add the sauerkraut, onions, caraway seeds and ½ cup water; cook, covered, until the liquid evaporates and the sauerkraut and onions are very tender, about 15 minutes. Remove from the heat and cool completely.

2. Preheat the oven to 400° F. Cut the kielbasa into two 8″ lengths, then cut the pizza dough in half. On a lightly floured surface, roll out each half of dough into a rectangle about 2″ longer than the kielbasa and wide enough to wrap around it. Spoon half of the sauerkraut mixture down the center of each piece of dough, then place a kielbasa half on the sauerkraut. Fold up the dough to enclose the kielbasa completely, pinching the edges to seal. Transfer to an ungreased baking sheet. Bake until golden, 15–20 minutes. Cut into slices; serve warm or at room temperature, with the honey mustard on the side.

Per serving: 270 CALORIES, 5 G TOTAL FAT, 1 G SATURATED FAT, 26 MG CHOLESTEROL, 975 MG SODIUM, 45 G TOTAL CARBOHYDRATE, 2 G DIETARY FIBER, 14 G PROTEIN, 35 MG CALCIUM.

POINTS PER SERVING: 5

This take on the French classic uses a flavorful low-fat kielbasa, but any already cooked lean sausage would work. Try smoked sausage, or one of those gourmet-style flavored chicken sausages like scallion-and-herb flavor.

Dumplings with Ginger Dipping Sauce

Makes 8 servings

Dipping Sauce

¼ cup red-wine vinegar

¼ cup reduced-sodium soy sauce

2 tablespoons sugar

1 tablespoon Asian sesame oil

1 scallion, thinly sliced

2 teaspoons grated peeled gingerroot

¼ teaspoon crushed red pepper flakes

Dumplings

½ pound lean ground pork

1 scallion, finely minced

1 tablespoon reduced-sodium soy sauce

1 tablespoon Asian sesame oil

1 teaspoon cornstarch

1 teaspoon dry sherry

1 teaspoon grated peeled gingerroot

1 garlic clove, minced

One 12-ounce package (about 48) wonton skins

1. Bring a large pot of water to a boil.
2. In a small bowl, mix the dipping sauce ingredients, stirring until the sugar dissolves; set aside.
3. In a medium bowl, mix the pork, scallion, soy sauce, sesame oil, cornstarch, sherry, gingerroot and garlic.
4. Place the wonton skins on a work surface and cover them with a damp towel. Remove the wonton skins one at a time and place about 1 teaspoon filling in the center; do not overstuff or the wontons won't seal securely. Moisten the

edges of the wontons with water. Bring 2 opposite corners to the center, pinching the points to seal, then bring remaining 2 corners to center, pinching the points to seal. Repeat with the remaining wonton skins and filling.

5. Add the wontons in batches (if you add too many at once they may stick together) to the boiling water. Stir gently with a wooden spoon and bring back to a boil; boil 5 minutes. With a slotted spoon, transfer the wontons to a platter. Serve with dipping sauce.

Per serving: 186 CALORIES, 6 G TOTAL FAT, 1 G SATURATED FAT, 16 MG CHOLESTEROL, 525 MG SODIUM, 21 G TOTAL CARBOHYDRATE, 0 G DIETARY FIBER, 10 G PROTEIN, 23 MG CALCIUM.

POINTS PER SERVING: 4

Tip

You'll be surprised how easy these delicate little morsels are to make; if you like, use shrimp or ground skinless turkey or chicken instead of pork. For something different, add the boiled dumplings to your favorite soup. If your supermarket doesn't sell lean ground pork, cut ½ pound pork tenderloin into chunks and grind it in your food processor. Look for wonton skins in the produce department of your supermarket.

Spiced Olives with Lemon and Fennel

Makes 10 servings

1 cup kalamata olives

1 cup oil-cured black olives

1 cup Sicilian (green) olives

1 cup fennel, trimmed and thinly sliced

1 garlic clove, thinly sliced

1 tablespoon grated lemon zest

1 tablespoon chopped fresh rosemary, or 1 teaspoon dried, crumbled

1 tablespoon chopped fresh thyme, or 1 teaspoon dried, crumbled

1 tablespoon fresh lemon juice

1 teaspoon olive oil

In a large bowl, mix all the ingredients. Serve at room temperature.

Per serving: 88 Calories, 9 g Total Fat, 1 g Saturated Fat, 0 mg Cholesterol, 925 mg Sodium, 3 g Total Carbohydrate, 1 g Dietary Fiber, 1 g Protein, 43 mg Calcium.

POINTS PER SERVING: 2

Tip

Use whatever olives you prefer, as any variety will work well with the other flavors. We don't call for pitted olives, as they wouldn't look as attractive as those left whole. If you've never encountered a fennel bulb before, see Step 2 of the Fennel and Blood Orange Salad recipe (page 63) for trimming how-tos.

A Formal Luncheon

Royal Ascot is the British equivalent of America's Kentucky Derby: a grand social occasion at which parties are held after the races.

In my Mum's day, Ascot was as it is today, a highly fashionable event where the hats receive more notice than the horses. Nowadays, I rarely attend, but I will never forget the first time I went: I spent the week playing games and attending the races, cocktail parties and grand dinners. At times, I felt awkward. Yet that first Ascot was the most memorable and special because out of such humble beginnings came a great and lasting friendship, one that endures to this very day. I came to know Andrew that week.

While the meals I ate that Ascot week were extraordinary, the one thing I remember was the chocolate profiteroles. Andrew and I joked about them over lunch.

Serves 4

Sesame Breadsticks*

Roast Chicken and Chutney Tea Sandwiches

Minted Carrot Salad with Lemon Vinaigrette

Orange Tea Biscuits with Citrus Glaze

Chocolate Profiteroles

Kir Royales

Roast Chicken and Chutney Tea Sandwiches

Makes 4 servings

2 teaspoons vegetable oil

2 onions, chopped

1 teaspoon ground ginger

2 Granny Smith apples, peeled, cored and diced

⅔ cup dried cranberries or raisins

½ cup apple cider

¼ cup cider vinegar

3 tablespoons packed dark brown sugar

8 slices pumpernickel or raisin-pumpernickel bread

½ cup watercress, cleaned and torn

2 cups sliced skinless roast chicken breast

1. In a large nonstick skillet, heat the oil. Add the onions and ginger; cook, stirring as needed, until the onions are tender and lightly browned, about 10 minutes. Add the apples, cranberries, cider, vinegar and brown sugar; reduce the heat and simmer, uncovered, stirring as needed, until the liquid evaporates and the chutney thickens, about 30 minutes. Cool to room temperature, then refrigerate until ready to use.

2. To assemble the sandwiches, line 4 slices of bread with the watercress, then the chicken. Dollop each with 1 tablespoon of the chutney before covering with another slice of bread; cut the sandwiches in half and serve at once.

Per serving: 492 CALORIES, 8 G TOTAL FAT, 2 G SATURATED FAT, 60 MG CHOLESTEROL, 496 MG SODIUM, 80 G TOTAL CARBOHYDRATE, 7 G DIETARY FIBER, 29 G PROTEIN, 99 MG CALCIUM.

POINTS PER SERVING: 9

This easy apple chutney is a great accompaniment for roast pork as well as poultry. Adjust the texture to suit your taste: for a chunky relish, cut the fruit more coarsely, for a jamlike chutney, cut it finer. Make the chutney a day ahead to allow its flavors to develop fully. Refrigerate any leftover chutney in a tightly sealed jar for up to 1 week.

Minted Carrot Salad with Lemon Vinaigrette

Makes 4 servings

2 tablespoons fresh lemon juice

2 teaspoons olive oil

1 teaspoon sugar

4 carrots, shredded

1 cup golden raisins

3 tablespoons chopped mint

1. In a small bowl, mix the lemon juice, oil and sugar.
2. In a large bowl, mix the carrots, raisins and mint. Drizzle with the dressing; toss to coat.

Per serving: 182 Calories, 3 g Total Fat, 0 g Saturated Fat, 0 mg Cholesterol, 32 mg Sodium, 42 g Total Carbohydrate, 4 g Dietary Fiber, 2 g Protein, 46 mg Calcium.

POINTS PER SERVING: 3

Tip

With its hint of mint, this salad is wonderfully refreshing on a hot summer's day. You can serve it right away if you like, but the sweetness of the raisins is more pronounced if you let it stand at room temperature for 30 minutes.

Orange Tea Biscuits with Citrus Glaze

Makes 12 servings

2 cups all-purpose flour

¼ cup granulated sugar

2 teaspoons baking powder

½ teaspoon salt

5 tablespoons cold margarine or butter

½ cup dried currants

½ cup low-fat (1%) buttermilk

2 tablespoons orange juice

1 tablespoon fresh lemon juice

3 tablespoons confectioners' sugar

1. Preheat the oven to 400° F; spray a 12-cup muffin tin with nonstick cooking spray.
2. In a large bowl, mix the flour, granulated sugar, baking powder and salt. With a pastry blender or two knives, cut in the margarine until the mixture resembles coarse crumbs. Stir in the currants and buttermilk until just blended; do not overmix. Spoon the batter into the muffin cups. Bake until golden, 12–15 minutes. Cool on a wire rack 10 minutes.
3. Meanwhile, prepare the glaze. In a small bowl, mix the orange juice and lemon juice; stir in the confectioners' sugar. Brush the tops of the slightly cooled biscuits with the glaze; cool completely before serving.

Per serving: 158 CALORIES, 5 G TOTAL FAT, 1 G SATURATED FAT, 0 MG CHOLESTEROL, 222 MG SODIUM, 26 G TOTAL CARBOHYDRATE, 1 G DIETARY FIBER, 3 G PROTEIN, 50 MG CALCIUM.

POINTS PER SERVING: 3

Continued on next page.

Serve these biscuits with orange marmalade or apricot jam and a pot of Earl Grey or English Breakfast tea. Leftover biscuits may be kept for a few days in an airtight plastic bag.

Chocolate Profiteroles

Makes 8 servings

¼ cup + 4 teaspoons margarine

¾ cup all-purpose flour

2 eggs

¼ cup fat-free egg substitute

⅓ cup sugar

2 tablespoons unsweetened cocoa powder

2 tablespoons cornstarch

1 cup skim milk

2 teaspoons vanilla extract

2 teaspoons confectioners' sugar

1. Preheat the oven to 400° F; spray a large baking sheet with nonstick cooking spray.
2. In a medium saucepan, bring ¾ cup water and ¼ cup of the margarine to a full boil. Stir in the flour; cook, stirring constantly, until the dough pulls away from the sides of the pan, 1–2 minutes. Remove from the heat; stir in the eggs, one at a time, until the dough is smooth. Drop the dough, 1 heaping tablespoon at a time, onto the baking sheet, making 24 balls. (If you prefer, transfer the dough to a pastry bag; pipe the dough onto the baking sheet in 1½″ balls.) Bake until golden, 25–30 minutes. Slice a small portion off the top of each puff; cool on a wire rack.
3. Place the egg substitute in a small bowl. In a medium nonstick saucepan, combine the sugar, cocoa powder and cornstarch. Stir in the milk, vanilla and ½ cup water; bring to a boil, stirring constantly, and boil 1 minute. Slowly whisk a small amount of the cocoa mixture into the egg substitute, then slowly pour the egg mixture into the cocoa mixture, whisking quickly and constantly. Cook, stirring constantly, until just boiling. Remove from the heat; whisk in

Continued on next page.

the remaining 4 teaspoons of margarine. Transfer the chocolate pastry cream to a bowl; refrigerate, covered, until chilled and thickened, about 2 hours.

4. Spoon the pastry cream into the puffs; replace the tops. Put the confectioners' sugar in a small sieve and shake over the profiteroles. Serve at once.

Per serving: 193 Calories, 7 g Total Fat, 2 g Saturated Fat, 54 mg Cholesterol, 123 mg Sodium, 22 g Total Carbohydrate, 1 g Dietary Fiber, 5 g Protein, 50 mg Calcium.

POINTS PER SERVING: 4

— *Tip* —

Profiteroles are miniature cream puffs. Be sure to cut off the tops of the puffs when you remove them from the oven so that steam can escape. If you'd rather not make the pastry cream, fill the profiteroles with nonfat frozen yogurt. They're also delicious drizzled with chocolate syrup.

Kir Royales

Makes 4 servings

8 fresh raspberries
2 teaspoons crème de cassis (black-currant-flavored liqueur)
One 750-milliliter bottle dry champagne, well chilled

Place 2 raspberries in each of 4 champagne flutes; add ½ teaspoon crème de cassis to each. Pour the champagne over and serve at once.

Per serving: 142 Calories, 0 g Total Fat, 0 g Saturated Fat, 0 mg Cholesterol, 0 mg Sodium, 6 g Total Carbohydrate, 1 g Dietary Fiber, 0 g Protein, 2 mg Calcium.

POINTS PER SERVING: 3

Tip

If you prefer, use sparkling nonalcoholic cider, unflavored seltzer or ginger ale instead of the champagne.

An Argentinean Feast

In the past chapters of my life, my antidote for being unhappy had been food and more food. I remember the menu selections at home suffering after Mum left when I was twelve. I would have sausages for breakfast, then again for a snack, after lunch and at tea, when I would "balance" the meal out with boiled eggs and buttered white toast.

I loved visiting Mum and her new husband, Hector, in Argentina. I remember flying to Buenos Aires, then driving 300 miles across the Pampas, the great plains of South America, to Hector's farm. The country is breathtaking: the air pure and the sky unbroken. We had wonderful times: I rode the polo ponies (Hector was a world-class polo player) and spent a good deal of time with Mum—these are the memories that I cherish most.

Serves 4

Turkey Empanadas

Roasted Pork Loin

Baby Lamb Chops

Classic Roast Beef (served without the Wild Mushrooms) (see page 64)

Quinoa Salad

Shoestring Beets and Arugula Salad

Tarragon Vinaigrette

Alfajores

Turkey Empanadas

Makes 4 servings

1 onion, chopped

2 teaspoons canola oil

½ teaspoon ground allspice

1 garlic clove, minced

1 pound ground skinless turkey breast

1 teaspoon dried oregano

1 teaspoon salt

Twelve 12 x 17″ sheets phyllo dough, at room temperature

¼ cup fat-free egg substitute

1. Preheat a medium skillet over medium heat. Combine the onion, oil, allspice and garlic in the hot skillet; cook, stirring occasionally, until the onion just begins to brown, about 7 minutes. Add the turkey, oregano and salt; cook, breaking apart the turkey with a wooden spoon, until browned, 5–8 minutes. Refrigerate, covered, until the mixture is firm, at least 1 hour.

2. Preheat the oven to 375° F; line a baking sheet with parchment, or line it with foil or wax paper and spray with nonstick spray.

3. Place the sheets of phyllo on a work surface and cover them with a damp towel. Remove the first sheet and spray with nonstick cooking spray (garlic-flavored is nice). Remove a second sheet, lay it directly on top and spray it. Top with a third sheet and spray again. Cut the rectangle into three 5½ x 12″ strips. Put ¼ cup of the turkey filling in the bottom right-hand corner of each strip and fold the dough over the filling to make a triangle. Continue to fold each up like a flag. Repeat the process three more times to make 12 empanadas. Transfer the empanadas to the baking sheet and brush with the egg substitute. Bake until golden brown, 20–25 minutes.

Continued on next page.

Per serving: 333 Calories, 6 g Total Fat, 0 g Saturated Fat, 70 mg Cholesterol, 890 mg Sodium, 33 g Total Carbohydrate, 1 g Dietary Fiber, 26 g Protein, 45 mg Calcium.

POINTS PER SERVING: 7

—— *Tip* ——

In South America, the customary serving is three empanadas per person; they can also be passed on a platter. The filling can be prepared a day in advance and stored in the refrigerator. Tote any leftovers to the office for a great next-day lunch.

Roasted Pork Loin

Makes 4 servings

One 1–1¼-pound pork tenderloin
1 tablespoon fresh lemon juice
2½ teaspoons olive oil
1 garlic clove, minced
½ teaspoon freshly ground pepper
½ teaspoon ground cumin
½ teaspoon salt
¼ teaspoon cinnamon
¼ teaspoon ground cloves
2 large sweet potatoes, peeled and cut into chunks
1 green bell pepper, seeded, quartered lengthwise, then halved crosswise
One 6-ounce package large pearl onions, peeled

1. Place the pork on a sheet of plastic wrap. In a small bowl, mix the lemon juice, 1 teaspoon of the olive oil, the garlic, pepper, cumin, salt, cinnamon and cloves to make a paste. Rub the paste all over the pork, then wrap in the plastic and refrigerate 1 hour.

2. Preheat the oven to 350° F. Place the tenderloin in a shallow roasting pan. In a large bowl, toss the sweet potatoes, bell pepper and onions in the remaining 1½ teaspoons of oil; scatter around the pork. Roast until the pork reaches an internal temperature of 165° F, about 45 minutes. Transfer to a cutting board and let stand 10 minutes before slicing the pork into ½″ medallions. Serve the vegetables on the side.

Per serving: 355 CALORIES, 13 G TOTAL FAT, 4 G SATURATED FAT, 73 MG CHOLESTEROL, 357 MG SODIUM, 26 G TOTAL CARBOHYDRATE, 4 G DIETARY FIBER, 32 G PROTEIN, 64 MG CALCIUM.

POINTS PER SERVING: 7

Continued on next page.

This is an elegant one-dish meal. The spicy coating on the tenderloin pairs wonderfully with the sweet potatoes. The recipe can easily be doubled, with a second tenderloin, to serve 8.

Baby Lamb Chops

Makes 4 servings

2 garlic cloves, peeled
½ teaspoon kosher salt
Four 4-ounce boneless lamb chops

1. Spray the broiler rack with nonstick cooking spray; preheat the broiler.
2. Place the garlic and salt on a cutting board; with the flat side of a knife, crush to a paste.
3. Broil the lamb 4″ from heat until well browned, 3–4 minutes. Turn the chops over and spread with the paste. Broil until the lamb is cooked through and the paste is browned, 4 minutes longer. Let stand 5 minutes before serving.

Per serving: 202 Calories, 11 g Total Fat, 4 g Saturated Fat, 77 mg Cholesterol, 339 mg Sodium, 0 g Total Carbohydrate, 0 g Dietary Fiber, 24 g Protein, 18 mg Calcium.

POINTS PER SERVING: 5

Tip

A cleaver or chef's knife is best for crushing the garlic. If you don't have either, use a utensil like a cake server or even the bottom of a metal or plastic measuring cup.

Quinoa Salad

Makes 4 servings

1 cup quinoa, thoroughly rinsed and drained

½ pound fresh peas, shelled

1 roasted red pepper, broken up (about ½ cup)

2 tablespoons fresh lime juice

1 teaspoon dried thyme leaves, crumbled

1 garlic clove, coarsely chopped

¼ teaspoon ground white pepper

¼ teaspoon salt

1 carrot, diced

2 scallions, thinly sliced

1. In a medium saucepan, bring 2 cups water to a boil. Stir in the quinoa and bring back to a boil. Reduce the heat and simmer, covered, until the water is almost absorbed, about 11 minutes. Stir in the peas, re-cover and cook until the peas are bright green, the quinoa looks transparent and the water is completely absorbed, about 2 minutes longer. Transfer to a bowl.

2. To make the dressing, in a food processor, combine the roasted red pepper, lime juice, thyme, garlic, white pepper and salt; puree.

3. Add the carrot, scallions and dressing to the quinoa; toss to combine. Refrigerate, covered, until the flavors are blended, at least 30 minutes.

Per serving: 231 CALORIES, 3 G TOTAL FAT, 0 G SATURATED FAT, 0 MG CHOLESTEROL, 154 MG SODIUM, 44 G TOTAL CARBOHYDRATE, 7 G DIETARY FIBER, 10 G PROTEIN, 60 MG CALCIUM.

POINTS PER SERVING: 3

Quinoa, which was cultivated by the ancient Incas, contains more protein than any other grain. Be sure to rinse the quinoa thoroughly—it has a coating that, if not rinsed off, can make the grain bitter. The fresh peas can be replaced with ½ cup frozen baby peas, completely thawed; add them with the carrot and scallions. The salad can be made in advance and keeps well in the refrigerator for up to 3 days.

Shoestring Beets and Arugula Salad

Makes 4 servings

1 bunch watercress, cleaned and torn
1 bunch arugula, cleaned and torn
1 head Belgian endive, cleaned and cut lengthwise into thin strips
2 cups fresh cooked or drained canned beets, cut into thin strips
1 batch Tarragon Vinaigrette (recipe follows)

On a platter, combine the watercress, arugula and endive; mound the beets in the center, then drizzle with the vinaigrette.

Per serving: 87 CALORIES, 4 G TOTAL FAT, 0 G SATURATED FAT, 0 MG CHOLESTEROL, 240 MG SODIUM, 12 G TOTAL CARBOHYDRATE, 3 G DIETARY FIBER, 3 G PROTEIN, 113 MG CALCIUM.

POINTS PER SERVING: 1

Tip

If you use fresh beets, cook them according to Step 1 of the recipe for Beet and Apple "Napoleon" (page 201).

Tarragon Vinaigrette

Makes 4 servings

2 tablespoons cider vinegar

1 tablespoon olive oil

2 teaspoons Dijon mustard

¼ teaspoon salt

¼ teaspoon freshly ground pepper

1 tablespoon chopped tarragon

In a small bowl, mix the vinegar, oil, mustard, salt and pepper. Refrigerate, covered, until ready to use. Whisk in the tarragon just before drizzling over the salad.

Per serving: 34 Calories, 4 g Total Fat, 0 g Saturated Fat, 0 mg Cholesterol, 148 mg Sodium, 1 g Total Carbohydrate, 0 g Dietary Fiber, 0 g Protein, 5 mg Calcium.

POINTS PER SERVING: 1

— Tip —

There is something very special about the combination of fresh tarragon and beets. If you can't find fresh tarragon, substitute 1 teaspoon dried.

Alfajores

Makes 12 servings

One 14-ounce can sweetened condensed skimmed milk
One 3″ cinnamon stick
One 8″ round sponge cake
¼ teaspoon confectioners' sugar
¼ teaspoon ground cinnamon

1. In a small, heavy saucepan over medium heat, cook the condensed milk, stirring constantly, until liquefied, about 30 seconds. Reduce the heat to the lowest possible setting and add the cinnamon stick; cook, stirring occasionally, until the consistency is custardlike, 2¼–2½ hours. Remove from the heat, discard the cinnamon stick and stir for 1 minute to cool. Transfer the custard to a bowl.

2. Cut the cake twice horizontally to form 3 layers. Spread about ½ cup of the custard between each layer. In a small bowl, mix the confectioners' sugar and cinnamon; dust the top of the cake with the mixture.

Per serving: 154 Calories, 1 g Total Fat, 0 g Saturated Fat, 26 mg Cholesterol, 104 mg Sodium, 34 g Total Carbohydrate, 0 g Dietary Fiber, 4 g Protein, 112 mg Calcium.

POINTS PER SERVING: 3

Tip

Alfajores are usually made as individual pastries. A storebought cake or a cake mix (freezing the second layer) simplifies preparation. Using sweetened condensed milk cuts the cooking time of the custard in half—and the custard, by the way, is delicious on its own.

A Perfect Picnic

I am, without question, an outdoors person. I hate being trapped indoors, and when I am, I soon find myself longing for the quiet fields of Dummer, the soothing rivers of Scotland or the solitude of the mountains.

I will never forget when Andrew and I headed to Canada for our first overseas tour together. We had an exhausting schedule, and after a week, I must say, I wanted nothing more than to head for the nearest beach and collapse. Yet Andrew had a different type of holiday in mind: a two-week canoe trip with a team of six others in the remote Northwest Territories.

When I look back at my diaries from that trip, I am amazed I survived. Never mind the grueling trip down the Hanbury River. There were mosquitoes and blackflies everywhere! For twelve days, we had the same lunch of salami and cheese. And the river was unyielding—enormous and unforgiving.

Nowadays, I try to make sure my picnics are slightly more relaxing!

Serves 4

Chilled Honeydew Soup

Spinach Chicken Salad

Tomato Parmesan Toasts

Mixed Berry Turnovers

Chilled Honeydew Soup

Makes 4 servings

1 small (about 1½-pound) honeydew melon
¾ cup plain nonfat yogurt
1½ tablespoons white-wine vinegar
4 slices hard salami, chopped

1. Peel, seed and cube the melon; you will need 2 cups cubed melon.
2. In a food processor or blender, puree the melon, yogurt and vinegar. Refrigerate, covered, until thoroughly chilled, about 1 hour.
3. Serve the soup in small, chilled bowls. Garnish each serving with about 1 tablespoon of the chopped salami.

Per serving: 83 Calories, 3 g Total Fat, 1 g Saturated Fat, 6 mg Cholesterol, 201 mg Sodium, 12 g Total Carbohydrate, 1 g Dietary Fiber, 4 g Protein, 91 mg Calcium.

POINTS PER SERVING: 2

Tip

This complex-tasting soup takes only minutes of hands-on preparation. You may have some melon left over; save it for a fruit salad or a snack. If you like, garnish each serving with a dollop of yogurt or ⅓ cup chopped, peeled cucumber in addition to the salami.

Spinach Chicken Salad

Makes 4 servings

¼ cup + 2 tablespoons red-wine vinegar

¼ cup honey

2 tablespoons fresh lemon juice

1 tablespoon packed dark brown sugar

1 tablespoon Dijon mustard

1½ teaspoons Worcestershire sauce

One 10-ounce package triple-washed spinach, stemmed,
leaves broken in half and rinsed

2 cups shredded cooked chicken breast

1 small red onion, thinly sliced

6 slices turkey bacon, cooked crisp

1. In a small saucepan over medium heat, mix the vinegar, honey, lemon juice, brown sugar, mustard and Worcestershire sauce; cook, whisking constantly, until steaming, about 3 minutes.
2. Divide the spinach among 4 salad plates; top with the chicken and onion. Drizzle with the warm dressing, then crumble the bacon over the salads.

Per serving: 326 CALORIES, 5 G TOTAL FAT, 1 G SATURATED FAT, 40 MG CHOLESTEROL, 580 MG SODIUM, 27 G TOTAL CARBOHYDRATE, 2 G DIETARY FIBER, 17 G PROTEIN, 90 MG CALCIUM.

POINTS PER SERVING: 7

Tip

For a novel alternative to chicken, try the salted codfish known as baccala: Soak ½ pound salt cod overnight in water; drain. Bring 2 cups water to a boil in a medium saucepan, then simmer the cod with 2 celery stalks until the fish is tender and flakes easily, about 10 minutes. Cool the cod, discard the celery, then flake the fish over the spinach.

Tomato Parmesan Toasts

Makes 4 servings

Four ½″ slices French baguette
1 teaspoon reduced-calorie margarine
1 Roma or plum tomato, cored and cut lengthwise into 4 slices
1 garlic clove, minced
1 teaspoon grated Parmesan cheese

Preheat the broiler. Lightly toast the baguette slices on one side under the broiler. Flip and coat the untoasted sides with the margarine. Place a slice of tomato on each, then sprinkle with the garlic and cheese. Broil until the bread is toasted on the second side and the cheese is beginning to melt but is not yet browned, about 30 seconds.

Per serving: 46 CALORIES, 1 G TOTAL FAT, 0 G SATURATED FAT, 0 MG CHOLESTEROL, 96 MG SODIUM, 8 G TOTAL CARBOHYDRATE, 0 G DIETARY FIBER, 2 G PROTEIN, 18 MG CALCIUM.

POINTS PER SERVING: 1

Tip

We call for Roma, or Italian plum, tomatoes because they have few seeds; beefsteak tomatoes sliced crosswise can be substituted in a pinch. This dish lends itself to a number of variations: Try shredded mozzarella in lieu of the Parmesan, or add a little chopped fresh oregano on top of the cheese. Double or triple the recipe for hors d'oeuvres.

Mixed Berry Turnovers

Makes 4 servings

½ pint blueberries, picked over

½ pint raspberries, picked over

¼ cup + 1 teaspoon sugar

3 tablespoons all-purpose flour

3 tablespoons amaretto liqueur

One 9″ square frozen puff pastry, thawed

2 tablespoons fat-free egg substitute

1. In a small, heavy saucepan over high heat, combine the blueberries, raspberries, and ¼ cup of the sugar; bring to a boil, stirring constantly. Reduce the heat to medium and cook, stirring occasionally, until the berries start to give off juices, about 3 minutes. Meanwhile, in a small bowl, whisk the flour and amaretto to a smooth paste.

2. Remove the berries from the heat and stir in the paste. Return to medium heat and cook, stirring constantly, until thick, about 2 minutes. Transfer to a bowl and place in the freezer until chilled, about 20 minutes.

3. Preheat the oven to 375° F; line a baking sheet with parchment paper, or line it with foil or wax paper and spray with nonstick cooking spray.

4. On a lightly floured surface, roll out the puff pastry to an 11″ square. Cut into four 5½″ squares and brush off any excess flour. Put about ¼ cup of the chilled filling in the center of each square, then brush the outside borders with some of the egg substitute. Fold in half on the diagonal to form a triangle, pressing the edges together.

5. Transfer the turnovers to the baking sheet. Make 3 slits in the top of each turnover with the tip of a sharp knife. Brush the tops of the turnovers with the remaining egg substitute and sprinkle each with ¼ teaspoon of the remaining sugar. Bake until puffed and browned, about 30 minutes. Cool on wire racks.

Continued on next page.

Per serving: 203 Calories, 4 g Total Fat, 1 g Saturated Fat, 0 mg Cholesterol, 41 mg Sodium, 35 g Total Carbohydrate, 3 g Dietary Fiber, 3 g Protein, 13 mg Calcium.

POINTS PER SERVING: 4

Tip

When fresh blueberries and raspberries are out of season, use 1 cup each of frozen berries, thawed and drained. Make sure the slits in the tops of the turnovers are sufficiently small to let out the steam but not the filling.

A Winter Weekend Supper

Drowning my sorrows in food is one habit I have worked diligently at breaking. I remember when I was pregnant and Andrew was away at sea, I numbed my emotions in mayonnaise, sausage rolls and smoked mackerel pâté sandwiches. I got bigger and bigger. Just prior to the birth, I weighed a bit over 200 pounds.

Eating becomes a form of therapy. It is what I call the missing link, the connection between happiness or unhappiness and one's eating habits. When I was tense or aggravated, I used to reach for food instead of trying to uncover the underlying cause of why I was feeling disheartened.

It is critical to resolve those emotional problems that swirl about in your head, nagging and chipping away at your self-esteem and sense of self-worth. Nowadays, I still have my favorite treats, but only because I am physically hungry for food.

Serves 4

Rosemary Roast Chicken

Herbed Parmesan Biscuits

Radicchio Salad

Crumbled Parmesan Vinaigrette

Strawberry-Rhubarb Compote

Rosemary Roast Chicken

Makes 6 servings

2 garlic cloves, peeled

1 tablespoon fresh rosemary, or 1 teaspoon dried

2 teaspoons olive oil

½ teaspoon salt

¼ teaspoon freshly ground pepper

One 3–3½-pound chicken

1 lemon, halved

1. Preheat the oven to 350° F. In a mini food processor, combine the garlic, rosemary, oil, salt and pepper; puree.
2. Rinse the chicken thoroughly inside and out; pat dry with paper towels. Discard the giblets and remove any visible fat. Gently loosen the skin over the breast; rub the rosemary mixture under the skin. Squeeze the lemon over the chicken and place the halves in the cavity. Tuck the wings under the back. Place on a rack in a roasting pan. Roast, basting occasionally with the pan juices, until the juices run clear when the thigh is pierced with a fork, about 1 hour–1 hour 20 minutes. Transfer to a cutting board and let stand 10 minutes before carving. Remove the skin before eating.

Per serving: 201 Calories, 8 g Total Fat, 2 g Saturated Fat, 90 mg Cholesterol, 263 mg Sodium, 1 g Total Carbohydrate, 0 g Dietary Fiber, 30 g Protein, 20 mg Calcium.

POINTS PER SERVING: 5

Tip

Use any leftover chicken in Roast Chicken Salad (page 200) and Roast Chicken and Chutney Tea Sandwiches (page 154).

Herbed Parmesan Biscuits

Makes 8 servings

1½ cups all-purpose flour
¼ cup + 2 tablespoons grated Parmesan cheese
1 teaspoon baking powder
½ teaspoon baking soda
½ teaspoon dried oregano leaves, crumbled
½ teaspoon fennel seeds
¼ teaspoon salt
¼ teaspoon freshly ground pepper
Pinch cayenne pepper
1 cup plain nonfat yogurt

1. Preheat oven to 425° F; spray a baking sheet with nonstick cooking spray. In a medium bowl, mix the flour, cheese, baking powder, baking soda, oregano, fennel seeds, salt, pepper and cayenne; stir in the yogurt and 2 tablespoons water.
2. On a lightly floured surface, turn out the dough. With lightly floured hands, pat it into a rectangle about ½″ thick; cut into 8 pieces. Transfer to the baking sheet. Bake until the biscuits are golden brown and crispy, about 20 minutes.

Per serving: 140 Calories, 3 g Total Fat, 2 g Saturated Fat, 7 mg Cholesterol, 378 mg Sodium, 21 g Total Carbohydrate, 1 g Dietary Fiber, 8 g Protein, 207 mg Calcium.

POINTS PER SERVING: 3

Tip

No yogurt on hand? Put 1 tablespoon lemon juice or white vinegar in a 1-cup glass measure, then add milk to make 1 cup; let stand 5 minutes before using. Leftover biscuits can be kept in an airtight plastic bag or container for 1 or 2 days. They make a delightful accompaniment to a soup such as Twenty-Minute Minestrone (page 92).

Radicchio Salad

Makes 4 servings

1 head radicchio
1 batch Crumbled Parmesan Vinaigrette (recipe follows)

Remove the tough outer leaves from the radicchio and trim a thin slice from the bottom of the core; discard. Pull off the remaining leaves, wash in cold water; pat dry with paper towels. Divide the radicchio among 4 plates; drizzle with the vinaigrette.

Per serving: 61 CALORIES, 4 G TOTAL FAT, 1 G SATURATED FAT, 4 MG TOTAL CHOLESTEROL, 101 MG SODIUM, 3 G TOTAL CARBOHYDRATE, 1 G DIETARY FIBER, 2 G PROTEIN, 69 MG CALCIUM.

POINTS PER SERVING: 1

Tip

Drizzle leftover Crumbled Parmesan Vinaigrette on thick slices of day-old bread—the vinaigrette soaks into the bread, which gets wonderfully flavorful and softened.

Crumbled Parmesan Vinaigrette

Makes 4 servings

2 tablespoons balsamic vinegar
2 teaspoons extra virgin olive oil
¼ cup crumbled Parmesan cheese
Freshly ground pepper, to taste

In a small jar with a lid, shake the vinegar and oil. Add the cheese and pepper; shake again.

Per serving: 50 Calories, 4 g Total Fat, 1 g Saturated Fat, 4 mg Cholesterol, 94 mg Sodium, 2 g Total Carbohydrate, 0 g Dietary Fiber, 2 g Protein, 69 mg Calcium.

POINTS PER SERVING: 1

Tip

The older the Parmesan, the better it crumbles. Be sure you use authentic Parmigiano-Reggiano that's been aged at least 2 years when you make this robust and flavorsome dressing.

Strawberry-Rhubarb Compote

Makes 4 servings

1 cup orange juice
¼ cup sugar
2 cups diagonally sliced rhubarb (1″ pieces)
1 teaspoon grated orange zest
2 cups sliced strawberries

In a medium saucepan over medium heat, mix the orange juice and sugar, stirring until the sugar dissolves. Stir in the rhubarb and orange zest; bring just to a boil. Reduce the heat and simmer until the rhubarb is tender, about 5 minutes. Stir in the strawberries.

Per serving: 112 CALORIES, 0 G TOTAL FAT, 0 G SATURATED FAT, 0 MG CHOLESTEROL, 3 MG SODIUM, 27 G TOTAL CARBOHYDRATE, 3 G DIETARY FIBER, 1 G PROTEIN, 69 MG CALCIUM.

POINTS PER SERVING: 2

Tip

Strawberries and rhubarb are a classic pair, and even though spring is when they're both in season, we love this robust flavor combination in winter, too. Just use the frozen varieties when fresh are scarce.

A Poolside Lunch

My Mum is the most beautiful, most brilliant woman I have ever known. When Dads was consumed with his polo, we'd be left to Mum, who organized our ski trips abroad, the family holidays and the most wonderful birthday parties. She would instigate parties for my friends: swimming, ice-skating or to the movies or circus.

Mum would frequently bring Jane and me to one of our favorite childhood places to eat in London, Fortnum & Mason, where mayonnaise ruled supreme. My lunch order seldom varied: ham salad, then "three in a boat," a wonderful treat that consisted of one scoop each of mandarin, raspberry and lemon sorbet with raspberries and mandarin oranges.

Although my luncheon menus—and tastes!—have grown, I still look back on those days with fond memories. Not so much for the food, but for the time I spent with Mum and Jane. Nowadays, I work hard at creating great memories for my daughters.

Serves 4

Watermelon Slush

Summer Vegetable Salad with Sirloin Tips

Spicy Pita Chips

Fresh Blueberries with Sliced Mango and Kiwi*

Watermelon Slush

Makes 4 servings

4½ cups seedless watermelon chunks
2 tablespoons fresh lemon juice
1 tablespoon chopped mint
2–3 ice cubes
Fresh mint sprigs, to garnish

In a blender, combine the watermelon, lemon juice, mint and ice cubes; puree. Pour into 4 tall glasses; garnish with the mint sprigs.

Per serving: 60 Calories, 1 g Total Fat, 0 g Saturated Fat, 0 mg Cholesterol, 4 mg Sodium, 14 g Total Carbohydrate, 1 g Dietary Fiber, 1 g Protein, 16 mg Calcium.

POINTS PER SERVING: 1

Tip

For a refreshing summertime cocktail, add ½ cup chilled vodka.

Summer Vegetable Salad with Sirloin Tips

Makes 4 servings

2 tablespoons fresh lemon juice

2 tablespoons orange juice

1 tablespoon chopped rosemary

1 tablespoon extra virgin olive oil

1 garlic clove, minced

½ teaspoon freshly ground pepper

¼ teaspoon salt

1½ cups thinly sliced cooked sirloin steak

1 red bell pepper, seeded and slivered

1 medium zucchini, thinly sliced

½ red onion, thinly sliced

4 cups torn assorted salad greens

1. In a small bowl, whisk the lemon juice, orange juice, rosemary, oil, garlic, pepper and salt.
2. In a large bowl, mix the steak, bell pepper, zucchini and onion. Drizzle with the dressing; toss to combine. Refrigerate, covered, until chilled, at least 1 hour.
3. Divide the greens among 4 salad plates. Top with the steak mixture.

Per serving: 237 CALORIES, 10 G TOTAL FAT, 3 G SATURATED FAT, 76 MG CHOLESTEROL, 198 MG SODIUM, 9 G TOTAL CARBOHYDRATE, 3 G DIETARY FIBER, 28 G PROTEIN, 66 MG CALCIUM.

POINTS PER SERVING: 5

Tip

If you're interested in saving fat calories, roasted chicken breast without the skin can be substituted for the sirloin.

Spicy Pita Chips

Makes 4 servings

¾ teaspoon salt
¼–½ teaspoon cayenne pepper
4 large pitas or flour tortillas, cut into wedges

1. Preheat the oven to 350° F; line a baking sheet with foil, then spray with non-stick cooking spray.
2. In a small bowl, combine the salt and cayenne. Spray the pitas with nonstick cooking spray (olive-oil flavored is nice), sprinkle with the spice blend and place on the baking sheet in a single layer. Bake 15 minutes, then turn off the oven; let the pitas cool in the oven until crispy.

Per serving: 166 Calories, 1 g Total Fat, 0 g Saturated Fat, 0 mg Cholesterol, 722 mg Sodium, 34 g Total Carbohydrate, 1 g Dietary Fiber, 5 g Protein, 54 mg Calcium.

POINTS PER SERVING: 3

Tip

Try ¼–½ teaspoon flavored spice mix (like fajita or Cajun) instead of the cayenne for a slightly subtler taste.

Afternoon Tea

A typical British tea used to be traditional in some households. It included cucumber sandwiches, sausage rolls, butterfly cakes, which are little sponge cakes, and scones with cream and jam. A high tea is a cross between a tea and a light dinner and is usually served to children. It would include all of the above plus fish sticks and peas.

In my darkest days, tea with the children was one of the highlights of the day, as I relished the thought of all those comforts laid out before me. Tea is still important for us. Now, I know that I can enjoy some of these treats if they are made in a healthier way. Yet if I am served a regular tea, I simply watch the girls and sip my tea—willing myself not to reach out and overindulge. This tea menu has been adjusted to suit more American tastes.

Serves 8

Open-Face Ham Sandwiches

Cucumber Sandwiches

Blackberry Scones

Almond Biscotti

Pear-Port Quick Bread

Chocolate Mousse Tartlets

Open-Face Ham Sandwiches

Makes 8 servings

Eight ½″ slices French baguette
4 teaspoons Dijon mustard
4 paper-thin slices Parma ham (about 2 ounces), cut in half crosswise
½ pound buffalo mozzarella, cut into 8 slices
8 large basil leaves

Coat the baguette slices with the mustard. Layer each with the ham and mozzarella, then top with a basil leaf.

Per serving: 159 Calories, 7 g Total Fat, 4 g Saturated Fat, 22 mg Cholesterol, 342 mg Sodium, 14 g Total Carbohydrate, 1 g Dietary Fiber, 9 g Protein, 170 mg Calcium.

POINTS PER SERVING: 4

Tip

Parma ham is the authentic prosciutto di Parma, until recently unavailable in the United States. Buffalo mozzarella (sometimes called mozzarella *di bufala*) is indeed made from the milk of water buffalo; it is sweeter than the far more common cow's-milk mozzarella, with a deeper, richer flavor. If you can't find it, substitute fresh cow's-milk mozzarella.

Cucumber Sandwiches

Makes 8 servings

¼ cup reduced-fat blue cheese dressing
8 slices pumpernickel cocktail bread (3″ squares)
½ cucumber, peeled, seeded and sliced paper-thin
4 large dill sprigs

Spread the dressing on the bread. Top with the cucumber slices and a dill sprig.

Per serving: 34 CALORIES, 1 G TOTAL FAT, 0 G SATURATED FAT, 0 MG CHOLESTEROL, 160 MG SODIUM, 5 G TOTAL CARBOHYDRATE, 1 G DIETARY FIBER, 1 G PROTEIN, 17 MG CALCIUM.

POINTS PER SERVING: 1

Tip

To seed a cucumber easily, cut it in half lengthwise and run the tip of a spoon down the center, scooping out the seeds. The firmer and denser the bread, the better. For variety, substitute any creamy reduced-fat salad dressing for the blue cheese dressing.

Blackberry Scones

Makes 12 servings

1½ cups rolled oats

1½ cups all-purpose flour

⅓ cup sugar

1 tablespoon baking powder

½ teaspoon baking soda

½ teaspoon salt

½ cup (1 stick) cold reduced-calorie margarine,
cut into small pieces

¾ cup low-fat (1%) buttermilk

3 tablespoons seedless blackberry all-fruit spread

2 tablespoons fat-free egg substitute

1. Preheat the oven to 375° F; lightly spray a baking sheet with nonstick cooking spray.

2. In a food processor, combine the oats, flour, sugar, baking powder, baking soda and salt; whirl until the oats are finely ground, about 1 minute. Add the margarine and pulse until coarsely granular, about 40 times. With the machine running, drizzle the buttermilk through the feed tube to form a dough.

3. On a floured surface, turn out the dough. With lightly floured hands, pat it into a 10 x 8″ rectangle about ½″ thick. With the side of your finger, make a shallow spiral-shaped furrow in the dough; fill with the fruit spread, then gently press the fruit spread into the furrow. With a 2½″ biscuit or cookie cutter dipped in flour, cut out 12 scones, pushing the dough scraps together for the last. Transfer the scones to the baking sheet and brush the tops with egg substitute. Bake until golden, about 12 minutes. Cool on wire racks.

Per serving: 161 Calories, 5 g Total Fat, 1 g Saturated Fat, 1 mg Cholesterol, 452 mg Sodium, 26 g Total Carbohydrate, 1 g Dietary Fiber, 4 g Protein, 120 mg Calcium.

POINTS PER SERVING: 3

—— Tip ——

If available, use Irish steel-cut oats; they'll add a pleasantly chewy texture to these dense, moist scones. Wrap any leftovers for breakfast.

Almond Biscotti

Makes 36 servings

3 cups all-purpose flour
⅔ cup sugar
1 ½ teaspoons baking powder
¼ teaspoon salt
½ cup almonds, coarsely chopped
1 cup fat-free egg substitute
⅓ cup honey
1 teaspoon almond extract

1. Preheat the oven to 350° F; line a baking sheet with parchment, or line it with foil or wax paper and spray with nonstick cooking spray.
2. In a sifter or large strainer, combine the flour, sugar, baking powder and salt; sift into a large bowl. Stir in the almonds. In a medium bowl, whisk the egg substitute, honey and almond extract. Add to the dry ingredients, stirring to combine. Set aside about 5 minutes.
3. On a lightly floured surface, divide the dough in half and form into two 10 x 3″ logs. Transfer to the baking sheet. Bake until the logs are golden and beginning to crack on top, about 30 minutes. Remove from the oven and let cool about 10 minutes.
4. With a serrated knife, cut the loaves into ½″ slices, making 36 biscotti. Lay the slices flat onto the baking sheet. Bake the biscotti until dry and lightly toasted, about 10 minutes on each side. Cool completely on wire racks. Store in an airtight container.

Per cookie: 71 Calories, 1 g Total Fat, 0 g Saturated Fat, 0 mg Cholesterol, 43 mg Sodium, 14 g Total Carbohydrate, 0 g Dietary Fiber, 2 g Protein, 16 mg Calcium.

POINTS PER COOKIE: 2

Tip

For slightly chewier biscotti, in Step 4, stand the biscotti upright and toast for a total of 15 minutes. Stored in an airtight container, biscotti will keep 1–2 months.

Pear-Port Quick Bread

Makes 12 servings

6 ounces dried pears, chopped

¼ cup tawny port

2½ cups bread flour

¾ cup sugar

1 tablespoon baking powder

1 teaspoon baking soda

¼ teaspoon salt

1 cup low-fat (1%) buttermilk

¼ cup fat-free egg substitute

1 tablespoon reduced-calorie margarine, melted

1. In a small bowl, combine the pears and port. Preheat the oven to 350° F; lightly spray a 9″ loaf pan with nonstick cooking spray, then lightly dust it with flour.

2. In a sifter or large strainer, combine the flour, sugar, baking powder, baking soda and salt; sift into a large bowl. In a medium bowl, whisk the buttermilk, egg substitute and margarine until frothy. Add to the dry ingredients, stirring with a wooden spoon to combine. Stir in the pears and their soaking liquid. Transfer the dough to the loaf pan. Bake until the loaf begins to pull away from the edges of the pan and a tester inserted into the center of the loaf comes out clean, 50–60 minutes. Cool on a wire rack.

Per serving: 208 CALORIES, 1 G TOTAL FAT, 0 G SATURATED FAT, 1 MG CHOLESTEROL, 292 MG SODIUM, 45 G TOTAL CARBOHYDRATE, 1 G DIETARY FIBER, 5 G PROTEIN, 117 MG CALCIUM.

POINTS PER SERVING: 4

Tip

For variety, fold in ½ cup chopped pecans along with the pears. To make 3 mini loaves, divide the dough among three 5¾" loaf pans and reduce the baking time by about 10 minutes. Toast any leftovers for breakfast.

Chocolate Mousse Tartlets

Makes 12 servings

¼ cup + 2 tablespoons sugar

1 egg white

⅛ teaspoon cream of tartar

1½ ounces unsweetened chocolate, melted

12 mini phyllo dough shells, at room temperature

1. In a small saucepan over medium heat, combine ¼ cup of the sugar and 2 tablespoons water; cook, swirling the pan periodically to dissolve the sugar, until the syrup reaches a temperature of 240° F, 8–9 minutes.

2. Meanwhile, in a large bowl with an electric mixer on low speed, beat the egg white until frothy. Add the cream of tartar and the remaining 2 tablespoons of sugar and beat at medium-high speed until stiff, glossy peaks form.

3. When the syrup reaches 240° F, beat it into the egg-white mixture at medium-high speed, mixing until the bowl is no longer hot. With a rubber spatula, fold in the chocolate. Spoon 1 tablespoon of the mousse into each phyllo shell. Refrigerate, covered, for 1 hour before serving.

Per serving: 72 Calories, 3 g Total Fat, 1 g Saturated Fat, 0 mg Cholesterol, 51 mg Sodium, 12 g Total Carbohydrate, 1 g Dietary Fiber, 1 g Protein, 4 mg Calcium.

POINTS PER SERVING: 1

Tip

Look for phyllo dough shells in the freezer case of supermarkets; they need not be cooked, only thawed. Heating the sugar syrup to 240° F (candy makers call this the soft-ball stage) cooks the egg-white mixture sufficiently to kill any bacteria. If you don't have a candy thermometer, drop a little of the syrup into a glass of cold water. It should form a ball that, when lifted out of the water, flattens slightly.

A Girlfriends' Get-Together

I have been fortunate to have some of the most extraordinary friends. My good friend Charlotte set off with me on a New World journey that took us from Rio to San Francisco. The two of us—18 years old and broke—finally landed in Squaw Valley in the high Sierras, and quickly secured a variety of odd jobs: we cleaned lavatories at our youth hostel, carried disabled children up the mountain and skied down with them and made strudel at the local bakery. I got huge from eating too much strudel, but the memory of it all still brings a smile to my face.

We were young and fearless! Full of energy and a sense of adventure. As I have grown older, I constantly try to learn from the mistakes I have made. Yet I also want to hold on to some of the bravery and fearlessness possessed by that young redhead.

Serves 4

Roast Chicken Salad (with Afghani bread)
Beet and Apple "Napoleon"
Chardonnay*

Roast Chicken Salad

Makes 4 servings

1 tablespoon olive oil

1 red bell pepper, seeded and finely diced

1 carrot, peeled and shredded

2 garlic cloves, minced

¼ teaspoon crushed red pepper flakes

2 cups shredded roast chicken breast

¼ cup fresh lemon juice

6 large green olives, pitted and sliced

8 arugula or radicchio leaves

1. In a medium nonstick skillet, heat the oil. Sauté the bell pepper, carrot, garlic and pepper flakes until the bell pepper is softened and the garlic is lightly golden, 1–2 minutes. Remove from the heat; stir in the chicken, lemon juice and olives.
2. Divide the arugula among 4 salad plates; top with the chicken mixture.

Per serving: 165 Calories, 7 g Total Fat, 1 g Saturated Fat, 48 mg Cholesterol, 115 mg Sodium, 9 g Total Carbohydrate, 2 g Dietary Fiber, 19 g Protein, 61 mg Calcium.

POINTS PER SERVING: 3

Tip

Turkey breast substitutes for chicken easily in this recipe, as does slivered celery in place of the carrot. Serve this robust salad with Afghani bread or pocketless pita (available at supermarkets or specialty stores).

Beet and Apple "Napoleon"

Makes 4 servings

4 beets
1 red onion, thinly sliced
2 tablespoons cider vinegar
1 Granny Smith apple, cored and thinly sliced into rings
1 tablespoon chopped parsley

1. Preheat the oven to 400° F. Trim the greens from the beets, leaving 1" of greens; save the greens for another use. Scrub the beets, then wrap in foil. Bake until a tester pierces the beets easily, 1¼–1½ hours. Remove the foil and let the beets cool enough to handle. Hold the beets under cold running water so the skins will slip off; you may have to rub gently. Thinly slice the beets and, in a medium bowl, combine them with the onion and vinegar. Refrigerate, covered, until chilled, at least 1 hour.
2. On each of 4 plates, layer the beets and onion with the apples; sprinkle with the parsley.

Per serving: 51 Calories, 0 g Total Fat, 0 g Saturated Fat, 0 mg Cholesterol, 44 mg Sodium, 12 g Total Carbohydrate, 3 g Dietary Fiber, 1 g Protein, 17 mg Calcium.

POINTS PER SERVING: 0

Tip

For the most attractive presentation, choose beets and apples that are about the same size in diameter.

A Midday Snack

The most soul-searching and difficult book I have authored has to be my autobiography, *My Story*. The book forced me to collect the emotions and thoughts I had amassed over my lifetime and try to put them into words, words that didn't always show me in a flattering light for the world to see. In retrospect, however, the book was a triumphant release. It marked a new beginning in my life: a fresh start for feeling better about myself and about my body.

In my travels across America, I have met many Weight Watchers members who have made their own fresh starts. From San Francisco and Denver to Chicago and New York, I have met new friends who share an old problem. Their courage to talk about their weight and how it has affected their lives is tremendous.

I am learning how to confront my issues with food. Taking a cue from the people I have met in the States, I try to use my new habits when dealing with my old problems. Now, if it's midday and I'm famished, I don't wait until I am out of control, which can lead to bingeing. If I have had a particularly trying and exhausting day, I enjoy a plate of fresh fruit with Parma ham and shavings of Parmesan. I also enjoy raw vegetables and a low-fat dip. All good, healthy foods that can keep me going.

Serves 4

Assorted Breadsticks*

Parma Ham and Honeydew Wedges with Parmesan Shavings*

Platter of Crudités*

White Bean-Basil Dip

Roasted Red Pepper Dip

White Bean–Basil Dip

Makes 4 servings

One 19-ounce can white beans, rinsed and drained
⅓ cup coarsely chopped basil
3 tablespoons fresh lemon juice
4 teaspoons extra virgin olive oil
1 large garlic clove, peeled
½ teaspoon salt

In a blender or food processor, combine all the ingredients; puree. Let stand at room temperature, covered, until the flavors are blended, 2–3 hours.

Per serving: 193 Calories, 5 g Total Fat, 1 g Saturated Fat, 0 mg Cholesterol, 643 mg Sodium, 28 g Total Carbohydrate, 7 g Dietary Fiber, 10 g Protein, 70 mg Calcium.

POINTS PER SERVING: 3

Tip

This Tuscan-inspired dip is delicious with crusty bread, or try it with Spicy Pita Chips (page 188).

Roasted Red Pepper Dip

Makes 4 servings

2 red bell peppers
2 teaspoons tomato paste
2 teaspoons balsamic vinegar
1 garlic clove
⅛ teaspoon cayenne pepper

1. Line a baking sheet with foil; preheat the broiler. Place the peppers on the baking sheet; broil, turning frequently with tongs, until the skin is lightly charred on all sides, about 10 minutes. Transfer the peppers to a paper bag; fold the bag closed and let the peppers steam 10 minutes.
2. Fit a strainer over a small bowl. Peel the peppers over the strainer, removing and discarding the stems and seeds, allowing the juices to drip into the bowl.
3. In a food processor, combine the peppers and pepper juice with the remaining ingredients; puree until almost smooth.

Per serving: 22 CALORIES, 0 G TOTAL FAT, 0 G SATURATED FAT, 0 MG CHOLESTEROL, 4 MG SODIUM, 5 G TOTAL CARBOHYDRATE, 1 G DIETARY FIBER, 1 G PROTEIN, 7 MG CALCIUM.

***POINTS PER SERVING:* 0**

Tip

Dollop any leftover dip on a baked potato or fresh steamed asparagus.

Wining and Dining

You don't have to have a wine cellar, spend hours at wine tastings or live in France to appreciate wine. Today, many of the stodgy "rules" of wine appreciation are obsolete: gone is the notion that white wine only goes with chicken or fish and red wine with meat. Today, wine experts acknowledge two principles: A good wine—regardless of whether it is red, white or blush—simply makes good food better, and when it comes to wine, pricier does not necessarily mean better. (Plenty of exceptional wines can be found for as little as ten dollars.)

Be adventurous with wine. Experiment by asking your local wine merchant or, when eating out, the sommelier (who is responsible for choosing the wines on the restaurant's menu) for his or her favorites. Keep the following tips in mind:

1. As a general rule, serve white and blush wines chilled to about 45° F by refrigerating or immersing in an ice bucket for about 30 minutes. The same rule is true for sparkling wines, which may also be served colder still. Red wines can be served cool (55° to 65° F) by placing the bottle in the refrigerator for a short period—about 20 minutes. A good rule of thumb: the simpler the wine, the more it will benefit from being chilled.

2. Don't be intimidated when tasting wine at a restaurant. Follow this protocol and you will impress even the stuffiest sommelier: First, observe the color and clarity of the wine (older wines often have a duller color than do young wines). Next, swirl the wine in the glass to release the aromas and the bouquet—the smell should be pleasing and aid in your appreciation of the wine. Now sip the wine, holding a small amount in your mouth; roll it around. Note if it's tart, sweet or bitter, or all of the above. These observations constitute the most important elements of wine appreciation—an experience you will likely want to build on. One point about tasting wine in a restaurant: Unless the wine is spoiled, which is extremely rare, returning a wine is generally not accepted.

3. Drink wine from the proper glass. An all-purpose wineglass will do the job, but the right glass makes for an even more captivating experience. White-wine glasses have tall, narrow bowls while red-wine glasses are large and rounded.

4. Unless you're a wine collector, you probably do not need a wine cellar, but you should still store wines properly. To store small amounts of wine for less than a year, simply keep the bottles on their sides where they won't be disturbed at a fairly stable temperature and out of direct sunlight.

5. To open a bottle of wine: First cut the plastic or metal wrapper (the capsule) covering the cork well below the lip of the bottle. Next, insert the corkscrew and pull to remove the cork. Wipe the lip of the bottle to remove any deposits left from the capsule or cork—pour and enjoy!

The following chart is a primer for the best-selling wines in the United States. Use it as your starting point for developing an appreciation of wines. Cheers!

Some Popular Varieties of Wine	Description	Try With
White		
Chardonnay	Dry, with an appealing balance of fruit, acidity and texture.	Red Snapper Primavera; Gorgonzola and Pear Pizza
Sauvignon Blanc	Grassy, herbal flavors.	Roast Chicken and Chutney Tea Sandwiches
Chenin Blanc	Light and well-balanced with a fresh delicate floral character.	Open-Face Ham Sandwiches; Cider Pork Chops
Gewürztraminer	Spicy aroma and full flavors; range from dry to sweet.	Barbecue Beef Sandwiches

Some Popular Varieties of Wine	Description	Try With
White Riesling	Floral, with fruity-yet-delicate aromas and flavors.	Parma Ham and Honeydew Wedges; Mushroom-Caraway Soup
Red		
Cabernet Sauvignon	Full-bodied, rich, intense wine with cherry-currant, sometimes herbal, flavors and noticeable tannins.	Roasted Pork Loin; Lamb Chops with Mint Salsa
Merlot	Medium- to full-bodied red with herbaceous flavors.	Classic Roast Beef; Chicken Calvados
Pinot Noir	Light- to medium-bodied red that is delicate, smooth and rich in complexity.	Provençal Beef Tenderloin
Zinfandel	Light-, medium- or full-bodied; rich in berrylike— sometimes spicy—flavors.	Steak Frites
Blush		
White Zinfandel	Off-dry flavor.	Summer Vegetable Salad with Sirloin Tips; Mesquite Chicken Salad

Information supplied by The Wine Institute, San Francisco, CA.

Index

Dieting with The Duchess

Also by Sarah, The Duchess of York

WHAT I KNOW NOW: SIMPLE LESSONS LEARNED THE HARD WAY

ENERGY BREAKTHROUGH: JUMP-START YOUR WEIGHT LOSS AND FEEL GREAT

REINVENTING YOURSELF WITH THE DUCHESS OF YORK:
INSPIRING STORIES AND STRATEGIES FOR CHANGING YOUR WEIGHT AND YOUR LIFE

WIN THE WEIGHT GAME: SUCCESSFUL STRATEGIES FOR LIVING WELL

DIETING WITH THE DUCHESS: SECRETS AND SENSIBLE ADVICE FOR A GREAT BODY

DINING WITH THE DUCHESS: MAKING EVERYDAY MEALS A SPECIAL OCCASION

MY STORY

THE PALACE OF WESTMINSTER

VICTORIA AND ALBERT: LIFE AT OSBORNE HOUSE

TRAVELS WITH QUEEN VICTORIA

Also by Weight Watchers

WEIGHT WATCHERS GREATEST HITS

WEIGHT WATCHERS COOK IT QUICK

WEIGHT WATCHERS TAKE-OUT TONIGHT

WEIGHT WATCHERS SIMPLY DELICIOUS

GREAT COOKING EVERY DAY

NEW COMPLETE COOKBOOK

SIMPLY THE BEST ITALIAN

SIMPLY THE BEST: 250 PRIZEWINNING FAMILY RECIPES

STOP STUFFING YOURSELF: 7 STEPS TO CONQUERING OVEREATING

THE FIT FACTOR

. . . and many more

Dieting with The Duchess

SECRETS & SENSIBLE ADVICE FOR A GREAT BODY

SARAH, THE DUCHESS OF YORK
AND WEIGHT WATCHERS

A Word About Weight Watchers

Since 1963, Weight Watchers has grown from a handful of people to millions of enrollments annually. Today, Weight Watchers is recognized as the leading name in safe and sensible weight control. Weight Watchers members form diverse groups, from youths to senior citizens, attending meetings virtually around the globe. Weight-loss and weight-management results vary by individual, but we recommend that you attend Weight Watchers meetings, follow the Weight Watchers food plan and participate in regular physical activity. For the Weight Watchers meeting nearest you, call 1-800-651-6000.

WEIGHT WATCHERS PUBLISHING GROUP

EDITORIAL DIRECTOR: NANCY GAGLIARDI
SENIOR EDITOR: MARTHA SCHUENEMAN, C.C.P.
ASSOCIATE EDITOR: CHRISTINE SENFT, M.S.

WRITER: STACEY COLINO, M.S.J.
RECIPE DEVELOPERS: BARRY BLUESTEIN AND KEVIN MORRISSEY
PHOTOGRAPHER: RITA MAAS
FOOD STYLIST: MARIANN SAUVION
FOOD ASSISTANT: GRETCHEN IRWIN
PROP STYLIST: CATHY COOK

This text has been reviewed by the following members of the Weight Watchers community:
Karen Miller-Kovach, M.S., R.D., *General Manager of Program Development*
Palma Posillico, *General Manager Service Design, Training and Organizational Development*
William D. McArdle, Ph.D., *Professor of Health and Physical Education, Queens College, Flushing, NY*

Contents

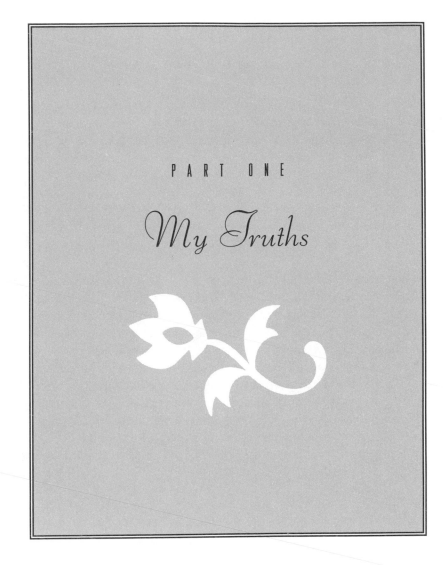

PART ONE

My Truths

1. FREE YOUR MIND AND THE WEIGHT WILL FOLLOW

I want to tell you that no matter how insurmountable your problems may seem, you can change your life for the better. If I can do it, so can you.

In many ways, I feel everything finally came together for me last summer, I went to Washington, D.C., to receive the first *Journal of Women's Health* award from Bernadine Healy, M.D., the well-respected editor of the *Journal* and the former head of the National Institutes of Health. When I went to the podium to receive the award, I was truly moved. Here I was, being recognized for what I call my truths: to help others and speak out for those who don't have a voice.

As many people know, I wasn't always so strong or sure of myself—and much of that insecurity had to do with my weight. I have had a weight problem practically all my life and I always will. But now, things are different—and they can be for you, too.

When I look back, I can clearly see the real problem with my weight began at an age when my world should have only revolved around riding my beloved horses. At 12 years of age, the world should be a thrilling and exciting place, filled with endless possibilities. Yet when I was 12, it was starting to crumble like a house of cards. Mum had just left for Argentina. Although I always admired her and never blamed her for following her heart, her absence left a tremendous hole. I ate to compensate for that loss.

For years, I did the craziest things to lose weight, like the fad diets, the vitamin pills, the fasts. By now, everyone has heard about the bizarre meat and oranges diet, the one I lived on for weeks before my wedding to Andrew. On this diet, I could eat all the meat and oranges I wanted, so I'd have my huge steak night after night and think all was right with the world. In hindsight, I can see that going on that diet was the act of a desperate woman, but at the time, the only thing that filled my mind was my wedding and the fact that I'd be walking down the aisle. Although I got great comfort from the thought of Dad being there with me, I was terrified—the entire world would be watching as Sarah Ferguson become Sarah, wife of Prince Andrew and The Duchess of York. I couldn't hide. I would be on display and I just had to look good.

Little did I know (I was only 26 after all) that the wedding was just the start of life under the microscope. Despite being married to the man I loved, my weight was still an issue and life at the Palace did little to make my world seem more in control. There were endless events and meetings to attend, people to report to. On top of this, my husband was frequently away at sea; Andrew and I were together an average of 42 days out of the entire year. Needless to say, I felt isolated and alone. Food (my favorite snacks were sausage rolls and egg mayonnaise sandwiches) was my one constant comfort.

Being in the public eye, I couldn't simply fill up and then retreat from the world. Others always noticed my weight. The press took great joy in reporting the ups and downs of my size. When I had Beatrice, my weight hit an all-time high; needless to say, after the birth the press was on a roll. "Great Fun Fergie" became "Fat, Appalling Fergie."

The stress was overwhelming. It's terrible when you walk into a room and see people nudge one another, wink and say, "Check out her backside," then give a little laugh. I've always had a rebellious streak so my reaction to this behavior was, "OK, fine, you don't like me like this, well, OK, then, I'll just eat more." And I would eat and eat. On the outside I was defiant and headstrong. On the inside I felt horrible and was terribly judgmental of my body and myself.

I was on this weight roller coaster for years. When my marriage disintegrated, I truly thought I couldn't handle much more: the press was unrelenting, the British establishment was watching my every move and I was heavily in debt. Looking back, I can see I was at the end of my rope. I had finally reached rock bottom.

When Weight Watchers approached me to act as a spokesperson I was surprised. Here I was, a single working mother who certainly had her share of highs and lows, in life as well as with my weight. How could I motivate others to take control of their lives when I was still struggling with mine?

I had been on Weight Watchers before, when I was 19, and lost a good amount of weight. I knew the program was safe, smart and effective. And I believed in it. Truth is a big thing with me. I don't—won't—do anything I don't believe in because it would be a lie. So, I thought if I do this, follow the Weight Watchers **1•2•3 Success®** Weight Loss Plan, people just might say, "If she can do it, so can I." I said yes. That was two years ago.

What have I discovered about the world and myself in the last two years? I've learned a good deal about good nutrition, eating well, exercising and the importance of having a support network. I get great satisfaction out of helping others, whether it's through my charity work or my role as a spokesperson for Weight Watchers.

I now understand that in the past I derailed because people expected me to be something I was not. They wanted me to be demure and sit quietly and do as I was told. Now I know I can't—I won't—be someone I am not. I'm opinionated and spontaneous and, at times, difficult. I'm a redhead with a bit of fire in her. I'm living my life as I see fit, despite what others think or what the press say about me. Today, I'm living my life according to *my* truth.

2. FOOD IS NOT THE ENEMY

When I did a promotional tour for my cookbook with Weight Watchers, *Dining with The Duchess: How to Make Everyday Meals a Special Occasion*, I would answer the first question that was on every interviewer's mind before he or she asked it: "I don't cook," I would begin, "but I know what I like, I know what tastes good and I'm a perfectionist when it comes to food." While many may say, "She has it easy, she has a cook," the truth is I still have to sit down with her and plan my family's meals. I also think it's amazing that at almost 40 years of age, I suddenly have found a healthier and more enjoyable way to eat.

Not surprisingly, one of the biggest changes in my life since I've lost weight involves my eating habits. They had to change, otherwise I wouldn't have the stamina to maintain the hectic pace of my schedule and be a good mother to my girls. I realized that in the past I had been eating to fill a painful empty space deep inside me. I did not want to look at my true feelings, so I suppressed the pain by eating.

In the past, I would starve myself, shed a few pounds, then go straight back to my old ways and regain the weight (plus some, more often than not!). Now, I've learned that once you find a sensible eating plan, no food is off limits or "bad." To lose weight, you mustn't be on a diet. You have to develop an eating routine that can become a way of life for *your* life.

I've found a plan that's safe and sensible and works for me. I like real food—like the pastas and risottos in my cookbook, as well as cold ham with chutney, baked potatoes with butter, and a glass of wine with dinner. In the past I did what a lot of women who try to lose weight would do: I'd cut back drastically during the week and go mad on the weekends, eating whatever I wanted. I would then get "back on track" and go on a diet on Monday. Somehow, I always felt sad because I thought I had to give up the foods I loved in order to lose weight. Now I've found that's just not the case. I can follow my eating plan anywhere in the world, at restaurants, and with my family and friends. Like any parent, I'll occasionally take my girls out to a fast-food restaurant. We sit on the toadstool chairs and have our fizzy drinks and burgers. I'll take a handful of fries, knowing that I don't have to feel guilty—and that I can stop at that handful.

Of course, watching portion sizes and making smart choices on a regular basis are also important. I know I can't have a huge plate of creamy risotto every night. It comes back to the control issue: I needed to educate myself and learn what a sensible portion of pasta or just a pat of butter looks like. I also needed to learn when to stop, whether it's after one bite or one cookie. When I'm traveling and just dying for a sweet, I might order it but take just one spoonful—like the time on a recent flight when the flight attendant on the airline wheeled the cart of butterscotch sundaes down the aisle. I didn't have to totally give in. A few spoonfuls satisfied me.

But like most women, controlling my eating habits isn't always so easy—or private. For example, sometimes I just say to myself, I'm going all out. For example, one evening I went to a favorite restaurant with a group of friends and decided it was my night off. I had my roll with butter, my favorite risotto and my wine. It's natural and healthy to go off your eating plan once in a while. However, with me, the difference is that the next day, it was written up in the papers, suggesting I shouldn't be a spokesperson for Weight Watchers. Well, the truth is, if they really knew anything about the Program, they'd know that you can eat what you like, as long as you watch your portions and plan a big meal into your whole day.

3. ONE STEP AT A TIME

I was an active child. I rode horses from a young age and was always the first in line to be a part of any game. I still ride today and I love to ski or play a game of squash or tennis.

Because I've always been so active, you'd think that exercising is an integral part of my life. But I'm very much like most women when it comes to working out: It's something I will constantly have to make an effort to do for the rest of my life. Exercise is different from activity. Activity reminds me of children playing: moving, jumping, running or just doing something that is fun and spirited. Exercise, on the other hand, can be a chore. But it is imperative for your well-being.

Through the years, I have learned to change my attitude toward exercise because, ultimately, I know that exercise has helped me lose weight and provides me with the stamina I need for my busy schedule. For instance, when I filmed my television special, *Adventures with The Duchess*, I had to scuba dive, mountain climb, even swing on a trapeze! Some of the things I did were fun (the trapeze); others were terrifying (like the mountain climbing). Yet I know it would have been impossible for me to do any of these activities if I didn't exercise regularly.

My longtime trainer, Josh Salzmann, has been a big help with my exercise program. We've been working together since the late 1980s and he's the one who encourages me to push harder when I think I've had enough. Josh also knows when to tell me to ease up. I can be very competitive with myself, but Josh reminds me that there are times when I just have to, as he would say, "chill out."

Workout time with Josh is important to me. It's one of the few times I won't allow myself to be interrupted. We have a schedule: Sometimes I ride the exercise bike, other times I use the stair climbing machine. I'll do some strength training and stretches. Our sessions vary because, as Josh has told me, I need to listen to my body and respect its limits from day to day.

When I'm feeling trapped and can't even think about exercising, I remember what Josh always tells me: "If you're really healthy and fit, you'll have a good resistance to illness and a high energy level—you'll also look your best."

I've also learned it is critical to make your workout appealing and convenient. For instance, I prefer morning workouts at a health club or at my home. I like listening to music when I work out; I'm a big Elton John fan. My favorite part of the routine is when I'm pedaling on my bike, meditating and listening to music; it's one of the few times I get to turn off my mobile phone! The part I hate: push-ups!

4. IT TAKES SUPPORT TO SLIM DOWN

I have discovered that learning about sound nutrition is relatively easy compared to using that information wisely. For me, using my head—and not my heart—to make food decisions is always a challenge. One incident that I clearly remember occurred recently after I had started the Program. Things were going swimmingly until I was preparing for a trip to the States. I was feeling anxious and suddenly found myself falling into my old habits, seeking out my trusty "comfort" foods. I also had great difficulty controlling my portions: I would have two croissants or a few more cookies than I really wanted. I didn't know what was wrong, but clearly I felt like I was beginning to spin out of control.

I immediately called my friend Sarah, a fellow Weight Watchers member, and she came over. As we talked, I unearthed the nasty root of my sudden overeating: I was anxious about leaving my girls to travel (this also was shortly after the death of Princess Diana and the girls understandably didn't want me out of their sight). Now I know that this is a trigger for me. I'm aware of it and try to keep it in mind.

Discovering triggers helps you understand yourself better. While I have been working on my weight issues, I have discovered other interesting facts about myself—for instance, I now know I'm a people pleaser. I always want others to like me and think well of me. I remember recently having to make an appearance on an American television program. I wanted to pick up my girls from school before I left, so I took a rather late flight from London to New York the day of the show. I knew it was going to be tight, but I really wanted to spend the time with my girls. Of course, things went wrong. We ended up taking off late because the airplane had a major problem with its navigating system. We sat on the runway for hours and I just kept thinking over and over, "What am I going to do?" I couldn't be late. I was so nervous. I truly did not want to let the host or the audience down. After several minutes of this, I realized I had to calm down, telling myself to relax since there was nothing I would do to change the situation. We eventually took off and I made it to the taping (although it was close!).

When I go to a Weight Watchers meeting, there is always support. We are all there for the same reason: primarily to lose weight, but also to understand how we got ourselves into our predicaments. So if you gain a pound or two, everyone knows what it's like and will try to help you figure out why.

A good support network should be a positive force in your life. At the meetings I've attended, everyone is so up, it just lifts you. It's like a tonic. I love the sense of support and friendship; it leaves you feeling you are not on your own or isolated. This time around, I learned that you don't have to be an island, all alone, when you're on a weight-loss program. Seek out support, be it your spouse, a friend, family member, even your children. Use their shoulders; you'll do the same for them at one time or another. If you find it might be too difficult relying on close friends or family members for your weight support, find a support group that makes you feel comfortable and welcome.

The day I reached my weight goal was one of the proudest of my life. Everyone was so supportive and positive. Like most women, I will always want to lose a few more pounds, but knowing that I reached my goal through my own sheer will and the help of my friends was incredibly satisfying.

5. I CONTROL MY WEIGHT, IT DOESN'T CONTROL ME

Weight is not just a "fat issue." When I talk about weight, I know I'm talking about a major health issue. I also am not afraid to say that dealing with weight is a mood-altering experience. If you gain a pound or simply wake up one morning feeling fat, it can leave you mad, frustrated, difficult, cranky. It affects your marriage and your self-esteem; it causes problems at work. And it can make you feel worthless.

How I feel about my body and my weight can dictate how I feel for the rest of the day. For instance, even if someone says casually, "You look fine," I might reply, "Thank you," but deep down I know I don't feel fine. Maybe I know I've eaten too much and that the new black swimsuit I've bought for a family

> "At the end of the day, I want my epitaph to say: A Loyal, Dedicated Mother and Friend. A Humanitarian for Children. A Spokesperson for Women's Health."

holiday is a little too snug. I know I have pushed the suit back further and further away in my drawer. Ultimately, I know I can only push the suit so far: Like my weight issue, it's there and eventually I'll have to deal with it.

I also see that I need to keep my stress level down if I am going to stay in control. I use my workouts to keep myself focused and in control. Josh always tells me that fitness is more than muscle: I have to be physically, emotionally and spiritually fit to be well. My workouts are about decompressing; they reduce my stress and clear my head so I can concentrate on the important matters at hand.

So when things get rough and the world seems insane, how do I get back on track and in control? I keep the truth. I think one of the greatest things in life is to be able to gather the courage in yourself, hold your head high and ask yourself, "Am I being true to myself?" When you can answer with a resounding yes, then you've reached your goal and you are a success.

PART TWO

Nutritional Know-How

Understanding the basics of good nutrition is critical for losing weight smartly and safely. If you're like most women, you probably have a good idea of the basics of sound nutrition. It's putting the principles into practice, however, that's likely to be the problem. Although 39 percent of Americans say they are doing everything they can to achieve a healthful diet, according to a 1997 survey by the American Dietetic Association, many are encountering serious obstacles to their good intentions. Four out of ten people surveyed confessed that they don't want to give up the foods they like; nearly a quarter said they were confused by conflicting studies on food and nutrition issues; and one out of five people said it simply takes too much time to eat well.

These findings really aren't surprising. Healthful meal-planning can be confusing, especially since nutrition research seems to produce findings that contradict each other. You know that eating too much fat is bad for you, for example, but which fats are the worst culprits? Carbohydrates, on the other hand, are good for you, but which ones pack the biggest nutrient bang for their buck? The recommendations on how much protein you should consume seem to change with each decade: In the seventies, protein was hot, in the eighties, it was *not*. Today, with high-protein diets back in vogue, many people have the impression that eating more protein is the secret to controlling weight.

In addition to this nutritional conundrum, many women are juggling work and home responsibilities and simply don't have the time or energy to revamp their diets. The good news in this nutritional quagmire is that, even if you don't think you have the time or energy to change your eating habits, you can. All it takes is a little know-how about applying the basic tenets of sound nutrition to your diet, sprinkled with a few dashes of inspiration.

Food Fundamentals

YOU'VE PROBABLY HEARD ABOUT THE FOOD GROUPS from the time you were in elementary school. Back then, there were four basic food groups—meat, dairy, fruits/vegetables, and cereals/grains. But times have changed, and so have the food groups. In 1992, the U.S. Department of Agriculture banished the basic four and replaced them with the Food Guide Pyramid, a more contemporary and detailed definition of a balanced diet. Meanwhile, research on which types of fats and grains are healthiest has also fine-tuned the picture. If you haven't kept up with the shifts—and many busy women haven't—your diet may be constructed around outdated notions. If this is the case, it may be time to give your diet a makeover.

CALORIES COUNT

All foods have calories and whether you get them from carbohydrates, proteins or fats, calories still count. The word *calorie* refers to the amount of energy a particular food gives your body. Ounce for ounce or gram for gram, different types of foods supply your body with different amounts of calories. A gram of protein and a gram of carbohydrates, for example, each contain four calories. A gram of fat, by contrast, has about nine calories, which explains why foods that are high in fat are also high in calories. And a gram of alcohol (which isn't considered a food because it doesn't have any nutrients; that's why beer, wine or spirits are often referred to as "empty calories") has seven calories.

Proponents of many fad diets would like you to believe that some calories count less than others when it comes to managing your weight. The truth is, every single calorie that enters your body can affect your weight. No matter who you are, if you consume more calories than you expend, you'll gain weight; if you burn off more calories than you take in, you'll lose weight.

CARBOHYDRATE COMPLEXITIES

Carbohydrates are a potent source of energy for the body, fueling the brain with energy in the form of glucose (a.k.a. blood sugar). Not all carbohydrates are created equal, however. There are the simple ones (such as the sugars in fruits or certain vegetables, and table sugar or honey) which are easily digested by the body and provide a fleeting energy burst. Then there are the complex carbohydrates (found in rice, grains, beans, many vegetables, pastas and breads), which take longer for the body to break down; as a result, complex carbohydrates give you a more sustained flow of energy and help you feel full longer.

Energy issues aside, it's important to make savvy carbohydrate selections for other reasons. For instance, while a cupcake contains plenty of carbohydrates from flour and refined sugar, it's also a nutritional wasteland; a whole-wheat bagel, on the other hand, is a nutritious source of complex carbohydrates that's loaded with fiber and vital minerals. Overall, most nutritionists recommend that carbohydrates make up 50 percent or more of your total calories on a daily basis.

One of the secret weapons in carbohydrates is dietary fiber. It may not contain any vitamins or minerals, but fiber is important for your diet both for weight loss and for your overall health. Fiber can help you feel full; it also helps keep things moving through your digestive tract, lowering your risk of constipation and other ailments. In fact, recent research has found that a high-fiber diet can lower your blood cholesterol and decrease your risks of heart disease, high blood pressure, colon cancer and Type II diabetes.

Basically, there are two types of dietary fiber. Soluble fiber (which is found in oat bran, barley, fruits, beans and other legumes) can help lower blood cholesterol, thereby protecting against heart disease. On the other hand, insoluble fiber (which is found in whole grains, wheat bran and the skins of fruits and vegetables) passes through the digestive tract basically undigested while absorbing lots of water. As a result, eating plenty of insoluble fiber has a laxative effect and can reduce the risk of colon cancer, as well as other digestive disorders.

Most Americans eat only half the daily fiber they should. The current recommendation calls for 20 to 35 grams of fiber a day. While this recommendation may sound like a tall order, it's easily achievable if you include at least one fiber-rich item in every meal: a bowl of high-fiber cereal for breakfast, whole-wheat pita bread stuffed with lots of veggies for lunch, a pear for a snack, and a bowl of split pea or bean soup with your dinner, for example.

PROTEIN PRIMER

As the body's major construction material, protein is crucial for building and maintaining muscles, blood cells, enzymes, hair, nails and connective tissue, as well as disease-fighting antibodies in the immune system. It's also important for key body functions like metabolism and the healing of wounds. The reason protein is so essential is that it's composed of amino acids: Your body needs more than 20 different amino acids.

Despite its crucial role, protein is often misunderstood and misused. Most Americans, for example, consume more protein than they need (sometimes twice as much). The average healthy adult needs about .8 grams of protein for every kilogram (or 2.2 pounds) of body weight. Translated, that means a 140-pound woman needs about 51 grams of protein a day—an amount that is easily fulfilled by eating a three-ounce serving of chicken and a three-ounce piece of swordfish. In recent years, protein has also become unfairly equated with fat. While it's true that some protein sources (such as red meat and cheese) are high in fat, there are plenty of low-fat options (like white-fleshed fish and nonfat yogurt) as well.

THE FAT FINDINGS

Fat has become Diet Enemy Number One, blamed for all sorts of evils from increasing your risk of heart disease and cancer to packing on extra pounds. The effort to cut back on dietary fat has given rise to a feeding frenzy of astonishing proportions. The fat-free or low-fat processed food craze that's swept the nation in recent years, for example, has spurred normally rational consumers to stock up on fat-free cookies, cakes, chips and ice cream. What many consumers don't realize, however, is that many of these products contain the same amount of, if not more, calories than their full-fat counterparts.

There's no question that consuming too much fat is harmful—or that fat contains double the calories found in an equal amount of carbohydrates or protein—but some dietary fat is actually needed by the body. Dietary fat performs a variety of crucial functions in the body, including making hormones, aiding digestion and promoting the absorption of the fat-soluble vitamins A, D, E and K. Plus, fats make eating more pleasurable by adding flavor and texture to foods.

While the total amount of fat you consume is important, the type of fat you consume is also a critical issue. The "good" fats, such as monounsaturated fats, found in olive or canola oils, reduce artery-clogging LDL cholesterol without affecting HDL (the "good") cholesterol. The worst fats are the saturated variety, found in meats and dairy foods, and trans unsaturated fats (a.k.a. trans fatty acids), which are found in margarines and baked goods, both of which increase the risk of heart disease. In addition, polyunsaturated fats found in seafood and corn oil appear to decrease heart disease risk, but some evidence suggests that the type in corn oil may be linked with an increased breast cancer risk.

Most reputable health associations now recommend that you restrict your fat intake to less than 30 percent of your total calories. What's more, less than 10 percent of the day's calories should come from saturated fat, less than 10 percent from polyunsaturated fats, and up to 15 percent of total calories can be derived from monounsaturated fats. Tracking the fat in your diet is easier now that packaged foods have labels that contain specific nutritional information, including the fat and saturated fat content. If you get in the habit of reading labels and checking a fat-gram chart for commonly eaten foods, the job of eating healthfully becomes much easier.

What About Dairy?

Milk has received a bad reputation in recent years, largely because it's thought to be high in fat. But the fact is, milk is a good source of protein as well as vital source of calcium and vitamin D, which many women don't get enough of in their diets. The Recommended Dietary Allowance (RDA) for calcium is 1,000 mg a day (for those under 50), while the RDA for vitamin D is 200 IU (for those under 50).

Unfortunately for those who don't like milk, it's difficult to get enough calcium and vitamin D from nondairy sources. As you probably know, calcium is essential for building and maintaining bone density (thus lowering your risk of osteoporosis), but so is vitamin D. In addition, recent research suggests that vitamin D may also reduce your risk of breast and colon cancer. This vitamin, which occurs naturally in very few foods, is added to milk, but seldom added to other dairy products.

While some dairy products, such as cheese and whole milk, are high in fat, others aren't. It all depends on the choices you make. If you include plenty of fat-free milk (a cup of milk provides 300 mg of calcium and 100 IU of vitamin D) in your diet, you'll consume plenty of calcium and vitamin D—without sending your fat intake soaring.

HOW FIT IS YOUR DIET?

Rating your eating habits amounts to more than simply hitting the basic food groups. It also has to do with all the choices you make throughout the day. Answer these questions to see how your diet fares.

1. **What do you usually have for breakfast during the week?**
    a) Nothing (except maybe coffee). You don't like to eat—or don't have time to—first thing in the morning.
    b) A bagel with cream cheese or jam.
    c) A bowl of whole-grain cereal topped with fresh fruit.

2. **How would you describe your eating habits in general?**
    a) Erratic—some days you skip meals; other days you eat three squares.
    b) Frequent—you often munch all day on whatever is handy.
    c) Balanced—usually breakfast, lunch and dinner plus a snack.

3. **If you have a midmorning snack, it's usually:**
    a) A doughnut or piece of pastry.

b) A bran muffin from the nearest coffee shop.

c) A piece of fruit.

4. **It's a hectic day, and you need to have lunch at your desk. Which of the following are you likely to choose for fullness and energy without too much fat?**

   a) A slice of pepperoni pizza.

   b) A tuna sandwich with mayo on multi-grain bread.

   c) A bowl of black bean soup with a small whole-wheat roll.

5. **You've hit the midafternoon energy slump and you're craving something sweet. Which are you most likely to reach for?**

   a) A small package of fat-free chocolate-chip cookies.

   b) A granola bar.

   c) A low-fat chocolate-pudding cup.

6. **How do you usually prepare fish or poultry?**

   a) Fried or sautéed.

   b) Grilled with a little olive oil.

   c) Baked, poached or broiled.

7. **You're making hamburgers (or turkey burgers) for your family. Approximately how big will they be?**

   a) The size of a videotape.

   b) The size of a box of animal crackers.

   c) The size of a deck of cards.

8. **When cooking something that calls for oil, you are most likely to use:**

   a) Margarine or butter.

   b) Vegetable or corn oil.

   c) Olive oil.

9. **To get enough fiber in your diet, you eat:**

   a) A nightly salad with iceberg lettuce.

   b) A high-fiber cereal such as All-Bran for breakfast.

   c) Plenty of fruits, vegetables, legumes and whole grains.

10. **When dining out at a restaurant that serves hefty portions, you usually:**

   a) Clean your plate and have dessert, and try to eat less the next day to compensate.

   b) Skip dessert so you don't overdo it.

   c) Order an appetizer and share an entrée—or take half of it home.

If you chose mostly A's, your diet needs an overhaul. Don't worry, though: By reading up on the basics, you'll get a better idea of how to make healthier choices and how to work them into your day.

If you chose mostly B's, your diet is headed in a healthy direction but it probably contains too much fat, not enough fiber, and overly large portions. It may be time to give your diet a tune-up.

If you chose mostly C's, congratulations! You're making smart choices all day long without skimping on variety or flavor. Looks like you're on the road to Wellville—and Slimville.

What's Weight Watchers Got to Do with It?

What role do the Pyramids play in the Weight Watchers scheme of things?

A good part of what makes **1•2•3 Success** unique is that it's so adaptable to various cultures and individual lifestyles. Thus, since there are no good and bad foods on **1•2•3 Success,** you can easily use any of the Pyramids to help plan your daily meals and menus.

If you're following **1•2•3 Success,** you are given a range within the **POINTS®** food system that can be eaten throughout the day; *all* foods are given a **POINTS** value. If you were raised eating foods that resemble the diet of the Asian Pyramid, you probably can continue eating most of those foods—you simply need to keep track of the **POINTS.** Ditto for all the other Pyramids.

Be aware that all the Pyramids—whether it's the ubiquitous USDA version or the one outlining the Latin American diet—offer guidelines for choosing a wide selection of foods, so that a person ultimately will consume a healthier, more varied diet. If you're watching your weight or trying to lose some, you need to be especially vigilant about fat and calories, as well as portions and serving sizes.

> "My weakness is savory food: egg and mayonnaise mixed together, baked potatoes with loads of butter, cold ham with chutney. I still crave toast with boiled eggs and sausage."

THE VALUE OF VITAMINS AND MINERALS

Vitamins and minerals are nearly as essential to our health as air and water. For their part, vitamins—which are organic substances that are derived from animal or plant foods—regulate all sorts of functions, from building body tissues and metabolizing other nutrients to promoting healing and preventing deficiency-related diseases such as scurvy. Minerals, on the other hand, are inorganic substances that originally come from soil and water and make their way into plants and animals; they are important for a variety of body functions such as transporting oxygen to cells, regulating your heartbeat and maintaining your body's fluid balance. There is also increasing evidence that consuming more of certain vitamins and minerals can have health-protective effects such as warding off heart disease and various forms of cancer.

For years the debate has raged on about whether it's best to get all your essential vitamins and minerals from food sources or supplements. In an ideal world, food would provide all the nutrients you need. But the truth is, many Americans don't eat a balanced diet and aren't meeting their Recommended Dietary Allowances (RDAs) for these nutrients. Others—such as pregnant and breast-feeding women, vegetarians and often dieters—are at a special risk of not getting what they need, in which case it's smart to take a multivitamin. For most people, though, taking supplements is like buying insurance: You hope you won't need that safety net but it's there just in case.

The following chart lists various vitamins and minerals, what they do, and good food sources:

VITAMIN (FAT-SOLUBLE)	WHAT IT DOES	GOOD SOURCES
Vitamin A	Keeps skin, hair and nails healthy. Helps maintain gums, glands, bones, teeth. Helps ward off infection. Promotes eye function, prevents night blindness.	Low-fat or skim dairy products. Fortified cereals. Organ meats.
Vitamin D	Helps build and maintain teeth and bones. Needed for body to absorb calcium.	Egg yolks. Fish and cod-liver oil. Fortified milk and butter. Exposure to the sun.
Vitamin E	Helps form red blood cells, muscles and other tissues. Preserves fatty acids.	Poultry and seafood. Seeds and nuts. Cooked greens. Wheat germ and fortified cereal. Eggs.
Vitamin K	Needed for normal blood clotting, bone metabolism.	Made by intestinal bacteria. Spinach and other green leafy vegetables. Oats, wheat bran and other whole grains. Potatoes, cabbage. Organ meats.

VITAMIN (WATER-SOLUBLE)	WHAT IT DOES	GOOD SOURCES
Thiamin (Vitamin B_1)	Enhances energy by promoting metabolism of carbohydrates. Promotes normal appetite, digestion and proper nerve function.	Pork. Fortified grains/cereals. Seafood.
Riboflavin (Vitamin B_2)	Needed for metabolism of all foods. Instrumental in release of energy to cells. Maintains mucous membranes. Helps maintain vision.	Organ meats, beef, lamb and dark meat of poultry. Low-fat dairy products. Fortified cereals, grains. Dark green leafy vegetables.

continues

VITAMIN (WATER-SOLUBLE)	WHAT IT DOES	GOOD SOURCES
Niacin (Vitamin B_3)	Needed in many enzymes that convert food to energy. Promotes normal appetite and digestion. Promotes proper nerve function. In very large doses (which can lead to abnormal liver function, ulcers, elevated blood sugar and uric acid, and cardiac arrhythmias), lowers cholesterol.	Poultry and seafood. Seeds/nuts. Peanuts, potatoes. Fortified whole-grain breads and cereals.
Pantothenic acid ("Vitamin B_5")	Essential in converting food to molecular forms needed by body. Needed to manufacture adrenal hormones and chemicals that regulate nerve function.	Manufactured by intestinal bacteria. Also found in almost all plant and animal foods.
Pyridoxine (Vitamin B_6)	Essential to protein metabolism and absorption. Also important in carbohydrate metabolism. Helps form red blood cells. Promotes proper nerve function.	Meats/fish/poultry. Grains and cereals. Spinach, sweet potatoes, white potatoes. Bananas, prunes, watermelon.
Cobalamin (Vitamin B_{12})	Builds genetic material (nucleic acid) needed by all cells. Helps form red blood cells.	All animal products, including meats, poultry, eggs and seafood. Low-fat dairy products.
Biotin	Needed for metabolism of glucose and formation of certain fatty acids. Essential for many bodily processes.	Made by intestinal bacteria. Meats, poultry, fish and eggs. Nuts, seeds and legumes. Vegetables.
Folic acid	Needed to make genetic material (DNA and RNA). Needed in manufacture of red blood cells.	Poultry and liver. Dark green leafy vegetables and legumes. Fortified whole-grain cereals and breads. Orange and grapefruit juice.
Vitamin C (Ascorbic acid)	Helps bind cells together. Strengthens blood vessel walls. Keeps gums healthy. Helps resist infection. Promotes healing of cuts and wounds.	Citrus fruits, citrus juices, strawberries, cantaloupe, watermelon. Sweet potatoes, cabbage, cauliflower, broccoli, green or red pepper, plantains, snow peas.

MINERAL (MACROMINERAL)	WHAT IT DOES	GOOD SOURCES
Calcium	Helps build strong bones and teeth. Promotes proper muscle and nerve function. Helps blood to clot. Helps activate enzymes needed to convert food to energy.	Milk and milk products. Canned salmon (with bones). Oysters. Broccoli. Tofu.

MINERAL (MACROMINERAL)	WHAT IT DOES	GOOD SOURCES
Phosphorus	Works with calcium to build and maintain bones and teeth. Needed by certain enzymes to convert food to energy. Helps maintain body's chemical balance. Promotes proper nerve and muscle function.	Dairy products and egg yolks. Meat, poultry and fish. Legumes.
Magnesium	Activates enzymes needed to release energy in body. Promotes bone growth. Needed to make cells and genetic material.	Green leafy vegetables. Beans and nuts. Fortified whole-grain cereals and breads. Oysters, scallops.

MINERAL (TRACE)	WHAT IT DOES	GOOD SOURCES
Iron	Essential to make hemoglobin, the red substance in blood that carries oxygen and myoglobin, the substance that stores oxygen in muscles.	Red meat and liver. Shellfish and fish. Legumes. Dried apricots. Fortified breads and cereals. Acidic foods cooked in cast-iron pots.
Zinc	Element in more than 100 enzymes that are essential to digestion and metabolism.	Beef, liver and oysters. Yogurt. Fortified cereals and wheat germ.
Selenium	Interacts with vitamin E to prevent breakdown of fats and body chemicals.	Chicken, seafood. Whole-grain breads and cereals. Egg yolks. Mushrooms, onions and garlic.
Copper	Component of several enzymes, including one needed to make skin's pigment. Stimulates iron absorption. Needed to make red blood cells, connective tissue and nerve fibers.	Lobster. Organ meats. Nuts. Dried peas, beans, prunes. Barley.
Iodine	Essential to normal thyroid-gland function.	Iodized salt. Seafood or vegetables grown in iodine-rich soil.
Fluoride	Promotes strong teeth and bones, especially in children. Improves body's uptake of calcium.	Fluoridated water, food cooked in fluoridated water. Tea.
Manganese	Needed for normal tendon and bone structure. Component of some enzymes important in metabolism.	Tea and coffee. Bran. Dried peas and beans. Nuts.

continues

MINERAL (TRACE)	WHAT IT DOES	GOOD SOURCES
Molybdenum	Component of enzymes needed in metabolism. Helps regulate iron storage.	Dried peas and beans. Dark green leafy vegetables. Organ meats. Whole-grain breads and cereals.
Chromium	Works with insulin for proper glucose metabolism.	Whole-grain breads and cereals. Brewer's yeast. Peanuts.
Sulfur	Needed to help make hair and nails. Component of several amino acids.	Wheat germ. Dried pasta and beans. Beef. Peanuts. Clams.

MINERAL (ELECTROLYTE)	WHAT IT DOES	GOOD SOURCES
Potassium	With sodium, helps to regulate body's fluid balance. Promotes transmission of nerve impulses and proper muscle contraction. Needed for proper metabolism.	Bananas, citrus fruits and dried fruits. Deep yellow vegetables, potatoes and legumes. Low-fat milk. Bran cereal.
Sodium	Helps maintain body fluid balance.	Salt. Processed foods. Milk. Water in some areas.
Chloride	Helps maintain proper acid-base balance. Component of hydrochloric acid, found in gastric juices and important in digestion.	Same as sodium.

THE WONDERS OF WATER

> "I drink plenty of water—up to 2 quarts—throughout the day. It's the big weight-loss secret for keeping you full. I like my water plain with no ice, or I'll sip weak Earl Grey tea."

Water is the most plentiful substance on the planet—not to mention in our bodies, making up 50 to 70 percent of our weight. With a quick twist of the tap, it's easily accessible day or night. Nevertheless, many of us don't drink as much water as we should. Not only does simple water carry waste products out of our bodies, it also aids digestion, regulates body temperature, lubricates our joints—and doesn't contain a single calorie. What's more, water can provide a feeling of fullness, leading us to eat less than we might otherwise. In fact, many people mistake thirst for hunger and end up eating when their bodies really want fluids. If we start getting in the habit of drinking water throughout the day, we'll begin to recognize true hunger when it strikes.

Water is present in many of the foods we eat, from fruits and vegetables to breads and cheeses, but it's still important to drink plenty in its purest form: a minimum of six eight-ounce glasses per day, more if you're exercising or live in a hot climate. Thirst is not always an accurate indicator, either: By the time you're thirsty, you may already be dehydrated. The best way to tell if you're drinking enough water is by the color of your urine; it should be pale yellow. If it's bright yellow, you need to drink more water. It's also smart to increase your water intake if you're adding fiber or protein to your diet because extra water is needed to carry fiber through your gastrointestinal tract and to metabolize the added protein. So drink up.

IN SEARCH OF THE PYRAMIDS

It's one thing to understand the tenets of basic nutrition, another to put them into practice. In 1992, the U.S. Department of Agriculture (USDA) tried to make it easier for consumers by releasing the Food Guide Pyramid, which spells out in graphic form the types and amounts of foods you should eat on a daily basis. It breaks foods into six categories and offers recommendations for how many servings you should have from each category every day. The plan encourages balance, variety and moderation.

The idea is to use foods from the base of the Pyramid—those from the bread, cereal, rice and pasta group—as the basis or framework of your meals, then to build from there. The government recommends that you have between 6 and 11 servings of bread, cereal, rice and pasta per day. (Keep in mind that 1 slice of bread, ½ cup of cooked cereal or 1 ounce of ready-to-eat cereal, or ½ cup of cooked rice or pasta counts as one serving.) As far as the range of servings goes, most sedentary adults should stick to the lower end of this range, while those who are physically active may be closer to the middle and those who are extremely active may need to aim for the upper end.

Next comes the recommendation of three to five servings of vegetables and two to four servings of fruit per day. A total of five from the two groups is considered the bare minimum, but you can't go wrong if you set your sights on the higher end of the spectrum. One vegetable serving, for example, consists of 1 cup of raw, leafy vegetables or ½ cup of cooked or chopped raw veggies; a serving of fruit is equal to 1 medium apple, banana, orange or peach.

As you move up the Food Pyramid, a little restraint is in order. The U.S. government recommends two to three daily servings from the milk, yogurt and cheese group and two to three servings from the meat, poultry, fish, dried beans, eggs and nuts group. This advice reflects the concern that Americans typically eat too much protein. A serving from this group consist of: 1 cup of milk or yogurt or 1½ ounces of natural cheese from the dairy group, 2 to 3 ounces of lean meat, fish or poultry or 1 egg from the other group. At the top of the Food Pyramid are fats, oils and sweets, which the government recommends you use sparingly. Meaning: The less you use, the better.

FOOD GUIDE PYRAMID
A Guide to Daily Food Choices

Fats, Oils & Sweets
USE SPARINGLY

KEY
□ Fat (naturally occurring and added)   ■ Sugars (added)
These symbols show fats, oils, and added sugars in food.

Milk, Yogurt, & Cheese Group
2-3 SERVINGS

Meats, Poultry, Fish, Dry Beans, Eggs, & Nuts Group
2-3 SERVINGS

Vegetable Group
3-5 SERVINGS

Fruit Group
2-4 SERVINGS

Bread, Cereal, Rice, & Pasta Group
6-11 SERVINGS

Source: U.S. Department of Agriculture &
U.S. Department of Health and Human Services

What's in a Serving?

When it comes to gaining control of your weight and eating habits, one of the biggest hurdles may be curbing the size of your portions. Let's face it: Unless you're a nutritionist, it's not easy to gauge what 3 ounces of lean beef or a cup of pasta look like on a plate. It helps if you visualize servings of common foods as everyday objects. Here are a few examples:

3 OUNCES OF COOKED MEAT=A DECK OF CARDS

3 OUNCES OF FISH=ONE AND A HALF CASSETTE TAPES

1 CUP OF PASTA=A TENNIS BALL

1 PANCAKE=A COMPACT DISC

2 SERVINGS OF MOST BREADS=A VIDEOCASSETTE TAPE

1 CUP OF FRUIT OR RAW VEGGIES=A BASEBALL

½ CUP OF COOKED VEGGIES=A CLENCHED FIST

1 OUNCE OF CHEESE=A PAIR OF DICE OR A 1-INCH CUBE

1 TABLESPOON OF BUTTER OR SALAD DRESSING=A HALF DOLLAR OR THE TIP OF YOUR THUMB

Putting the Pyramid into practice may seem complicated, but it really isn't. Since most of us don't eat items from each food group in isolation, it's easy to knock off a few recommendations in a single meal. For example, by having chicken fajitas, you could incorporate a serving from the meat group, one from the bread group, one from the cheese group and at least one from the vegetable group. Here's what a sample day's menu, based on the Food Guide Pyramid, might look like if you're trying to lose weight.

BREAKFAST: 1 SLICE HIGH-FIBER BREAD SPREAD WITH 2 TEASPOONS OF PEANUT BUTTER

½ BANANA

1 CUP FAT-FREE MILK

LUNCH: 1 CUP LENTIL SOUP

CHEESE MELT MADE WITH 1 SLICE MULTI-GRAIN BREAD AND 1 SLICE REDUCED-FAT CHEESE

SLICES OF TOMATO AND CUCUMBER WITH FAT-FREE ITALIAN DRESSING

1 CUP LOW-FAT YOGURT

SNACK: 1 CUP FRUIT SALAD

DINNER: 1 CUP PASTA TOSSED WITH ½ CUP MARINARA SAUCE AND 1 CUP SAUTÉED ZUCCHINI, SEASONED WITH MINCED GARLIC AND OREGANO

1 CUP BERRIES TOPPED WITH ½ CUP LOW-FAT FROZEN YOGURT

PYRAMID SCHEMES

In addition to the basic USDA Pyramid, there's now the Mediterranean Diet Pyramid, the Asian Diet Pyramid, the Latin American Diet Pyramid, and the Vegetarian Diet Pyramid. Coming soon: the African-American Diet Pyramid. It's enough to make your head spin. So it's important to remember that these are simply alternatives to the original Food Guide Pyramid, only they're placing popular foods from these cultures within the same framework.

Each of the Pyramids do have some important distinctions. The Mediterranean Food Pyramid, for example, permits the use of more olive oil than the USDA Pyramid does (to mirror the traditional diet of countries such as Italy and Greece). The Asian Diet Pyramid, on the other hand, places fish and dairy products in the same block since dairy foods are generally not key in the traditional Asian diet. The Latin American Diet Pyramid recommends having fruits, vegetables, beans and grains (such as tortillas and quinoa) at every meal. And the Vegetarian Diet Pyramid advocates fruits, vegetables, legumes (such as soybeans and lentils) and whole grains at every meal. Only the basic Food Guide Pyramid spells out how many servings you should have from any given food group on a daily basis.

While all of these Pyramids are intended to help consumers make healthful food choices, remember that none of them are specifically geared to help you lose weight. It is possible to lose weight using any of these guides as long as you make smart choices within the recommendations, stay on the lower end of the serving spectrum and watch your fat intake. The bottom line is: You can continue to enjoy some of the dietary patterns you've grown accustomed to, start eating a more healthful diet, *and* begin to manage your weight, if you make some simple adjustments.

You don't have to completely revamp your diet, nor do you have to sacrifice the tastes you crave. The idea is to use any of the Pyramids as the framework for a nutritious diet while including many of the foods you love and skimming the fat. It's entirely possible; it just takes a little planning and creativity.

Here are examples of how a day's menu from the other Pyramids can be modified to conform to the guidelines of the USDA Food Guide Pyramid. This way, you can incorporate the cultural foods you prefer into the basic framework, while minimizing your fat intake and meeting your dairy (i.e., calcium) requirements.

The Mediterranean Diet

BREAKFAST: 1 ORANGE

2 SLICES HIGH-FIBER BREAD TOPPED WITH 1½ TABLESPOONS SPREADABLE FRUIT

1 CUP FAT-FREE MILK

LUNCH: MIXED GREENS WITH 1 TEASPOON EACH OLIVE OIL AND BALSAMIC VINEGAR

¼ CUP HUMMUS WITH 1 SMALL WHOLE-WHEAT PITA, CUT INTO WEDGES

1 CUP LOW-FAT VANILLA YOGURT

1 CUP MELON

SNACK: 3 CUPS LOW-FAT MICROWAVE POPCORN

DINNER: 1 CUP COOKED COUSCOUS TOPPED WITH 1 CUP BLACK BEAN SOUP AND 1 TABLE-SPOON REDUCED FAT CHEDDAR CHEESE

1 CUP STEAMED GREEN BEANS

1 CUP SLICED BERRIES

1 GLASS RED WINE

The Asian Diet

BREAKFAST: 1 CUP CREAM OF RICE CEREAL TOPPED WITH 1½ TABLESPOONS SPREADABLE FRUIT

1 CUP FAT-FREE MILK

LUNCH: 1 CUP HOT-AND-SOUR SOUP

1 CUP STEAMED CHINESE VEGETABLES WITH TOFU

1 APPLE

SNACK: 1 NECTARINE

DINNER: SHRIMP STIR-FRY MADE WITH 1 CUP SHRIMP; ½ CUP EACH SLICED CARROTS, SNOW PEAS AND RED BELL PEPPER STRIPS; ¼ CUP SLICED SCALLIONS, 2 TEASPOONS PEANUT OIL; 1 TABLESPOON SOY SAUCE, 2 TEASPOONS WATER, 1 TEASPOON SHERRY AND A PINCH OF GROUND GINGER

1 CUP WHITE OR BROWN RICE

1 CUP LOW-FAT YOGURT

The Latin-American Diet

BREAKFAST: ¼ CANTALOUPE

2 SLICES HIGH-FIBER BREAD, TOASTED AND SPREAD WITH 2 TABLESPOONS LIGHT CREAM CHEESE

1 CUP FAT-FREE MILK

*H*ERE I AM AT FOUR
YEARS OF AGE, GATHERING
LEAVES IN THE YARD.

*A*T 29 YEARS OF AGE. BY THIS TIME,
I WAS STARTING TO BATTLE WITH MY
WEIGHT. I SELDOM FELT COMFORT-
ABLE BEING THE CENTER OF ATTEN-
TION, AND MY WEIGHT PROBLEM
DIDN'T HELP.

I WAS ABOUT 28 WHEN THIS SHOT WAS
SNAPPED ON A TOUR OF MAURITIUS. JUST MAR-
RIED, I WAS BEGINNING MY NEW LIFE AND AD-
JUSTING TO MY NEW ROLE.

THE CHARITIES I DEVOTE MY TIME TO ARE A BRIGHT LIGHT IN MY LIFE. I WAS DEEPLY MOVED BY THE BOMBING IN OKLAHOMA; MY ORGANIZATION CHANCES FOR CHILDREN DONATED FUNDS TO HELP THE CHILDREN WHO WERE INJURED IN THE BLAST. HERE I AM WITH P.J., ONE OF THE YOUNGEST, BRAVEST VICTIMS OF THE BOMBING.

AT CHANCES FOR CHILDREN WE'RE ALWAYS LOOKING FOR NEW WAYS TO RAISE MONEY FOR THE YOUNGSTERS WE TRY TO HELP. WE'VE ORGANIZED BLACK-TIE GALAS, IN-STORE PROMOTIONS, EVEN FASHION SHOWS WITH TOP DESIGNERS. I'M HAPPY THAT I AM ABLE TO DO SOMETHING TO HELP THOSE WHO HAVEN'T HAD SUCH EASY LIVES.

I AM WITH TWO CHILDREN FROM THE INCARNATION CHILDREN'S CENTER (ICC), THEIR ADOPTIVE MOTHER, AND SISTER BRIDGET KINIRY, THE ASSISTANT DIRECTOR OF ICC. ICC IS A REMARKABLE PLACE AND ONE OF NEW YORK CITY'S ONLY RESIDENCES FOR CHILDREN WITH HIV AND AIDS. CHANCES FOR CHILDREN HAS DONATED BOOKS, CLOTHES, TOYS, AND SUPPLIES TO ICC.

Another bright light came into my life when Weight Watchers asked me to serve as spokesperson. Here I am at the launch of 1•2•3 Success. This program has helped millions of women—myself included—lose weight smartly and safely. I know it's a plan I'll follow for years to come.

Here I am with Vivian Pinn, M.D., Director of the Women's Health Initiative, National Institutes of Health. Dr. Pinn is truly a remarkable woman, who has done important work for women's health issues.

*I*T'S ALWAYS GOOD TO MEET OTHER WEIGHT WATCHERS MEMBERS; THEIR STORIES TRULY INSPIRE ME. MY TRAVELS WITH WEIGHT WATCHERS HAVE TAKEN ME ALL OVER THE UNITED STATES. HERE I AM AT A MEETING WITH LEADERS AND MEMBERS.

*M*Y LIFE IS CERTAINLY A LOT DIFFERENT THAN IT WAS FIVE YEARS AGO. THIS IS MY SECOND BOOK WITH WEIGHT WATCHERS. I HAVE ALSO JUST COMPLETED TAPING MY OWN TALK SHOW IN THE UK CALLED "SURVIVING LIFE," WHICH FOCUSES ON PEOPLE WHO HAVE GONE THROUGH EXTRAORDINARY EXPERIENCES. I KNOW I COULDN'T HAVE DONE ALL THIS TEN YEARS AGO. NOWADAYS, I KNOW SO MUCH MORE ABOUT MYSELF.

LUNCH: MEXICAN PIZZA MADE WITH 1 TORTILLA SPREAD WITH ½ CUP FAT-FREE REFRIED BEANS, ¼ CUP SALSA AND 2 TABLESPOONS GRATED REDUCED-FAT CHEDDAR CHEESE (BAKE AT 400° F UNTIL CHEESE IS MELTED AND TORTILLA IS CRISP, ABOUT 10 MINUTES)

½ MANGO

1 CUP FAT-FREE MILK

SNACK: 1 BANANA

DINNER: SPINACH LEAVES WITH SLICED TOMATO, 1 TABLESPOON SUNFLOWER SEEDS AND 1 TEASPOON EACH CANOLA OIL AND FLAVORED VINEGAR

ONE 3-OUNCE RED SNAPPER FILLET, GRILLED AND SEASONED WITH SALT, FRESHLY GROUND PEPPER AND FRESH LEMON JUICE

½ CUP WHITE OR BROWN RICE

1 CUP STEAMED BROCCOLI, WITH 1 TEASPOON REDUCED-CALORIE MARGARINE

1 CUP PINEAPPLE CHUNKS

The Vegetarian Diet

BREAKFAST: 1 SMALL BAGEL SPREAD WITH 2 TABLESPOONS LIGHT CREAM CHEESE

1 CUP LOW-FAT YOGURT

LUNCH: MIXED GREENS, SHREDDED CARROTS AND SLICED CUCUMBER, TOSSED WITH 1 TEASPOON EACH OLIVE OIL AND FLAVORED VINEGAR

1 COOKED VEGETARIAN BURGER, WITH LETTUCE LEAVES AND TOMATO SLICES ON 1 TOASTED ENGLISH MUFFIN

1 CUP CHOCOLATE PUDDING

SNACK: 3 CUPS LOW-FAT MICROWAVE POPCORN

DINNER: 1 CUP COOKED PASTA MIXED WITH ¼ CUP EACH STEAMED SLICED ZUCCHINI, YELLOW SQUASH, CARROT AND MUSHROOMS, ⅓ CUP COOKED CHICKPEAS, ½ CUP TOMATO SAUCE (SEASONED WITH GARLIC, OREGANO AND BASIL), AND ⅓ CUP PART-SKIM RICOTTA CHEESE

1 CUP GRAPES

The key to healthful eating is to make savvy choices from the Food Pyramid and balance your favorite foods with those that promote good health. No food should be taboo; if you exercise in moderation and keep the big picture in mind, your diet can be varied, enjoyable and healthful. If you're trying to lose weight, however, you may need to tinker with the items you select from the various food groups. When choosing from the milk, yogurt and cheese group, for example, it's best to opt for fat-free milk or low-fat milk, low-fat yogurt and reduced-fat cheese. Also, since a range is given for serving guidelines, it's important to find the number of servings from each group that's right for you. For instance, if you're trying to lose weight, nine servings from the bread, cereal, rice and pasta group may be too much, whereas six may be just right.

Key Points

♦ To get the most from your carbohydrates, choose the complex variety—grain products, vegetables, and dried beans and legumes—over simple ones whenever possible. They're a better source of energy, nutrition and fiber.

♦ Choose your fat sources wisely, use the monounsaturated variety whenever possible and limit your total intake.

♦ Increase your fiber intake gradually, and be sure to drink plenty of water as you do so. Your gastrointestinal tract will thank you.

♦ Instead of plopping a big piece of meat on the center of your plate, put a smaller serving on the side and fill your plate with lots of veggies and grains.

♦ In trying to follow the Food Guide Pyramid, don't be afraid to adjust the number of servings from any one group, according to what works for you. Also, be sure to pay attention to serving sizes.

Goals

◇ *Spend most of your time shopping the perimeter of the grocery store, where the healthiest choices lie—produce, dairy, and the fish, poultry and meat counters.*

◇ *Try to include a fiber-rich item with every meal and you'll easily fulfill the recommended daily intake for fiber.*

◇ *Start sipping water throughout the day by keeping a water bottle at your desk, in the car, at the table. Before you know it, you'll increase your intake without sweating it.*

◇ *Get into the habit of reading Nutrition Facts labels—they're full of helpful information, from fat content to nutrient values, as well as calorie counts. The new design is easy to decipher.*

◇ *Try new food preparation methods: Instead of frying your fish or chicken, broil or roast it. Instead of topping a baked potato with a hefty dollop of sour cream, substitute a low-fat version or low-fat yogurt.*

◇ *Make changes to your diet gradually and keep your goals realistic. Your current eating habits have been established over a number of years, so it's unrealistic to think you can revamp them overnight. Adjust your patterns at a comfortable pace and make a long-term commitment to improving the way you eat.*

Four Weeks to a Better Body

*I*F YOU'RE READY to lose weight, but not ready to spend hours pondering questions about protein and portion sizes, consider the following eating plan. It's based on the basic tenets of good nutrition and promotes a safe, steady weight loss of up to two pounds per week. Chock-full of delicious meal ideas and mini-recipes, the following plan stresses variety and simplicity. Use it as a springboard for starting a healthful, new lifestyle. (Recipes with asterisks can be found in Part Five: Elegant, Everyday Eating.)

WEEK ONE

Sunday

BREAKFAST

Breakfast Bruschetta (Split and toast 1 whole-wheat English muffin; spread with ⅓ cup part-skim ricotta cheese. Top with ½ cup chopped tomato and 1 tablespoon chopped parsley.) (5)

½ cup orange juice (1)

6 POINTS

LUNCH

Leek and Potato Soup* (1)

Mini Crudité Platter with Tangy Dipping Sauce (On a plate, arrange ⅓ cup each fennel slices, baby carrots and red bell pepper slices. For dipping sauce, mix together 3 tablespoons light sour cream, 1 tablespoon balsamic vinegar and 2 teaspoons Dijon mustard.) (1)

Herb-Crusted Grilled Chicken Breast (Combine 1 teaspoon minced garlic with ½ teaspoon each dried basil and dried oregano. Dip a 4-ounce skinless boneless chicken breast in 1

tablespoon low-fat buttermilk, then into the basil mixture before grilling.) (3)

1 cup fat-free milk (2)

7 POINTS

DINNER

Citrus-Seared Tuna (Brush a 6-ounce tuna steak with 1 teaspoon each olive oil and fresh lemon juice; sprinkle with a pinch each salt and freshly ground pepper. Cook in ridged grill pan over medium-high heat 3–4 minutes on each side.) (5)

Mango Salsa (Toss ½ diced mango with ½ cup diced red bell pepper, 1 tablespoon chopped cilantro, 2 teaspoons fresh lime juice and a pinch each cayenne pepper and salt. Serve over the tuna.) (1)

1 cup steamed green beans (0)

1 cup cooked couscous (2)

8 POINTS

SNACK

1 cup aspartame-sweetened vanilla nonfat yogurt with 1 cup sliced strawberries (3)

3 POINTS

*TOTAL FOR THE DAY: **24 POINTS***

Monday

BREAKFAST

Sweet Cherry Oatmeal (1 cup cooked oatmeal topped with ¼ cup dried cherries and 1 teaspoon packed brown sugar.) (4)

1 cup fat-free milk (2)

1 cup cubed papaya (1)

7 POINTS

LUNCH

Tarragon Chicken Salad Sandwich (Cube one 3-ounce skinless cooked chicken breast and combine with ½ cup finely chopped carrot, 1 tablespoon tarragon mustard and 2 teaspoons each scallion slice and reduced-calorie mayonnaise. Spoon into a small whole-wheat pita with lettuce and tomato.) (5)

1 Anjou pear (1)

6 POINTS

DINNER

Fish and Chips* (4)

Red and Orange Slaw (Combine 1 cup shredded red cabbage, 1 shredded carrot and ¼ cup fat-free mayonnaise with salt, freshly ground pepper and fresh lemon juice to taste.) (1)

5 POINTS

SNACK

1 cup lemon nonfat yogurt with 1 cup blueberries (4)

4 POINTS

*TOTAL FOR THE DAY: **22 POINTS***

Tuesday

BREAKFAST

Breakfast Burrito (In a nonstick skillet coated with nonstick cooking spray, scramble 1/4 cup fat-free egg substitute until almost firm. Stir in 3 tablespoons shredded cheddar cheese and 1 tablespoon salsa. Spoon into warmed 6" flour tortilla; roll up.) (5)

1 whole pink grapefruit, cut in half and sprinkled with 1 teaspoon sugar (2)

Café latte made with 1 cup fat-free milk (2)

9 POINTS

LUNCH

Cavatappi with Broccoli Rabe (Sauté 1 crushed garlic clove in 2 teaspoons olive oil; toss with 1 cup cooked cavatappi pasta and 1 cup steamed broccoli rabe. Top with 1 chopped plum tomato and 1 tablespoon grated Parmesan cheese.) (6)

1 sliced peach, drizzled with 1 teaspoon honey (1)

7 POINTS

DINNER

Asian Glazed Pork (Brush one 3-ounce boneless pork loin chop with 1 tablespoon hoisin sauce; grill in ridged grill pan.) (3)

½ cup each steamed broccoli and cauliflower tossed with 1 teaspoon butter (1)

½ cup cooked short-grain brown rice (2)

6 POINTS

SNACK

1 cup aspartame-sweetened raspberry nonfat yogurt with 1 cup blackberries (3)

3 POINTS

TOTAL FOR THE DAY: 25 POINTS

Wednesday

BREAKFAST

Berry-Banana Smoothie (In a blender, puree 1 cup fat-free milk, ½ sliced banana, 1 cup semifrozen strawberries and 1 teaspoon honey.) (4)

1 slice toasted raisin bread with 1 tablespoon apple butter (3)

7 POINTS

LUNCH

Pizza Provençal* (5)

1 cup mixed endive, radicchio and arugula drizzled with 1 teaspoon olive oil and 2 teaspoons balsamic vinegar (1)

1 cup cubed honeydew melon (1)

7 POINTS

DINNER

Sausage and Pepper Hero (In a nonstick skillet, sauté ½ cup each sliced green bell pepper and onions in 1 teaspoon olive oil; place a grilled

pork sausage link on a hard roll and top with the pepper and onions.) (7)

Diet root beer (0)

7 POINTS

SNACK

Cinn-fully Sweet Baked Apple (Peel a strip from the top of an apple; core and stuff with 1 teaspoon packed brown sugar mixed with ¼ teaspoon cinnamon. Bake with 2 tablespoons water in dish at 350° F until tender, about 30 minutes. Serve with 1 cup aspartame-sweetened caramel-apple nonfat yogurt.) (3)

3 POINTS

TOTAL FOR THE DAY: 24 POINTS

Thursday

BREAKFAST

Cherry Muffin with Amaretto Glaze* (3)

Café latte made with 1 cup fat-free milk (2)

5 POINTS

LUNCH

Sahara Wrap (Spread ¼ cup hummus on a 6" flour tortilla. Top with ½ cup chopped tomato; roll up.) (4)

1 cup cucumber spears and carrot sticks (0)

½ cup each cubed honeydew and cantaloupe (1)

1 cup fat-free milk (2)

7 POINTS

DINNER

Steak au Poivre (Press 1 teaspoon cracked black pepper into a 6-ounce filet mignon. Melt 1 teaspoon butter in heavy skillet. Cook steak over high heat, 3 minutes on each side for medium-rare.) (6)

1 cup tossed green salad with 2 tablespoons fat-free Italian dressing (0)

Roasted Rosemary Potatoes (On a baking sheet, toss 1 cup halved new potatoes with 1 teaspoon each olive oil and chopped fresh rosemary, and ¼ teaspoon each salt and freshly ground pepper; roast at 450° F, about 20 minutes.) (4)

10 POINTS

SNACK

Hawaiian Sundae (½ cup vanilla nonfat frozen yogurt topped with ½ cup fresh pineapple chunks and 2 teaspoons shredded coconut.) (3)

3 POINTS

TOTAL FOR THE DAY: *25 POINTS*

Friday

BREAKFAST

Piquant Poached Egg Sandwich (Place a poached egg on a slice of reduced-calorie toast; top with ¼ cup salsa and another piece of toast.) (3)

½ cup orange juice (1)

4 POINTS

LUNCH

Potato Parmigiana (Split a large baked potato and top with ½ cup tomato sauce. Sprinkle with 3 tablespoons shredded part-skim mozzarella cheese and bake until melted, about 10 minutes.) (5)

⅓ cup each broccoli florets, red bell pepper strips and jicama spears (0)

1 cup fat-free milk (2)

7 POINTS

DINNER

Lamb Kebabs with Couscous* (9)

1 cup steamed asparagus spears (0)

Wine-Poached Pear (Peel, halve and core a pear; poach in ½ cup dry red wine with 1 star anise pod and ½ cinnamon stick.) (3)

12 POINTS

SNACK

1 cup aspartame-sweetened crème-caramel nonfat yogurt (2)

2 POINTS

TOTAL FOR THE DAY: *25 POINTS*

Saturday

BREAKFAST

Power Parfait (Alternately layer 1 cup sliced strawberries, ⅓ cup part-skim ricotta cheese and 3 tablespoons wheat germ in a tall glass.) (5)

Café au lait made with 1 cup fat-free milk (2)

7 POINTS

LUNCH

Turkey Sandwich with Chipotle Mayonnaise
(Combine 2 teaspoons reduced-calorie mayonnaise with 1 teaspoon mashed chipotle in adobo sauce; spread over 2 slices sourdough bread. Top 1 slice of the bread with 2 slices lean smoked turkey breast luncheon meat, 2 tomato slices and 2 lettuce leaves; top with remaining slice of bread.) (7)

1 cup red seedless grapes (1)

8 POINTS

DINNER

Greens and Beans (Sauté 1 minced garlic clove in 1 tablespoon olive oil; toss with 2 cups steamed escarole and ⅔ cup canned cannellini beans, rinsed and drained.) (5)

1 slice semolina bread (2)

7 POINTS

SNACK

1 cup aspartame-sweetened vanilla nonfat yogurt with 1 cup mixed fruit (3)

3 POINTS

TOTAL FOR THE DAY: *25 POINTS*

Sunday

BREAKFAST

First Frost Bagel Breakfast (Spread 1 small toasted sesame bagel with 2 tablespoons light cream cheese and 1 tablespoon pumpkin butter.) (5)

½ cup apple cider (1)

6 POINTS

LUNCH

Cobb Salad (On a plate, arrange in rows: one 3-ounce sliced grilled skinless chicken breast, ½ cup each chopped yellow and red bell pepper, 1 chopped plum tomato and 1 cup chopped romaine lettuce. Sprinkle with 1 slice crumbled cooked bacon, then drizzle with 2 tablespoons fat-free blue cheese dressing.) (5)

1 cup fat-free milk (2)

Orange Juice Spritzer (Mix ½ cup fresh orange juice and ½ cup seltzer water; pour over ice.) (1)

8 POINTS

DINNER

Veal Ragout* (3)

1 cup cooked fusilli (3)

1 cup mixed baby greens with 2 tablespoons reduced-calorie lemon–poppy-seed dressing (2)

8 POINTS

SNACK

1 cup aspartame-sweetened raspberry nonfat yogurt mixed with 1 tablespoon fat-free fudge sauce (3)

3 POINTS

TOTAL FOR THE DAY: *25 POINTS*

Monday

BREAKFAST

1 cup bran flakes with 1 sliced banana (3)

1 cup fat-free milk (2)

5 POINTS

LUNCH

Portobello Mushroom Panini (Brush 1 teaspoon each olive oil, balsamic vinegar and soy sauce over 1 large portobello mushroom cap; broil 2 minutes on each side. Place mushroom, 2 tomato slices, 2 arugula leaves and ½ cup part-skim ricotta cheese inside a ciabatta roll.) (7)

1 fig (1)

Seltzer with lemon slice (0)

8 POINTS

DINNER

Sesame Tofu with Asian Vegetables (Toss ⅔ cup cubed firm tofu with 1 teaspoon Asian sesame oil. Sauté in nonstick skillet over medium-high heat until crispy and brown, about 3 minutes. Remove from heat; stir in 1 tablespoon tamari sauce and 1 teaspoon grated peeled gingerroot. Meanwhile, in small skillet, cook ½ cup each chopped bok choy, sliced onion, mushrooms and red bell pepper in ½ cup chicken broth until vegetables are softened, about 8 minutes. Serve over the tofu.) (5)

½ cup cooked short-grain brown rice (2)

1 cup fat-free milk (2)

9 POINTS

SNACK

Pineapple and Orange Sorbet* (2)

2 POINTS

TOTAL FOR THE DAY: *24 POINTS*

Tuesday

BREAKFAST

½ seeded papaya topped with ⅓ cup nonfat cottage cheese and 1 teaspoon honey (2)

1 slice high-fiber bread (1)

Frozen Café Latte (In a blender, puree ½ cup espresso or strong coffee, 1 cup fat-free milk and 3 ice cubes.) (2)

5 POINTS

LUNCH

One 6-ounce Dover sole fillet, broiled (4)

1 cup sugar-snap peas tossed with ½ teaspoon each grated peeled gingerroot, minced garlic and soy sauce (0)

1 small sliced Japanese eggplant, brushed with 1 teaspoon olive oil and grilled (1)

1 cup orange sections and 1 chopped kiwi fruit (2)

7 POINTS

DINNER

Penne Bolognese (In a nonstick skillet, brown 4 ounces lean ground beef [10% or less fat]. Stir in 1 cup fat-free tomato sauce, 1 tablespoon fat-free milk and a dash of nutmeg; heat through. Pour over 1 cup cooked penne.) (8)

1 cup watercress tossed with 1 grated carrot and ½ chopped cucumber; drizzle with 2 tablespoons fat-free Italian dressing (0)

1 small glass red wine (2)

10 POINTS

SNACK

1 cup aspartame-sweetened coffee nonfat yogurt (2)

2 POINTS

TOTAL FOR THE DAY: *24 POINTS*

Wednesday

BREAKFAST

Soy Smoothie (In a blender, puree 1 cup calcium-fortified vanilla-flavored soy milk, ½ chopped mango, 1 cup semifrozen raspberries, 2 ice cubes and 1 teaspoon honey.) (4)

½ large corn muffin (3)

7 POINTS

LUNCH

Pita Veggie Burger (Slice a small whole-wheat pita and place a grilled vegetarian burger inside; top with ½ cup each arugula and sliced yellow tomatoes.) (3)

1 cup shiitake mushrooms sautéed in 1 teaspoon olive oil (1)

1 cup fat-free milk (2)

6 POINTS

DINNER

Spicy Gazpacho* (0)

Paella Valenciana* (7)

1 cup bing cherries (1)

8 POINTS

SNACK

1 cup reduced-calorie butterscotch pudding (prepared with fat-free milk) with ½ sliced banana (3)

3 POINTS

TOTAL FOR THE DAY: *24 POINTS*

Thursday

BREAKFAST

Italian Omelet (Sauté 1 chopped plum tomato and 1 teaspoon chopped basil in 1 teaspoon olive oil. Add ¼ cup fat-free egg substitute and 2 tablespoons grated part-skim mozzarella cheese; stir until firm.) (4)

2 slices reduced-calorie whole-wheat toast (1)

1 cup fat-free milk (2)

7 POINTS

LUNCH

Lemon-Caper Tuna (Combine ½ cup drained light tuna canned in olive oil, 2 tablespoons chopped onion, 1 tablespoon fresh lemon juice

and 2 teaspoons capers with salt and freshly ground pepper to taste; place on 1 cup watercress.) (5)

1 cup steamed green beans (0)

5 POINTS

DINNER

Steak Fajita (Thinly slice 5 ounces flank steak; sprinkle with 2 tablespoons fresh lime juice. Heat 1 teaspoon olive oil in nonstick skillet; sauté steak until cooked through, 4–5 minutes. Add ⅓ cup each sliced red and yellow bell pepper and Vidalia onion. Spoon onto a warmed 6" jalapeño-flavored flour tortilla. Serve with ¼ cup salsa, 3 tablespoons nonfat sour cream and 2 tablespoons mashed avocado.) (10)

10 POINTS

SNACK

2 graham crackers (1)

1 cup fat-free milk (2)

3 POINTS

TOTAL FOR THE DAY: *25 POINTS*

Friday

BREAKFAST

½ cup low-fat granola cereal (3)

1 cup sliced strawberries (1)

1 cup fat-free milk (2)

6 POINTS

LUNCH

Classic BLT (Toast 2 slices reduced-calorie whole-wheat bread; spread 1 slice with 2 teaspoons reduced-calorie mayonnaise; layer with 3 slices cooked bacon, ½ thinly sliced tomato and 2 iceberg lettuce leaves. Top with remaining slice of toast.) (5)

1 cup baby carrots (0)

5 POINTS

DINNER

Grilled lean turkey burger with lettuce and tomato (4)

Sweet Potato Fries (Cut 1 large sweet potato into wedges and toss with 1 teaspoon oil and salt and freshly ground pepper to taste; bake at 450° F, about 20 minutes.) (4)

Creamy Coleslaw Dijon (Combine 1 cup shredded cabbage, 1 shredded carrot, ¼ cup fat-free mayonnaise and 1 tablespoon Dijon mustard with salt, freshly ground pepper and fresh lemon juice to taste.) (1)

9 POINTS

SNACK

1 cup aspartame-sweetened blackberry-pie nonfat yogurt with 1 cup blackberries and chopped mint (3)

3 POINTS

TOTAL FOR THE DAY: *23 POINTS*

Saturday

BREAKFAST

Chocolate Chip Scone* spread with ⅓ cup part-skim ricotta cheese (7)

1 cup orange sections (1)

8 POINTS

LUNCH

French Country Pork (Brush one lean 3-ounce pork loin chop with 1 tablespoon grainy mustard and grill; serve with 1 cup warmed unsweetened applesauce.) (4)

½ cup cooked brown rice (2)

1 cup sliced tomato sprinkled with ¼ teaspoon salt and drizzled with 1 tablespoon balsamic vinegar (0)

1 cup fat-free milk (2)

8 POINTS

DINNER

1 slice thin-crust cheese pizza (4)

Insalata Tri-Colore (Combine 2 cups arugula, endive and radicchio with 2 tablespoons fat-free Italian dressing; sprinkle with 2 teaspoons grated Parmesan cheese and 1 teaspoon fresh lemon juice.) (0)

1 bottle light beer (2)

6 POINTS

SNACK

Cappuccino made with 1 cup fat-free milk (2)

2 POINTS

TOTAL FOR THE DAY: *24 POINTS*

Sunday

BREAKFAST

1 cup cooked cream of wheat cereal topped with 1 teaspoon packed brown sugar, ¼ teaspoon cinnamon and 2 tablespoons raisins (3)

1 cup fat-free milk (2)

½ banana (1)

6 POINTS

LUNCH

Tuscan Wrap (Sprinkle 3 tablespoons shredded part-skim mozzarella cheese on a 6" sun-dried tomato-flavored flour tortilla; melt in a toaster oven. Top with ½ cup each chopped tomato and zucchini; sprinkle with 1 tablespoon chopped flat-leaf parsley and roll up.) (4)

1 cup each sliced fennel and red bell pepper (0)

1 Comice pear (1)

5 POINTS

DINNER

Honey-Ginger Chicken with Orange-Parsley Rice* (7)

1 cup steamed broccoli spears (0)

1 cup mixed fruit drizzled with 1 teaspoon honey (1)

8 POINTS

SNACK

Vanilla Hot Chocolate (In a small saucepan over low heat, whisk 1 cup fat-free milk and 1 tablespoon unsweetened cocoa powder until cocoa is dissolved. Cook, whisking constantly, until heated through. Stir in 1 tablespoon sugar and ½ teaspoon vanilla extract.) (3)

3 POINTS

TOTAL FOR THE DAY: *22 POINTS*

Monday

BREAKFAST

Palm Beach Parfait (In a tall glass, alternate layers of ½ chopped mango, 1 chopped kiwi fruit and ½ cup fresh pineapple chunks with 1 cup aspartame-sweetened coconut cream pie nonfat yogurt and 3 tablespoons wheat germ.) (6)

6 POINTS

LUNCH

Open-Face Croque Monsieur (Layer 2 slices lean luncheon meat ham and 1 slice Jarlsberg cheese on 1 slice whole-wheat bread; melt under broiler.) (6)

½ cup each arugula and cherry tomato halves drizzled with 2 tablespoons fat-free French dressing (1)

1 Fuji apple (1)

8 POINTS

DINNER

Lemon Chicken Stir-Fry (Cut one 4-ounce skinless boneless chicken breast into strips; stir-fry in 1 teaspoon peanut oil with ½ teaspoon each minced peeled gingerroot, garlic, lemon zest and juice and a dash of soy sauce.) (4)

½ cup each spinach and sliced shiitake mushrooms (0)

½ cup cooked brown rice (2)

6 POINTS

SNACK

1 **Orange Madeleine*** (1)

1 cup fat-free milk (2)

3 POINTS

TOTAL FOR THE DAY: 23 POINTS

Tuesday

BREAKFAST

1 toasted whole-grain frozen waffle topped with 1 cup sliced peaches and 1 tablespoon maple syrup (5)

Cappuccino made with 1 cup fat-free milk (2)

7 POINTS

LUNCH

Roast Beef on Rye (Spread 1 tablespoon reduced-calorie Russian dressing on 1 slice reduced-calorie rye bread; top with 2 slices lean deli roast beef, 2 tomato slices and 2 lettuce leaves. Top with another slice of the bread.) (4)

1 cup red grapes (1)

5 POINTS

DINNER

Gnocchi Marinara* (6)

1 cup shredded romaine lettuce with 2 tablespoons fat-free Italian dressing (0)

1 cup roasted red and yellow bell peppers (0)

6 POINTS

SNACK

1 cup fat-free milk (2)

1 Granny Smith apple (1)

3 POINTS

TOTAL FOR THE DAY: 21 POINTS

Wednesday

BREAKFAST

Breakfast Muffin* (3)

Cinnamon-Orange Stewed Prunes (In ½ cup water, simmer 4 orange essence–flavored prunes with a cinnamon stick until slightly softened, about 10 minutes.) (2)

Café latte made with 1 cup fat-free milk (2)

7 POINTS

LUNCH

Greek Quesadilla (Sprinkle ⅓ cup each chopped tomato, green bell pepper and red onion and 3 tablespoons crumbled feta cheese onto one half of a 6" flour tortilla. Fold tortilla in half and bake in a toaster oven until lightly browned, turning once. Cut into thirds.) (4)

Dilly Cold Cucumber Salad (Toss 1 cup chopped cucumber with 1 cup plain nonfat yogurt, 1 tablespoon chopped fresh dill and 2 teaspoons fresh lemon juice; refrigerate at least 30 minutes.) (3)

7 POINTS

DINNER

Bengali Broiled Lamb (Broil one 3-ounce lean lamb chop; top with 1 tablespoon mango chutney.) (4)

1 cup cooked basmati rice (5)

1 cup steamed baby carrots tossed with 1 teaspoon butter and ¼ teaspoon toasted cumin (1)

10 POINTS

SNACK

1 cup grapes (1)

1 POINT

TOTAL FOR THE DAY: *25 POINTS*

Thursday

BREAKFAST

PB & J Bagel (Spread 1 small toasted oat bran bagel with 1½ tablespoons strawberry spreadable fruit and 1 tablespoon peanut butter.) (6)

½ cup orange juice (1)

7 POINTS

LUNCH

Turkey Waldorf Salad (Cube one 3-ounce skinless cooked turkey breast and combine with ¼ cup each chopped carrot, celery, apple,

raisins and fat-free mayonnaise. Serve on 2 cups baby greens; sprinkle with raspberry vinegar.) (6)

7 fat-free crackers (1)

7 POINTS

DINNER

Salmon Tiles* (6)

½ cup each steamed zucchini and yellow squash tossed with 1 teaspoon butter (1)

1 cup fat-free milk (2)

9 POINTS

SNACK

Creamy Carrot Smoothie (In a blender, puree 1 cup aspartame-sweetened vanilla nonfat yogurt, ½ cup carrot juice and 3 ice cubes.) (2)

2 POINTS

TOTAL FOR THE DAY: *25 POINTS*

Friday

BREAKFAST

1½ cups puffed rice cereal topped with ½ cup each blueberries and sliced strawberries (2)

1 cup fat-free milk (2)

4 POINTS

LUNCH

Cracked Wheat Salad (Combine 1 cup cooked bulgur with ⅓ cup each chopped cucumber, tomato and red onion; toss with 2 teaspoons each chopped mint and fresh lemon juice and 1 teaspoon olive oil.) (3)

¼ cup dried dates (2)

5 POINTS

DINNER

Chinese Takeout:

1 cup hot-and-sour soup (2)

1 cup Chinese vegetables with shrimp (5)

1 cup steamed snow pea pods (0)

½ cup steamed brown rice (2)

1 fortune cookie (1)

10 POINTS

SNACK

1 cup aspartame-sweetened tangerine chiffon nonfat yogurt with 1 cup orange sections (3)

3 POINTS

TOTAL FOR THE DAY: *22 POINTS*

Saturday

BREAKFAST

1 cup cooked Irish oatmeal with 6 dried chopped apricot halves (3)

1 cup fat-free milk (2)

5 POINTS

LUNCH

Mango Chicken Salad (Cube one 3-ounce skinless cooked chicken breast and combine with ½ chopped red bell pepper, ½ chopped mango, ¼ cup nonfat sour cream and 1 tablespoon sliced scallion. Serve over 1 cup mesclun.) (5)

Diet lemon-lime soda (0)

5 POINTS

DINNER

Gingered Shrimp (Heat 1 teaspoon olive oil in nonstick skillet. Sauté 1 teaspoon each minced garlic and grated peeled gingerroot with 1 cup diced red and yellow bell pepper. Add 1 cup shrimp; sauté until shrimp are pink.) (3)

1 cup broccoli florets sautéed with 1 minced garlic clove in 1 teaspoon olive oil (1)

½ cup cooked jasmine rice (5)

9 POINTS

SNACK

Peaches and Cream Shortcakes* (4)

Café au lait made with 1 cup fat-free milk (2)

6 POINTS

TOTAL FOR THE DAY: *25 POINTS*

Sunday

BREAKFAST

Lean Eggs Florentine (Divide ½ cup chopped cooked spinach between 2 toasted whole-wheat English muffin halves. Top each with a poached egg.) (6)

½ cup orange juice (1)

7 POINTS

LUNCH

Baked Eggplant* (4)

1 cup tossed greens with 2 tablespoons fat-free Italian dressing (0)

1 slice semolina bread (2)

1 cup fat-free milk (2)

8 POINTS

DINNER

1 baked chicken breast (with skin) (5)

1 small ear corn on the cob with 1 teaspoon butter (2)

½ cup each steamed sugar-snap peas and carrots (0)

7 POINTS

SNACK

1 cup aspartame-sweetened banana cream pie nonfat yogurt (2)

2 POINTS

TOTAL FOR THE DAY: *24 POINTS*

Monday

BREAKFAST

1 **Tutti-Frutti Muffin*** (3)

1 banana (2)

Café latte made with 1 cup fat-free milk (2)

7 POINTS

LUNCH

Mushroom and Cheese Pizza (Top a large pocketless pita with ¼ cup fat-free tomato sauce, ½ cup chopped mushrooms and 3 tablespoons shredded part-skim mozzarella; broil in a toaster oven until the cheese melts.) (4)

1 cup canned tomato soup (2)

1 cup carrot sticks (0)

6 POINTS

DINNER

Piedmontese Braised Turkey* (4)

½ cup cooked brown rice (2)

1 cup broccoli rabe sautéed with 1 teaspoon olive oil (1)

1 small glass dry red wine (2)

9 POINTS

SNACK

1 cup reduced-calorie chocolate pudding (prepared with fat-free milk) with 1 cup strawberries (3)

3 POINTS

TOTAL FOR THE DAY: *25 POINTS*

Tuesday

BREAKFAST

½ cup high-fiber cereal with 1 sliced banana (3)

1 cup fat-free milk (2)

5 POINTS

LUNCH

Barbecue Beef Sandwich (Mix ½ cup lean shredded cooked beef with 1 tablespoon barbecue sauce. Serve on a sourdough roll.) (6)

1 cup steamed collard greens with 1 teaspoon butter (1)

1 cup watermelon chunks (1)

8 POINTS

DINNER

Sea Bass with Yellow Pepper Sauce* (4)

1 cup *haricots verts* and 1 crushed garlic clove sautéed in 1 teaspoon olive oil (1)

½ cup cooked barley (1)

Cranberry Spritzer (Mix ½ cup cranberry juice cocktail, ½ cup seltzer water and 1 teaspoon fresh lime juice in a glass; pour over ice.) (1)

7 POINTS

SNACK

1 cup aspartame-sweetened vanilla nonfat yogurt mixed with 1 tablespoon fat-free butterscotch sauce (3)

3 POINTS

TOTAL FOR THE DAY: *23 POINTS*

Wednesday

BREAKFAST

1 slice toasted raisin bread with 1 tablespoon apple butter (3)

1 cup aspartame-sweetened cherry nonfat yogurt (2)

5 POINTS

LUNCH

Pecan-Crusted Grilled Chicken Breast (Dip one 4-ounce skinless boneless chicken breast in 1 tablespoon low-fat buttermilk and 5 chopped pecans; bake at 400° F for 20 minutes, turning once.) (6)

1 cup steamed sliced zucchini (0)

Iced tea with mint (0)

6 POINTS

DINNER

Tuna Provençal (Brush a 6-ounce tuna fillet with 1 teaspoon each olive oil and fresh lemon juice; sprinkle with ¼ teaspoon each salt and freshly ground pepper. Cook in ridged grill pan over medium-high heat for 3–4 minutes on each side. Meanwhile, combine 1 cup chopped plum tomatoes, 10 pitted chopped niçoise olives, 1 tablespoon chopped basil and a splash of balsamic vinegar; serve over the tuna.) (6)

1 cup steamed asparagus (0)

½ cup cooked orzo (2)

8 POINTS

SNACK

Banana-Butter Smoothie (In a blender, puree 1 sliced banana, 1 cup aspartame-sweetened banana cream pie nonfat yogurt, 1 tablespoon smooth peanut butter and 3 ice cubes.) (6)

6 POINTS

TOTAL FOR THE DAY: *25 POINTS*

Thursday

BREAKFAST

1 **Bacon Biscuit*** (2)

1 cup aspartame-sweetened blueberry nonfat yogurt with 1 cup blueberries (3)

5 POINTS

LUNCH

Jalapeño Corn Soup with Cilantro* (2)

Quickie Quesadilla (Sprinkle a 6" flour tortilla with 3 tablespoons shredded low-fat Monterey Jack cheese; toast in a toaster oven until the cheese is melted. Top with ¼ cup salsa.) (4)

1 cup cubed honeydew (1)

7 POINTS

DINNER

Skinny Buddha's Delight (Sauté ¼ cup each chopped Chinese eggplant, broccoli florets, sliced carrots, chopped mushrooms, shredded bok choy and chopped celery, and ⅓ cup firm tofu chunks in 2 teaspoons peanut oil; stir in 1 tablespoon each hoisin sauce and

soy sauce; serve with ½ cup cooked brown rice.) (6)

1 Bosc pear (1)

7 POINTS

SNACK

Lemon Curd Tartlet* (4)

1 cup fat-free milk (2)

6 POINTS

TOTAL FOR THE DAY: *25 POINTS*

Friday

BREAKFAST

Seaside Smoothie (In a blender, puree 1 cup fat-free milk, ½ diced papaya, ½ sliced banana, ½ teaspoon coconut extract and 3 ice cubes.) (4)

1 slice whole-grain toast with 1 teaspoon butter (3)

7 POINTS

LUNCH

Roasted Ratatouille Lasagna* (5)

1 cup tossed salad with 2 tablespoons fat-free Italian dressing (0)

5 POINTS

DINNER

1 cooked lean hamburger patty on a whole-wheat English muffin with 2 each lettuce leaves, tomato slices and sliced pickles (7)

Sweet Potato "Chips" (Peel and very thinly slice a large sweet potato; spread on a baking sheet and spray with nonstick cooking spray, then sprinkle with salt. Bake at 350° F until crispy, about 25 minutes.) (3)

1 bottle diet cola (0)

10 POINTS

SNACK

1 cup aspartame-sweetened chocolate nonfat yogurt (2)

2 POINTS

TOTAL FOR THE DAY: *24 POINTS*

Saturday

BREAKFAST

Greek Isles Omelet (Sauté 1 cup chopped spinach in 1 teaspoon olive oil. Add ¼ cup fat-free egg substitute and 3 tablespoons crumbled feta cheese; cook until firm. Serve with 1 cup chopped plum tomatoes.) (4)

1 small onion pita (1)

1 cup aspartame-sweetened lemon chiffon non-fat yogurt (2)

7 POINTS

LUNCH

1 cup canned lentil soup (2)

1 small sesame pita with 1 teaspoon butter (2)

1 cup mesclun with 2 tablespoons fat-free Italian dressing (0)

⅛ casaba melon (1)

5 POINTS

DINNER

Cornish Hens with Apricot Sauce* (6)

½ cup cooked brown rice (2)

1 cup steamed yellow squash (0)

1 cup fat-free milk (2)

10 POINTS

SNACK

Chocolate Mousse* (3)

3 POINTS

TOTAL FOR THE DAY: *25 POINTS*

The Hidden Protection in Produce

THEY'RE NATURE'S WONDER FOODS—naturally low in calories, chock-full of vitamins and minerals and filled with dietary fiber. Fruits and vegetables are incredibly good for you, and they should play a starring role in your diet. What you probably don't know about produce is that it also contains lots of health-promoting compounds called phytochemicals. These aren't exactly vitamins or minerals; nor are they nutrients in the classic sense of the word. Rather, phytochemicals are naturally occurring substances in fruits, vegetables, grains, nuts, seeds and legumes that carry the potential to enhance your health and prevent life-threatening diseases such as heart disease, cancer and diabetes; they may also ward off other medical ailments such as macular degeneration (a leading cause of blindness) and osteoporosis.

The National Cancer Institute estimates that one in three cancer deaths in the United States is related to diet. By contrast, hundreds of clinical trials have found that people who consume higher amounts of fruits and vegetables have dramatically lower risks of numerous forms of cancer, including breast cancer and cancers of the gastrointestinal and respiratory tracts. In fact, a study recently published in *The Journal of the National Cancer Institute* found that Greek women who consumed four to five servings of vegetables a day had a 46 percent lower risk of breast cancer compared to those who ate fewer than two servings of vegetables per day; in addition, women who consumed six servings of fruit per day had a 35 percent lower risk of breast cancer compared to those who ate less than two servings of fruit per day. What's more, the consumption of soy-based foods in the traditional Japanese diet has been linked with a lower incidence of breast cancer among Japanese women. And other studies have found that people who consume a lot of fruits and vegetables have a lower risk of cardiovascular disease.

Experts don't think these connections are a fluke. They believe the difference in disease rates is due to the power of phytochemicals. So far, thousands of phytochemicals have been identified, but researchers are only beginning to pinpoint what these compounds are and how they work their magic. Some of these substances—such as limonenes in citrus fruits and lycopene in cooked tomatoes and guavas—have antioxidant properties, preventing those unstable molecules called free radicals from wreaking cellular damage. Others—like indoles and sulforaphanes in cruciferous vegetables (like cabbage and broccoli) and lignans in flaxseed and grapes—appear to prevent carcinogens from forming, prohibit them from reaching their targets, or promote the production of enzymes that detoxify or excrete carcinogens. Still others, such as isoflavones in soy foods and allium compounds in onions and garlic, may help to lower blood cholesterol or enhance immune function. In addition, herbs such as basil, oregano, thyme and rosemary appear to contain small amounts of cholesterol-inhibiting substances.

The evidence supporting the cancer-fighting power of fruits and vegetables is so convincing that the

American Cancer Society (ACS) now recommends Americans eat most of their foods from plant sources. Specifically, the ACS advocates eating five or more servings of fruits and vegetables each day and consuming foods such as breads, cereals, grain products, rice, pasta or beans (all of which are derived from plants) several times per day, recommendations that are in keeping with the Food Guide Pyramid.

Yet surveys have found that few Americans are meeting the recommended minimums in their consumption of fruits and vegetables. Given the reality of how Americans are eating, it may be tempting to opt for a dose of phytochemicals in pill form. These supplements promise all the benefits of eating loads of fruits and vegetables, thanks to extracts of their healthful essence, without having to lift a single forkful to your mouth. Sounds simple enough, but the trouble is that because scientists are still identifying specific phytochemicals and what they do, manufacturers may not be extracting the right compounds in the right amounts, or all the ones that are needed to reap the health benefits. Plus, it's not clear how phytochemicals are compromised when they're taken from their original source and processed. After all, in its natural habitat, a particular phytochemical lives with an extended family of other phytochemicals, and it may be that they work together rather than individually or that they balance each other, preventing you from overdosing on any one. These are a few of the reasons why nutrition experts don't recommend popping a pill to get your phytochemicals.

THE NEW HEROES: PHYTOCHEMICALS

Although the research on phytochemicals is very preliminary, there is promising evidence to suggest that they may be capable of enhancing health in a variety of ways. The following chart spells out which foods contain particular phytochemicals and some of their purported benefits:

PHYTOCHEMICAL	POTENTIAL BENEFITS	FOOD SOURCE(S)
Alpha-linoleic acid	Reduces inflammation, lowers blood cholesterol, protects against breast cancer, enhances immunity.	Flaxseed, soy, walnuts.
Beta-carotene	Reduces risk of cataracts, coronary artery disease, breast cancer; enhances immunity (elderly).	Green and yellow fruits and vegetables.
Capsaicin	Reduces risk for colon, gastric and rectal cancer.	Chile peppers.

continues

PHYTOCHEMICAL	POTENTIAL BENEFITS	FOOD SOURCE(S)
Catechin theaflavins, thearubigins	Reduces risk of gastric cancer; antioxidant increases immune function; decreases cholesterol production.	Green and black tea, berries.
Curcumin	Reduces risk of skin cancer.	Turmeric, curry, cumin.
Cynarin	Decreases cholesterol levels.	Artichoke.
Ellagic acid	Reduces cancer risks, reduces LDL cholesterol while increasing HDL cholesterol.	Wine, grapes, currants, nuts (pecans), berries (strawberries, blackberries, raspberries), seeds.
Genistein	Reduces risk of hormone-dependent cancers; reduces cholesterol levels; reduces thrombi formation, risk of osteoporosis, menopausal symptoms.	Soybeans.
Indoles	Reduce risk of hormone-related cancers, inactivate estrogen.	Cabbage, broccoli, Brussels sprouts, spinach, watercress, cauliflower, turnips, kohlrabi, kale, rutabaga, horseradish, mustard greens.
Isothiocyanates, such as sulforaphane	Reduce risk of tobacco-induced and other tumors.	Cabbage, cauliflower, broccoli and broccoli sprouts, Brussels sprouts, mustard greens, horseradish, radishes.
Lignans	Reduce cancer risk (colon), reduce blood glucose and cholesterol.	High-fiber foods, especially seeds.
Lycopene	Antioxidant; reduces risk of prostate cancer, reduces cardiovascular disease.	Tomato sauce, ketchup, red grapefruit, guava, dried apricots, watermelon.
Terpenes, such as limonene	Antioxidant; reduce cancer risk, reduce cholesterol production, reduce premenstrual symptoms.	Citrus fruits.
Organosulfur compounds, such as allylic acid	Decrease lipid peroxidation, reduce risk of gastric cancer, antithrombotic, reduce cholesterol.	Garlic, onions, watercress, cruciferous vegetables, leeks.
Phenolic acid	Inhibits cancer through or by inhibition of nitrosamine formation, reduces risk for lung and skin cancers.	Cruciferous vegetables, eggplant, peppers, tomatoes, celery, parsley, soy, licorice root, flaxseed, citrus, whole grains, berries.

If the disease-fighting potential isn't reason enough to increase your intake of real produce, consider this: Fruits and vegetables are also naturally low in fat and calories, and high in fiber, which means they'll fill you up. You can eat practically as much of them as you want (as long as your intestines can tolerate it). In short, you can't go wrong by eating more produce: It's good for your waistline as well as your health.

Key Points

- Phytochemicals are naturally occurring compounds in fruits, vegetables, grains and legumes, and they can enhance your health and protect you from heart disease, cancer and other debilitating diseases.
- Research has found that women who have a high intake of fruits and vegetables have a dramatically lower risk of breast cancer.
- The American Cancer Society now recommends that Americans eat most of their foods from plant sources.
- Most Americans are still woefully low on their fruit and vegetable intake and should aim to eat at least five a day.
- To get the best nutritional benefits from your produce, you need to pick fruits and vegetables that are at their peak of freshness.

Goals

◇ *Start the day with two servings of fruit—a glass of orange juice and sliced banana or strawberries on your cereal, for example—and you'll be on your way to hitting the magic number.*

◇ *Aim for a minimum of five different colors of fruits and vegetables each day. Try eating something from every color of the rainbow—red, orange, yellow, green, blue, purple—and not only will you consume plenty of produce, but you'll get a variety of disease-fighting phytochemicals in the process. (If you eat two fruits of the same color, go for different ones—an orange and a slice of cantaloupe, for example—for optimal benefits.)*

◇ *Try to add a new fruit or vegetable to your plate each week. If you don't know what to do with exotic or unfamiliar produce, ask one of the clerks in the produce aisle for tips.*

◇   *Don't be afraid to experiment with fresh herbs; they can punch up any dish and provide health benefits, too.*

◇   *Eat more fruit for dessert; it's naturally sweet and good for you, too. And it doesn't have to be boring. You can have poached pears, a baked apple with cinnamon, fruit crumbles or compotes, sautéed banana slices. Be creative in how you prepare fruit desserts.*

Dieting Traps

BY UNDERSTANDING THE BASICS OF GOOD NUTRITION and using the Food Pyramid as your guide, you can start to construct meal plans that can help you lose weight and get healthier. But if you've been around the weight-loss block before, you know that good nutrition is only part of the battle. Being able to manage difficult situations and emotions also is key to being successful at weight loss. The road to losing weight is paved with potholes and marked by roadblocks. Let your guard down and your weight-management efforts can take a sharp detour and you may lose sight of where you're trying to go. If you keep your eye fixed on the route ahead, however, you can steer clear of such glitches or navigate your way through them without compromising your diet. Here are eight commonly encountered situations that can snare your weight-loss efforts, along with suggestions on how to handle them.

Situation: You're stressed to the nth degree and craving chocolate as if your life depended on it.

Your kids are acting up, your boss just gave you an extra project, your house is a mess, and you hardly have time to catch your breath. Is it any wonder that you feel like eating an entire box of chocolates or a whole cake? The debate continues as to whether cravings are physiological or psychological in nature, but the answer is academic if your urge to nosh is practically irrepressible. Many people tend to reach for their favorite foods when the snacking instinct kicks in, and studies of overweight adults have found very strong gender differences along these lines. In particular, men tend to prefer meat (such as hot dogs and hamburgers), pizza, chips and other fat-protein-salt combinations, whereas women go for carbohydrates and sweets (like cookies, chocolate and popcorn).

Fortunately, you can handle cravings without becoming a victim of them. The first step is to give yourself a 10-minute breather before reaching for cake, a candy bar or whatever you think you have to have. Most cravings last about 10 minutes, so if you can distract yourself by taking a walk or doing deep-breathing exercises, many cravings will pass on their own. If that doesn't do the trick, first identify what you've truly got a hankering for. Then indulge your craving instead of eating around it; otherwise, you may find yourself eating more in the long run. But exercise portion control and make smart choices that won't be too damaging. If it's chocolate that you want, have a few chocolate kisses, a miniature candy bar or a cup of chocolate sorbet. You'll get the taste you desire without wrecking your diet.

If you can't pinpoint what you're craving, however, you may need to think about what you're hungry for emotionally. Maybe you need a good laugh, a friendly shoulder to cry on or a good night's sleep. If it's an emotional need you're trying to fulfill, eating all the food in your pantry won't do it. So you're better off figuring out what will.

Situation: You're eating out a lot and having a hard time managing your food choices.

Taking healthful eating habits on the road can be challenging. When you don't have control over what's cooking in the kitchen, or how it's being prepared, you may feel like you're at the mercy of your host or a restaurant's chef. Since you're still responsible for your food choices, it's crucial to seize control any way you can. Here's how:

IF YOU'RE EATING OUT:

◆ **Ask how dishes are prepared.** Be specific in asking about the dish's ingredients, how it's prepared (poached, steamed, baked, broiled or grilled are good choices), and whether any extra oil is added (some restaurants brush fish or vegetables with olive oil before grilling them, for example). If you don't like the answer, order something else or ask if the chef will modify the cooking method. According to a recent survey by the National Restaurant Association, the vast majority of restaurants will alter their preparation methods at a customer's request.

◆ **Request sauce or salad dressing on the side.** It's a good way of conserving fat calories because it allows you to control how much goes on the food. If you dip your fork into the sauce or dressing then spear the meat or several leaves of lettuce, you'll get plenty of flavor but much less fat with every bite.

◆ **Stick with leaner choices.** Whenever possible, opt for leaner cuts of meat such as round steak, filet mignon or center-cut pork or lamb chops. Whenever there's a coating or sauce, ask that the skin be removed *before* cooking. You can also ask for a smaller portion of meat and more vegetables; many restaurants will happily oblige.

◆ **Remember: There are no rules.** You don't have to order an appetizer and a main course. In fact, you could order an appetizer and a salad and skip the main course altogether; or have your own appetizer and split a main course with a dining companion.

◆ **Divide and conquer.** As soon as your main course arrives, split the portion in two. These days, restaurant plates are generally oversized and so are the portions. Since they're really designed for more than one person, why not eat half and take the rest home for lunch or dinner tomorrow?

- ◆ **Split a dessert.** Yes, you can have your cake and eat it too but you don't have to have the whole piece. Share it with a friend. Or have an espresso or a flavored coffee instead.

IF YOU'RE GOING TO A PARTY:

- ◆ **Plan ahead.** Eat lighter meals during the day (don't skip meals, though!) and "bank" some extra calories so you can splurge that night.

- ◆ **Have a substantial snack beforehand.** Drink a large glass of water and eat a whole-wheat bagel, some vegetables and low-fat dip, or something else that will fill you up. That way you'll eat less and socialize more at the party.

- ◆ **Survey the buffet.** Before filling your plate, take a look at all the offerings and set priorities. That way you can stock up on lower-fat fare and have a taste of what you really want without overeating.

- ◆ **Decide how to deal with "food-pushers" in advance.** If your host insists that you try her homemade double-chocolate cake and you really don't want to, have a response at the tip of your tongue. You might tell her, for example, that you ate so much of all the other delicious foods that you're too full but you'd love to take a piece home for tomorrow. (She doesn't need to know whether you eat it or give it to the kids; just remember to compliment her on it later.)

Situation: You've cut calories as much as possible and the pounds aren't dropping off as expected.

The problem may be that you're eating too little. Many dieters think they're hastening weight loss when, in fact, cutting calories to less than 800 per day, or skipping meals, can send the body into starvation mode. The body slows down its metabolic rate to conserve energy, and as a result, you burn calories more slowly and your rate of weight loss can actually decrease. As if that weren't upsetting enough, you'll be setting yourself up for a fall psychologically: You'll end up feeling deprived and frustrated, which can lead you to binge.

To keep your metabolism revving high and your hunger in check, many weight-loss experts recommend that you eat regular meals and consume at least as many calories as your body burns at rest. If you're a woman, calculate how much that is using the following formula: Multiply your weight by 4.3 and your height in inches by 4.7. Add these numbers together, plus another 655 calories. Next, multiply your age by 4.7 and subtract this number from the previous total. The number you end up with refers to the amount of calories your body requires at rest. So a woman who weighs 150 pounds, is 5 feet 4 inches and 40 years old, would need 1,413 calories to fulfill basic body functions such as heart rate, breathing and digestion. If you've dipped below your basic calorie needs, gradually increase your calorie intake to an appropriate amount and you'll help your metabolism begin to function more efficiently, allowing you to burn calories faster even when you're not exercising; plus, you're likely to have more energy.

Situation: You're retaining water and you don't know why.

If it's not related to premenstrual hormonal surges—which can cause your kidneys to retain salt and water—check your salt or alcohol intake. Overdoing it on the dietary sodium or the cocktails usually has a temporary effect, but it can cause your body to retain water, making you feel puffy and as though you've ballooned a dress size overnight. You can prevent this by staying within the recommended daily limit of 2,400 milligrams of sodium and by drinking moderately (one glass of wine, beer or hard alcohol per day for women), if at all. Keep in mind that salt is often hidden in many so-called diet foods, including low-calorie salad dressings, low-fat soups and prepackaged foods, so read labels carefully. If

Smart Snacks

Does your energy plummet about midafternoon, leaving you with the undeniable urge to munch? Do you get so hungry between meals that you become a bear to be around? Don't despair: Many people love to snack, and snacking can actually be a part of a healthful diet.

Smart snacking is what you do when you reach for something that has some nutritional value that can supply you with a true energy boost. Mindless snacking is what you do when you're feeling bored, stressed out, lonely, or you do it simply out of habit.

For busy people, snacking can be an incredibly convenient and healthful way to eat, as long as you plan ahead. If you use snacks to fulfill nutritional voids in your diet you can treat snacks as minimeals or pick-me-ups during the day. Plus, if you watch the portion size, snacks can actually help you control your weight by taking the edge off your hunger. Contrary to traditional wisdom, they won't spoil your appetite for dinner. Here are several quick and healthful snacks that are easy to keep on hand:

IN THE FRIDGE:
- ♦ Cartons of nonfat yogurt or low-fat chocolate milk.
- ♦ A bag of baby carrots or cut-up pita strips along with a jar of low-fat bean dip or a container of low-fat hummus.
- ♦ Whole-grain bagels and low-fat cottage cheese for a high-carb protein snack.
- ♦ A bag of precut veggies and a container of low-fat yogurt-based dip for an instant crudité plate.

AT THE OFFICE:
- ♦ Keep a bowl of fruit—oranges, pears, bananas—on your desk.
- ♦ Stash a container of low-fat ready-made pudding in your briefcase.
- ♦ Place packages of low-fat microwave popcorn, small servings of pretzels or dried fruit, individual boxes of dry cereal, or cups of soup in your desk drawer.
- ♦ For sweet-tooth emergencies, have a favorite fun-size candy bar, a small bag of jelly beans or a package of sugar-free cocoa mix on hand.

> **"** I like using little things to jazz up traditional fare, like some balsamic vinegar on my pasta or soy sauce with my chicken. **"**

you're currently suffering a case of the bloating blues, aerobic exercise can help hasten water loss through sweat; so can natural diuretics such as cranberry juice, parsley or tea.

Situation: You've fallen off your diet and you're on the verge of bingeing.

You strayed at lunch, snacked on cookies all afternoon, had second helpings of comfort food at dinner, and now the carton of ice cream and the leftover birthday cake in the fridge are calling your name. Hold it right there! Before you put one more bite of anything in your mouth, it's not too late to regain control. Falling off the plan happens to every dieter at some point. One setback won't ruin your efforts, so don't beat yourself up about it. The important thing is to put the brakes on this runaway eating—*now!*—and get back on track. Forget about what you've already eaten; it's history. Instead, do something enjoyable to distract yourself, whether it's reading a book, playing with your kids or engaging in a hobby such as knitting or needlepoint, and focus on getting back to the plan tomorrow. Above all, don't let a lapse of willpower turn into a complete collapse.

Situation: Your weight loss has plateaued.

You were making great progress in the losing game when suddenly the number on the scale won't budge, regardless of what you do. Rest assured: You're hardly alone. Nearly every person who has ever tried to lose weight has hit a plateau and felt the intense frustration you're now feeling. Whether they last weeks or months, plateaus can happen for a variety of reasons. It may be that your body simply needs a break from all the changes that have been taking place. (This is one reason many weight-loss experts recommend that if you want to lose a considerable amount of weight that you aim initially for a 10 percent drop, which will lead to significant medical benefits, then try to maintain it for a while.) Or it could be that you've gone back to some of your old habits without your realizing it.

It's worth taking a close look at your eating and exercise patterns to make sure you've been sticking with your plan. If you are, then you may be dealing with a bona fide plateau. In this case, it's generally best to try to relax, keep up your current eating regimen and continue exercising. In all likelihood, once your body adjusts to its new, lower weight, you'll begin to shed pounds again. In the meantime, try to focus your energy on maintaining your motivation and cultivating patience.

Situation: You're stuck in a food rut and you can't climb out.

As the saying goes, "Variety is the spice of life," and that's especially true when it comes to the taste buds. In your quest to lose weight, you might find yourself drawing up inflexible food plans (consciously or not) and eating the same things, thinking this will help control your eating habits. If you do this, not only will you miss out on the variety of vitamins, minerals and other nutrients that a diverse diet brings, but you'll be more likely to fall into a food rut and grow bored with your diet. And that can set you up for trouble with overeating. Plus, you won't learn how to splurge occasionally or adjust your diet for special circumstances, while sticking to your plan in the long run. To avoid falling into this trap, it's important to add variety to your diet by including choices from all the major food groups and plenty of different tastes, textures, colors and aromas. Don't be afraid to branch out and try new healthful foods. Your taste buds and your health will appreciate the adventure.

Situation: You weigh yourself as often as you brush your teeth——and you don't like the numbers you're seeing.

Not only can hopping on the scale too often put you on an emotional roller coaster—you may feel elated if you like what you see, depressed if you don't—but the numbers don't tell the whole story. The truth is, the scale doesn't accurately reflect the healthy changes that may be going on in your body, especially if you're losing body fat and gaining lean muscle through regular exercise. Pound for pound, muscle is one-seventh the size of body fat, so even if you're not losing as many pounds as you think you should, you may look considerably slimmer. Plus, your weight can fluctuate on a daily basis thanks to hormonal shifts, whether you're retaining water, and a variety of other factors.

Instead of stepping on the bathroom scale every day, try weighing in no more than once a week, preferably at the same time of day with the same amount of clothing on (or, better yet, naked). Plot the results on a graph so that you can see if you're on a general losing trend rather than focusing solely on the numbers. In the meantime, you can measure your progress by considering how your clothes fit and how your body feels—both of which are better gauges than the scale.

Key Points

♦ Learn how to handle your cravings by distracting yourself from them or by initiating dietary damage control (giving in to them in small quantities, for example).

♦ To lose weight steadily and to keep your metabolism functioning smoothly, don't cut calories drastically or skip meals. Such actions will only come back to thwart your weight-loss efforts.

♦ Give yourself permission to splurge from time to time. It'll help you stick to your plan over the long haul. If you forbid yourself certain foods, on the other hand, you'll probably just want them even more.

♦ Watch your salt intake and drink plenty of water to prevent water retention. Pay attention to hidden sources of dietary sodium—salad dressings, soups and the like—by reading labels. And don't overdo it on the alcohol: An occasional drink or two won't harm your health but the calories can add up quickly.

♦ Become a smart snacker. Plan ahead and stock up on healthful items that can keep your energy high and your mind alert between meals.

♦ Don't weigh yourself more than once a week. Instead, focus on all the other positive changes your weight-loss efforts have brought: better muscle definition, more energy, a smaller clothing size, a sleeker shape. Not only are these better indicators of how you're doing, but they'll keep your motivation strong for the long haul.

Goals

◇ *Try eating a varied diet that's full of different tastes and textures. This way, you're less likely to get bored with your meals and binge.*

◇ *Map out a plan for dining out. Don't improvise or you're likely to lose control. Likewise, decide ahead of time how you'll deal with food pushers, whether you're dining out with friends or eating at a relative's house.*

◇ *Cultivate patience. The road to weight loss is a winding one and plateaus are inevitable. Try not to get discouraged. Remind yourself that in all likelihood, your body simply needs a little time to adjust and you'll be able to continue peeling off extra pounds soon enough.*

◇ *Keep a food diary. If you have a hard time monitoring your eating patterns, there's no better way to keep track of them than to write down everything you eat during the day. Gradually, this will help you become more mindful about your eating, which can help you lose weight.*

◇ *Start being kind to yourself by keeping your goals in perspective and not beating yourself up about temporary setbacks. One bad dieting day won't wreck your long-term efforts; if you let that bad day turn into a habit, however, that's another story.*

PART THREE

Moving and Losing

$\mathcal{U}$nless you've just arrived from a galaxy far, far away, you've heard time and again that exercise is as essential to losing weight as changing your eating habits. Exercise helps you control your weight by spurring your body to burn more calories, both while you're exercising and afterward. It helps build muscle, which also boosts your metabolism (the rate at which you burn calories) and strengthens bones; it can also curb your appetite, lift your mood, reduce the effects of stress and promote other healthy lifestyle changes.

Despite knowing all this, does exercise still feel like just one more chore to wedge into an already overbooked schedule? If so, you're hardly alone. These are common and legitimate issues for busy women. But it's also possible to overcome them without overburdening yourself.

First, it's important to pinpoint the reasons why you may not be exercising regularly. Maybe you haven't found activities you truly enjoy or have bad memories of being the resident klutz in your physical education class. Maybe you haven't noticed all the other health and mood-boosting benefits that exercise can bring or you haven't figured out how to squeeze workouts into your life without making it horrifically hectic. Or perhaps you haven't discovered how to maintain your motivation to exercise over the long haul.

While all of the above are widespread problems, they can be remedied. Once you get a sense of how to surmount these obstacles, you can create a game plan that will not only help you peel off pounds, but will help you feel healthier and more vibrant than ever.

$\mathcal{N}ote:$ It's smart to get a doctor's clearance before beginning any fitness program.

Fitness Factors

"My trainer, Josh, and I have a schedule that focuses on the three elements of fitness: cardiovascular work, strength training and flexibility. We work out Monday, Wednesday and Friday for about an hour. On Monday, I'll ride the stationary bike for 45 minutes, then do some strength training. I may use weights or my own body weight as a resistance (on a good day, I can do 30 straight-leg push-ups!). And we always stretch before and after a workout. On Wednesday, I'll just do the weight training, and on Friday a mixture of both."

THE PHRASE *GETTING IN SHAPE* is tossed around so easily these days. But what does it really mean? Getting in shape is more than just slimming down and toning up. It has to do with the three cornerstones of physical fitness: aerobic exercise, strength-training and flexibility. While each of these cornerstones requires different types of exercise, all three components complement the others, making it easier for you to move through everyday life.

Aerobic exercise refers to any sustained activity that uses large muscle groups and is intense enough to challenge and condition your heart and lungs. As you jog, swim, bicycle or dance over a period of time, your heart starts pumping harder in order to deliver blood and oxygen throughout your body, thus burning greater amounts of calories. As a result, your heart and lungs get a good workout, along with your muscles. To be considered truly aerobic, you'll need to exercise in your target heart rate zone—between 60 and 80 percent of your maximum heart rate (see page 72). (Before exercising, always warm up for five to ten minutes by walking or biking at a gentle pace, then stretching; this will reduce your risk of injury.)

While aerobic benefits begin to come fairly quickly after starting an exercise program, they can begin to diminish soon after stopping as well. Unfortunately, aerobic conditioning, which often goes by the term *cardiovascular conditioning* (the two are basically synonomous), can easily slip away within a few weeks of lapsing into sedentary ways. The good news is, you can maintain the fitness and health benefits of aerobic conditioning if you scale back the length of your workouts (if your schedule suddenly gets insanely hectic, for example) but maintain their intensity. Not only is aerobic exercise crucial for weight loss and fitness, but it's vitally important for your overall health as well.

Strength-training is often referred to as resistance training. The idea is to perform specific exercises against resistance. You can get resistance by moving against gravity if you do sit-ups or push-ups; lifting free weights, using machines such as Nautilus, or performing exercises with rubber tubing or Dyna bands is also effective. Whatever method you choose, you should use enough resistance so that your muscles feel fatigued after working out, but they shouldn't feel pain; that's a signal that you've overdone it.

Don't worry about morphing into a body-builder: Most women do not have the hormones and the initial muscle mass to build such bulging muscles. Women can, however, increase muscle mass, which can, in turn, cause our bodies to burn more calories all the time. Here's why: Each pound of muscle naturally burns 35 calories a day even when you're inactive; by contrast, a pound of body fat burns only two calories a day when you're resting. In fact, building and maintaining muscle mass is one of the keys to keeping your weight stable as you get older. Strength-training can also help prevent bone loss, improve your posture and prevent back problems, and make it easier for you to perform everyday activities more comfortably. What's more, it can create more well-defined muscles and give you a more toned appearance.

Flexibility, on the other hand, won't do a thing for your waistline, which may be partly why it's often overlooked as an aspect of fitness. Developing and maintaining flexibility—through stretching, yoga or tai chi, for example—will, however, help you move through everyday activities and exercise more comfortably, decreasing your chances of injury in the process. It can also help improve your posture.

Maintaining flexibility becomes even more important as you age because muscle fibers and tendons naturally shorten with the passing years. As a result, you lose some of the range of motion that you once took for granted and you become more susceptible to injury. To maintain flexibility, it's important to stretch all the major muscle groups—the ankles, calves, quadriceps, hamstrings, glutes, pelvis, lower back, arms and shoulders, as well as any problem areas you might have—after walking or biking for five to ten minutes to warm up your body's temperature and your muscles. You should stretch gently to the point where you feel mild tension and hold it for 30 seconds; don't push it to the point of pain and don't bounce, which can cause injury.

Drink Up

It's even more important to drink plenty of fluids when you're exercising. Not only does it replenish body fluids you've lost through sweat, but it can help ward off heat-related illnesses and muscle cramps. Try to consume two cups of water about 30 minutes before you exercise, then take a break every 20 minutes during your workout and drink another cup; afterward, have two more. (To get a more precise sense of how much fluid you lose during a typical workout, and how much you need to replenish, weigh yourself before and afterward. Remember: Two cups of water are equal to one pound—the difference in pounds reflects fluid loss through sweat and breathing.) Plain old water will do the trick—and it's a bargain at zero calories—but whatever you do steer clear of caffeinated or alcoholic beverages, which are dehydrating.

WORKOUT BASICS

Before you begin a workout, you need to focus on what you are trying to accomplish. If you want to improve your health, the U.S. Surgeon General recommends 30 minutes of physical activity, most and preferably all days of the week. Keep in mind that it doesn't have to be vigorous, nor does it have to be

How It All Adds Up

The following chart gives you an idea of how many calories you can expect to burn while doing popular activities for 30 or 45 minutes. The numbers apply to someone who weighs 150 pounds; if you weigh more, you'll probably burn more calories, and if you weigh less, you'll burn slightly fewer calories.

ACTIVITY	30 MINUTES	45 MINUTES
Aerobic dance	276	414
Basketball	282	423
Bicycling	206	308
Cross-country skiing	282	423
Dancing socially	105	158
Gardening	189	284
Golf (if you carry your clubs)	174	261
Golf (if you use a cart)	80	119
Hiking	168	252
In-line skating	222	333
Jogging (10-minute miles)	348	522
Kayaking	180	270
Racquetball (competitive)	360	540
Running (8-minute miles)	425	637
Skiing (water/downhill)	213	320
Swimming (crawl, moderate pace)	290	434
T'ai chi	144	216
Tennis	222	333
Volleyball	144	216
Walking (briskly)	245	367
Weight-lifting	200	320
Yoga	144	216

continuous. Research has found that doing aerobic exercise for three 10-minute stretches offers almost the same health benefits as one 30-minute session.

If you want to reap substantial health benefits from exercise, many experts recommend that you expend at least 1,000 calories per week in physical activity. If you exercise six days a week, for example, you'd want to burn off about 165 calories each day, which is easily done with 30 minutes of brisk walking. Alternatively, you could expend that many calories with 45 minutes of social dancing or 30 minutes of gardening or yard work every day. Or you could reach the 1,000-calorie mark by jogging (at the pace of a nine-minute mile) for 30 minutes three days per week or by playing tennis for 45 minutes three times per week if you weigh 150 pounds (if you weigh more, you'll burn even more calories). Remember, too, that 30 minutes of continuous, repetitive resistance exercise training twice a week would burn off 400 calories for someone who weighs 150 pounds.

Of course, expending all these calories through exercise will help you peel off extra pounds more easily. But to lose weight, the exercise prescription is slightly different. In a nutshell, it doesn't matter what you do, just that you expend more energy through everyday activities and exercise than you take in from food. Basically, for every 3,500 calories you burn above and beyond the calories you consume, you'll lose one pound of body fat. To make losing weight easier and more fluid, many experts recommend exercising every day. In general, you'll be able to perform weight-bearing activities that involve big muscle groups—walking, biking and swimming, for example—for longer, which can help you burn more calories.

Don't be surprised, though, if the numbers on the scale don't budge initially. Some people actually do not lose weight when they first start exercising (especially when performing resistance exercises) because they're increasing their ratio of muscle to fat. For example, if you replace one pound of fat with one pound of muscle, the scale won't change, but you'll certainly notice a difference physically. When the more dense muscle replaces fat, it occupies less space. (That's why the best way to gauge your first signs of progress is by how your clothes fit. When previously snug clothes start becoming loose on you, you'll know you're headed in the right direction, regardless of what the scale says.)

Another Pyramid to Consider

Recently, fitness experts from Arizona State University devised a simple prescription for physical activity in the form of an Exercise Pyramid, which describes various activities, their recommended frequency and intensity, and how long you should perform them. The Pyramid encompasses all three components of fitness—aerobic exercise, strength-training and flexibility—and makes it easy to incorporate these activities into your day.

The base of the Pyramid, or Level 1, includes moderate everyday activities such as walking to work instead of driving, using the stairs instead of the elevator and cleaning the house. Engaging in such activities for a total of at least 30 minutes on most, if not all, days of the week, will fulfill the basic guidelines for physical activity set by the U.S. Surgeon General.

The next level (Level 2) of the Pyramid includes both aerobic activities, such as jogging or biking, and more vigorous sports and recreational activities, such as tennis or volleyball and hiking; these should be performed for at least 20 minutes on three or more days per week. It's best to participate in activities from both categories to achieve optimal health benefits.

Level 3 of the Pyramid focuses on activities that involve flexibility and muscle fitness; the latter refers to muscle strength (how much you can bench press, for example) and muscle endurance (how many times or how long you can do it). Although some of the activities from the first two levels of the Pyramid will enhance flexibility, experts recommend performing stretching exercises that take the muscles and joints through their full range of motion three to seven days a week. Develop a routine that stretches the ankles, calves, quadriceps, hamstrings, glutes, pelvis, lower back, arms and shoulders, then work on any problem areas you might have.

At the third level, the American College of Sports Medicine (ACSM) also recommends strength-training exercises at least two days per week with a day of rest in between; a good routine should include at least one set (8 to 12 repetitions) of 8 to 10 exercises that targets all the major muscle groups (i.e., the neck and shoulders, the back, arms, chest, abdomen, buttocks, the fronts and backs of the thighs, and the calves). If you want to increase the calorie-burning and toning effects of strength-training, you can do up to three sets of exercises, using lighter weights and more repetitions.

Occupying the least amount of space at the top of the Pyramid is inactivity, which means that you should rarely be inactive for substantial periods of time—except, of course, when you're sleeping.

Overall, the goal is to incorporate activities from the first three levels of the Exercise Pyramid into your life on a regular basis. If you're new to exercise—as more than 25 percent of sedentary Americans are—your best bet is to start slowly with activities from the most basic tier (Level 1), then to build gradually from there. If you're already meeting the basic requirements, it's time to step up your activity level and begin to incorporate exercises or sports that are more vigorous into your life (Level 2). All it takes is a little planning. If you do active aerobics or active sports or recreation activities three days a week, plus flexibility and muscle-strength exercises on the other days, you can fit in these workouts in less than an hour per day and master the Exercise Pyramid.

If your goal is to improve your health, here's what a sample workout schedule for a week might look like:

Monday: Take a brisk walk for 15 minutes twice today.
Tuesday: Do strength-training exercises for 15 minutes; stretch for 10 minutes.
Wednesday: Take a bike ride or go in-line skating for 30 minutes.
Thursday: Do strength-training exercises for 15 minutes; stretch for 10 minutes.
Friday: Take the day off from exercise; relax.
Saturday: Play tennis for 45 minutes or dance for an hour.
Sunday: Spend half an hour gardening; stretch for 10 minutes.

If your goal is to lose weight, here's what a sample workout schedule for a week might look like:

Monday: Brisk walking, jogging, stair-climbing or cycling for at least 30 minutes; 10 minutes of stretching.
Tuesday: Strength-training exercises for 20 minutes; take a 10-minute brisk walk.
Wednesday: Swimming, aerobic dance or in-line skating for 30 to 45 minutes; 10 minutes of stretching.
Thursday: Strength-training exercises for 20 minutes; take a 10-minute brisk walk.
Friday: Brisk walking, jogging, stair-climbing or cycling for at least 30 minutes; 10 minutes of stretching.
Saturday: Aerobic dance or cross-country skiing for 30 to 45 minutes; 10 minutes of stretching.
Sunday: Hiking or cycling with your family—the longer, the better.

REAPING THE BENEFITS

Deciding whether you're exercising hard or hardly exercising may seem like a subjective issue, but it isn't. For optimal aerobic and weight-loss benefits, you should be exercising at 60 to 80 percent of your maximum heart rate (a.k.a., your target zone). It is possible to lose weight by exercising at a lower intensity, but you won't reap the greatest fitness benefits and you may have to work out longer. To figure out your maximum heart rate, subtract your age from 220—this number estimates your maximum heart rate in beats per minute. Now multiply the resulting number by .60 to figure out the lower limit of your target zone. To gauge the upper limit, multiply your maximum heart rate by .80. The resulting number is the intensity bracket within which you should be exercising.

You can tell if you've reached this target zone by taking a break and immediately doing a pulse-check on your wrist: Simply count the number of beats in 15 seconds then multiply the result by 4 to figure out your heart rate in beats per minute.

If you'd prefer to skip the math, there are two additional ways to determine if you're in the target zone. A Rating of Perceived Exertion is achieved by simply asking yourself to gauge the intensity or difficulty of the activity you are performing. If you rate the intensity of the activity you're doing as "somewhat hard," you're right where you should be. If you'd rate it as "easy," upping the difficulty is in order, and if you'd rate it as "very hard," it's time to slow down. An even easier way to gauge whether or not you're working hard enough and have reached your target zone is the conversation test. You should be able to talk while exercising (if you're exercising solo, give yourself a pep talk); however, you shouldn't be able to sing. If you can, it's a clear signal that you need to step up your pace.

What's Weight Watchers Got to Do with It?

When it comes to exercise, Weight Watchers promotes a comprehensive program that begins with 20 minutes of daily physical activity to help you achieve optimal health benefits while losing weight. As you already know, there are substantial advantages to converting sedentary behavior into a more active lifestyle, like increased energy, decreased stress and a reduced risk of chronic diseases to name just a few (below, "Great Reasons to Exercise"). Fortunately, Weight Watchers makes it easy to start reaping these healthy benefits, even if you've never exercised before, by providing just the right combination of aerobic, toning and stretching activities (on the 1•2•3 Success Weight Loss Plan they're called Fat Burners, Lean Builders and Stretches).

The Weight Watchers Activity Plan takes you step by step, explaining everything from what you need to get started, to how to gauge the intensity of your workouts as well as when you'll see results and how to tell when you're ready for more. With all the information you need to start and maintain an exercise plan, you'll be on your way to feeling healthier, while supporting your weight loss, and making strides toward physical fitness.

GREAT REASONS TO EXERCISE

The payoffs you reap from getting physical extend well beyond weight loss. Not only do regular exercisers lead healthier, longer lives according to research, but their quality of life improves, too. If you knew just how broad the benefits are, you'd have more incentive to start and stick with an exercise program. After all, it's an investment in your health and longevity. Here are nine more reasons to start exercising as soon as possible:

Reason 1: Boost Your Immune System

Numerous studies have found that moderate exercise can improve immune function and bolster resistance to colds and infections. In one study of 36 overweight women, David C. Nieman, Dr.P.H., a professor of health and exercise science at Appalachian State University in Boone, North Carolina, and colleagues found that those who walked briskly for 45 minutes, five days a week, reported half the days with cold symptoms during a 15-week period as their sedentary counterparts. In a similar study, the walkers experienced a 57 percent increase in natural killer cell activity (natural killer cells are a type of immune cell that are able to kill certain types of cancer cells) after six weeks, compared to nonexercisers.

Reason 2: Lift Your Mood

Exercise is one of the most potent stress-busters around, and it can even boost a bad mood. In fact, a recent series of studies at California State University, Long Beach, found that exercise appears to be *the* most effective mood-regulating behavior, better than listening to music, talking to a friend or eating comfort food. For one thing, it sparks the release of endorphins and other brain chemicals that have mood-enhancing properties. For another, exercise improves blood and oxygen flow throughout the body, which can reduce tension and raise energy.

Reason 3: Lower Your Cancer Risk

In recent years, exercise has shown great promise as a weapon against several different types of cancer. In an ongoing study of 18,000 Harvard alumni, moderately and highly active participants reduced their risk of both lung cancer and colon cancer considerably compared to their sedentary counterparts; in fact, those who expended 1,000 calories or more per week through exercise cut their risk of colon cancer in half. In addition, a few epidemiologic studies suggest that breast cancer risk is lower among physically active women. A Norwegian study recently published in *The New England Journal of Medicine* found the risk of breast cancer dropped dramatically in premenopausal women who exercised at least four hours per week. This may be because exercise changes the levels of female reproductive hormones and reduces body fat, which may in turn cut breast cancer risk.

Reason 4: Heat Up Your Sex Life

Researchers have confirmed that exercise buffs do, indeed, have better sex lives. In a survey of 500 women who participated regularly in aerobic dance, calisthenics or weight-training classes, nearly 60 percent reported greater satisfaction with their "sexual selves" since they started their exercise program, according to researchers from Chicago State University. The study was not a fluke. Research at the Center for Marital and Sexual Studies in Long Beach, California, also found that exercisers had much easier orgasms than those who were not physically fit. Whether these benefits stem from the physical effects of exercise—namely, increased circulation and the release of endorphins—or a psychological boost and a sense of greater well-being, there's more pleasure to be had.

Reason 5: Prevent Osteoporosis

You may have heard that weight-bearing exercises—running, walking, aerobics and even gardening—protect against the bone-weakening effects of osteoporosis. The latest research indicates that strength-training may also ward off bone loss. A recent study of 40 postmenopausal women found that a year of high-intensity strength-training exercises, performed two days per week, preserved bone density, while also promoting increased muscle mass, strength and balance, all of which reduce the risk of osteoporotic fractures.

Reason 6: Sleep Better at Night

There's considerable evidence that if you tire out your body by exercising, you may sleep better at night. In fact, a recent study found that 16 weeks of regular, moderate exercise—consisting of four 30- to 40-minute sessions a week of low-impact aerobics or brisk walking—helped improve the quality of sleep for adults between the ages of 50 and 76 who were previously sedentary and suffered sleep difficulties. The theory, according to sleep experts, is that exercise causes body temperature to rise, then drop a few hours later, promoting sleepiness. Just be sure to finish your workout at least four hours before bedtime so that it doesn't interfere with your slumber.

Reason 7: Lower Your Risk of Heart Disease

It's no secret that a sedentary lifestyle is considered a major risk factor for cardiovascular disease. Many studies have found that heart disease is almost twice as likely to develop in inactive people as in those who exercise. What's more, in a series of studies at Stanford University since 1973, researchers have found that active middle-aged men and women have higher blood levels of HDL (the "good") cholesterol, which protects against heart disease, and lower levels of artery-clogging LDL (the "bad") cholesterol. Exercise also helps control high blood pressure and reduces the risk of Type II diabetes—both of which are risk factors for cardiovascular disease. Even short bouts of exercise are beneficial. According to a new report from The Physicians' Health Study, working out for 11 to 24 minutes at a relatively moderate intensity confers benefits in reducing the risk of heart disease; so does exercising at least five times per week.

Reason 8: Improve Memory and Other Mental Skills

When it comes to exercise, the old adage "Use it or lose it" applies to the mind as well as the body, especially as you get older. In fact, a four-year study at Baylor College of Medicine in Houston found that retirees who stayed physically active by walking, jogging, bicycling, dancing or engaging in other exercise regularly scored better on cognitive tests than those who became inactive. This is partly the result of the fact that physical exercise fosters blood and oxygen flow to the brain.

Reason 9: Enhance Your Body Image

Many people who suffer from a poor body image believe that if they just lose weight, the change in their self-image will come naturally. So they wait and wait . . . and wait. But what they should be doing is exercising. A recent survey of more than 200 college students at the University of Arkansas found that men and women who exercise have a more positive body image. Although most studies examining the relationship between exercise and self-esteem have focused on aerobic training, a recent study from Brigham Young University in Utah compared the effects of walking and weight training on the body image of 60 women. After working out three times per week for 12 weeks, the weight-lifters gained more muscle strength than the walkers and saw their body image improve more than twice as much, even though neither group experienced significant changes in body weight.

Key Points

- ◆ Aerobic exercise includes any sustained activity that uses large muscle groups and is intense enough to challenge your heart and lungs.

- ◆ Strength-training builds muscle strength and mass by having you exercise against gravity (as in sit-ups or push-ups), lifting weights or using resistance bands.

- ◆ Flexibility, often the forgotten fitness factor, helps preserve range of motion as you age, which can decrease your risk of injury and help you move more comfortably through everyday activities. It's best to stretch for at least a few minutes at least three days per week.

- ◆ Aerobic exercise offers all sorts of health benefits from boosting your immune system to lowering your risks of heart disease, Type II diabetes and cancer to improved sleep and memory function. Strength-training, on the other hand, can help prevent osteoporosis and enhance your body image.

- ◆ The U.S. Surgeon General recommends 30 minutes of physical activity, most and preferably all days of the week. It doesn't have to be vigorous or continuous; it just has to add up to half an hour a day.

Goals

◇ *Aim to participate in aerobic activities such as walking, jogging, cycling, swimming or aerobic dance for at least 20 minutes at a time three to six days per week.*

◇   *Perform strength-training—by using free weights, Nautilus or other weight machines or elastic Dyna bands—two or three days per week.*

◇   *Stretch before and after an aerobic workout to decrease your chances of injury. Warm up slowly for 5 to 10 minutes—by walking, jogging lightly or riding an exercise bike—then stretch gently; don't bounce.*

◇   *Try to work out every day of the week to make losing weight easier. That way, you'll be able to burn the 3,500 calories required to lose a pound of body fat more quickly.*

◇   *Pay attention to how your clothes fit and how your body feels. These are better indications of whether your new exercise program is starting to pay off. You may be slimming down even if the scale doesn't budge since muscle occupies less space than an equivalent amount of fat.*

Discovering Your Exercise Style

HALF THE BATTLE IN MAKING EXERCISE A HABIT is finding activities you truly enjoy. Research has found that half of people who start an exercise program drop out after just three to six months. When exercise feels like one more chore to add to an already overburdened "To Do" list, it's likely to be the last one to be crossed off.

Think about it: How many times have you said to yourself that *this* is the year you're going to get in shape or take up tennis or go to the gym regularly, then not followed through on your resolution? When it came right down to it, after an exhausting day at work, or with the kids, stretching out on the couch with a good book or in front of the TV was probably a lot more appealing. These activities may help you unwind but they won't do a thing to get rid of the extra padding on your hips or to boost your energy.

If you discover workouts or sports that are fun and make you feel good, you'll not only make them a priority in your life, but you'll actually begin to look forward to them. Why? Because they won't feel like exercise; they'll be something that gives you pleasure. After all, it's a lot easier to stick with an exercise plan that boosts your mood and energy level, and fosters a can-do spirit. If you can glean these benefits from your workouts, you might even become an exercise convert.

When it comes to choosing physical activities, many people play it safe, gravitating toward what's familiar or easy for them. But after a while, that can start to feel less than challenging, even tedious. It's wise to broaden your repertoire of activities in ways that suit your goals, your personality and your lifestyle.

Gearing Up

You don't have to blow your budget on flashy workout attire, but it is important to dress appropriately for the activity you plan to do as well as for the weather. For starters, invest in good-quality shoes that are made specifically for the activity you'll be doing—running shoes for running, tennis shoes for tennis, aerobics shoes for aerobics and so on; make sure they offer ample cushioning and toe and heel support. Wear cotton athletic socks that are soft and absorbent.

If you'll be exercising in hot, sunny weather, choose loose, light-colored, lightweight clothes, made of cotton or a wicking fabric that draws sweat away from skin. And don't forget to buy a good sports bra. It should offer ample support, preventing your breasts from bouncing but without causing friction or rubbing against your skin. If it looks like rain or wind may be headed your way, wear a Gore-Tex jacket to prevent yourself from getting soaked. For cold-weather workouts, dress in layers so that you can peel them off as needed.

ASSESSING YOUR PHYSICAL SELF

It's important to know certain things about yourself when choosing activities. Otherwise, it's a bit like forcing a square peg into a round hole. To discover what kinds of activities might appeal to you, check the following diamonds that best describe you:

◇ *Do you enjoy the camaraderie and team spirit that come with being part of a group?*

If so, consider joining a local soccer, volleyball, basketball or ultimate Frisbee team.

◇ *Is the time spent exercising the only time you have to yourself or to hang out with a friend?*

If so, your best choice might be an activity such as walking, jogging, swimming, in-line skating or riding a bike.

◇ *Do you enjoy playing competitive sports?*

If so, try taking up tennis, squash or racquetball or a team sport.

◇ *Do you love being out in nature, amid rolling hills, pastoral landscapes or gorgeous seaside settings?*

If so, consider hiking, mountain-climbing, mountain-biking, kayaking or rowing; in winter, try cross-country skiing or go snow-shoeing.

◇ *Do you prefer to exercise in a gym environment where lots of people are doing the same thing?*

If so, sign up for an aerobics or spinning class.

◇ *Do you prefer kinder, gentler forms of exercise that are simultaneously relaxing and invigorating?*

If so, try a mind-body workout such as yoga or t'ai chi.

A point to keep in mind: once you've discovered your style and pinpoint an activity or several activities that suit you, don't be surprised if you find that you're partial to a particular category of fitness. Many people are. But for optimal fitness benefits, as well as lasting motivation, it's best to design an exercise regimen that includes complementary activities. For example, if jogging or aerobic dance is the mainstay of your exercise program, consider adding nonimpact exercises activities such as biking or swimming or mind/body techniques like yoga or t'ai chi. If, on the other hand, you love team sports such as soccer or basketball, try a solo activity like walking, swimming or in-line skating for variety. If rowing or kayaking is your thing, consider adding in-line skating, jogging, walking or stair-climbing to work different muscle groups. This is known as cross-training. Not only does cross-training add variety to your exercise regimen but it helps prevent injuries that result from placing too much stress and strain on the same muscles.

Now that you have an idea of what activities may appeal to you, here's what you need to know about what's involved, the level of conditioning that's required and other salient points.

Team sports: Sports such as volleyball, soccer, basketball and ultimate Frisbee require varying levels of conditioning. Not surprisingly, they also vary in their intensity. Volleyball, for example, requires bursts of energy as you dive for a falling ball, whereas soccer, basketball and ultimate Frisbee provide a more continuous and a more intense aerobic workout. For these reasons, volleyball is a good choice to supplement or add variety to a regular exercise program. A note of caution: If you're new to exercise, competitive sports may increase your chances of injury, especially if you're overweight, since you can't regulate the intensity of play—so be careful.

Solo or buddy activities: Walking, jogging, swimming, in-line skating or riding a bike are all good choices for the foundation of an aerobic exercise plan. With the exception of swimming, all of these can be done solo as well as with a friend. Each of these offers an excellent aerobic workout and all, except for jogging, are low-impact activities, so they're gentle on your joints. But in-line skating has a high injury rate so be sure to protect yourself with appropriate gear—a helmet, wrist and elbow guards, and knee pads. Since swimming is the only total body workout in this group, you may want to complement the others with upper-body workouts such as rowing or cross-country skiing.

Racquet sports: Tennis, racquetball and squash all require a certain amount of skill when it comes to technique. If you're brand-new to these sports, it may be worth taking a lesson or two to get you started the right way. While there's some crossover in skills, it's not as much as you think: A proper tennis stroke is a bit different from a racquetball stroke, for example. The intensity of these activities depends largely on the level of skill you and your partner display. All three are great aerobic workouts—if you're playing singles, that is—and each is good for conditioning your whole body. A note of caution: If you're new to exercise, these sports can be intense, which may increase your chances of injury, especially if you're overweight.

The great outdoors: If you crave beautiful scenery while you exercise, hiking, mountain-biking, kayaking, cross-country skiing and rowing (outdoors) may suit your style. The first two are especially great lower-body workouts; the others produce upper body exercise like few others, which makes these great complementary forms of exercise. All develop cardiovascular fitness and muscular endurance without putting a lot of wear and tear on your joints since they're low-impact activities. Golf is another appealing outdoor sport that's also social; however, it's only a good calorie-burner if you walk the course. Keep in mind that the motions involved in kayaking, cross-country skiing and rowing can be tricky, so if you're a novice it's best to have an instructor show you the basics.

Gym classes: At health clubs across the country, you'll find aerobic dance and spinning classes that offer fun workouts set to energizing music, and they're guaranteed to make you sweat. Keep in mind that the high-impact and step aerobics classes can be hard on your joints, especially your knees, whereas the low-impact version poses a lower risk of injury. In spinning classes, participants pedal specially designed stationary bikes while an instructor coaches them through bouts of hill climbing, fast pedaling and pedaling in various positions while high-charged music plays in the background. Good complements to these workouts include gentler ones like swimming and cross-country skiing.

Mind-body exercises: Yoga and t'ai chi can work wonders in enhancing flexibility and muscular strength, and they both promote a sense of relaxation and inner calm; they're great stress-busters. What they *won't* do is improve your level of aerobic fitness or help you burn a great amount of calories. For these reasons, they're excellent choices to complement an aerobic exercise program that involves jogging, aerobics or other high-intensity activities that can result in tight muscles.

Gym machines: One of the greatest advantages to joining a health club is the diversity of aerobic machines that are at your disposal: Treadmills, stair-climbers, stationary bikes, Versaclimbers, cross-country skiers and rowing machines all offer terrific cardiovascular workouts. But what appeals to one person may seem monotonous to another, so try them all to see which strike your fancy. Treadmills, stair-climbers and stationary bikes offer a good lower-body workout, which means they'll tone your butt and thighs, so if one of these is your machine of choice be sure to complement your workouts with an upper-body activity like swimming. Or try using a Versaclimber, cross-country skier or rowing machine, each of which is a total-body trainer, involving lots of muscles in the upper *and* lower body. Depending on the intensity you choose, every one of these contraptions can help you work up a good sweat. With each, however, proper posture is important, so have a trainer on staff give you a few pointers on your first try or two.

THE POWER OF PARTNERSHIP

When you exercise by yourself, it can be hard to maintain your enthusiasm day after day. Indeed, researchers at Indiana University found that people who joined a fitness program with a partner were much more likely to stick with it a year later than those who exercised on their own. Working out with a partner or a trainer offers instant camaraderie and support that can provide a much-needed lift when you're suffering from an energy slump. But there are certain strategies that can make the partnership more fruitful. Here's what you should know:

◆ **The Buddy System:** Of course, you'll want to choose an exercise partner who enjoys similar activities as you do and who you enjoy being with, but it's also important to pick someone who is equally committed to getting fit, and who won't cancel your workouts at the last minute. To get the best match, talk openly about the plan from the outset: how often and when you'll exercise together, what your mutual goals are, how you can help each other when motivation is missing, and what kind of encouragement you both prefer. That way big surprises won't surface.

◆ **Working with a Personal Trainer:** Even if you don't have deep enough pockets to afford a personal trainer on a regular basis, it may be worth splurging on one for a session or two. Why? Because it can help you create a tailor-made exercise program and give you a potent shot of motivation. Some trainers may also be willing to work with two clients—a sort of two-for-one deal—so consider hiring one with a friend. Just make sure the prospective trainer's personality and style appeals to both of you. In order for this arrangement to work, you need to like each other and be able to communicate freely and honestly. A qualified trainer should have a college background in exercise science or physical education and be certified by the American Council on Exercise (ACE), the Aerobics and Fitness Association of America (AFAA), or the American College of Sports Medicine (ACSM), according to industry experts.

♦ **Joining a Health Club:** In recent years, another fitness boom has taken place in gyms and health clubs around the country, as facilities have begun to offer more personalized service. Many health clubs now offer on-site trainers who are available to assist exercisers in their workouts. Some health clubs even offer a free session with a trainer when you join. And if you make yourself visible and let staff members know that you have a keen interest in getting fit, they're more likely to help you down the road. When shopping around for a health club, it's a good idea to find out what the ratio is between on-site trainers and the exercising population and whether they are certified by the American Council on Exercise (ACE), Aerobics and Fitness Association of America (AFAA), or American College of Sports Medicine (ACSM). Also, on your trial visit, try to gauge how friendly and helpful staff members are and whether you'd feel comfortable working closely with them.

Key Points

♦ The secret to making a commitment to exercise is to find activities you enjoy. Try different activities until you find a couple that suit your preferences and your lifestyle.

♦ To prevent overuse injuries and create variety, it's best to choose exercises that complement each other by using different muscle groups—jogging and swimming, for example, or in-line skating and rowing.

♦ If you want to work with a trainer—either a personal trainer or one at a health club—find one who has a college background in exercise science or physical education and is certified by the ACE, AFAA, or the ACSM.

♦ It's smart to dress appropriately for your chosen activity, not just for the sake of style but for comfort and proper movement. Always wear sport-specific shoes and loose, comfortable clothing.

♦ If you're new to a particular activity or machine at the gym, have an instructor show you the ropes so you get started in proper form from day one.

Goals

◇ Aim for a mix of indoor and outdoor activities, weather permitting. Varied scenery keeps your workouts more interesting.

◇ Try to broaden your horizons by participating in a new form of exercise every month.

◇ Make your workouts social, at least occasionally, by joining up with a friend or relative who shares your commitment to exercise.

◇ Join a local soccer, volleyball or basketball team by contacting your local YWCA or parks and recreation department.

◇ Aim to build upper- and lower-body strength. You'll be able to move more comfortably and you'll have more energy.

Fitting It In

SQUEEZING REGULAR WORKOUTS INTO A BUSY LIFE can be an enormous challenge. In fact, surveys have found that too little time is the number-one reason cited by women for not exercising regularly. But having a busy life doesn't mean it's utterly impossible to find the time. The key is to find what works for you when it works for you—and to be absolutely clear about why you're trying to find time for exercise. Here are seven steps that will help you fit fitness into your lifestyle:

STEP ONE: CREATE A PERSONAL GAME PLAN

If you're always pressed for time and you've been putting off exercising until a convenient opportunity presents itself, you're going to just keep procrastinating. What you need to do is make a commitment and devise a concrete plan for getting fit. First, though, you'll need to consider your goals. Sure, you want to slim down, but maybe you also want to decrease your risk of heart disease if it runs in your family. Do you want to boost your energy or play tag with your kids in the backyard without struggling for breath? What's important is that you want to do this for yourself—not because someone else has been nagging you.

Next you'll need to set specific goals, for both the short term and the long term. Think of this as the fitness equivalent of a financial plan: just as you wouldn't invest your money without thinking through your long- and short-term goals, it doesn't make sense to start an exercise regimen without considering the returns you desire. Taking the time to think this through will solidify your commitment. Research has found that setting goals not only helps people stick with an exercise regimen, but it also helps them derive more satisfaction from it.

The key is to set concrete goals that are focused on the act of exercising, rather than the result you want to achieve. Instead of saying that you will exercise so that you can lose five pounds in the next two weeks, for example, it's more productive to set a goal of jogging for 30 minutes three days a week and riding your bike in the park for half an hour on the other days. While the unstated aim may still be to lose those extra pounds, these acknowledged goals focus on what it will take for you to begin to slim down. By emphasizing what you can do, rather than the desired result, you are placed in the driver's seat: You have control over whether you exercise, whereas you don't have complete control over the numbers that appear on a scale.

Whether your ultimate goal is to run a 10-K race, lose 15 pounds in six months or swim across the

English Channel, breaking your long-term goal into short-term goals—such as jogging for 20 minutes four days a week or swimming 20, then 30, then 40 laps without stopping—will provide you with stepping-stones and plenty of satisfaction along the way to the Big One.

STEP TWO: WRITE DOWN YOUR GOALS IN AN EXERCISE JOURNAL

Putting pen to paper makes your goals official and serves as a reminder when your motivation wanes. Similarly, keeping a workout diary can help you track your progress and the results; it also helps you see what works and what doesn't in your exercise routine. To reinforce your motivation and commitment, reward yourself when you reach important short-term and long-term goals. If you keep up your jogging routine for a month, you might treat yourself to a new sports watch. If you run a 10-K race or lose those 15 pounds, reward yourself with a massage or another nonfood treat you've been wanting. Write your rewards down, too, so that you can get a sense of what things are especially motivating for you over time.

STEP THREE: CONSIDER WHAT TIME OF DAY WORKS FOR YOU

Exercising first thing in the morning may seem like the perfect way to jump-start your day but not if you can't drag yourself out of bed. One of the secrets to making exercise a regular part of your life is to schedule it when it works for you. And do schedule it. Block out specific time for exercise, then pen it into your calendar, as if it were a business appointment. That way, you'll be less likely to cancel it.

How can you tell what time is best for you? Consider your energy level, your tendency to procrastinate and your various responsibilities. If it's difficult for you to find time to exercise as the day goes on, consider scheduling your workouts for first thing in the morning; get up half an hour earlier if need be. Studies have found that morning exercisers are more likely to stick with their regimens. On the other hand, if you often need an energy boost about midday, working out during your lunch hour may be a good option for you (don't skip eating lunch; have something light after your workout on your way back to the office); exercising at this time of day may help curb your appetite and give you a potent shot of energy to get you through the afternoon. If you need to recharge your batteries after a day at the office, before you hit your second (home) shift, going to the gym after work may be a good idea so long as it doesn't make you too crunched for time in the evening. Likewise, if you want to take advantage of your body's maximum aerobic capacity, your best hours for exercising may be in the late afternoon, according to research. Keep in mind that you may need to experiment and try exercising at a few different times of day to see what works best for you.

STEP FOUR: MAP OUT A CONTINGENCY PLAN

The best-laid exercise plans can easily go awry, especially in a busy life. So it's wise to count on surprises and be ready for them. If it's raining, for example, you may have to skip your bike ride or jog but that doesn't mean you have to forgo a workout altogether. Think of ways ahead of time to bring your workout indoors—whether it's by following an exercise video, jumping rope, walking up and down the stairs or riding a stationary bike.

Similarly, if your exercise buddy can't make it on a particular day, that doesn't have to turn into a rest day for you. Psych yourself up for a solo activity or seek out a temporary replacement if what you really want to do requires two. One of the best ways to maximize your chances of success is to think ahead and create backup plans for those days when arrangements unexpectedly change.

STEP FIVE: SNEAK EXERCISE IN WHEREVER YOU CAN

Maybe you've learned from a financial plan that saving even small amounts of money here and there can add up significantly. Well, the same is true of exercise. Each time you move your body—whether it's by playing tag with your kids or walking to the bank instead of driving—that counts as exercise, which means that it burns calories, which will help you lose weight. For example, if a 150-pound woman were

Should You Exercise When You're Sick?

Many experts agree that while a common cold needn't sideline a workout, it's wise to rest if you have symptoms that might signal the flu or a systemic infection. Some physicians recommend drawing the line at the neck: If symptoms are isolated above the line—such as nasal congestion, sneezing, a scratchy throat and a slight headache—they probably indicate a run-of-the-mill head cold, in which case it's probably safe to continue exercising.

The best approach is to start slowly and if after 10 minutes you feel okay, keep going. But if you start feeling worse—if your head starts pounding and you feel like you're exercising in quicksand, stop and wait until you feel better. Remember that with a cold you may get dehydrated faster than usual, so drink lots of fluids during and after your workout. Be aware, too, that some cold remedies may make you drowsy and impair coordination and balance, which can increase your risk of injury.

On the other hand, symptoms that occur below the neck, such as muscle aches and pains, a hacking cough, vomiting, diarrhea, severe fatigue or a fever, could indicate the flu or a systemic infection, in which case doctors advise taking a break from exercise until the illness has passed.

to take a brisk 10-minute walk during her lunch hour every day of the work week, she'd lose four pounds in a year. If she played actively with her kids for 15 minutes every day of the week, she'd drop seven pounds in a year. And if she rode a stationary bike, while reading the paper, for 10 minutes five mornings a week, she'd be able to shave off five pounds in a year. This is all in addition to the calorie-burning effects of her formal exercise program.

It also helps if you try to combine exercise with another activity. For example, instead of meeting a friend for lunch, suggest that you go for a brisk walk during your lunch hour. Similarly, make a date with a friend to meet at the health club instead of going shopping. Trying to fit in quality time with your kids? Why not go for a family bike ride instead of choosing a sedentary activity? The point is, there are ways around your time-crunch; it just takes a little creativity to find them.

> **"** *J*ust because I travel doesn't mean that the workouts come to a screeching halt. In my hotel room, I'll do push-ups, leg lifts and squats. Sometimes I'll jump rope (Josh just got me started on that!) or climb the hotel stairs (my security men hate when I do that). Eating on the road can be a challenge. I tend to skip meals because I'm running around so much (not good!). When traveling, I generally have several mini meals throughout the day, rather than three large ones. **"**

STEP SIX: TAKE YOUR EXERCISE ROUTINE ON THE ROAD

No matter how committed you are, it can be especially challenging to keep up your exercise program while you're traveling. After all, you're away from your usual setting, your usual equipment, your usual schedule. But if you suddenly become inactive, you'll start to lose the strength and endurance—not to mention the weight-loss benefits—you've been building within 10 days.

Fortunately, it is possible to keep fit while traveling with some simple measures. Try to stay at a hotel that has a pool or a fitness center and pay those facilities a visit whenever your schedule permits. Or you can take a 30-minute walk or jog each day; it's a great way to do some sightseeing while also squeezing in a workout. You can also exercise in the privacy of your room if you pack elastic Dyna bands for strengthening and toning exercises. If you do these activities a few times per week, you'll have no trouble maintaining the fitness level you've worked so hard to attain.

STEP SEVEN: ADJUST YOUR WORKOUT TO SUIT THE WEATHER

When the mercury soars, so does your risk of becoming overheated while exercising. To avoid heat-related illnesses, it's important to take frequent breaks, to avoid exercising during the hottest part of the day (10 A.M. to 3 P.M.) and to allow yourself three to four weeks to get accustomed to the heat. Don't forget to wear a sunscreen with an SPF of at least 15; even activities that keep your body relatively cool (like swimming or biking) can expose your skin to the sun's damaging rays, making you susceptible to burning. If you're sensitive to smog, consider exercising in the morning before air pollution has a chance to build up; also, steer clear of vehicle-clogged streets and freeways.

When exercising in cold weather, in contrast, it's smart to dress in layers that you can peel off as needed. Also, if you're prone to coughing while exercising in cold temperatures, consider wearing a mask or handkerchief around your nose and mouth to warm and humidify the air as you inhale.

Key Points

♦ Creating a mission statement and/or a game plan for your exercise program will help clarify why you want to get fit and bolster your resolve to do so.

♦ Schedule your workouts as if they were very important appointments and write them into your calendar. That way, you'll be less likely to cancel these plans.

♦ Find the time of day that makes the most sense for you to exercise, depending on your energy level and your other responsibilities. Experiment to see what works best for you.

♦ Even well-thought-out exercise plans can go awry, so be ready for surprises like inclement weather and have a backup plan in place.

♦ While it's fine to exercise with a mild head cold, hold off if you have a fever or other symptoms of a more serious illness.

Goals

◇ *Start an exercise journal in which you can log your workouts as well as how you feel during and after them and what helped and hindered your energy level.*

◇ *Find inventive ways to keep fit while you're traveling, whether it's going on a walking sightseeing tour or renting a bicycle on which to cruise the town. You'll enjoy your trip all the more.*

◇ *Make getting fit a family affair by going on bike rides or hikes together and bringing along a healthful picnic.*

◇ *Look for clever little ways to sneak in a bonus bout of exercise whenever you can, whether it's by playing vigorously with your kids or taking your dog for an extra walk.*

◇ *Keep an eye on your long-term fitness goals as you embark on this weight-loss journey and set smaller goals to use as stepping-stones. This will help you stay motivated and give you plenty of satisfaction along the way.*

Staying Motivated

WITHOUT QUESTION, IT'S EASY TO FALL OFF THE FITNESS WAGON when your life is filled with all sorts of conflicting demands and when you do the same routine day in and day out. Just as you'd get tired of eating the same foods over and over again on a diet, the same is true when it comes to exercising. That's why it's important to include variety in your activities and where you do them, for starters.

But everybody—even the most die-hard gym rat—suffers from motivational crises now and then. If you develop a plan of action on how you'll deal with them, you'll be able to get through them much more easily without having your exercise program suffer. The key is to use whatever tactics you can think of to rev up your resolve to get fit and stay that way.

When it comes right down to it, you'll need to be your own personal coach, cheerleader, protector and star player all rolled into one. That may sound like a lot of responsibility, but no one else is going to play those roles for you. To make these jobs easier, it helps to fill your gym bag with these psychological tips and tricks.

Create your own mantra. Remember *The Little Engine That Could*? How she kept saying, "I think I can, I think I can" as she chugged her way up seemingly insurmountable hills? You can apply the same principle to your workouts to keep yourself going when you feel like quitting. The idea is to talk yourself through difficult situations by using positive affirmations, such as, "I'm tough, I'm strong, I cannot go wrong," or, "Nothing can stop me now!" that you silently repeat over and over to yourself. Not only will this give you a shot of motivation, but the repetitive chant can make you feel like you're on automatic pilot, which means that you'll be able to keep going.

Imagine success. Visualize yourself crossing the finish line in a bicycle or running race or hitting a winning passing shot on the tennis court, as a crowd of spectators cheers with delight. Imagine a scenario that might be appropriate to your chosen activity, one that focuses on the result you crave. By seeing yourself doing things in prime form, you'll be able to fine-tune your concentration skills and tap into reserves of energy you didn't know you had.

Challenge yourself. When your workouts begin feeling lusterless or uninspired, try presenting yourself with a new challenge. It could be sprinting for 30 seconds every 10 minutes during a 30-minute jog or pushing yourself to swim for an extra five minutes beyond your usual time. Setting new goals periodically adds variety to your workouts, and it can make you feel more pumped up to complete them.

Tune in to energizing music. Choose tunes that have an upbeat tempo and make you feel like dancing. Just as certain types of music can help you relax, others can rev up your energy. The key is to select the type of music that appeals to you and that provides you with the effect you desire. It will also make the time pass much more quickly.

Strike a bargain with yourself. On those days when you really don't feel like going out for a fast walk or a jog but you know you should, make a deal with yourself. Force yourself to hit the trail anyway and give yourself permission to quit after 10 or 15 minutes if you feel terrible. Chances are you'll just keep going. Alternatively, promise yourself a treat such as a relaxing soak in the tub after your exercise session. It'll give you something to look forward to.

Recall a time when you were bursting with energy. Try to conjure up a time in your life when you had so much energy that you didn't know what to do with it. Imagine how your body felt, how vibrant and alert your mind was, how your body must have looked when it was in motion. Now try to recapture that positive feeling and pour it into your current workout.

Find an exercise mentor. Look around you and find someone or a few people whose exercise commitment and style you admire. It could be that woman at the gym who can bench-press twice her weight, a neighbor who took up running marathons after being sedentary for most of her life or even an elderly aunt who began tap-dancing a few years ago and hasn't stopped moving her feet since. Talk to these people about how they train and what keeps them moving when they lose motivation. Also, watch them to discover secrets to their success that they may not even be aware of. Then borrow these techniques and think of these people for inspiration when you need it.

Don't overdo it. Zeal is a good thing when it comes to exercise and many other things in life. But working out too much too quickly can make you burn out—physically (if you injure muscles that have been overused) or psychologically (if you see your motivation go up in smoke). Instead, it's better to take the long view: Think of your exercise program as an ongoing commitment—which means there's no rush!—and increase the intensity and duration of your workouts gradually. That way you'll continue to have goals to work toward and you won't abuse your body in the process.

NO MORE EXCUSES!

Excuses, excuses. Many of us use them to weasel out of doing all sorts of things we don't feel like doing; why should exercise be any different? Because in this case, you're only hurting yourself by avoiding something that's good for you. So the next time you catch yourself making excuses for not exercising, try talking yourself into working out instead. You'll be happy you did later.

Excuse 1: I Don't Have Enough Time

The truth is, you have the time if—and only if—you *make* the time. If you make exercise a priority and think of it as an investment in your health and well-being, you'll be able to find all sorts of ways to carve out enough time for regular workouts. All it takes is 20 to 30 minutes here and there: waking up half an hour earlier, exercising on your lunch break, squeezing in a run to the gym before heading home from the office. If that's too much to ask, it may be time to revamp your schedule so that you can fit in one of the most powerful stress-relievers and health-boosters around. Sneak in short bouts of exercise whenever you can—by taking the stairs at work instead of the elevator, by walking on your errands instead of driving and so on. As long as you can piece together a total of 30 minutes of physical activity in a day, you'll be fulfilling the Surgeon General's minimal recommendation for exercise.

Excuse 2: I'm Not Coordinated Enough

You're adept enough to walk, aren't you? Lots of people feel as though they're not coordinated or athletic enough to play certain sports, but that's not a legitimate reason for not exercising. After all, there are plenty of activities you already know how to do that count as exercise—walking, riding a bike and swimming. Besides, what have you got to lose if you try something new? You just might surprise yourself, and even if you don't, what's the big deal? You can't be great at everything; it wouldn't be fair to the rest of us mere mortals.

Excuse 3: I Don't Have the Energy

At the end of a long, exhausting day, it's easy to fall into the trap of thinking you're too tired to exercise, but rather than draining you, working out is likely to boost your energy level, leaving you feeling refreshed or invigorated. By promoting the flow of blood and oxygen throughout your body—not to mention mood-boosting endorphins—exercise can help you reduce tension and refuel your energy for the rest of your day.

Excuse 4: I'm Too Fat to Exercise

Unless your doctor has advised you not to exercise—in which case you shouldn't—this excuse falls into the category of catch-22 thinking. If you wait until you're thin to start exercising, you'll probably wait a long time because exercise helps you to lose weight. It's understandable if you're reluctant to join an aerobics class, but who says that's the only way or place to exercise? Head out for a brisk walk in your neighborhood, push back the coffee table and follow an exercise video in the privacy of your own home, or invest in home exercise equipment such as a treadmill or a stationary bike. You've got plenty of choices, no matter how much you weigh.

Excuse 5: I'm Afraid of Getting Hurt

Many injuries, as well as cases of severe muscle soreness, result from trying to do too much too quickly. If you're new to exercise, start slowly and increase your distance or time gradually; also, try to incorporate a less strenuous day between vigorous workouts and at least one rest day (meaning a day of no exercise) into each week. To minimize the chance of injury, you can also stick with activities that are among the safest around—namely, walking or swimming, both of which are gentle on the joints.

Besides, look at it this way: If you don't exercise, your muscles will gradually atrophy and you may actually increase your chances of getting hurt in everyday life.

Key Points

♦ Everyone suffers from motivational crises occasionally. The way to get through them is to know how to handle them ahead of time and to be prepared to act as your own coach and cheerleader.

♦ Even when you feel tired, exercise can boost your energy level by promoting the flow of blood and oxygen throughout your body, along with mood-boosting endorphins. Exercise can also help you reduce tension.

♦ You can learn to talk yourself through your workouts and motivational lapses by using positive affirmations. They're the equivalent of an abbreviated pep talk.

♦ Find an exercise mentor to learn from and look up to. Talk to that person about how she or he maintains motivation, about training secrets that have worked for her or him. Then borrow these techniques—shamelessly!

♦ If you're new to exercise, start slowly and increase your distance or time gradually to minimize your chances of injury. Many injuries stem from trying to do too much too quickly. Also, try to incorporate a less strenuous day between vigorous workouts and at least one day of rest into each week.

Goals

◇ *Harness the power of your imagination to rev up your motivation. Use visualization techniques to complete a grueling run, for example, or recall a time when you were brimming with excess energy and tap into that reserve to keep going.*

◇ *Make exercise a priority. You may not think you have the time for it but somehow you manage to snatch time for movies, shopping and other pleasurable activities. Do the same for your workouts.*

◇ *Start differentiating between excuses and legitimate reasons for not exercising. If you're injured, that's valid. If you're tired, that's not. Do it anyway, then take a nap if you need to.*

◇ *Don't stop setting goals. Celebrate the ones you've achieved, then set new ones. They'll keep your workout life interesting and they'll keep your motivation high for the long haul.*

◇ *Reward yourself for making fitness an integral part of your life. You're doing one of the best things you could possibly do for yourself so give yourself a pat on the back regularly.*

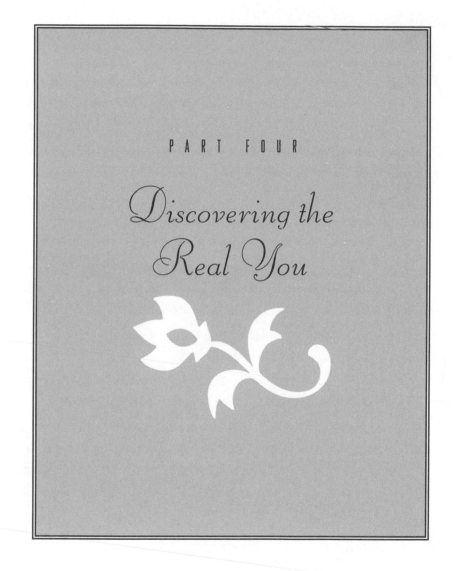

PART FOUR

Discovering the Real You

These days, many women wear so many different hats in their lives—mother, wife, daughter, sister, friend, professional—that it can be hard to tell who's really underneath. After all, when your life is loaded with responsibilities, time with your own thoughts—much less time to reflect on how you see yourself—can seem like an unaffordable luxury. But how you view yourself affects how you act and who you appear to be in the eyes of the world. It can influence many aspects of your behavior from your willingness to take chances to how you interact with others. As the circumstances of your life shift and change, *you* are the one constant that's always there—which means that how you see yourself has the power to affect the quality of your life, regardless of how it changes.

Whether you realize it or not, body image plays a starring role in many women's images of themselves. Yet for many women, issues involving perceptions of body shapes and sizes are often complicated: On the one hand, they determine how you feel about and treat yourself; on the other hand, they often stand in the way of losing weight and changing your behavior for the better. Plus, it's very difficult to feel good about your body unless you feel good about yourself—or vice versa. Feeling good about your body and feeling good about yourself are so closely intertwined.

That's why it's important to get comfortable in your own skin—physically and emotionally—no matter what you weigh. The key is to figure out what you stand for and how you'd like to treat yourself before you start to get in shape or lose weight. Otherwise, you're bound to be disappointed when your weight loss doesn't magically alter your image of yourself. Those changes need to come from within, but they're well worth making. As the late, great actress and comedienne Lucille Ball once said, "Love yourself first and everything else falls into line. You really have to love yourself to get anything done in this world."

Who Are You?

WHEN YOU THINK ABOUT YOUR IDENTITY, do you refer to yourself by name, role(s) or the qualities that make you unique? When you look in the mirror, who do you actually see: a likable woman whose talents and attributes you value or someone who strikes you as inadequate or with numerous shortcomings? Do you ever wake up in the morning and wish you'd see someone else's face in the mirror? More importantly, do you ever wish you were someone else?

Self-esteem and self-image affect your emotional and physical well-being; they can also have a profound impact on the quality of your life. Simply put, they shape your reality. They influence the activities you participate in and the chances you take. Self-esteem and self-image also affect how you see the world and how you relate to other people; your ability to weather life's storms; and your skill in rebounding from hardship. Indeed, researchers have found that the best predictor of one's satisfaction with life isn't how you feel about your family, your friendships or your bank-account balance, but how satisfied you are with yourself.

Many people suffer from low self-esteem, which can cast a black cloud over your outlook on life, as well as create an enormous obstacle to going after what you want and achieving it—whether the goal is a promotion at work, organizing the school fund-raiser or losing weight. After all, if you're struggling with negative feelings toward yourself, it can sap your motivation and determination to slim down and shape up. It's hardly surprising, then, that researchers have found a strong link between low self-esteem and psychological problems, especially depression and anxiety. If you don't feel good about yourself, it's awfully hard to feel good about life in general.

Part of the complex issue of women and self-esteem has to do with the enormous societal pressure on women to be thin. There's no getting around the fact that we live in an appearance-obsessed culture. Even if you don't think you succumb to such definitions of success, you probably do on some level. Take a moment to consider how you truly see yourself now. If you're like many women, you may focus on appearance-related goals like having a slender figure, looking your absolute best or being successful professionally, financially, socially—in other words, achieving those external trappings of worth. You might

> **"**When I was a young girl, I loved ponies. Nowadays, girls are discussing the size of their bottoms. Weight is a topic of discussion, not just an issue, in our house. I think it's important to be honest with yourself and your children. If my child comes up to me and says, "Mom, I'm not comfortable in my ballet outfit," I won't dismiss her. Rather than pushing her aside and telling her not to worry, I'll say, "OK, let's deal with it," and we'll talk it out.**"**

even admire or envy people who are thin, gorgeous and seemingly successful. You also might believe that if you could just attain these goals, then you would *finally* feel great about yourself.

The truth is, many people who achieve these benchmarks do wear veneers of self-confidence but they're often an illusion. Deep down, they don't feel particularly good about themselves, and often they feel like frauds, afraid that others will reject the real them. Why? None of these *external* measures—of beauty, appearance, social or professional stature, or wealth—takes into account who you really are. Only *internal* measures—personality attributes, personal values, morals—do. Besides, if your sense of self is constructed around such rickety, changeable factors, how strong can it really be?

THE ORIGINS OF SELF-ESTEEM

If your sense of self is shaky, don't despair. You can fortify it, but first it's helpful if you examine the foundations of your self-esteem. After all, your self-esteem and self-image didn't develop in a vacuum. They evolved over the course of your life and were shaped by factors ranging from issues in your family, to the quality of relationships in your life, to how you've handled emotional issues in relation to your own body.

If your parents were overly critical about how you looked or how well you performed in school or socially while you were growing up, you may have internalized those negative messages and come to believe them yourself. Similarly, if your parents often used you as a scapegoat for their problems, you may have developed a habit of blaming yourself when things don't go according to plan. If you have a history of close relationships that have been mired by conflict, knowingly or not, you may have placed the blame squarely at your own feet, which also may have eroded your self-esteem. And if you've never felt comfortable with your own body, how could you possibly feel comfortable with your self?

People who have high self-esteem, on the other hand, basically like and respect themselves. They're

Self-Esteem Versus Self-Absorption

When it comes to trying to enhance their self-esteem, some people worry that it might make them overly self-absorbed or think *too* highly of themselves. In most cases, it's an unfounded worry.

After all, there's a world of difference between having high self-esteem, which is healthy, and being self-absorbed or narcissistic, which isn't. Self-esteem involves having respect and a favorable impression of oneself. Narcissism, on the other hand, involves passionately wanting to think well of oneself and being emotionally invested in establishing your superiority over others.

In other words, people with high self-esteem have opinions of themselves that are fairly stable. As a result, they are not easily threatened by negative feedback from others; nor are they overly preoccupied with proving themselves to the world at large. They simply feel good about themselves from the inside, which is a very pleasant way to go through life.

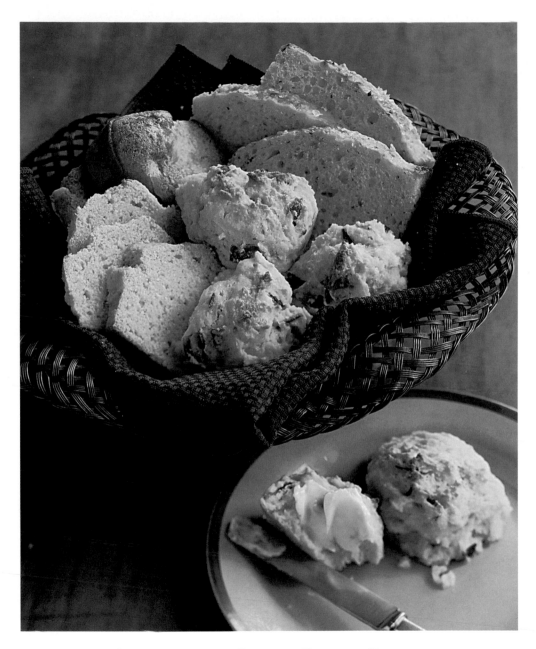

Anise Polenta Bread, Peppery Popovers,
Rosemary Bread, and Bacon Biscuits

Wild Mushroom Strudel

Marinated Shellfish in Endive and Tuna Crostini

Jalapeño Corn Soup with Cilantro and Mexican Chicken Salad

proud of their accomplishments and feel capable of performing and handling different kinds of situations. As a result, they feel fairly secure and successful in life. They're not arrogant, narcissistic or self-absorbed. They simply believe that they have inherent value as human beings and that they can face most challenges that head their way. Part of this stems from a sense of what psychologists call self-efficacy: a can-do spirit, a sense that with some effort you can control the outcome of various circumstances of your life. People with self-efficacy believe, for example, that they can achieve and maintain a thin body—and often their efforts to do so become a self-fulfilling prophecy. They're not afraid to take chances because they know that even if they don't succeed in reaching their goal, they will have learned something from the experience, which is a success in itself.

WEIGHTY MATTERS

If you've been heavy all your life or you've been a yo-yo dieter, repeatedly losing and regaining the same excess pounds, the numbers on the scale may have taken a serious toll on your self-esteem. Given the fact that we inhabit a culture that values a slim, fit physique and attractive appearance, it's no surprise that so many women don't feel good about themselves when they can't attain the cultural ideal of a fashion model or a triathlete.

Although it may not be in your genes to have such a figure, that reality probably doesn't stop you from trying. Many women cut their calorie intake almost to the point of starvation, aerobicize until they're ready to drop from exhaustion, and fall victim to all sorts of fad diets. When they still can't achieve that dream body, their self-esteem—not to mention their mood!—takes a serious nosedive. Is it any wonder? So many women set themselves up for failure simply because they're striving for unrealistic, if not completely unattainable, goals. They're destined for disappointment. What's more, women take failure to heart more than men do, according to some psychologists. Women are simply more ashamed to fail in any domain, whether it's the world of work, at the gym or at losing weight.

Even those who are successful at losing weight often struggle with the maintenance part of the equation. One of the reasons this is so difficult is that people often expect their lives to change dramatically, for the better, of course, once they've slimmed down. When that doesn't happen, it's all too easy to lose willpower and suffer a relapse of unhealthy eating habits. The biggest changes that weight loss will bring is that there will be less of you and you'll be healthier, so if you're unhappy with other aspects of your life (your work, your family life or your civic involvement) you'll need to do something about them separately.

When it comes to changing your eating habits, Weight Watchers knows that you'll probably need to do more than restock your pantry and refrigerator. Although making healthy food choices is important, it is also crucial to develop positive attitudes and effective strategies for dealing with weight-loss challenges. To help, Weight Watchers has developed **Weight Watchers Tools for Living**. Think of them as your own personal arsenal of techniques to help you get what you want and to combat difficult situations that get in your way.

Mental Rehearsing: Special occasions, for example, can be perilous when you're trying to lose weight. How to deal with that big holiday feast? Create a picture in your mind and repeatedly imagine yourself saying, "No, thank you. That was wonderful, but I'm satisfied," to offers of a second serving *before* the big event. When you're in the situation, recall your rehearsals.

Winning Outcomes: Specific goals that are stated in the positive, fit your lifestyle and that you can do on your own.

Empowering Beliefs: Ideas that you believe are true, the ones coming from deep within you, helping you achieve your goals.

Anchoring: A technique that helps you call up your personal strengths and characteristics whenever you need them to achieve something.

Storyboarding: A step-by-step action plan that you draw up, much like a sequence of scenes in a film, to help you get closer to a goal.

Motivating Strategy: A visualization technique to inspire your continued efforts toward a Winning Outcome.

Reframing: This tool can help you find positive behaviors to replace negative ones.

Positive Self-Talk: Thinking, speaking or writing positive thoughts to yourself to inspire a positive action.

CULTIVATING SELF-ESTEEM

Of course, garnering self-esteem is not about accepting yourself the way you are if you're unhappy with some aspect of yourself or your life, like your weight. The goal should be to strive to be the best person *you* can be, not to be or look like some cultural ideal. So while you're working on the physical transformation, it's wise to start the internal, psychological one simultaneously. If you can begin to feel good about yourself now, before you lose weight, peeling off the pounds will be that much easier. You'll be less likely to regain the weight because you'll already feel good about yourself on the inside; you won't be relying on your appearance to change your feelings for you.

Make a list that charts what personal values are important to you (such as giving of yourself to others or maintaining a personal honor code) and why. You may begin to notice qualities in yourself that you've liked in other people and that you may not have been able to see until now. Next, consider how you'd like to be. Maybe you'd like to have a more upbeat attitude toward life in general, or be less afraid of taking chances. Or maybe you'd like to feel and project an air of confidence in more situations. The more specific you can be with your wish list, the better because you'll know what to work on.

To get the ideas flowing, it helps to think about qualities you admire in other people and wish you had as well. It's a little bit like making a sketch of your ideal character, in which you hold on to your own desirable attributes and simply add to them. Here's what a sample wish list might look like:

I WISH:

I WERE MORE OUTGOING IN SITUATIONS WHERE I DON'T KNOW PEOPLE.
I FELT MORE SELF-ASSURED WHEN MAKING PRESENTATIONS AT WORK.
I WERE BETTER AT SETTING BOUNDARIES OR LIMITS WITH FAMILY MEMBERS.
I COULD LOOK AT THE BRIGHT SIDE OF LIFE MORE OFTEN.
I WEREN'T AFRAID TO SAY NO TO REQUESTS FROM FRIENDS OCCASIONALLY.
I COULD STOP TAKING CRITICISM SO PERSONALLY.
I COULD HELP PEOPLE IN THE COMMUNITY WHO ARE LESS FORTUNATE THAN I AM.
I HANDLED CRISES MORE SMOOTHLY AND WITHOUT GETTING PANICKY.

Once you've set your agenda, the aim is to start singing your own praises, minimizing your faults, learning to love yourself unconditionally and treating yourself with kindness—just as you would your partner, your children or your best friend. For most women, this may be an entirely new operating procedure. Many are socialized to do this for those they love but not for themselves. In fact, most women take better care of others than themselves. But the truth is, you are just as worthy of such treatment as anyone else is. And if you start acting as though you're entitled to nurture yourself, it can gradually transform the foundation of your self-esteem from quicksand into bedrock.

Many women feel guilty spending the time and energy on nurturing themselves. But why should they? Think about it: Does anyone else in your family feel guilty about carving out time for his or her needs and wants? Probably not. So why treat yourself like a second-class citizen? Kindness is a much more effective way to promote change than self-flagellation, which will only make your spirits plummet and lead you to rebel against your own good intentions. After all, if you treat yourself the way you would a dear friend while you're trying to make these lifestyle changes, you'll appreciate your own support and encouragement; you'll feel as though you have a partner, rather than an enemy, in yourself, one who will help you reach your goals.

Just as bad eating habits can pack on unwanted pounds, so can bad emotional habits sabotage your emotional well-being in subtle ways. The trick is to kick the negative emotional and psychological habits so that you can begin to feel good about yourself now.

How to do this? All it takes is a little attitude adjustment. Rather than striving for perfection, for example, it's smarter to set reasonable, achievable goals. When you meet them, don't quickly move on to the next ones: Pause and revel in your successes, the big and the small. While you're at it, try to stop being so hard on yourself, a hazard that often comes with the territory of womanhood. Perfectionism is a dangerous pursuit, partly because it's linked with depression, according to psychologists. It can also be

Acting the Part

One of the best ways to change your self-image is to *act* as if you are the totally confident, self-assured, put-together woman you've always wanted to be. In other words, a positive self-image can become a self-fulfilling prophecy if you nudge it in the right direction. If you *act* as if you feel talented, smart, gorgeous or prosperous, other people will perceive and respond to you as if you are. Slowly but surely you'll begin to feel that way. What follows are eight ways to fake self-assurance until your self-image catches up:

Stand tall, stand proud: Your posture and carriage speak volumes about how you see yourself. Walking into a room with your head held high, your back and shoulders straight, signals that you feel in command of your life. People with long strides are generally viewed as more gregarious, independent and happier than those who shuffle along or drag their feet. Keep in mind, too, that steady eye contact communicates honesty, poise and self-assurance.

Smile: Besides alerting people that you're approachable, keeping a pleasant smile on your face can trigger feelings of happiness. How is that possible? One theory maintains that as you observe your own behavior you infer that you must be feeling that way. It may also be that smiling creates some physiological feedback within the brain that sparks the genuine feeling.

Dress the part: Choose clothing and colors that boost your spirits, that make you feel put-together, sexy, powerful, sophisticated—whatever the effect is you desire. Keep in mind that certain hues communicate specific messages: in general, darker shades project authority while brighter ones are viewed as outgoing and attention-grabbing and pastel colors are seen as gentle and friendly. Select your attire accordingly.

Become an impersonator: From time to time, everybody gets stuck in certain ways of behaving and it's hard to find an exit. It helps if you think of someone whose style and qualities you truly admire, whether it's a celebrity or a woman you know, and try to borrow those traits when you need them the most. For example, you might try "impersonating" a friend who's a natural-born charmer if you're shy by nature and you feel nervous about throwing an important dinner party. With each successful experience, you'll grow more comfortable making these shifts in your own style.

Rehearse in your head: Actors do it, dancers do it, musicians do it, and so do athletes. They picture themselves performing the way they want to before the Big Event, and they do it again and again and again. Not only does this mental rehearsal help them prepare for the nerve-racking event, but it enhances their performance. You can do the same for any situation where you want to act more self-assured—whether it's an important business meeting or a social gathering.

Be assertive: If it doesn't come naturally, acting assertive can be difficult but it gets easier with practice. Imagine how you would look, act and feel if you were an assertive woman. Silently remind yourself why you're trying to be more assertive—because "I am taking charge of my life"—then put your strongest foot forward. It helps to start by requesting what you want in low-risk situations—at the grocery store or the dry cleaner's, for example—then to work up to more challenging situations—say, with your boss or your mother-in-law. With practice, assertiveness will become second nature before you know it.

Compliment yourself: Just as hearing compliments from other people can give your mood and outlook a potent boost, paying yourself compliments can do the same. Instead of attributing a particular success—whether it's preparing a fabulous meal or writing a first-rate report—to something other than your abilities or actions, take credit for it and praise yourself. If you can begin to really hear and absorb your own compliments, your confidence will rise.

Talk up your strengths: Rather than focusing on your weaknesses, play up your strengths to yourself. If you were meeting someone for the first time, what would you want them to know about you right away? Once you've pinpointed those qualities, play them up to yourself. Or consider writing a glittering bio of yourself, then remind yourself of those accomplishments when you need a shot of confidence.

damaging to your psyche and your self-esteem because you'll inevitably be disappointed when you don't attain perfection, which is nothing more than an illusion. Instead, when setbacks occur—on the job, in relationships, with lifestyle changes—try to take them more lightly by reminding yourself that they happen to everyone. Look for factors that contributed to the lapse, try to learn something from the experience, then forge ahead.

Another tactic that can help bolster your self-esteem: Stop saying mean things to yourself. Psychologists call this negative self-talk and it can be truly harmful to your state of mind. Instead, stick up for yourself just as you would for a friend. Or try to find something endearing about your quirks and blemishes just as you would with your husband's, for example. When confidence wanes, give yourself a pep talk or focus on all the things that could go right, rather than wrong, if you were to, say, take a smart chance on a new job. If you feel racked by guilt (women are especially vulnerable as emotional caretakers to family and friends) sit with it long enough to decide whether it's a sign that you're betraying your values. If you are, do something about it; otherwise, send your guilt packing instead of letting it send you on a trip.

Most of all, focus on the future—how you want to be, not how you've been. Start taking action, whether it's by trying new experiences, enhancing your intellectual prowess or reaching out to others, that will set you on the road to that destination. Learn to trust your inner voice instead of automatically running to others to help you with decisions. The more you can begin to rely on yourself, the better you'll begin to feel about your judgment, your abilities and your mindset. The tools for boosting your self-esteem are already in place; they just need to be used.

Key Points

♦ Your self-image affects not only your state of mind but the quality of your life. It influences how you act and who you appear to be in the minds of other people.

♦ Many women suffer from low self-esteem, which can cast a shadow over their lives, making them more susceptible to depression, anxiety and other psychological disorders.

♦ Self-esteem is shaped by myriad factors, including your family of origin, the quality of your relationships, how you handle emotional issues and your body image.

♦ A woman's weight history—especially if she's been heavy all her life or a yo-yo dieter—can wreak havoc with her self-esteem, especially if she strives for cultural ideals of thinness and attractiveness.

♦ Losing weight won't automatically improve your self-esteem; in order for self-esteem to improve, the changes have to come from within.

Goals

◇ *Take a few minutes each day for a little self-examination to figure out who you are, what you believe in and what you stand for. Getting in touch with your true self can help you notice qualities you like about yourself.*

◇ *Try to love yourself unconditionally, simply for who you are, not for what you do or how you look.*

◇ *Dare to define your own standards of attractiveness based on what's reasonable for you to achieve.*

◇ *Start being nicer to yourself by treating yourself as a dear friend. Sing your own praises, celebrate your accomplishments and rally to your own defense in the face of self-criticism.*

◇ *Pretend you're already confident by acting as if you were. Walk the walk, talk the talk and dress as if your opinion of yourself were high—and you'll begin to feel that way before you know it.*

Your Body Is Your Friend

ASK ANY WOMAN HOW SHE FEELS ABOUT HER BODY and there's likely to be a long pause. For most women, this seemingly simple question is problematic; it's a rare person who is completely satisfied at all times with the way she looks. But the truth is, a woman's vision of her body often has nothing to do with assessing her body's shape and size; her body image is a matter of perception that's often divorced from reality. What's more, a woman's feelings about her body can vary considerably from week to week, sometimes even from day to day.

Many women's emotional well-being can swing like a pendulum, depending on how they feel about their bodies. If a woman feels like she's having a fat day or doesn't like the number that appears on the scale, it can color her whole outlook on life. It's hardly surprising when you consider that a woman's body image—the picture she has of her body in her mind's eye—relates to all the other visions and attitudes she embraces about herself. Research from Old Dominion University in Norfolk, Virginia, has found that body image makes up about 25 percent of a person's self-esteem; body perceptions constitute a more significant part of a woman's feelings about herself and her sense of self-worth than they do for a man. If a woman feels dissatisfied with her body, she's likely to feel emotionally distressed and self-conscious about her appearance, and these feelings of distress can make it difficult, if not impossible, for her to feel in control of her life.

Survey after survey has found that the vast majority of American women are unhappy with their bodies, no matter where they fall on the weight spectrum. What's more, studies have found that most women consistently overestimate their size. According to research from the University of South Florida, more than 95 percent of women overestimate their body size, guessing that they are about one-quarter larger than they really are. The body parts most likely to be perceived as larger than the reality are the cheeks, the waist, the thighs and the hips (the latter two are not surprising since they are the primary areas of fat storage for women). It turns out that the more inaccurate a woman's perception is of her body size, the worse she's likely to feel about not just her body, but herself as well, according to psychologists. Men's self-esteem, by contrast, isn't as predicated on whether they see their body realistically.

BODY-IMAGE BASICS

Whether your body image is positive or negative, its roots can be traced to both historical sources and current experiences. As children, people begin to evaluate their bodies in terms of how well they conform to cultural standards as depicted, for example, in fairy tales, movies and the media. Yet these standards have varied with the decades. Women's body types have gone in and out of vogue nearly as frequently as long and short hemlines—from the hourglass figure of Marilyn Monroe in the 1950s to Twiggy's skinny shape in the 1960s to the lithe, strong look of Cindy Crawford in the mid-1980s to the reed-thin Kate Moss of the 1990s.

The environment where you grew up also affected the way you perceive your body. For example, children who were teased or criticized about their appearance often grow up to have a poor body image as adults. Likewise, growing up in a household where your mother constantly criticized or obsessed about her appearance can cause you to turn a similarly faultfinding eye upon your own. Psychologists call this modeling, and it can have a lasting impact on how you see yourself: A parent's distorted perception can become your distorted perception.

In addition, how you've weathered various phases of your life has also influenced your body image. Adolescence can be a pivotal time for the formation of body image; how accepted or popular you felt and whether you felt you had the right look probably took on monumental importance and made an indelible impression on your self-image. Adults who were overweight as kids or teenagers, for example, often experience a phenomenon called "phantom fat": No matter how slim or svelte they eventually become, they don't quite lose the feeling of being fat; they still feel physically flawed in some way. In addition, pregnancy and menopause can also change—for better or worse—the way women think and feel about their bodies; so can the way important people in your life respond to you.

To some extent, cultural standards of beauty are unavoidable. They aren't really the problem, though. Trouble arises when people adopt those cultural standards as their own and put enormous pressure on themselves to meet them. Striving for these unrealistic standards can set you up for a dramatic fall, physically and emotionally. Studies conducted by Thomas Cash, Ph.D., a professor of psychology at Old Dominion University, have found that people who embrace extreme standards for how they should look are vulnerable to a wide array of disturbing emotions including shame, anxiety and depression. If that weren't worrisome enough, these emotions can lead to self-damaging behaviors, from excessive dieting to eating disorders to overspending problems related to trying to achieve a certain look. Not surprisingly, having a negative body image is also linked with low self-esteem and self-consciousness, and it can interfere with having a satisfying sex life and healthy relationships. In short, it can overshadow much of your life.

Part of this effect stems from the fact that many people with body-image disorders use the body as a target for their negative emotions. Feelings of being out of control, ineffective or angry get twisted into criticisms and are then aimed and tossed like poison darts at the vision a woman has of her body.

How Is Your Relationship with Your Body?

No woman loves the way she looks every single moment of every day. But most women have a prevailing opinion of their bodies, consciously or not. To figure out how you really feel about yours, read each statement and decide whether it generally applies to you by marking it True or False.

1. On most days, I feel reasonably attractive and satisfied with my looks.
2. When I gain weight, I feel flawed in some way.
3. When I don't make an effort to look my best, I feel ashamed of myself or worry that I come across as a bad person.
4. I would be mortified if people knew what I really weigh.
5. Generally, I think more about what my body can do or how it feels than how it looks.
6. I feel proud of at least a few things about my body.
7. I often compare how my body looks to how other people look—and it stacks up badly.
8. I'm glad I look like me.
9. I'm always trying to change how I look because I'm so unhappy with the status quo.
10. I usually cringe when I see myself in snapshots or catch my reflection in the mirror.

Now, tally up your responses, then read the corresponding analysis:

1. T: 2 F: 1
2. T: 1 F: 2
3. T: 1 F: 2
4. T: 1 F: 2
5. T: 2 F: 1

6. T: 2 F: 1
7. T: 1 F: 2
8. T: 2 F: 1
9. T: 1 F: 2
10. T: 1 F: 2

17–20: FRIENDLY WITH YOUR BODY

You're at peace with your body and reasonably pleased with what you see, quirks and all. You also keep things in perspective. Your looks aren't of paramount importance to you; you're more focused on what your body can do and how it feels.

13–16: SO-SO ABOUT YOUR BODY

Your relationship with your body runs hot and cold. Sometimes you feel good about it; other times, you feel really, really bad. Maybe you're falling into the judgment trap; or maybe you're spending too much time comparing curves and dress sizes. Instead, focus your energy on bolstering your body image from within.

10–12: ON THE WARPATH WITH YOUR BODY

You wouldn't dare be this critical of a friend's body. So why are you of your own? The trouble may be that you have too much of your self-esteem tied up in appearance issues; or that you're so busy envying other people's looks that you haven't even tried to appreciate your own. To grow more comfortable in your own skin, stop thinking about your body's shortcomings and start noticing its good qualities.

GIVING YOUR BODY IMAGE A MAKEOVER

Fortunately, there are steps you can take to improve your body image from the inside out. First, it helps to test your perception versus the reality. Take out a tape measure and before you use it, guess your measurements for your waist, hips and thighs; then check your estimates against the reality. If you're like most women, you'll discover that these body parts aren't as big as you thought they were. This exercise can help you begin to see your body as it actually is.

Then the trick is to alter your perception of your physical self, or shape up your body image in other ways. The goal: to feel better about your body and yourself now, regardless of whether you lose weight. As difficult as this goal may sound, it is possible. In a study at the University of Vermont, 24 women who weighed within the normal range for their height but had disturbed body images underwent cognitive behavior therapy to improve their body image. Each week for two hours they met in small groups and talked about different facets of body image such as cultural and familial influences, the negative consequences of being so preoccupied with their weight and body shape, the issue of size perception, and how feelings about their appearance related to other beliefs about their self-worth. As homework, the participants practiced saying self-enhancing things and refuting negative statements to themselves; they also began exposing themselves to situations that scared them because of their body-image issues. At the end of the study, the women's body images improved substantially. Not only did they feel more satisfied with their bodies, but they stopped being so preoccupied with their weight or shape, reduced their minds' distortion of their size, began feeling less fat and self-conscious around others, and stopped avoiding situations in which attention would be drawn to their appearance. What's more, they showed less dietary restraint in their eating habits, less guilt about eating, and they overate less frequently.

Indeed, there's some evidence that improving your body image may even facilitate the weight-loss process by making it less stressful. After all, if you can relax your ideals about your body and your eating habits, you'll feel less pressure while trying to slim down, which will make you less prone to stress-related overeating. What follows are eight ways to befriend your body while you're making lifestyle changes that will improve your health and appearance:

1) Silence your inner critic. The next time that little voice inside your head calls you *fat* or *thunder thighs*, tell it to pipe down. Defend yourself to yourself with compliments or remind yourself of all the things you're doing to improve your health and to take care of yourself.

2) Accept your body today. Asking you to start loving your body is probably too tall an order if you've spent a lifetime disliking it, but you can at least make peace with it. That means accepting your body and acknowledging how it looks without judging it. Instead, use positive or neutral affirmations such as "My body is strong and healthy" to reassure yourself that your body is acceptable as it is. If you do this every day, you'll probably start to think less frequently and less critically about your body.

3) Imagine how you'd like to look. Close your eyes and picture how you'd look if you were at your optimal weight, if you truly adored your body. Think about how you'd feel inside that body, how you'd move, act and express yourself. Now practice walking down the street or into a room as if you felt that way right now. Keep that vision in mind as you go through your daily routine and you'll be able to conjure the feeling from the inside.

4) *Pamper the part you're most critical of.* From this moment on, stop considering that body part as flawed and start thinking of it as quirky or part of what makes you unique. In reshaping your body image, it helps if you celebrate your quirks by treating them as if they were special—by treating your thighs to a rub with an aromatic lotion, for example. If you begin to nurture the body parts you're least fond of, you'll grow to love, or at least accept, them as your own.

5) *Confront situations that produce body anxiety.* It's all too easy to get into the habit of avoiding situations that send your body image into the depths of despair, whether it's heading to the beach, wearing shorts to a picnic or even going to the gym. But the only way to get over this anxiety is to gradually face these situations. If you're afraid to wear a bathing suit in public, you might try wearing it in the privacy of your bedroom and look at yourself in the mirror without voicing criticism. Then gradually work up to wearing it in your backyard, then to a pool where you don't know anyone, and finally to the beach with friends. By facing your body-image fears head on, you'll gradually overcome them.

6) *Start a body-talk journal.* Chronicle situations when you begin to criticize your body and what kinds of factors seem to trigger the body bashing. Take note of anything else that could be upsetting you; it may be that you're using your body as a scapegoat when you're really bothered by something completely unrelated (such as getting chewed out by your boss or having a fight with your spouse). If you can detect patterns in what sparks negative thoughts about your body, you'll be in a position to short-circuit them (through relaxation exercises, for example) before they take a toll on your body image.

7) *Look in the mirror.* Many women who have a history of being heavy have spent much of their adult lives going out of their way to avoid mirrors, especially full-length ones. They don't really have any idea what they actually look like; they've simply distorted their vision of themselves in their minds. Start occasionally looking in the mirror. The aim is simply to grow more comfortable with what you see.

8) *Focus on your body's health.* If you pour your energy and commitment into leading a healthier lifestyle and doing the best things you can for your body—by improving your eating habits and exercising regularly, for instance—you'll be doing yourself three favors: You will be treating your body with love and respect; you will get in touch with how your body feels rather than just how it looks; and finally, you will have a more constructive goal instead of simply aiming for improving your appearance. If you don't love and take care of your body unconditionally, who will?

DRESSING RIGHT

Many women who don't feel good about their bodies wear baggy clothes in an attempt to hide their figures. Often this just adds to the problem, making them feel frumpy or unattractive. It is possible to dress with style while you're trying to lose weight, and it can help you feel better about your body—and yourself—in the meantime.

Do:

- **Go monochromatic.** Dressing in one color from your neck to your shoes creates a streamlined effect. If you don't want to stick with just one hue, choose colors that are in the same family. Keep in mind: Darker colors tend to be more slimming.
- **Select drapey fabrics.** If you opt for classic but slightly loose styles made from supple fabrics like cotton, rayon, silk and lightweight knits, you'll flatter your figure because the fabric will gently caress your curves.
- **Choose a long, slightly fitted jacket.** It can add a touch of elegance while hiding your hips and derriere. And it can be worn with both long and short skirts, as well as pants.
- **Take the straight route.** An A-line or straight skirt emphasizes the length of your frame, while downplaying width.
- **Create a leggy look.** To make your legs look longer and leaner, wear the same color panty hose as your skirts or shoes.

Don't:

- **Be bold.** Stay away from large floral or horizontal patterns, bold prints, and bulky fabrics. These tend to magnify size.
- **Wear large shoulder pads.** They'll only give you a linebacker look, adding bulk to your frame.
- **Pick styles with oversized buttons or trims.** While trouser cuffs and pockets can add width to the body, double-breasted tops and breast pockets create a top-heavy look.
- **Choose flared skirts or elastic waists.** These cause fabric to pouf out below the waist, adding unwanted girth to your hips.
- **Wear out-of-proportion accessories.** Keep the scale suitable to your body frame: If you're petite, dainty jewelry and accessories will look fine on you; if you're large boned, on the other hand, bigger and bolder may be better.

Key Points

♦ Body image constitutes about 25 percent of a person's self-esteem; it's a particularly potent factor for a woman's feelings about herself and her sense of self-worth, according to psychologists.

♦ An overwhelming number of American women are dissatisfied with their bodies, regardless of their weight. What's more, most women overestimate their body size.

♦ A negative body image can color your entire world, making you more susceptible to depression, anxiety, shame and unhealthy eating habits.

♦ Your body image is the result of accumulated family influences, peer acceptance issues, positive and negative feedback you've received about yourself from key people in your life, and whether you've adopted cultural standards of beauty as your own.

♦ You can improve your body image from the inside out while you're making lifestyle changes that will enhance your figure.

Goals

◇ *Identify the parts of your body that you love and think about why you're fond of them. Do the same for those you dislike, then think about how you can begin to make peace with them.*

◇ *Try to stop your distorted ways of thinking about your body. Instead of criticizing your looks, answer that criticism with a nod to reality—that your thighs are not huge, they're simply a bit larger than you'd like, for example.*

◇ *Expose yourself to situations that produce anxiety about your body, but do it gradually. Start with low-risk situations and work up to more challenging ones. Do it with a friend for moral support.*

◇ *Force yourself to get to know your body. Look at yourself in the mirror and try to simply see, not judge, yourself. By getting in the habit of looking at yourself uncritically, you'll probably start to notice aspects of your body that you actually like—aspects you've never bothered to notice before.*

◇ *Start treating yourself as if your body were flawless now. Think about how it would feel and try to capture that feeling in the way you move and act. If you do this regularly, you can boost your appreciation of your body from the inside.*

How Do You Handle Stress?

> "Support is key when it comes to handling stress. My network includes my best friends—my children, my former husband, the people who spend many hours working for me and Josh, my trainer."

STRESS. IT'S EVER PRESENT, maybe even unavoidable, in modern life, especially for a working parent whose plate of responsibilities is always full. It's blamed for all sorts of physical and emotional ills, from headaches and digestive problems to depression and anxiety.

When it comes to losing weight, stress can be one of the largest potholes in the dieting journey. According to weight-loss experts, stress is one of the biggest predictors of gaining or regaining weight. When research scientists at the Massachusetts Institute of Technology surveyed people about their tendency to overeat when under stress, they found that anger, exhaustion, depression and boredom were especially big triggers for women; not far behind were frustration, tension and worry.

Indeed, stress can turn even the most determined dieter into a spineless snacker. Many people use food as a way to pacify themselves in times of stress. On happy occasions, they may eat to celebrate; in distressing times, they may use comfort foods to console themselves. This overuse of food is not surprising considering that in our culture food is a more socially acceptable substance for overindulgence than, say, alcohol or drugs. Plus, it's readily available.

Research has found that life's major sources of stress stem from situations that are either unknown, unpredictable or uncontrollable. Whether the stress is positive (getting married, having a baby or buying a new house) or negative (suffering financial or marital problems) it can produce physiological changes, including a surge of adrenaline and other stress hormones that have widespread effects on the body.

But everyone reacts to stress differently, and what may be highly stressful for one person is easy to shrug off for another. Moving to a new home could be a positive stressor for one woman and a source of negative stress for another, depending on the circumstances and her feelings about the move. While shopping for clothes may be an enjoyable pastime for one woman, it could be anxiety producing for someone who's dissatisfied with her looks.

Dieting can be a stressor in its own right. After all, it probably involves a foreign way of eating and the outcome isn't altogether predictable. It involves a period of sustained change and challenge, which can be emotionally difficult. Moreover, the quest for the perfect figure can create stress that comes from within: Holding yourself to impossible physical standards and creating rigid rules about eating can be enormously stressful because you can't ever meet them. A study conducted at Pennsylvania State University examined how women and men adjust their food intake in response to stress. Not only did the researchers find that women are more likely to eat more in response to stress, but they concluded that for women "the inability to maintain control of self-imposed rules concerning food intake is an important factor in the relationship between stress and eating."

The good news about this cause of stress is that you can revamp your definition of fitness and beauty, making them more realistic and attainable and, hence, less stressful to aim for. Other sources of stress aren't so easily controlled. Since stress is here to stay, the best you can do is to pinpoint the sources of stress that are difficult for you, then learn how to reduce or manage them more effectively. This is a goal that is achievable and it can make a big difference for your day-to-day life. Not only will learning to manage stress help you stay on a more even emotional keel, but it can help you gain control of your weight, too.

EATING OUT OUR EMOTIONS

For some people, it's often easier to numb negative emotions with food than to tolerate, get in touch with or articulate them. Many stress-eaters can't stand feeling bad emotionally; they want to fix their feelings as soon as possible but they don't know how, so they eat. Others have a hard time distinguishing anger from disappointment, or anxiety from fatigue—they simply don't have the words at their disposal

The Physiology of Stress

Whether you're faced with an acute stressor, such as narrowly avoiding a car accident, or ongoing stress, such as deadline pressure at work, the way you react to stress has a lot to do with a cascade of events that occur in the body. Anxiety-producing situations often set off what's known as the "fight-or-flight" response: The hypothalamus in the brain triggers the release of adrenaline, cortisol and other stress hormones, which in turn cause blood sugar, blood pressure, heart rate and body temperature to rise. This puts your body into a superalert mode, preparing you to fight or run for your life.

In fact, just sitting around worrying about stressful things can turn on this same physiological chain of events. And if this response is repeatedly turned on—or if you can't turn it off *after* a stressful event—there's considerable evidence that this adaptive response can become damaging in itself, contributing to a variety of stress-related diseases and ailments.

Research has found, for example, that these stress hormones can suppress the immune system, cause the blood to clot more quickly, and produce muscle contractions as if to prepare the body for sudden movement; they can also block the release of pain-killing chemicals in the brain, making you more sensitive to pain. In addition, stress can trigger headaches, indigestion, backaches, cold sores and insomnia, as well as exacerbating chronic illnesses such as asthma, diabetes, ulcers and arthritis. Given all this, it's hardly surprising that an estimated 75 percent of all doctor's visits are for stress-related complaints.

> **"** *Being a people pleaser, I've discovered, is a very problematic trait to have when you are in the public eye. I find it terribly difficult when I read something negative about myself in the press. My friends just shrug and tell me to brush it off like an annoying fly, but I can't. I do care what others say about me. What I have learned is not to care quite so much.* **"**

to describe their feelings. It's hard for them to distinguish between physical sensations and emotional ones. As a result, they may rush to the fridge when they feel needy, mistaking emotional fragility for physical hunger. They might reach for a candy bar as their heart starts racing when they're stuck in a traffic jam in route to an important appointment. In other words, overeating becomes their way of dealing with emotions they don't understand or the physical symptoms they produce. It's an approach that's probably so ingrained that it becomes automatic.

These patterns are particularly common among people-pleasers or people who are more focused on fulfilling other people's needs than their own, some psychologists say. This is a phenomenon that's especially common to women, given how we're socialized to tune in to others' feelings. Sometimes these habits can also be developed during your early years, particularly if your parents comforted you with food rather than their attention or if they used food to console their own distress. In some instances, emotional overeating can also reflect a lack of tolerance for emotions. Rather than sitting with a feeling or exploring it, emotional eaters want to act on it; they try to quash the feeling with food. And they want that feeling to go away *now*.

Part of this has to do with a need for immediate gratification. Eating a box of chocolates might help you feel better briefly after, say, a fight with your husband. But the effect doesn't last long, especially when you realize the damage you've done to your diet. Indeed, a recent study conducted at Wesleyan University in Connecticut found that depression, stress, low self-esteem and the need to avoid certain situations were major factors leading to weight gain among women; what's more, women who'd lost weight were more likely to feel terrible about a relapse to unhealthy eating habits and end up regaining pounds as a result.

STRESS 911

While you're learning to handle stress differently, crises are bound to come up that truly test your resolve. In those instances, you need an emergency plan that will reduce stress without blowing your weight-control plan. The next time your stress-meter registers overload, try these diet-saving strategies:

♦ Give yourself a 10-minute break and do something distracting such as calling a friend or taking a walk around the block (or up and down the stairs in your office building). Most cravings last about 10 minutes, so if you can impose an alternate activity for that long, the urge to nibble will probably pass.

- Breathe away your stress. Inhale slowly for five seconds, breathing deeply almost as if you were sighing into yourself; hold the breath for five seconds, then slowly exhale for another five seconds. Repeat this 5 to 10 times, focusing on the rhythm of your breathing to relax. This will help calm your body's reaction to stress.

- Expose yourself to a soothing scent. Research has found that the aromas of vanilla and green apples are particularly effective at reducing stress but it's important to find one that appeals to you. Buy a small bottle of the essential or aromatic oil or scent and keep it handy for when stress strikes.

- Close your eyes and repeat a soothing mantra to yourself, such as "This too shall pass." Spend a few moments visualizing a less stressful time in your life, picturing yourself feeling relaxed and at ease. This can help spark the feeling when you need it.

- If all else fails, eat what you crave *in small amounts*. The key is to exercise portion control. At only 25 calories apiece, three chocolate kisses won't harm your diet, and getting the fix could prevent you from overeating.

TUNING IN TO YOURSELF

Getting in touch with your feelings can seem like a Herculean task if you've spent much of your life trying to avoid them, but it can be done. The key is to learn to sit with them and mull them over without obsessing about them, instead of rushing into action. One way to do this is to start keeping a journal: Before you turn in for the night, spend about 10 minutes writing about your foremost concerns and emotions. Don't worry about the quality of the writing; just spill your thoughts onto paper, letting the words flow the best you can. This can help you clue in to your feelings, and gradually you'll begin to feel more comfortable with them.

Not only can keeping a journal help you cope with stress better, but it can improve your physical health, too. For more than a decade, James Pennebaker, Ph.D., now a psychology professor at the University of Texas in Austin, has investigated the benefits of writing about personal subjects. In one study, students who wrote about their intimate feelings about entering college for 20 minutes three days per week had many fewer visits to the health center for physical illnesses over the next several months. He believes this helps because translating emotional experiences into language helps organize them so that you understand them better. This, in turn, can eliminate the urgency to act—by rushing to the refrigerator, for instance.

The first step to handling stress more constructively is to begin using stress-busting techniques—such as working out, doing deep-breathing or progressive muscle relaxation exercises, performing meditation or yoga—on a regular basis. Doing this can help relieve tension and make you less emotionally reactive.

The second step is to identify situations that are highly stressful for you and develop a plan of action for coping ahead of time. For example, if family squabbles typically incite the urge to nosh, think about a more constructive way to handle those frustrations: Take a break and listen to music or go for a jog. Or if you suffer frequent snack attacks whenever you feel lonely, make a date to visit, or at least call, a close friend the next time your husband goes out of town on business.

By mapping out healthier alternatives, you'll know how to help yourself the next time stress floods you with negative emotions. Although you may not be able to control the source of stress, you can control your response to it. And that will have a positive impact on your emotional life as well as your weight-control efforts.

Do You Abuse Food?

1. **You are most likely to eat more than usual when you:**
   a) are ravenously hungry.
   b) need to comfort yourself because you're feeling blue, anxious or frazzled.
   c) are celebrating a special occasion—whether it's a promotion at work or a visit with a close friend.

2. **Last night, you vastly overate at a dinner party and today you feel guilty. What are you likely to do?**
   a) Compensate by cutting way back on what you'll eat today.
   b) Chalk it up to a mistake and return to your healthy diet plan.
   c) Skip breakfast and eat normally the rest of the day.

3. **When you overeat, what do you usually indulge in?**
   a) Larger portions of a balanced meal.
   b) Sweet or starchy foods.
   c) Salty or crunchy foods.

4. **True or false: Your eating habits vary considerably, depending on how you feel about yourself on a given day.**

5. **Where do you usually eat dinner?**
   a) At the table with your family.
   b) In front of the TV.
   c) On the fly between tending to your kids or getting things done around the house.

6. **Yes or no: Do you ever punish yourself by withholding favorite foods or treats?**

7. On those days when you have the luxury of a quiet meal, what's likely to be going through your mind while you eat?

    a) The events of the day.
    b) Nothing special; you simply try to enjoy the food.
    c) Guilt about what you're putting in your mouth.

8. True or false: Your weight varies considerably depending upon how much stress you're under.

9. Yes or no: Do you keep a mental list of forbidden foods ("bad" foods that you will not allow yourself to have)?

10. It's your birthday and you really have a hankering for a piece of flourless chocolate cake. Which of the following are you most likely to do?

    a) Deny yourself. It has too many calories.
    b) Enjoy a piece then sneak a second sliver before putting it away.
    c) Treat yourself to a piece and savor every mouth-watering bite.

Now, tally up your points, then read the corresponding section for advice.

    1. a) 1 b) 3 c) 2

    2. a) 3 b) 1 c) 2

    3. a) 1 b) 2 c) 2

    4. True: 3 False: 1

    5. a) 1 b) 2 c) 2

    6. Yes: 3 No: 1

    7. a) 2 b) 1 c) 3

    8. True: 3 False: 1

    9. Yes: 3 No: 1

    10. a) 3 b) 3 c) 1

22–28: FELONY ABUSE

It looks like you're using food as a weapon—against yourself, that is. How to clean up your eating habits? Throw out your list of forbidden foods; all foods are fine in moderation so long as you maintain a low-fat, balanced diet over the long haul. The truth is, indulging from time to time will reduce the urge to cheat or binge.

16–21: MISDEMEANOR INFRACTION

Your eating habits seem to be slightly erratic, occasionally veering into dangerous territory. Start making an effort to eat only when you're hungry and to find other activities to relieve bad moods, boredom or fatigue. Second, stop skipping meals because it hurts more than it helps. Not only can meal-skipping disrupt your routine, it can set you up for overeating at the next meal. Instead, aim for consistency.

10–15: HEALTHY RESPECT

Congratulations! You seem to be abiding by the healthy laws of food consumption. You eat regular meals, find other ways to deal with your emotions and treat yourself to foods you love on occasion. In other words, you allow yourself to take pleasure in food but not too much. During meals, you probably try to experience and appreciate a variety of flavors and textures but you exercise portion control. Keep up the good habits.

Key Points

- People who struggle with overeating often have trouble dealing with emotional issues; instead, they use food to comfort themselves.

- Everyone reacts to stress differently, and what may be highly stressful for one person may be no big deal to another.

- Even dieting can be stressful, especially since it involves changing your eating habits, which can be difficult. Setting unrealistic weight-loss goals and creating rigid rules about eating can add to the burden, making you more susceptible to emotional overeating.

- Emotional overeating is especially common among people-pleasers or people who are more focused on tending to other people's needs than their own, according to psychologists.

- By pinpointing positive and negative sources of stress in your life, you can then figure out healthier ways to cope with them rather than eating.

Goals

◇   *Identify the biggest sources of stress in your life—both the ones you can do something about and the ones you can't control—and write them down. Next to each stressor jot down how you typically deal with it. This will help you pinpoint your usual responses to stress.*

◇   *Map out a list of healthier ways to react to stress—by making a reciprocal agreement with a friend to chat on the phone when your kids start driving you crazy, for example; or by relaxing with a bubble bath after an especially taxing day at work—and post it on your refrigerator.*

◇   *Start a mood journal, in which you record your most intimate thoughts and feelings. This will help you get in touch with your emotions and become more comfortable tolerating them.*

◇   *Try to make meals a sacred time, during which you do nothing but enjoy the food. Savor the tastes and textures, and let dining be a relaxing, sensory experience.*

◇   *Treat yourself to your favorite foods occasionally. There's no such thing as an inherently good or bad food; all foods are fine in moderation if you maintain a low-fat, balanced diet over the long haul.*

Changing Your Behavior

THERE'S NO DOUBT ABOUT IT: OLD HABITS ARE HARD TO SHAKE. But hard doesn't mean impossible. Whether your aim is to reform your sofa spud ways and become an exercise convert, clean up your eating habits so they're healthier, lose those extra pounds you've been toting around, or get rid of self-damaging behavior such as emotional overeating, you can be successful if you use a variety of strategies and learn how to deal with setbacks.

The key is to find what works for you. Don't be afraid to reinvent your own strategies; what helps today may not next week. While diet and exercise guidelines are helpful in giving you a framework for making these types of changes, ultimately it's up to you to devise your own rules and come up with your own ideas for leading a healthy lifestyle. Then, you'll need to practice them, with patience and awareness. Remember: Your eating, exercise and emotional habits evolved over years, so it's just not going to be possible to change them overnight. You'll need to cultivate patience with yourself for slipups (because they *will* happen), and you'll need to develop awareness of your eating, exercise and emotional habits, which will have a powerful effect on your ability to lose weight.

Of course, it's also important to keep a close eye on what you can do today. In order to maintain your motivation as you make these changes, you'll need to start living in the here and now, not in yesterday's unsuccessful dieting history, or in tomorrow's vision of a svelte new you. If you remind yourself of the outcome you desire and outline a plan for how to get there, you'll be able to take concrete steps toward your goals. Then you can use some of the motivation-boosting strategies you've learned—talking up your strengths, visualizing success, repeating your personal mantra and so on—to keep yourself going in challenging times. By now, you undoubtedly realize that there are no magical measures that will melt off the pounds. But there are tried-and-true steps that will help you shed excess weight and keep it off for good—if you make these changes slowly but steadily.

SECRETS OF SUCCESSFUL LOSERS

In the largest study, to date, of people who have been successful at losing weight and maintaining their slimmer, sleeker shapes over the long term, researchers from the University of Pittsburgh School of Medicine and the University of Colorado Health Sciences Center have unearthed some surprising secrets. Nearly 800 women and men have participated in the project, called the National Weight Control

> **"My** schedule can be mad! Sometimes, I'll be running from meeting to meeting and before I know it the day is over and I haven't eaten a thing. To offset this, I may pack a lunch—maybe cherry tomatoes, chicken salad and a roll—to take with me and eat in the car on my way to the next meeting.**"**

Registry, and have lost and kept off at least 30 pounds for more than a year. These dieters had tried to lose weight before but hadn't been successful.

What made this time the charm? While they used a variety of dietary strategies to slim down, sticking with a low-fat, low-calorie diet and exercising regularly were essential to losing weight and maintaining their loss. As expected, too, many participants restricted their intake of certain types of foods and limited their portion sizes. What *was* surprising: Most of the successful dieters ate nearly five times per day, including snacks. They didn't eat out at restaurants much, choosing to prepare most of their foods at home instead.

Another eye-opening factor: 92 percent of participants exercised at home while they lost weight, and most relied on one or two activities—usually walking and aerobic dancing for the women—to peel off the pounds. They all developed very active lifestyles, expending more than 2,500 calories per week through exercise—the equivalent of walking 28 miles per week. (This exceeds the fitness recommendations from both the Centers for Disease Control and Prevention and the American College of Sports Medicine.)

Now here's the real surprise: The majority of participants report that maintaining the weight loss is easier than losing the pounds. Perhaps that's because the payoffs really kick in during the maintenance phase. More than 85 percent of participants report that their general quality of life has improved and that they have more energy, physical mobility and self-confidence as a result of losing weight. Most experienced an upswing in their physical health and general mood, as well, and many claim that their relationships with others, even with strangers, have improved.

If there's one resounding message from the Weight Control Registry, it's that maintaining weight loss requires a lifetime commitment. Even now, most of the successful dieters continue to count calories and fat grams, which suggests that self-monitoring is one of the keys to their success. But they aren't obsessed: They don't check in with the scale several times a day. In fact, 38 percent weigh themselves daily and 31 percent weigh themselves just once a week.

Among the things that really distinguishes successful dieters from the not-so-successful ones (besides their weight loss, of course) is their willingness to do things their way, to find tactics that really work for them. In other words, they customized their approach: Some joined a program, others did it on their own or with the help of a dietitian. Another key factor: They truly discovered what would really motivate them. They lost weight for themselves, usually for medical reasons, such as varicose veins, fatigue or low back pain, or emotional ones, such as a divorce and a desire for a new start.

MONITORING YOURSELF

> "I feel great about turning 40. I've lived eight lives in one. My goals are to live every moment to its fullest—and to run down the beach in a black bikini."

When it comes to monitoring their habits, many people are resistant to the idea of writing down their eating, exercise and emotional behavior. Maybe it's because they feel like it's nothing more than policing themselves; or maybe they're worried that such record-keeping will remove the spontaneity from life.

But research has found that keeping a food diary, an exercise log or a mood journal really can help when you're trying to change your ways. It leads to accountability, for one thing, making you take responsibility for your actions; it can reinforce your commitment to lead a healthier lifestyle; and it creates a record that can help you draw connections between troublesome situations (such as parties) or difficult-to-handle emotions (such as anger) and unhealthy habits (like overeating). This, in turn, can help you figure out healthier ways to respond to those circumstances (by avoiding the buffet) or feelings (by going for a walk outside to cool off, rather than to the fridge).

In fact, a recent study published in *Health Psychology* found that people who diligently self-monitored their eating habits—by observing and recording every single bite of food they consumed—even managed to lose weight between Thanksgiving and New Year's Eve, a notorious danger zone for dieters. Besides jotting down what they ate, the dieters counted the calories in those foods, which likely helped them plan subsequent meals and budget calories for splurges. Those who didn't keep a record, by contrast, gained considerable weight during those weeks.

MANAGING SETBACKS

However you decide to lose weight, it's absolutely essential that you cultivate patience. You gained weight over a period of time, not overnight. Your eating habits developed over the course of your life, which means that it's not realistic to expect permanent changes to come right away, which also means that you can count on occasional setbacks. They're inevitable for anyone who's embarking on a major lifestyle change.

If you lose your willpower and really overindulge on fatty fare at a party one night, that's not a big deal unless you continue to overeat. Likewise, slipping back into sedentary ways during a particularly hectic week or while suffering a bout of the flu won't ruin your weight-management efforts; what's important is to get back on your exercise program as soon as possible. In other words, you'll need to keep the big picture in mind and try to be aware of how you handle eating and exercise hurdles. If you can become conscious of what emotional and circumstantial factors prompt you to overeat and learn to anticipate them, for example, you'll stay in better control of your weight-loss plan.

> *"I try to learn something new every day. I'm a single working woman who misses her children when she's away on business. I look to others who are doing it successfully and see what I can learn from their routine, habits and actions."*

When lapses do occur, it helps if you interpret them as a signal for self-examination. What's going on? Why did this particular situation—whether it's a work-related cocktail party or a family celebration—trigger the urge to overeat, for example? Did it conjure up certain feelings that are hard for you to handle? If so, how could you deal with them more constructively? If you can identify your feelings before you act, it may be helpful to give yourself a time-out—say, with a quick visit to the ladies' room during a social gathering—and to remind yourself how much progress you've made in your goals and why you're trying to improve your lifestyle.

If the lapse is history, don't beat yourself up about it. Forgive yourself and move on by plunging into action and employing the techniques you've developed for handling difficult diet challenges, whether it's asking a friend or family member for support, using a powerful stress-busting strategy, or distracting yourself from the risky situation. What's important is to put the brakes on this runaway train immediately and to get your plan back on track. That way you'll prevent a momentary lapse of willpower from turning into a relapse, in which case you'll begin to gain weight.

Above all, take your weight-loss program day by day. If you begin every morning with the idea that you have a fresh opportunity to eat more healthfully, to pack in plenty of exercise, and to begin to peel off excess pounds, you'll stay more motivated. So will ending each day by reminding yourself of what you did right and by commending yourself for making these healthy lifestyle changes. With each change that you adopt and each pound that you shed, you'll move that much closer to joining the winner's circle of successful dieters.

THE STAGES OF CHANGE

It's not enough to want to change, and being committed to change isn't enough, either. What can really make a difference in altering your behavior is to understand the structure of change and how you can maximize your opportunities for success by using appropriate problem-solving skills.

For more than a decade, a team of three psychologists—James O. Prochaska, Carlo C. DiClemente and John C. Norcross—has studied how people make lasting changes in their lives without the benefit of therapy. It's not a matter of luck, it turns out; nor is it solely a matter of willpower. What they've found is change occurs in six predictable stages. If you can identify the stage of change you are in, you can gain a sense of what strategies you're ready for and how to maintain motivation. Then you can take the following steps to push yourself to the next stage of changing your ways.

1. Precontemplation

At this point, people are often resistant to change. They don't really intend to alter their behavior or their diet, for example. Instead, they often deny that there's a problem or they rationalize why they should maintain the status quo. If they give lip service to wanting or trying to change, it's often in response to pressure from other people. But as soon as the pressure eases, they're likely to return to their usual ways.

Your best strategies: Start thinking about the self-defeating excuses that block your ability to make healthy changes in your life. Become conscious of when you use them, and why. This is a good time to gather information about what constitutes a healthy diet, about the benefits of exercise and other critical issues. It's also a prime opportunity to ask friends or family members to talk to you about why and how you should introduce these changes. Enlisting their support can make a big difference, but be specific in telling them how you'd like them to help: that you don't want them to nag, for example, but you would appreciate some gentle reminders.

2. Contemplation

By now, people have become aware that a problem (with their diet, sedentary lifestyle or emotional habits, for example) exists, and they've begun to think seriously about taking action to overcome it. On some level, however, they may still be grappling with resistance to change. Maybe they're waiting for the perfect time to launch their plan of action. Maybe they're still hoping that the whole issue would simply and magically go away. As a result, they can remain stuck at this phase for long periods of time, unable to move forward.

Your best strategies: Think about why you want to change your habits and what your real goals are. To kick-start your motivation, make two lists: one of the possible benefits of improving your habits (more energy, a healthier body, being able to play with your kids more vigorously and so on) and another of the potentially harmful consequences that could result from not altering your behavior (dying at a premature age or losing your mobility if you're considerably overweight or sedentary, for example). It also helps to begin monitoring your diet, exercise and emotional habits to gauge both your starting point and what really needs changing.

3. Preparation

At this point, someone's intentions are real and they're on the verge of taking action. They may have already taken baby steps toward their goals—by reducing their fat intake slightly, for example, or by starting to walk on errands instead of driving—but they're not yet ready to fully jump into the process of dramatically altering their habits. They may be slightly afraid of commitment, anxious about taking the plunge. As a result, this is more of a rehearsal phase, as they prepare mentally for what's ahead.

Your best strategies: The keys to getting over this hurdle are to make change a priority in your life, *then* to make a commitment. Don't keep it to yourself; go public with it. Tell your family and friends about what you plan to do so they're on board to help. Next, develop a plan of action that suits your lifestyle but also incorporates helpful hints from others who've taken similar steps and set a date to launch it. In the meantime, continue taking small steps in the right direction; think of it as your way of warming up.

4. Action

This is when people swing into action and start modifying their habits and behavior. But the hard part isn't necessarily over. Often people erroneously equate action with change when, in fact, change can be slow to come even at this phase. After all, change involves a major commitment of time and energy, and stumbling blocks will come up. The good news is, this is the time when their efforts are most visible to other people so there's more opportunity for positive reinforcement from others.

Your best strategies: To make these changes easier, it helps if you let your environment support you—by keeping your workout gear next to your bed to remind you to get moving first thing in the morning, for instance. Modifying your environment can also help avert high-risk situations from cropping up. If you keep healthful snacks in your desk drawer, you'll be less likely to hit the vending machine when you have to work late. To spur yourself on, try to keep positive thoughts in mind and be ready to counter negative ones when they pop up. You'll also need to think about healthful substitutes—such as exercise, attention-diverting hobbies or relaxation techniques—when you feel like lapsing into your old patterns of, say, emotional eating.

5. Maintenance

At this point, a person might have changed her eating and exercise habits, and possibly her emotional habits as well. Now the trick is to make them permanent. That's no easy feat. The challenges here are to prevent relapse and keep focusing on all the positive benefits she's reaped as a result of those changes—increased self-confidence, less fatigue, more energy, for example. She'll need to guard against slipups; when they do happen, it's wise to try to minimize them and learn from the experience.

Your best strategies: Have a plan ready for how you'll deal with high-risk situations, such as stress, parties, traveling or whatever makes it difficult for you to sustain your new, healthful habits. If you relapse, initiate damage control as soon as possible and climb back on your plan. Keep an eye on the long-term perspective: Making these changes permanent is a lengthy process and you'll need to exercise persistence and patience with yourself.

6. Termination

This phase is the ultimate goal for anyone trying to change her habits. It's the end of the road, the point where past unhealthy behavior is truly considered history. By this point, she will have complete confidence in her ability to handle difficult situations without lapsing into old patterns of eating, for example. The newfound habits will have become such an integral part of her life that she wouldn't think twice about having it any other way. She will, in effect, be leaving the cycle of change with a new image of herself, a can-do spirit and a healthier lifestyle.

Your best strategies: Congratulate yourself, you deserve it! From this point on, your life won't be problem-free but you're in fine shape to handle whatever comes your way. Don't rest on your laurels, though. Keep pursuing self-enhancing activities and dreams. Your life will be that much more gratifying and healthy for it.

Key Points

- Diet and exercise guidelines can provide you with a framework for making these healthy changes, but ultimately it's up to you to devise your own rules and come up with your own strategies for healthy living.

- In the largest study of successful dieters to date, researchers have found that sticking with a low-fat, low-calorie diet and exercising regularly helped the participants shed and keep off at least 30 pounds.

- Successful dieters aren't afraid to do things their way, to find tactics that really work for them—and to use them when they work for them.

- Along the road to change, lapses are inevitable for anyone. But in and of themselves, they're not necessarily setbacks; it all depends on how you handle them.

- Changing unhealthy habits involves six predictable stages, researchers have found. If you can identify the stage where you are, you can take steps to spur yourself forward.

Goals:

◇ *If you've tried to lose weight before, without success, think about your dieting history, which strategies helped (in terms of food plans, exercise programs and behavioral approaches), and which didn't.*

◇ *To make sure your eating habits stay on track, keep a food diary. Not only can it serve as a reality check when you begin to stray, but it increases your awareness of what you put into your mouth because it makes you accountable.*

◇ *The next time you lapse into old patterns, consider it a wake-up call and do a little self-examination. Consider why you're falling back into habits you're trying to kick and consider how you can handle those triggers more constructively.*

◇   *Go public with your program:* Announce to family members and friends what you're trying to do and enlist their support. But be specific: Let them know how they can best help you. Also, make tracking your improvements a family affair to keep your motivation high.

◇   *Create an environment that's conducive to the positive changes you're trying to make.* Don't keep lots of junk food or other high-fat fare around the house, but do keep your gym bag handy to remind you of your exercise commitment.

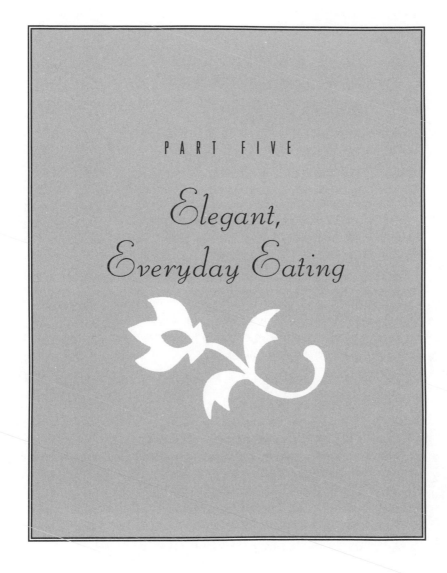

PART FIVE

*Elegant,
Everyday Eating*

Breads

Cherry Muffins with Amaretto Glaze

USE FRESH SOUR CHERRIES when they're plentiful during June and July; the rest of the year, thaw frozen sour cherries, or rinse and drain canned sour cherries. Make sure that the muffins have cooled completely before you glaze them; if you brush on the syrup when the muffins are still warm, it will be absorbed rather than harden into a topping.

MAKES 18 SERVINGS

1 cup low-fat buttermilk
2 eggs
4 tablespoons unsalted butter, melted
1 teaspoon almond extract
½ cup packed dark brown sugar
1⅔ cups all-purpose flour
½ tablespoon baking powder
1 teaspoon baking soda
½ teaspoon salt
1¼ cups sour cherries, pitted
¼ cup granulated sugar
¼ cup amaretto liqueur

1. Preheat the oven to 375° F; spray an 18-cup muffin tin with nonstick cooking spray.

2. In a large bowl, whisk the buttermilk, eggs, butter and almond extract. Whisk in the brown sugar. Add the flour, baking powder, baking soda and salt; stir to combine. Fold in the sour cherries.

3. Spoon the batter into the muffin cups, filling each about three-quarters full. Bake until a tester inserted in the center of a muffin comes out clean, 20–22 minutes. Cool in the pan on a rack 30 minutes; remove from the pan and cool completely on the rack.

4. To make the glaze, in a small saucepan, combine the granulated sugar and amaretto over medium heat; stir constantly until the sugar dissolves. Bring to a boil, reduce the heat to low and simmer until a thick syrup forms, about 10 minutes. Brush over the muffins.

PER SERVING: 129 CALORIES, 3 G TOTAL FAT, 2 G SATURATED FAT, 28 MG CHOLESTEROL, 178 MG SODIUM, 21 G TOTAL CARBOHYDRATE, 0 G DIETARY FIBER, 2 G PROTEIN, 28 MG CALCIUM.

POINTS PER SERVING: 3.

Tip: When you test the muffins, make sure your toothpick or cake tester is touching the bready part of the muffin, not a cherry. Cooling the muffins in the pan allows the muffins to reabsorb the juices that the cherries release.

Tutti-Frutti Muffins

TINY WILD BLUEBERRIES (commonly referred to as Maine wild blueberries) are preferable to cultivated blueberries for baking; they have a much more intense flavor and give off far less moisture. If you can't find fresh wild blueberries, use thawed frozen or canned; drain the liquid from either type.

MAKES 18 SERVINGS

2 cups all-purpose flour
½ tablespoon baking powder
1 teaspoon baking soda
¼ teaspoon salt
2 eggs
1 cup light sour cream
1 tablespoon unsalted butter, melted
½ cup packed dark brown sugar
1½ cups small wild blueberries
¾ cup sweetened dried cranberries

Topping:

3 tablespoons all-purpose flour
2 tablespoons granulated sugar
½ teaspoon cinnamon
2 tablespoons unsalted butter, at room temperature

1. Preheat the oven to 375° F; spray an 18-cup muffin tin with nonstick cooking spray.

2. In a medium bowl, whisk the flour, baking powder, baking soda and salt. In a large bowl, whisk the eggs until frothy. Whisk in the sour cream, butter and brown sugar; stir in the blueberries and cranberries. Add the flour mixture and stir just to blend (do not overmix). Spoon the batter into the muffin cups, filling each about two-thirds full.

3. To make the topping, in a small bowl, mix the flour, granulated sugar and cinnamon. With a fork, cut in the butter to coarse crumbs. Sprinkle a generous ½ teaspoon over each muffin. Bake until a tester inserted in the center of a muffin comes out clean, 20–22 minutes. Cool in the pan on wire racks.

PER SERVING: 149 CALORIES, 4 G TOTAL FAT, 2 G SATURATED FAT, 30 MG CHOLESTEROL, 140 MG SODIUM, 26 G TOTAL CARBOHYDRATE, 1 G DIETARY FIBER, 3 G PROTEIN, 30 MG CALCIUM.

POINTS PER SERVING: 3.

Tip: Sweetened dried cranberries are readily available in most supermarkets, but you might have to ask where they're kept; we've seen them in the baking section, with the other dried fruits, in the produce department and in the gourmet foods aisle! Other tasty substitutions include dried sour cherries (but not dried sweet cherries), golden raisins, currants or chopped dried apricots, dried peaches or even dried pears.

If you cannot find wild blueberries in any form, use the common variety, but toss them with a tablespoon or so of flour before stirring them into the batter. This will help to absorb some of the moisture they release when they're heated.

For a very sophisticated, somewhat savory variation, omit the topping and add 1 tablespoon of chopped fresh basil to the flour mixture. Serve these as part of a tea (use as the base of a sandwich spread with a soft fresh goat cheese like montrachet, or topped with a slice of fontina cheese) or as part of a breakfast with a goat-cheese omelet.

Breakfast Muffins

*I*F YOU PREFER A LITTLE CRUNCH, sprinkle each muffin with about 1 teaspoon of chopped pecans before baking. Use old-fashioned rolled oats in this recipe. Steel-cut Irish oats require more moisture and take longer to cook, and quick-cooking or instant oats would give the muffins a pasty texture.

MAKES 18 SERVINGS

1 cup seedless dark raisins
⅔ cup boiling water
1¾ cups all-purpose flour
1¼ cups old-fashioned rolled oats
¼ cup granulated sugar
2½ teaspoons baking powder
1 teaspoon cinnamon
½ teaspoon salt
2 eggs
1 cup low-fat buttermilk
¾ cup packed dark brown sugar
3 tablespoons unsalted butter, melted

1. Preheat the oven to 375° F; spray an 18-cup muffin tin with nonstick cooking spray. In a small bowl, combine the raisins and boiling water.

2. In a medium bowl, whisk the flour, oats, granulated sugar, baking powder, cinnamon and salt. In a large bowl, whisk the eggs until frothy; whisk in the buttermilk, brown sugar and butter. Stir in the raisins and their soaking liquid. Add the flour mixture and stir just to blend (do not overmix).

3. Spoon the batter into the muffin cups, filling each about three-quarters full. Bake until a tester inserted in the center of a muffin comes out clean, 20–22 minutes. Remove from the pan and cool on wire racks.

PER SERVING: 169 CALORIES, 3 G TOTAL FAT, 2 G SATURATED FAT, 26 MG CHOLESTEROL, 123 MG SODIUM, 33 G TOTAL CARBOHYDRATE, 1 G DIETARY FIBER, 4 G PROTEIN, 37 MG CALCIUM.

POINTS PER SERVING: 3.

Chocolate Chip Scones

Scones usually include milk or cream to provide moisture. Substituting orange juice means that you can use a bit more butter, and the orange juice adds a subtle flavor accent to the chocolate.

MAKES 12 SERVINGS

1¾ cups all-purpose flour
⅓ cup sugar
2 teaspoons baking powder
½ teaspoon salt
5 tablespoons cold unsalted butter, cut into bits
½ cup mini chocolate chips
3 tablespoons orange juice

1. Preheat the oven to 400° F; lightly spray a baking sheet with nonstick cooking spray.

2. In a large bowl, whisk the flour, sugar, baking powder and salt. With a pastry blender or a large fork, cut in the butter to coarse crumbs. Stir in the chocolate chips. Mix in the orange juice to form a dough.

3. On a floured surface, turn out the dough. Pat into a 9" circle about ½" thick. With a 2½" fluted biscuit cutter, cut out 12 scones, pushing the dough scraps together for the last, if necessary. Transfer the scones to the baking sheet. Bake until golden, about 12 minutes. Cool on wire racks.

Per serving: 168 Calories, 7 g Total Fat, 4 g Saturated Fat, 14 mg Cholesterol, 142 mg Sodium, 24 g Total Carbohydrate, 1 g Dietary Fiber, 2 g Protein, 18 mg Calcium.

POINTS PER SERVING: 4.

Tip: Make sure the butter is well chilled, which will produce a flakier texture.

Sun-Dried Tomato Biscuits

*T*HIS DINNER BISCUIT derives its savory character from sun-dried tomato paste. Look for the variety in the tube, which will keep for weeks in the refrigerator. If you can't find it, make your own: Reconstitute sun-dried tomatoes, then transfer the tomatoes to a food processor and puree, drizzling in as much of the soaking liquid as needed to make a paste.

MAKES 6 SERVINGS

1¾ cups self-rising flour
1 teaspoon chopped fresh oregano, or ¼ teaspoon dried, crumbled
¾ teaspoon baking powder
½ teaspoon salt
1 tablespoon sun-dried tomato paste
½ cup + 1 tablespoon fat-free milk
¼ cup vegetable oil

1. Preheat the oven to 450° F.

2. In a large bowl, combine the flour, oregano, baking powder and salt. In a small bowl, mix the tomato paste and 2 tablespoons water, then stir in ½ cup of the milk. Pour over the flour mixture, then add the oil; stir to form a dough. Knead the dough into a ball in the bowl, absorbing any excess flour.

3. On a lightly floured surface, turn out the dough. Pat into a 9 x 8" rectangle about ½" thick. With a 2½" biscuit cutter, cut out 12 biscuits, pushing the dough scraps together for the last, if necessary. Transfer the biscuits to a baking sheet and brush the tops with the remaining tablespoon of milk. Bake until golden, about 15 minutes. Serve at once.

PER SERVING: 110 CALORIES, 5 G TOTAL FAT, 0 G SATURATED FAT, 0 MG CHOLESTEROL, 352 MG SODIUM, 14 G TOTAL CARBOHYDRATE, 1 G DIETARY FIBER, 2 G PROTEIN, 77 MG CALCIUM.

POINTS PER SERVING: 2.

Tip: If you don't have self-rising flour on hand, sift together 1¾ cups all-purpose flour, 2½ teaspoons baking powder and ¼ teaspoon salt to use instead.

Bacon Biscuits

THESE OLD-FASHIONED SOUTHERN-STYLE BISCUITS are dropped, not rolled. Although using a ¼-cup measure or large spoon and a sharp snap of the wrist is one way to drop the dough onto the baking sheet, a 2" ice-cream scoop with a spring-release handle is easier.

MAKES 16 SERVINGS

2 cups all-purpose flour
2½ teaspoons baking powder
½ teaspoon salt
⅛ teaspoon baking soda
3 tablespoons cold unsalted butter, cut into bits
4 strips crisp-cooked turkey bacon, chopped
1 cup low-fat buttermilk
¼ cup fat-free milk

1. Preheat the oven to 425° F; lightly spray a 9" round cake pan with nonstick cooking spray.

2. In a large bowl, whisk together the flour, baking powder, salt and baking soda. With a pastry blender or a large fork, cut in the butter to coarse crumbs. Stir in the bacon. Mix in the buttermilk and milk to form a dough.

3. Drop the dough by ¼-cup measures into the pan, pushing the mounds together. Bake until golden, about 20 minutes. Serve at once.

PER SERVING: 92 CALORIES, 3 G TOTAL FAT, 2 G SATURATED FAT, 9 MG CHOLESTEROL, 183 MG SODIUM, 13 G TOTAL CARBOHYDRATE, 0 G DIETARY FIBER, 3 G PROTEIN, 27 MG CALCIUM.

POINTS PER SERVING: 2.

Tip: Turkey bacon is best baked in a 425° F oven for 12–15 minutes, until brown and very crispy. Chop it after cooking.

Anise Polenta Bread

COARSE CORNMEAL LENDS THIS BREAD its rich texture and hue; look for it in a health food or natural food market, or in the Italian section of many supermarkets, labeled "polenta."

MAKES 10 SERVINGS

1½ cups all-purpose flour
1 cup coarse cornmeal
½ cup sugar
2 teaspoons baking powder
½ teaspoon salt
2 eggs
½ cup fat-free milk
3 tablespoons anise-flavored liqueur
2 tablespoons unsalted butter, melted

1. Preheat the oven to 375° F; lightly spray a 5 x 9" loaf pan with nonstick cooking spray.

2. In a medium bowl, whisk the flour, cornmeal, sugar, baking powder and salt. In a large bowl, whisk the eggs until frothy. Whisk in the milk, liqueur and butter. Add the flour mixture and stir just to blend (do not overmix).

3. Scrape into the loaf pan and smooth the top with a spatula. Bake until the loaf begins to pull away from the sides of the pan and a tester inserted in the center of the bread comes out clean, about 40 minutes. Remove from the pan and cool on a wire rack.

PER SERVING: 207 CALORIES, 4 G TOTAL FAT, 2 G SATURATED FAT, 44 MG CHOLESTEROL, 181 MG SODIUM, 37 G TOTAL CARBOHYDRATE, 2 G DIETARY FIBER, 5 G PROTEIN, 24 MG CALCIUM.

POINTS PER SERVING: 4.

Tip: Although sambuca, the anise-flavored Italian liqueur, is perhaps a more authentic pairing with polenta, you may substitute an equal amount of the Greek liqueur ouzo or 1 teaspoon pure anise extract.

Ginger-Apple Tea Bread

THIS BREAD REMAINS WONDERFULLY FRESH AND FLAVORFUL for up to a week. The sweet Fuji apple holds its shape well, but Jonathan, Gala or Rome would be good as well. Don't choose particularly small apples; you'll need about 1 cup chopped apple.

MAKES 10 SERVINGS

2 Fuji apples, peeled and chopped (about 1 cup)
2 teaspoons fresh lemon juice
2 cups all-purpose flour
1 cup sugar
2 teaspoons baking powder
1¼ teaspoons ground ginger
¾ teaspoon cinnamon
½ teaspoon salt
1 egg
1 cup fat-free milk
2 tablespoons vegetable oil

1. Preheat the oven to 375° F; lightly spray a 5 x 9" loaf pan with nonstick cooking spray.

2. In a small bowl, combine the apples and lemon juice. In a medium bowl, whisk the flour, sugar, baking powder, ginger, cinnamon and salt. In a large bowl, whisk the egg until frothy; whisk in the milk and oil. Stir in the apples, then add the flour mixture and stir just to blend (do not overmix).

3. Pour into the loaf pan. Bake until the loaf is golden and a tester inserted into the center of the bread comes out clean, 55–60 minutes. Remove from the pan and cool on a wire rack.

PER SERVING: 225 CALORIES, 4 G TOTAL FAT, 0 G SATURATED FAT, 19 MG CHOLESTEROL, 182 MG SODIUM, 45 G TOTAL CARBOHYDRATE, 1 G DIETARY FIBER, 4 G PROTEIN, 39 MG CALCIUM.

POINTS PER SERVING: 5.

Bourbon-Sweet Potato Bread

FOR 1 CUP COOKED SWEET POTATO, cook a 1¼-pound sweet potato in a microwave oven on High power until fork-tender, about 10 minutes. Remove, wrap in foil and set aside for 15 minutes. Cut the potato open and scoop out the inside. You can also bake the potato in a 375° F oven for about 1 hour.

MAKES 8 SERVINGS

1¼ cups all-purpose flour
½ cup packed light brown sugar
⅓ cup quick-cooking oats
1 tablespoon baking powder
1 teaspoon grated orange zest
½ teaspoon baking soda
½ teaspoon salt
½ teaspoon cinnamon
½ teaspoon ground nutmeg
1 egg
½ cup low-fat buttermilk
½ cup fat-free milk
3 tablespoons unsalted butter, melted
5 tablespoons bourbon
1 cup cooked mashed sweet potato
½ cup golden raisins
1 cup confectioners' sugar

1. Preheat the oven to 375° F; lightly spray a 4 x 8½" loaf pan with nonstick cooking spray.

2. In a medium bowl, whisk the flour, brown sugar, oats, baking powder, orange zest, baking soda, salt, cinnamon and nutmeg. In a large bowl, whisk the egg until frothy; whisk in the buttermilk, milk, butter and 2 tablespoons of the bourbon. Whisk in the sweet potato until thoroughly blended. Add the flour mixture and raisins and stir just to blend (do not overmix).

3. Pour into the loaf pan. Bake until the loaf begins to pull away from the sides of the pan and a tester inserted into the center of the bread comes out clean, 55–60 minutes. Remove from the pan and cool on a wire rack.

4. To make the icing, in a small bowl, whisk the confectioners' sugar and the remaining 3 tablespoons of bourbon until well mixed. Drizzle over the loaf while it is still slightly warm.

Per serving: 278 Calories, 4 g Total Fat, 2 g Saturated Fat, 29 mg Cholesterol, 284 mg Sodium, 53 g Total Carbohydrate, 2 g Dietary Fiber, 4 g Protein, 58 mg Calcium.

POINTS PER SERVING: 5.

Tip: This sweet, moist bread is based on the Southern specialty sweet potato pie. If you like, drain an 8-ounce can of crushed pineapple very well (press the chunks with the back of a spoon to get out as much of the juice as possible) and add the fruit with the raisins. You can use the juice in lieu of the bourbon if you prefer to avoid alcohol.

For more crunch and less sweetness, sprinkle the bread with 1 tablespoon of chopped pecans before baking; omit the glaze.

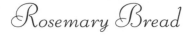

Rosemary Bread

*T*OP THE BREAD either with coarse kosher salt or sea salt. Both of these large-grained salts have a purer taste than table salt and are less likely to dissolve when baked.

MAKES 10 SERVINGS

2½ cups all-purpose flour
¼ cup sugar
1 tablespoon chopped fresh rosemary, or 1 teaspoon dried, crumbled
1 tablespoon baking powder
¼ teaspoon salt
1 egg
1¼ cups low-fat buttermilk
1 tablespoon vegetable oil
½ teaspoon coarse salt

1. Preheat the oven to 350° F; lightly spray a 5 x 9" loaf pan with nonstick cooking spray.

2. In a medium bowl, whisk the flour, sugar, rosemary, baking powder and salt. In a large bowl, whisk the egg until frothy; whisk in the milk and oil. Add the flour mixture and stir just to blend (do not over-mix).

3. Scrape into the loaf pan and smooth the top with a spatula. Sprinkle with the coarse salt. Bake until a tester inserted into the center of the bread comes out clean, about 40 minutes. Remove from the pan and cool on a wire rack.

PER SERVING: 165 CALORIES, 2 G TOTAL FAT, 0 G SATURATED FAT, 20 MG CHOLESTEROL, 282 MG SODIUM, 31 G TOTAL CARBOHYDRATE, 1 G DIETARY FIBER, 5 G PROTEIN, 45 MG CALCIUM.

POINTS PER SERVING: 3.

Tip: This makes great toast; the heating boosts the rosemary flavor.

Dried Cherry–Cocoa Bread

*T*HIS DENSE RICH BREAD is the perfect solution to satisfy a chocolate craving. Look for dried sweet (bing) cherries; their sweeter flavor works better than dried sour cherries in this recipe.

MAKES 10 SERVINGS

½ cup unsweetened cocoa powder
⅔ cup boiling water
2 cups all-purpose flour
2 tablespoons granulated sugar
2 teaspoons baking powder
½ teaspoon salt
1 egg
1 cup low-fat buttermilk
4 tablespoons unsalted butter, melted
¾ cup packed light brown sugar
½ cup dried cherries

1. Preheat the oven to 350° F; lightly spray a 5 x 9" loaf pan with nonstick cooking spray. In a small bowl, mix the cocoa powder and boiling water until smooth.

2. In a medium bowl, whisk the flour, granulated sugar, baking powder and salt. In a large bowl, whisk the egg until frothy; whisk in the buttermilk, butter and brown sugar, then stir in the cherries. Add the flour mixture and stir just to blend (do not overmix).

3. Pour into the loaf pan. Bake until the loaf begins to pull away from the sides of the pan and a tester inserted into the center of the bread comes out clean, 40–45 minutes. Remove from the pan and cool on a wire rack.

PER SERVING: 254 CALORIES, 6 G TOTAL FAT, 4 G SATURATED FAT, 32 MG CHOLESTEROL, 203 MG SODIUM, 47 G TOTAL CARBOHYDRATE, 3 G DIETARY FIBER, 5 G PROTEIN, 59 MG CALCIUM.

POINTS PER SERVING: 5.

Tip: For a decorative presentation, dust with 1 tablespoon confectioners' sugar through a sieve. To make a harlequin pattern, cut out diamond shapes from stiff paper. Dab a little vegetable oil on your fingertips and rub *very lightly* over the bread. Working quickly, arrange the cutouts on the bread, pressing them gently. Dust with the confectioners' sugar. Gently brush the sugar off the cutouts, then carefully remove them. Try this technique with other patterns as well.

Peppery Popovers

TAKE CARE NOT TO OPEN THE OVEN DOOR while the popovers bake, as this will allow the steam that makes them rise to escape. This dough is very wet. When heated, the moisture turns into steam, which causes the spectacular rise.

MAKES 8 SERVINGS

2 eggs
1 cup fat-free milk
1 cup all-purpose flour
½ teaspoon salt
¼ teaspoon freshly ground black pepper

1. Preheat the oven to 450° F; spray 8 cups of a popover pan or muffin tin with nonstick cooking spray.

2. In a medium bowl with an electric mixer at medium speed, beat the eggs until frothy. Beat in the milk, then the flour, salt and pepper. Spoon ¼ cup of the batter into each cup. Bake 15 minutes; reduce the oven temperature to 400° F and bake until browned, about 12 minutes longer. Serve at once.

PER SERVING: 85 CALORIES, 1 G TOTAL FAT, 0 G SATURATED FAT, 47 MG CHOLESTEROL, 176 MG SODIUM, 14 G TOTAL CARBOHYDRATE, 0 G DIETARY FIBER, 4 G PROTEIN, 46 MG CALCIUM.

POINTS PER SERVING: 2.

Tip: Use popover pans or single-weight muffin tins. Don't use insulated tins;
they won't get hot enough to generate sufficient steam.

Soups and Salads

Leek and Potato Soup

LIKE SPINACH, leeks grow in sandy soil, so it's important to clean them thoroughly (see the Tip for how-tos). Don't discard the green tops: Save them to toss into stocks for a subtle flavor. This soup can also be refrigerated and served chilled.

MAKES 4 SERVINGS

3½ cups low-sodium chicken broth
4 leeks, trimmed to white and light green parts and thinly sliced
1 large red potato, peeled and cubed
Snipped fresh chives, to garnish

1. In a medium saucepan, combine the broth, leeks and potato; bring to a boil. Reduce the heat and simmer, covered, until the vegetables are fork-tender, about 45 minutes.

2. Transfer to a blender or food processor and puree (in batches, if necessary). Pour the puree back into the saucepan and heat to serving temperature, 1–2 minutes. Serve, garnished with the chives.

PER SERVING: 64 CALORIES, 2 G TOTAL FAT, 1 G SATURATED FAT, 4 MG CHOLESTEROL, 101 MG SODIUM, 11 G TOTAL CARBOHYDRATE, 1 G DIETARY FIBER, 4 G PROTEIN, 26 MG CALCIUM.

POINTS PER SERVING: 1.

Tip: To trim a leek, cut off the dark green leaves and halve lengthwise. Fan open under cold running water to rinse off residual dirt. Lay flat on a board, trim the root ends and slice as desired.

Cream of Cauliflower Soup

*I*F YOU'D LIKE TO TRY MAKING YOUR OWN low-sodium chicken broth, use 1 celery stalk, 1 carrot, 4 parsley sprigs, ¼ onion and 4 cups water for every pound of chicken meat and bones (use at least 4 pounds). Combine in a large pot and simmer until the vegetables and the bones are very tender, about 1 hour for each pound of chicken scraps. Strain into a large bowl, bring to room temperature, cover and refrigerate. Skim off the fat once it has coagulated across the top. The most efficient way to store: Seal in 1-quart freezer bags, then stack the bags, flat, in the freezer.

MAKES 6 SERVINGS

2 teaspoons olive oil
1 white onion, chopped
1 head cauliflower, broken into florets
3 cups low-sodium chicken broth
¾ cup evaporated skimmed milk
¼ teaspoon freshly grated nutmeg
⅛ teaspoon ground white pepper
Salt, to taste
6 chervil or flat-leaf parsley sprigs

1. Preheat a large nonstick saucepan or Dutch oven over medium-high heat. Pour in the olive oil and swirl to coat. Sauté the onion, stirring constantly, until tender and translucent, about 5 minutes. Add the cauliflower and cook, stirring, until heated through, about 5 minutes. Add the broth; bring to a boil. Reduce the heat to medium-low and simmer, covered, until the vegetables can be easily mashed, about 10 minutes.

2. Transfer to a blender or food processor and puree. Pour the puree back into the saucepan. Over low heat, stir in the evaporated milk, nutmeg, pepper and salt; heat to serving temperature, about 1 minute. Serve, garnished with a chervil or parsley sprig.

PER SERVING: 83 CALORIES, 3 G TOTAL FAT, 1 G SATURATED FAT, 5 MG CHOLESTEROL, 121 MG SODIUM, 10 G TOTAL CARBOHYDRATE, 3 G DIETARY FIBER, 6 G PROTEIN, 35 MG CALCIUM.

POINTS PER SERVING: 1.

Roasted Garlic and French Onion Soup

Y OU'LL NEED ABOUT 2 POUNDS of onions for this recipe, but it doesn't matter whether you choose the common yellow onion, or red, sweet, white or a mix of varieties. If you love the flavor of freshly roasted garlic but not the time involved, look for vacuum-packed whole roasted garlic cloves, which can be found refrigerated with fresh pastas, or minced roasted garlic in jars, which can be found in the produce section.

MAKES 4 SERVINGS

4–5 yellow onions, thinly sliced
1 tablespoon olive oil
1 garlic bulb, roasted*
¼ cup dry Marsala wine
4 cups fat-free beef broth
4 tablespoons grated Gruyère cheese

In a large saucepan over medium heat, combine the onions and oil. Cook, stirring occasionally, until golden and beginning to caramelize, about 45 minutes. Add the garlic and stir until fragrant, about 30 seconds. Stir in the Marsala and broth; bring to a boil. Reduce the heat and simmer gently, covered, 15 minutes. Serve, topped with the cheese.

PER SERVING: 152 CALORIES, 6 G TOTAL FAT, 2 G SATURATED FAT, 7 MG CHOLESTEROL, 102 MG SODIUM, 14 G TOTAL CARBOHYDRATE, 2 G DIETARY FIBER, 9 G PROTEIN, 98 MG CALCIUM.

POINTS PER SERVING: 3.

Tip: If you have ovenproof soup crocks, replace the grated cheese with thin slices. Ladle the soup into the crocks, top each with a slice of Gruyère and broil until the cheese is lightly browned and beginning to melt.

*To roast garlic, preheat oven to 350° F. Wrap garlic bulb in foil and bake until softened, about 45 minutes; let cool 10 minutes, then remove foil. Cut the top off garlic bulb and separate cloves.

Jalapeño Corn Soup with Cilantro

THE AMOUNT OF CORN you can scrape from an ear varies considerably—you'll get between ½ cup and 1¼ cups, depending on its size; feel free to substitute frozen corn kernels. For a spicier soup, use one jalapeño.

MAKES 6 SERVINGS

2 teaspoons olive oil
1 white onion, chopped
2 garlic cloves, minced
2½ cups corn kernels
2 red potatoes, peeled and diced
½ jalapeño pepper, seeded, deveined and chopped (wear gloves to prevent irritation)
3 cups low-sodium chicken broth
Salt, to taste
Freshly ground pepper, to taste
½ red bell pepper, seeded and diced
1 tablespoon chopped cilantro

1. In a large nonstick saucepan, combine the oil and onion over medium-high heat. Cook, stirring occasionally, until translucent and beginning to brown, about 3 minutes. Add the garlic and stir 15 seconds. Stir in the corn, potatoes and jalapeño; cook, stirring, until the corn begins to soften, about 3 minutes. Add the broth; bring to a boil. Reduce the heat to low and simmer, covered, until the vegetables can be easily mashed, about 15 minutes.

2. Transfer to a food processor or blender and puree. Season with salt and pepper to taste. Serve, sprinkled with bell pepper and cilantro.

PER SERVING: 125 CALORIES, 3 G TOTAL FAT, 1 G SATURATED FAT, 3 MG CHOLESTEROL, 61 MG SODIUM, 24 G TOTAL CARBOHYDRATE, 3 G DIETARY FIBER, 5 G PROTEIN, 23 MG CALCIUM.

POINTS PER SERVING: 2.

Tip: If you prefer a chunkier soup, puree half of the mixture. Stir it back into the pot before seasoning with salt and pepper.

Chilled Curried Carrot Soup

THIS SOUP IS JUST AS GOOD made a day ahead and refrigerated, but be aware that the longer the soup sits, the stronger the curry flavor becomes.

MAKES 4 SERVINGS

4 carrots, chunked
½ white onion, roughly chopped
2 cups low-sodium chicken broth
½ tablespoon minced peeled gingerroot
½ teaspoon curry powder
Salt, to taste
½ cup light sour cream
2 tablespoons fat-free milk
Snipped chives

1. In a medium saucepan, combine the carrots, onion and broth, then stir in the gingerroot and curry powder; bring to a boil. Reduce the heat and simmer, covered, until the carrots can be mashed easily, 40–45 minutes.

2. Transfer to a blender or a food processor and puree. Transfer to a bowl, add salt to taste and refrigerate, tightly covered, at least 2 hours.

3. In a small bowl, whisk the sour cream and milk until smooth. Serve the soup, dolloped with the sour cream mixture and sprinkled with the chives.

PER SERVING: 93 CALORIES, 4 G TOTAL FAT, 3 G SATURATED FAT, 13 MG CHOLESTEROL, 105 MG SODIUM, 12 G TOTAL CARBOHYDRATE, 3 G DIETARY FIBER, 5 G PROTEIN, 83 MG CALCIUM.

POINTS PER SERVING: 2.

Tip: Curry powders come in a range from mild to madras (which is spicy). To add to the confusion, there are even different levels of madras curry powders; "mild madras," for example, is on the lesser end of the spiciest set. The soup will take on a very different character depending upon which you choose.

Spicy Gazpacho

THIS IS A VERY CHUNKY GAZPACHO, filled with bits of vegetables. If you prefer a smoother consistency, process for a longer time in the food processor. Different hot sauces will produce different results. For example, red pepper sauce is a bit hotter; green pepper sauce, made from jalapeño peppers, is somewhat mellower. For a milder soup, omit the hot sauce entirely and use a spicy vegetable juice.

MAKES 6 SERVINGS

1 cucumber, peeled, seeded and chunked
1 green bell pepper, seeded and chunked
2 celery stalks, chunked
1 white onion, chunked
1 garlic clove, peeled
1¼ cups low-sodium vegetable juice
¼ cup red-wine vinegar
½ teaspoon hot red pepper sauce
½ teaspoon salt
1 plum tomato, seeded and chopped

1. In a food processor, combine the cucumber, pepper, celery, onion and garlic; pulse 8–10 times to break up. Add the vegetable juice, vinegar, pepper sauce and salt; process to a fine dice. Transfer to a nonreactive bowl and refrigerate, tightly covered, at least 2 hours.

2. Serve, sprinkled with the tomato.

PER SERVING: 39 CALORIES, 0 G TOTAL FAT, 0 G SATURATED FAT, 0 MG CHOLESTEROL, 240 MG SODIUM, 8 G TOTAL CARBOHYDRATE, 2 G DIETARY FIBER, 1 G PROTEIN, 30 MG CALCIUM.

POINTS PER SERVING: 0.

Minted Pea Soup

THE APPLIANCE YOU USE to puree the soup will determine its texture. If you prefer a smoother soup, puree in the blender; a food processor will yield a slightly coarser puree.

MAKES 4 SERVINGS

4 cups fresh or frozen peas
2 cups low-sodium chicken broth
⅛ teaspoon ground white pepper
Salt, to taste
¼ cup chopped mint
¼ cup light sour cream
Mint sprigs

1. In a large saucepan, combine the peas and broth; bring to a boil. Reduce the heat and simmer, covered, until the peas are tender but still bright green, about 5 minutes.

2. Transfer to a blender or food processor and puree. Transfer to a bowl, stir in the white pepper and salt and refrigerate, tightly covered, at least 2 hours.

3. Stir in the chopped mint. Serve, garnished with the sour cream and a sprig of mint.

PER SERVING: 148 CALORIES, 3 G TOTAL FAT, 2 G SATURATED FAT, 8 MG CHOLESTEROL, 227 MG SODIUM, 22 G TOTAL CARBOHYDRATE, 7 G DIETARY FIBER, 10 G PROTEIN, 89 MG CALCIUM.

POINTS PER SERVING: 2.

Tip: For 4 cups fresh peas, start with 4 pounds of peas in the pod.

Chilly Dilly Cucumber Soup

*L*OOK FOR A LONG, THIN HOTHOUSE (or English) cucumber, which is bred to be seedless. They usually come wrapped in plastic, which seals in the moisture and helps to prolong freshness (it also means the cucumber doesn't need to be waxed).

MAKES 4 SERVINGS

1 hothouse cucumber, peeled and chunked
1½ cups vegetable broth
8 scallions, chunked (white and light green parts only)
¼ cup chopped dill
¼ cup light sour cream
Snipped dill

1. In a food processor or blender, puree the cucumber, broth, scallions and chopped dill. Transfer to a bowl and refrigerate, tightly covered, at least 2 hours.

2. Stir in the sour cream until well blended. Serve, sprinkled with snipped dill.

PER SERVING: 66 CALORIES, 3 G TOTAL FAT, 1 G SATURATED FAT, 5 MG CHOLESTEROL, 402 MG SODIUM, 15 G TOTAL CARBOHYDRATE, 3 G DIETARY FIBER, 6 G PROTEIN, 192 MG CALCIUM.

POINTS PER SERVING: 1.

Tip: Stir in a pinch of cayenne pepper before refrigerating if desired.

Chilled Tomato Soup with Pesto

*T*HIS LOW-IN-FAT PESTO is very versatile. Use it to top a piece of broiled white fish or to accent a rice salad, or combine it with chopped tomatoes on bread as an appetizer.

MAKES 4 SERVINGS

1 white onion, chopped
1 garlic clove, minced
1 teaspoon olive oil
2 large tomatoes, peeled, seeded and chopped
1 cup vegetable broth

Pesto:

2 cups loosely packed basil leaves
2 tablespoons fresh lemon juice
½ tablespoon pine nuts
1 garlic clove, smashed and peeled
¼ teaspoon salt
⅛ teaspoon freshly ground pepper
1 tablespoon olive oil

1. In a medium saucepan, combine the onion, garlic and olive oil. Sauté until the onion is translucent, about 5 minutes. Stir in the tomatoes and broth; bring to a boil. Reduce the heat and simmer until the tomatoes are falling apart, 15–20 minutes.

2. Transfer to a blender or food processor and puree. Put into a container with a tight-fitting lid and refrigerate at least 2 hours.

3. To make the pesto, in a food processor or blender, puree the basil, lemon juice, pine nuts, garlic, salt and pepper. With the machine running, drizzle in the oil; puree. Serve the soup, topped with a dollop of pesto.

PER SERVING: 96 CALORIES, 6 G TOTAL FAT, 1 G SATURATED FAT, 0 MG CHOLESTEROL, 406 MG SODIUM, 11 G TOTAL CARBOHYDRATE, 3 G DIETARY FIBER, 3 G PROTEIN, 79 MG CALCIUM.

POINTS PER SERVING: 2.

Tip: If you don't have time to peel and seed the tomatoes, you can start with 2 cups of commercially peeled, seeded and chopped tomatoes. Choose a high-quality brand imported from Italy, preferably the variety packed in a box rather than a can.

Mexican Chicken Salad

*T*OASTED TORTILLA STRIPS are a perfect garnish. To make, spray a 10" flour tortilla on each side with nonstick cooking spray, cut it into small, thin strips (about 3 x ½") and scatter in a single layer on a baking sheet. Bake in a 400° F oven until golden, 6–7 minutes.

MAKES 4 SERVINGS

1 tablespoon fresh lime juice
4 teaspoons olive oil
2 garlic cloves, peeled
¾ teaspoon chili powder
¾ pound skinless boneless chicken breasts, poached and cut into 1" chunks
1 tomato, seeded and cut into ½" cubes
1 avocado, peeled, pitted and sliced
2 scallions, minced (white and light green parts only)
2 tablespoons minced cilantro
4 cups shredded romaine lettuce

1. To make the dressing, put the lime juice in a small bowl. Drizzle in the oil, whisking constantly. Using a garlic press, press in the garlic and add the chili powder; whisk thoroughly.

2. In a large bowl, combine the chicken, tomato, avocado, scallions and cilantro. Pour the dressing over and toss to coat. Refrigerate, covered, until the flavors are blended, at least 2 hours.

3. Divide the lettuce among 4 plates, mound the chicken salad on top.

PER SERVING: 243 CALORIES, 14 G TOTAL FAT, 2 G SATURATED FAT, 49 MG CHOLESTEROL, 77 MG SODIUM, 9 G TOTAL CARBOHYDRATE, 5 G DIETARY FIBER, 22 G PROTEIN, 60 MG CALCIUM.

POINTS PER SERVING: 5.

Tip: To poach the chicken, bring 1 cup chicken broth to a simmer in a medium saucepan over medium heat. Add the chicken breasts, cover and simmer until cooked through, about 5 minutes on each side.

Sausage and Goat Cheese Salad

*T*HIS BRIGHTLY COLORED SALAD makes an ideal luncheon entrée. Serve individually and drizzle with 2 tablespoons of the dressing. If you prefer, sliver 4 ounces prosciutto to use in place of the sausage.

MAKES 4 SERVINGS

½ pound smoked turkey sausage, julienned
1 yellow bell pepper, roasted* and julienned
1 red bell pepper, roasted* and julienned
1 bunch watercress, stemmed
1 small head radicchio, shredded
¼ cup white-wine vinegar
3½ ounces goat cheese with garlic and herbs
1 teaspoon olive oil
¼ teaspoon freshly ground pepper

1. In a salad bowl, combine the sausage, roasted peppers, watercress and radicchio.

2. To make the dressing, in a small nonstick skillet, heat the vinegar over medium heat until it gives off steam, 1–2 minutes. Add the goat cheese; cook, stirring constantly, until melted and heated through, about 30 seconds. Remove from the heat and stir in the oil and pepper. Pour over the salad; toss to coat.

PER SERVING: 203 CALORIES, 12 G TOTAL FAT, 6 G SATURATED FAT, 58 MG CHOLESTEROL, 814 MG SODIUM, 10 G TOTAL CARBOHYDRATE, 1 G DIETARY FIBER, 14 G PROTEIN, 174 MG CALCIUM.

POINTS PER SERVING: 5.

Tip: Heating the dressing helps the cheese melt, resulting in a creamier, smoother dressing than one that is simply pureed in a blender.

*To roast bell peppers, preheat broiler. Line baking sheet with foil; place peppers on baking sheet. Broil 4–6" from heat, turning frequently with tongs, until skin is lightly charred on all sides, about 10 minutes. Transfer to paper bag; fold bag closed and steam 10 minutes. Peel, seed and devein peppers over a bowl to catch juices.

Melon, Prosciutto and Fig Salad

THE SALAD DERIVES MUCH OF ITS CHARACTER from robustly flavored salt-cured prosciutto, an Italian ham known as Parma ham in England. Although this is quite flavorsome with dried figs (which are available year-round), it is sublime with fresh figs. They are in season in summer and early fall; choose Calimyrna, Brown Turkey or Mission figs.

MAKES 4 SERVINGS

¼ cup + 2 tablespoons honey
2 teaspoons Dijon mustard
2 tablespoons balsamic vinegar
1 bunch watercress, stemmed
1 cantaloupe, seeded, peeled and thinly sliced
½ honeydew melon, seeded, peeled and thinly sliced
8 slices prosciutto, quartered and rolled
4 dried Calimyrna figs, quartered

1. To make the dressing, in a small bowl, whisk the honey and mustard; whisk in the vinegar.

2. Divide the watercress among 4 salad plates. Alternate the cantaloupe and honeydew slices in a spoke pattern; intersperse 8 prosciutto rolls between the melon slices and scatter the fig quarters over the salad. Drizzle with the dressing.

PER SERVING: 384 CALORIES, 6 G TOTAL FAT, 2 G SATURATED FAT, 45 MG CHOLESTEROL, 911 MG SODIUM, 67 G TOTAL CARBOHYDRATE, 4 G DIETARY FIBER, 20 G PROTEIN, 64 MG CALCIUM.

POINTS PER SERVING: 7.

Tip: This lovely fat-free dressing is versatile enough for just about any salad.

Orange and Red Onion Salad

CURLY ENDIVE IS SOMETIMES SOLD as chicory, but they're actually quite different. Curly endive is a deeper green and not as bitter; it's sometimes sold as frisée.

MAKES 4 SERVINGS

1 head curly endive, cleaned and torn
2 navel oranges, peeled and sliced into rounds
16 niçoise olives, pitted and halved
½ red onion, thinly sliced
2 teaspoons balsamic vinegar
4 teaspoons olive oil
Freshly ground pepper, to taste

1. Divide the endive among 4 salad plates. Top with the orange rounds, then scatter with the olives and onion.

2. To make the dressing, put the vinegar into a small bowl. While whisking, drizzle in the oil; whisk in the pepper. Drizzle over the salads.

PER SERVING: 115 CALORIES, 6 G TOTAL FAT, 1 G SATURATED FAT, 0 MG CHOLESTEROL, 142 MG SODIUM, 15 G TOTAL CARBOHYDRATE, 6 G DIETARY FIBER, 3 G PROTEIN, 109 MG CALCIUM.

POINTS PER SERVING: 2.

Tip: To pit niçoise olives, place them on a cutting board; push down with the side of a chef's knife or a similar kitchen utensil to flatten and split the olive. Pull the halves of the olive open, remove the pit and cut the halves apart.

Roasted Beet and Asian Pear Salad

Oɴᴇ ʙᴜɴᴄʜ ᴏꜰ ʙᴇᴇᴛs, which most commonly consists of 3 beets in varying sizes, usually weighs about 1 pound. Asian pears, also known as apple pears, are shaped like apples and have golden brown skins similar to Bosc pears. They are as sweet as a pear, but have more of the crunch of an apple.

MAKES 6 SERVINGS

1 bunch beets, trimmed
1 Asian pear, peeled and chopped
1 bunch arugula, cleaned and shredded
2 tablespoons tarragon vinegar
1 tablespoon fresh lemon juice
1 tablespoon olive oil
Salt, to taste
Freshly ground pepper, to taste

1. Preheat the oven to 400° F. Wrap the beets in foil and roast until fork-tender, about 1 hour and 15 minutes. Unwrap the foil and let the beets cool, then peel and chop. In a large bowl, combine the beets, half of the Asian pear, and the arugula; toss to combine.

2. To make the dressing, in a small bowl, whisk the vinegar and lemon juice. Drizzle in the oil, whisking constantly; whisk in the oil, then the salt and pepper. Pour over the salad and toss to coat. Serve, scattering the remaining Asian pear over the salads.

Pᴇʀ sᴇʀᴠɪɴɢ: 47 Cᴀʟᴏʀɪᴇs, 2 ɢ Tᴏᴛᴀʟ Fᴀᴛ, 0 ɢ Sᴀᴛᴜʀᴀᴛᴇᴅ Fᴀᴛ, 0 ᴍɢ Cʜᴏʟᴇsᴛᴇʀᴏʟ, 32 ᴍɢ Sᴏᴅɪᴜᴍ, 7 ɢ Tᴏᴛᴀʟ Cᴀʀʙᴏʜʏᴅʀᴀᴛᴇ, 2 ɢ Dɪᴇᴛᴀʀʏ Fɪʙᴇʀ, 1 ɢ Pʀᴏᴛᴇɪɴ, 8 ᴍɢ Cᴀʟᴄɪᴜᴍ.

POINTS PER SERVING: 1.

Tip: Leave about an inch of stem when you trim the beets, and don't touch the pointy root end until after they're roasted (this helps keep the color in the beets and off your hands, clothes and counters). Don't toss the tops—they're a good source of fiber and vitamins A and C, and they're tasty, too. Just cook them as you would spinach.

Roasted Pepper Salad with Feta Cheese

THIS LOVELY DISH has plenty of colors, but for even more contrast, use ½ bunch of watercress and 1 small head of Belgian endive, thinly sliced crosswise, instead of 1 bunch of watercress.

MAKES 4 SERVINGS

3 tablespoons balsamic vinegar
1 large garlic clove, chopped
½ teaspoon Dijon mustard
1 green bell pepper, roasted* and thinly sliced
1 yellow bell pepper, roasted* and thinly sliced
1 red bell pepper, roasted* and thinly sliced
Salt, to taste
Freshly ground pepper, to taste
1 bunch watercress, stemmed
¼ cup crumbled feta cheese
12 niçoise olives, pitted and halved
4 teaspoons shredded basil leaves

1. In a medium nonreactive bowl, whisk the vinegar, garlic and mustard. Add the peppers; toss to coat, then sprinkle with salt and pepper. Refrigerate, covered, until chilled, about 30 minutes.

2. Divide the watercress among 4 salad plates; top with the peppers, then scatter with the cheese, olive halves and basil.

PER SERVING: 75 CALORIES, 3 G TOTAL FAT, 2 G SATURATED FAT, 8 MG CHOLESTEROL, 209 MG SODIUM, 10 G TOTAL CARBOHYDRATE, 3 G DIETARY FIBER, 3 G PROTEIN, 121 MG CALCIUM.

POINTS PER SERVING: 1.

Tip: To shred basil, stack a few leaves on top of each other. Slice lengthwise through the layers of leaves, then stack the halves, roll them up lengthwise and thinly slice crosswise to create long, thin shreds.

*To roast bell peppers, preheat broiler. Line baking sheet with foil; place peppers on baking sheet. Broil 4–6" from heat, turning frequently with tongs, until skin is lightly charred on all sides, about 10 minutes. Transfer to paper bag; fold bag closed and steam 10 minutes. Peel, seed and devein peppers over a bowl to catch juices.

Small Plates

Sautéed Artichoke Hearts

*T*HIS CAN SERVE EQUALLY WELL as a side dish to accompany veal or poultry; omit the radicchio.

MAKES 4 SERVINGS

One 9-ounce box frozen artichoke hearts, thawed
2 teaspoons olive oil
1 tomato, peeled, seeded and diced
2 tablespoons chopped basil
½ teaspoon salt
⅛ teaspoon freshly ground pepper
4 radicchio leaves

Preheat a medium nonstick skillet over high heat. Add the artichoke hearts and oil; sauté until they just begin to brown, about 4 minutes. Stir in the tomato, basil, salt and pepper; cook until dry and blended, 1–2 minutes. Spoon into the radicchio leaves.

PER SERVING: 57 CALORIES, 2 G TOTAL FAT, 0 G SATURATED FAT, 0 MG CHOLESTEROL, 337 MG SODIUM, 8 G TOTAL CARBOHYDRATE, 4 G DIETARY FIBER, 2 G PROTEIN, 31 MG CALCIUM.

POINTS PER SERVING: 1.

Tip: For a festive presentation, serve tapas-style in little earthenware bowls instead of in the radicchio leaves.

Wild Mushroom Strudel

CREMINI MUSHROOMS are sometimes referred to as baby portobellos or simply as brown mushrooms. If you can't find them, substitute an equal weight of portobello mushrooms, chunked.

MAKES 8 SERVINGS

½ pound white mushrooms, stemmed
6 ounces cremini mushrooms, stemmed
3½ ounces shiitake mushrooms, stemmed
1 red onion, chunked
1 teaspoon dried thyme leaves
½ teaspoon ground coriander
½ teaspoon salt
½ teaspoon freshly ground pepper
½ cup evaporated skimmed milk
¼ cup dry white wine
Four 12 x 17" sheets phyllo dough, at room temperature

1. In a food processor, finely chop the mushrooms and onion. Transfer to a medium nonstick skillet. Cook, stirring frequently, until the onion is softened, about 5 minutes. Stir in the thyme, coriander, salt and pepper, then add the evaporated milk and wine. Simmer until the liquid is absorbed, 12–15 minutes. Transfer to a bowl; refrigerate, covered, until thickened and chilled, at least 1 hour.

2. Preheat the oven to 375° F.

3. Fit a baking sheet with a piece of baker's parchment or wax paper. Put 1 sheet of the phyllo in the center and spray with nonstick cooking spray. Layer the other 3 sheets on top, spraying between each. Spoon the mushroom filling onto a short end, leaving a ¼" border. Lift the short edge alongside the filling over the mixture and roll up into a log. Turn the log one quarter-turn so that it lies lengthwise in the center of the baking sheet; lightly spray the top. Bake until golden brown, 25–30 minutes. Cut into eight 1½" slices.

PER SERVING: 67 CALORIES, 1 G TOTAL FAT, 0 G SATURATED FAT, 1 MG CHOLESTEROL, 212 MG SODIUM, 11 G TOTAL CARBOHYDRATE, 1 G DIETARY FIBER, 3 G PROTEIN, 10 MG CALCIUM.

POINTS PER SERVING: 1.

Tip: This holds up well on a buffet. Bake it two hours ahead so the flavors have time to blend.

Spinach-Stuffed Mushrooms

*I*F YOU PREFER, use large cremini mushrooms instead of the white variety, but don't use portobellos (they're too big).

MAKES 4 SERVINGS

One 10-ounce bag triple-washed spinach, rinsed and cleaned (do not dry)
1 egg
2 tablespoons plain dried bread crumbs
1 tablespoon fat-free milk
1 teaspoon chopped oregano
¼ teaspoon salt
⅛ teaspoon freshly ground pepper
⅛ teaspoon ground nutmeg
4 large white mushrooms, cleaned and stemmed
¼ cup shredded Monterey Jack cheese

1. Preheat the oven to 400° F; spray a baking dish with nonstick cooking spray.

2. Preheat a large skillet over high heat. Cook the spinach, stirring as needed, until wilted, 2–3 minutes. Transfer to a cutting board and chop, then transfer to a bowl; mix in the egg, bread crumbs, milk, oregano, salt, pepper and nutmeg.

3. Place the mushrooms, stem-side down, in the baking dish. Bake 5 minutes. Turn the mushrooms stem-side up; stuff with the spinach mixture, then sprinkle with the cheese. Bake until the cheese is melted and browned, about 15 minutes longer.

PER SERVING: 81 CALORIES, 4 G TOTAL FAT, 2 G SATURATED FAT, 53 MG CHOLESTEROL, 285 MG SODIUM, 7 G TOTAL CARBOHYDRATE, 1 G DIETARY FIBER, 6 G PROTEIN, 148 MG CALCIUM.

POINTS PER SERVING: 2.

Tip: Monterey Jack cheese melts very well. If you like, use a flavored version such as pepperjack.

Melon, Prosciutto and Fig Salad

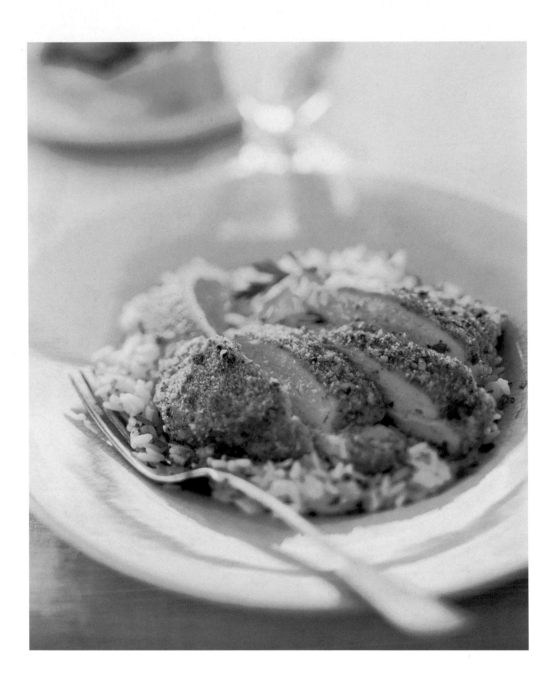

Honey-Ginger Chicken with Orange-Parsley Rice

Soy Steak and Noodles

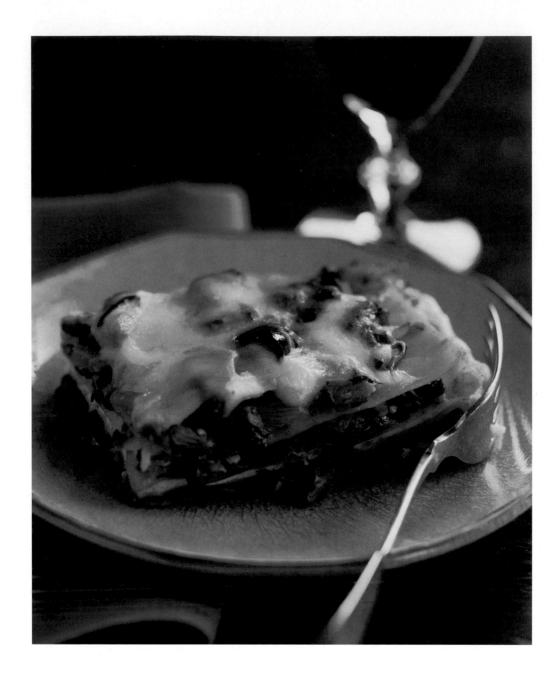

Roasted Ratatouille Lasagna

Garlic Potato Salad

THIS SALAD WILL KEEP, REFRIGERATED, for up to 3 days, and if you have the foresight to make it ahead, you should: Its flavor just gets more robust. For a spicier salad, use ½ teaspoon hot paprika in lieu of the 1 teaspoon sweet.

MAKES 4 SERVINGS

8 small red potatoes, cut into 8 pieces each
½ cup reduced-fat mayonnaise
2 scallions, thinly sliced
1 teaspoon sweet paprika
1 teaspoon snipped chives
½ teaspoon salt
⅛ teaspoon freshly ground pepper
8 garlic cloves, roasted* and peeled
2 cups mesclun

1. Steam the potatoes over boiling water until fork-tender, about 6 minutes.
2. In a bowl, mix the mayonnaise, scallions, paprika, chives, salt and pepper; press in the garlic. Fold in the potatoes. Refrigerate, covered, until chilled, at least 30 minutes.
3. To serve, divide the mesclun among 4 plates; top with the potato salad.

PER SERVING: 239 CALORIES, 6 G TOTAL FAT, 1 G SATURATED FAT, 7 MG CHOLESTEROL, 463 MG SODIUM, 43 G TOTAL CARBOHYDRATE, 4 G DIETARY FIBER, 5 G PROTEIN, 61 MG CALCIUM.

POINTS PER SERVING: 4.

To roast garlic, preheat oven to 350° F. Wrap 8 garlic cloves in foil and bake until softened, about 45 minutes; let cool 10 minutes, then remove foil.

Bean Cakes on Salsa

Be sure to use a high-quality fresh salsa, which you should be able to find in the dairy case of your supermarket. As a variation, make the cakes with pinto beans.

MAKES 6 SERVINGS

One 15-ounce can chickpeas, rinsed and drained
⅓ cup reduced-fat sour cream
4 garlic cloves, peeled
1 teaspoon ground cumin
½ teaspoon salt
¾ teaspoon green hot sauce
¼ cup + 2 tablespoons white cornmeal
1½ cups prepared salsa

1. In a food processor, puree the beans, sour cream, garlic, cumin, salt, hot sauce and 2 tablespoons of the cornmeal; scrape into a bowl. Refrigerate, covered, chilled, about 30 minutes.

2. Form the mixture into six 3" round cakes, about ½" thick. Put the remaining ¼ cup of cornmeal on a plate and coat the cakes on both sides with the cornmeal.

3. Heat a large nonstick skillet over medium heat; spray with olive oil–flavored nonstick cooking spray. Cook the cakes until browned on the bottom, 5–6 minutes. Spray the tops of the cakes, turn them over and cook until brown on the other side, about 5 minutes longer. Spoon the salsa onto each of 6 plates, then top with a bean cake.

Per serving: 137 Calories, 3 g Total Fat, 1 g Saturated Fat, 4 mg Cholesterol, 374 mg Sodium, 23 g Total Carbohydrate, 4 g Dietary Fiber, 6 g Protein, 76 mg Calcium.

POINTS PER SERVING: 2.

Tip: The spiciness of this dish depends on two factors: the salsa you choose as well as the green hot sauce.

Potato–Red Pepper Frittata

WHOLE EGGS AND EGG SUBSTITUTE made from egg whites reduce fat without compromising taste. If you'd rather use egg whites, you'll need eight to equal one cup of egg substitute.

MAKES 8 SERVINGS

4 small red potatoes, thinly sliced
1 sweet onion, thinly sliced
1 red bell pepper, seeded and cut into strips
1 cup fat-free egg substitute
2 eggs
¼ cup grated pecorino Romano cheese
½ teaspoon salt
¼ teaspoon freshly ground pepper
2 tablespoons chopped parsley

1. Preheat the oven to 350° F; place a 10" ovenproof skillet in the oven.

2. In a microwavable dish, combine the potatoes, onion and bell pepper. Cover with plastic wrap and microwave on High until fork-tender, about 5 minutes.

3. In a large bowl, mix the egg substitute, eggs, cheese, salt and pepper; mix in the vegetables. Carefully remove the skillet from the oven, spray with nonstick cooking spray and pour in the egg mixture. Bake until the edges are set and the frittata is lightly browned across the top, 20–25 minutes. Cool 15 minutes. Invert onto a plate, then sprinkle with the parsley.

PER SERVING: 101 CALORIES, 3 G TOTAL FAT, 1 G SATURATED FAT, 50 MG CHOLESTEROL, 256 MG SODIUM, 11 G TOTAL CARBOHYDRATE, 1 G DIETARY FIBER, 8 G PROTEIN, 64 MG CALCIUM.

POINTS PER SERVING: 2.

Tip: Pecorino Romano is a sheep's milk cheese that has a stronger taste than Parmesan; its hard texture makes it perfect for grating.

Goat Cheese Crostini

Although these are delicious as they are, broiling until the cheese just begins to brown, 1–2 minutes, will enhance the flavor. If you don't broil the crostini, they can be made 15–30 minutes ahead of time, but they should be served at once if broiled.

MAKES 4 SERVINGS

¼ cup goat cheese
1 tablespoon chopped flat-leaf parsley
⅛ teaspoon freshly ground pepper
1 garlic clove, peeled
1 teaspoon olive oil
Eight ½" baguette slices, toasted

In a small bowl, combine the goat cheese, parsley and pepper. Press in the garlic; add the oil and mix until smooth. Spread on the baguette slices.

Per serving: 200 Calories, 7 g Total Fat, 3 g Saturated Fat, 11 mg Cholesterol, 378 mg Sodium, 27 g Total Carbohydrate, 2 g Dietary Fiber, 8 g Protein, 83 mg Calcium.

POINTS PER SERVING: 4.

Tip: Chervil, a member of the parsley family, has a mild anise flavor; if you like, substitute an equal amount for the parsley. For a flavor boost, use roasted garlic if you have some on hand.

Tuna Crostini

Use a dark Mediterranean olive (niçoise could be substituted for kalamata) but make sure to choose a variety packed in vinegar rather than in oil to save on fat grams.

MAKES 8 SERVINGS

¾ pound tuna steak
Juice of 1 lemon
1 teaspoon anchovy paste
¼ teaspoon freshly ground pepper
1 plum tomato, chopped
4 scallions, thinly sliced
6 kalamata olives, pitted and chopped
2 tablespoons chopped flat-leaf parsley
8 slices Italian bread, halved crosswise

1. Preheat the broiler. Broil the tuna 4" from the heat until just opaque in the center, about 5 minutes on each side.

2. In a large bowl, combine the lemon juice, anchovy paste and pepper. Flake in the tuna, then add the tomato, scallions, olives and parsley; toss to combine. Mound onto the bread.

PER SERVING: 103 CALORIES, 2 G TOTAL FAT, 0 G SATURATED FAT, 1 MG CHOLESTEROL, 227 MG SODIUM, 18 G TOTAL CARBOHYDRATE, 2 G DIETARY FIBER, 4 G PROTEIN, 47 MG CALCIUM.

POINTS PER SERVING: 2.

Tip: For a stronger anchovy taste, substitute 3 anchovy fillets, rinsed, patted dry and minced for the paste. If you find salt-packed anchovies (in a Greek or Italian food market), use them; they're far superior in flavor to the common tinned variety. To use, rinse under running water and separate into 2 fillets; discard the tail and fins, and as much of the spine as you can, then mince.

Marinated Shellfish in Endive

THIS IS A SEVICHE FOR THE NINETIES, since the seafood is lightly cooked for safety. Feel free to vary the seafood with whatever looks best at your fish market. Try such alternatives or additions as calamari rings (not tentacles) or chunks of red snapper or sole.

MAKES 6 SERVINGS

½ red bell pepper, seeded and diced
2 scallions, thinly sliced
1 tablespoon chopped cilantro
⅛ teaspoon crushed red pepper flakes
½ cup dry white wine
1 bay leaf
¼ pound shrimp, peeled, deveined and diced
¼ pound bay scallops
¼ teaspoon salt
Juice of 2 limes
6 large Belgian endive leaves

1. In a bowl, combine the bell pepper, scallions, cilantro and pepper flakes.
2. In a medium saucepan, combine the wine, bay leaf and ¾ cup water; bring to a boil and boil 3 minutes. Reduce the heat and add the shrimp and scallops; simmer until the shrimp turn bright pink, about 1 minute. Drain, discarding the bay leaf, and add the seafood to the vegetables. Stir in the salt, then mix in the lime juice. Spoon into the endive leaves.

PER SERVING: 78 CALORIES, 1 G TOTAL FAT, 0 G SATURATED FAT, 35 MG CHOLESTEROL, 169 MG SODIUM, 7 G TOTAL CARBOHYDRATE, 3 G DIETARY FIBER, 8 G PROTEIN, 53 MG CALCIUM.

POINTS PER SERVING: 1.

Radicchio Bundles

WHEN A DISH HAS SO FEW INGREDIENTS, you want to make sure those you use are the highest quality. Seek out an Italian-style delicatessen to get authentic prosciutto di Parma and the freshest mozzarella.

MAKES 4 SERVINGS

12 radicchio leaves, blanched
2 ounces prosciutto di Parma, thinly sliced and halved
¼ pound fresh mozzarella cheese, thinly sliced

1. Preheat the oven to 350° F.

2. In the center of each radicchio leaf, place a piece of prosciutto and a slice of cheese. Fold the stem end of the leaf over the filling, then fold in the sides and roll up; secure the bundles with a toothpick. Place the bundles in a baking dish. Bake until the cheese is melted and the radicchio has given off its liquid, 20–25 minutes.

PER SERVING: 96 CALORIES, 5 G TOTAL FAT, 3 G SATURATED FAT, 23 MG CHOLESTEROL, 340 MG SODIUM, 2 G TOTAL CARBOHYDRATE, 0 G DIETARY FIBER, 10 G PROTEIN, 189 MG CALCIUM.

POINTS PER SERVING: 2.

Tip: Blanching the radicchio makes the leaves easier to work with. To blanch them, bring a small saucepan of water to a boil. Core the radicchio as you would a tomato and place it in the boiling water for no more than 10 seconds. Run briefly under cold water, then peel the leaves from the core end. You'll have a little radicchio left over, but it can be used in a salad.

Spicy Veal Skewers

CUBED VEAL STEW MEAT is from the same lean cut; buy it if you're pressed for time. A high-quality Hungarian paprika will give the richest flavor. Be warned that hot paprika is *hot*. When you see a recipe calling for this much, be sure to use sweet paprika (it's often not labeled as such, but simply "paprika").

MAKES 6 SERVINGS

1 pound veal top round, trimmed and cut into eighteen 1" cubes
1 cup dry red wine
2 scallions, cut into 1" lengths
2 tablespoons paprika
1 teaspoon freshly ground pepper
¼ teaspoon salt
8 sprigs parsley
4 garlic cloves, peeled

1. Soak six 8" bamboo skewers in water for at least 1 hour. Meanwhile, in a gallon-size sealable plastic bag, combine the veal, wine, scallions, paprika, pepper, salt and parsley; press in the garlic. Seal the bag, squeezing out the air; turn to coat the veal. Refrigerate, turning the bag occasionally, at least 1 hour.

2. Preheat the broiler. Thread 3 chunks of veal onto each skewer, leaving about ½" between chunks. Place the skewers on the broiler rack and broil 4" from the heat until well browned, 4–5 minutes. Turn the skewers and broil until browned on the second side, about 4 minutes longer.

PER SERVING: 132 CALORIES, 3 G TOTAL FAT, 1 G SATURATED FAT, 60 MG CHOLESTEROL, 172 MG SODIUM, 4 G TOTAL CARBOHYDRATE, 1 G DIETARY FIBER, 16 G PROTEIN, 39 MG CALCIUM.

POINTS PER SERVING: 3.

Tip: Bamboo skewers need to soak to avoid charring under the broiler; you can substitute metal skewers. These skewers are savory enough that they don't need a dipping sauce. Serve them alone, or with an assortment of small plates.

Smoked Turkey Tostadas

FOR THE BEST FLAVOR, look for smoked turkey breast that's still on the bone. You'll find it in your supermarket's meat section, near the other turkey products.

MAKES 6 SERVINGS

½ pound smoked turkey breast, chopped
4 plum tomatoes, diced
¼ cup chopped cilantro
4 garlic cloves, peeled
1 small red onion, diced
1 serrano pepper, seeded, deveined and minced (wear gloves to prevent irritation)
Juice of 1 lime
2 teaspoons chopped oregano
½ teaspoon salt
6 soft corn tortillas
3 cups mesclun

1. Preheat the oven to 400° F.

2. In a bowl, combine the turkey, tomatoes and cilantro; press in the garlic. Stir in the onion, pepper and lime juice, then add the oregano and salt.

3. Place the tortillas directly onto the middle oven rack and bake until toasted, 5–6 minutes. Transfer to plates; top with the mesclun and turkey mixture.

PER SERVING: 160 CALORIES, 3 G TOTAL FAT, 1 G SATURATED FAT, 16 MG CHOLESTEROL, 759 MG SODIUM, 24 G TOTAL CARBOHYDRATE, 2 G DIETARY FIBER, 10 G PROTEIN, 38 MG CALCIUM.

POINTS PER SERVING: 3.

Tip: If you have a toaster oven, the tortillas can be toasted in it
for the same number of minutes as in a full-size oven.

Family Meals

Thyme Roasted Chicken

*U*SE A GLASS MEASURING CUP for skimming the pan juices; it is heat-resistant and will allow you to see the layer of fat that will form on top. A hint: Drop in an ice cube to make the fat coagulate faster.

MAKES 4 SERVINGS

12 garlic cloves, roasted*
1 tablespoon thyme leaves
1 tablespoon olive oil
¾ teaspoon salt
¼ teaspoon + ⅛ teaspoon freshly ground pepper
One 3½–4-pound chicken, rinsed and patted dry
1 cup low-sodium chicken broth
½ cup apple juice
2 tablespoons packed dark brown sugar

1. Preheat the oven to 375° F. Place a roasting rack inside a roasting pan.

2. Squeeze the garlic pulp into a food processor, discarding the peels. Add the thyme, oil, ½ teaspoon of the salt and ¼ teaspoon of the pepper to the garlic; puree to form a paste. Gently lift the skin from the breast of the chicken; push the paste under the skin, spreading to cover the meat.

3. Place the chicken, breast-side up, on the rack, tucking the wings under. Roast until the chicken is cooked through and the juices run clear when the thigh is pierced with a fork, about 1 hour; an instant-

read thermometer inserted in the thigh, not touching any bone, should register 180° F. Transfer the chicken to a plate, wrap it in foil and let stand while you make the sauce.

4. Pour the pan juices into a glass measuring cup and skim the fat. Transfer the juices to a small saucepan. Add the broth and apple juice; bring to a boil and boil until reduced to about ¾ cup, about 10 minutes, then stir in the brown sugar, the remaining ¼ teaspoon of salt and ⅛ teaspoon of pepper. Carve the chicken, removing the skin before eating. Serve with the sauce on the side.

PER SERVING: 309 CALORIES, 12 G TOTAL FAT, 3 G SATURATED FAT, 102 MG CHOLESTEROL, 566 MG SODIUM, 14 G TOTAL CARBOHYDRATE, 1 G DIETARY FIBER, 34 G PROTEIN, 55 MG CALCIUM.

POINTS PER SERVING: 7.

Tip: Don't truss the chicken or even tie the legs together; leaving the cavity open allows greater heat circulation, so the bird cooks faster.

To roast garlic, preheat oven to 350° F. Wrap 12 garlic cloves in foil and bake until softened, about 45 minutes; let cool 10 minutes, then remove foil.

Honey-Ginger Chicken with Orange-Parsley Rice

For a more even coating, after you've rolled the chicken breasts in the cornmeal mixture, spread the mixture with a knife. White cornmeal is a better choice than yellow when broiling; yellow cornmeal is quicker to burn under the direct heat, while white cornmeal browns better.

MAKES 4 SERVINGS

⅔ cup orange juice
1 cup long-grain rice
1 tablespoon chopped parsley
1 teaspoon grated orange zest
½ cup pecan halves
¼ cup white cornmeal
¼ teaspoon freshly ground pepper
1 tablespoon honey
½ tablespoon reduced-sodium soy sauce
½ teaspoon grated peeled gingerroot
Four 4-ounce skinless boneless chicken breasts

1. Preheat the broiler.

2. In a medium saucepan, combine the orange juice and 1⅓ cups water; bring to a boil. Stir in the rice; reduce the heat and simmer, covered, until the liquid is absorbed and the rice is tender, about 15 minutes. Fluff with a fork, then stir in the parsley and orange zest.

3. Meanwhile, in a food processor, combine the pecans, cornmeal and pepper until the nuts are finely ground. Transfer to a plate. In a shallow bowl, combine the honey, soy sauce and gingerroot. Dip the chicken in the honey mixture, then roll it in the cornmeal mixture. Place on a broiler rack and broil until crusty brown and cooked through, about 4 minutes on each side. Serve with the rice.

PER SERVING: 335 CALORIES, 11 G TOTAL FAT, 1 G SATURATED FAT, 66 MG CHOLESTEROL, 142 MG SODIUM, 29 G TOTAL CARBOHYDRATE, 2 G DIETARY FIBER, 30 G PROTEIN, 30 MG CALCIUM.

POINTS PER SERVING: 7.

Tip: A small amount of nuts, crushed, adds wonderful flavor and richness with less fat than you might imagine. If you prefer to avoid nuts, however, use wheat-and-barley cereal nuggets instead.

Individual Shepherd's Pies

If you don't have ovenproof soup crocks (or if yours are smaller than 1½ cups), make one large pie in a 2-quart casserole.

MAKES 4 SERVINGS

2 cups low-sodium chicken broth
1 pound turkey breast tenderloin, cut into 1" pieces
One 10-ounce package frozen baby peas, thawed
One 8-ounce bag yellow pearl onions, peeled
2 carrots, diced
4 teaspoons unsalted butter
3 tablespoons all-purpose flour
1 tablespoon Old Bay seasoning
2 Yukon gold potatoes, peeled, cubed and cooked
½ cup low-fat buttermilk
½ teaspoon salt
¼ teaspoon freshly ground pepper

1. Preheat the oven to 350° F.

2. In a large saucepan, bring the broth to a boil. Add the turkey and poach until no longer pink, about 1 minute. Add the peas, onions and carrots; bring back to a boil, then cover and remove from the heat.

3. In a small skillet, melt the butter over medium heat. Stir in the flour; cook until the flour is browned and begins to smell nutty. Add ½ cup of the poaching liquid and stir until smooth, then stir in the Old Bay seasoning. Transfer this mixture to the saucepan, stirring to blend. Divide the turkey, vegetables and sauce among four 1½-cup soup crocks.

4. In a bowl, mash the potatoes until smooth; stir in the buttermilk, salt and pepper. Spread the mashed potatoes over the turkey mixture. Bake until the potatoes are browned and the filling is bubbling, about 25 minutes.

PER SERVING: 373 CALORIES, 6 G TOTAL FAT, 3 G SATURATED FAT, 84 MG CHOLESTEROL, 1,040 MG SODIUM, 41 G TOTAL CARBOHYDRATE, 6 G DIETARY FIBER, 37 G PROTEIN, 101 MG CALCIUM.

POINTS PER SERVING: 7.

Tip: To cook the potato cubes quickly, put them into a microwavable container along with 2 tablespoons water. Cover loosely with plastic wrap and microwave on High until fork-tender, about 3 minutes.

Piedmontese Braised Turkey

THE PIEDMONT REGION is in the northwestern part of Italy, bordering France and Switzerland. This preparation is typical of the red-wine braising done in the area.

MAKES 6 SERVINGS

2 cups low-sodium chicken broth
1 cup dry red wine
1½ pounds turkey breast tenderloin
1 small red onion, thinly sliced
2 tablespoons chopped sage
1 tablespoon cornstarch
½ teaspoon salt
¼ teaspoon freshly ground pepper

1. In a medium nonstick skillet, bring the broth and wine to a boil and boil 2 minutes. Add the turkey, onion and sage. Reduce the heat and simmer, covered, until the turkey is cooked through, about 15 minutes. Remove from the heat.

2. To make the gravy, transfer ¼ cup of the braising liquid to a small bowl and mix with the cornstarch. Transfer 1 cup of the braising liquid to a small saucepan; bring to a boil. Remove from the heat and whisk in the dissolved cornstarch. Return to the heat and cook until thickened and translucent, about 2 minutes. Stir in the salt and pepper.

3. Thinly slice the turkey and fan onto dinner plates. Scatter each plate with the onion and drizzle with the gravy.

PER SERVING: 177 CALORIES, 2 G TOTAL FAT, 1 G SATURATED FAT, 72 MG CHOLESTEROL, 289 MG SODIUM, 4 G TOTAL CARBOHYDRATE, 1 G DIETARY FIBER, 29 G PROTEIN, 36 MG CALCIUM.

POINTS PER SERVING: 4.

Tip: The tenderloin is the lean center portion of the turkey breast.
You could also use 1½ pounds skinless boneless breast.

Soy Steak and Noodles

*E*VEN IF YOU TYPICALLY AVOID SPICY INGREDIENTS like pepper flakes, don't omit them here; a small amount is needed to balance the sweetness of the hoisin and the sharpness of the ginger. Of course, if you prefer a spicier dish, increase the amount you use up to ½ teaspoon.

MAKES 6 SERVINGS

2½ tablespoons reduced-sodium soy sauce
1 tablespoon dry sherry
½ teaspoon grated peeled gingerroot
1 garlic clove, minced
1 pound flank steak, trimmed
One 8-ounce package lo mein noodles
2 tablespoons hoisin sauce
1 teaspoon Asian sesame oil
⅛ teaspoon crushed red pepper flakes, or to taste
1 red bell pepper, seeded and thinly sliced
1 green bell pepper, seeded and thinly sliced
2 scallions, thinly sliced

1. Preheat the broiler. In a shallow baking dish, mix 1 tablespoon of the soy sauce, the sherry, gingerroot and garlic. Add the steak, turning to coat. Let stand 20 minutes to marinate.

2. Meanwhile, cook the noodles according to package directions; drain and transfer to a large bowl. Toss with the remaining 1½ tablespoons of soy sauce, the hoisin sauce, sesame oil and pepper flakes, then add the bell peppers and scallions; toss to combine.

3. Broil the steak 5" from the heat until done to taste, about 4 minutes on each side for medium. Slice paper thin on the diagonal across the grain. Divide the noodles and vegetables among 4 plates; top with the steak.

PER SERVING: 244 CALORIES, 9 G TOTAL FAT, 4 G SATURATED FAT, 51 MG CHOLESTEROL, 376 MG SODIUM, 17 G TOTAL CARBOHYDRATE, 3 G DIETARY FIBER, 24 G PROTEIN, 31 MG CALCIUM.

POINTS PER SERVING: 5.

Tip: Look for wide, flat, white lo mein noodles in your supermarket's Asian food section; if you can't find them, use soba noodles or fettuccine.

Pork Tenderloin with Pearl Onion Sauce

Tiny PORK TENDERLOINS have liberated roast pork from the tyranny of lengthy roasting times! If you prefer, roast the tenderloin in a 425° F oven for 20 minutes, or cook it in a ridged grill pan on the stovetop for 5 minutes on each side. The grill pan produces crusty bands where the ridges sear the mustard into the meat.

MAKES 4 SERVINGS

½ tablespoon coarse-grain Dijon mustard
One 1-pound pork tenderloin
½ tablespoon olive oil
One 6-ounce bag pearl onions, peeled
1 garlic clove, minced
½ cup low-sodium chicken broth
½ tablespoon balsamic vinegar
1 teaspoon thyme leaves
1 teaspoon packed dark brown sugar

1. Spray the broiler rack lightly with nonstick cooking spray; preheat the broiler. Rub the mustard over the pork to coat; place on the broiler rack. Broil 5" from the heat until done to taste, about 5 minutes on each side for medium. Transfer the pork to a plate, wrap it in foil and let stand 10 minutes before thinly slicing.

2. Meanwhile, in a medium skillet, heat the oil. Sauté the onions, stirring constantly, until they begin to brown, about 4 minutes. Stir in the garlic, then stir in the broth, vinegar, thyme and brown sugar; bring to a boil and boil until the liquid is reduced by one-third and thickens into a sauce, 3–4 minutes. Spoon over the pork.

PER SERVING: 192 CALORIES, 6 G TOTAL FAT, 2 G SATURATED FAT, 74 MG CHOLESTEROL, 127 MG SODIUM, 8 G TOTAL CARBOHYDRATE, 1 G DIETARY FIBER, 25 G PROTEIN, 27 MG CALCIUM.

POINTS PER SERVING: 4.

Tip: To peel pearl onions, blanch for 2 minutes in boiling water, drain and rinse briefly under cold running water. Cut off the root ends and slip off the peels. Or use thawed frozen pearl onions, which are already peeled.

Lamb Kebabs with Couscous

THIS RECIPE ALSO WORKS WELL using beef cubes in place of lamb. Although couscous is most frequently associated with Moroccan cooking, it's fairly common in southern Italian cuisines, especially those of Sicily and Sardinia.

MAKES 4 SERVINGS

1 pound lamb, trimmed and cut into 1" cubes
2 tablespoons dried oregano, crumbled
1 cup dry red wine
2 garlic cloves, smashed and peeled
¼ teaspoon salt
¼ teaspoon freshly ground pepper
2 cups low-sodium chicken broth
1⅓ cups couscous
12 cherry tomatoes, quartered
2 tablespoons chopped parsley
1 teaspoon chopped thyme
1 teaspoon extra virgin olive oil

1. In a nonreactive bowl, combine the lamb and oregano; stir in the wine, garlic, salt and pepper. Refrigerate, covered, at least 1 hour.

2. Preheat the broiler. Thread about 5 pieces of lamb onto each of 4 skewers, leaving about ½" between each cube. Broil 5" from the heat until crusty brown on the outside, about 4 minutes on each side.

3. Meanwhile, in a medium saucepan, bring the chicken broth to a boil. Stir in the couscous, cover, remove from the heat and let stand until the liquid is absorbed, about 5 minutes. Stir in the tomatoes, parsley, thyme and oil. Divide the couscous among 4 plates and serve with a skewer of lamb.

PER SERVING: 461 CALORIES, 10 G TOTAL FAT, 4 G SATURATED FAT, 77 MG CHOLESTEROL, 292 MG SODIUM, 50 G TOTAL CARBOHYDRATE, 4 G DIETARY FIBER, 33 G PROTEIN, 67 MG CALCIUM.

POINTS PER SERVING: 9.

Tip: Leaving a space between the lamb chunks allows air to circulate, so the meat cooks faster. If you use bamboo skewers rather than metal, soak in water for at least 1 hour to prevent charring.

Roasted Ratatouille Lasagna

*I*F YOU THINK OF VEGETARIAN LASAGNA AS BLAND, wait till you try this version. Roasting intensifies the flavors and imparts an intriguing smoky nuance. Using no-boil lasagna noodles saves at least 30 minutes of preparation time, reduces the number of pots to wash and eliminates burned fingertips; the noodles break easily to fit in the casserole.

MAKES 6 SERVINGS

1 medium (1-pound) eggplant, chunked
2 medium zucchini, chunked
4 plum tomatoes, halved
1 yellow bell pepper, seeded and quartered
1 white onion, chunked
1 garlic bulb
1 cup part-skim ricotta cheese
2 tablespoons grated Parmesan cheese
2 tablespoons chopped basil
1 egg white
¼ teaspoon freshly ground pepper
8 no-boil lasagna noodles
1 cup shredded part-skim mozzarella cheese

1. Preheat the oven to 375° F. Spray a baking sheet with nonstick cooking spray. Scatter the eggplant, zucchini, tomatoes, bell pepper and onion on the baking sheet; spray lightly with additional cooking spray. Wrap the garlic in foil. Roast the vegetables until well browned, about 45 minutes, tossing every 15 minutes. Roast the garlic at the same time until softened, about 45 minutes. Peel the bell pepper, tomatoes and garlic. In a food processor, puree the tomatoes and garlic. Finely chop the bell pepper, eggplant, zucchini and onion. In a large bowl, combine all the vegetables.

2. In a small bowl, mix the ricotta, Parmesan, basil, egg white and ground pepper. Spray a 7 x 11" baking dish with nonstick cooking spray. Spread ¼ cup of the vegetable mixture over the bottom of the baking dish; top with 2 noodles. Spread an additional 1½ cups of the vegetable mixture over the noodles; top with 2 more noodles. Spread with all of the ricotta mixture; top with 2 more noodles. Spread with an additional 1 cup of the vegetable mixture, top with the last 2 noodles and the remaining vegetable mixture; sprinkle with the mozzarella. Cover with foil and bake 30 minutes. Remove the foil and bake until the cheese is melted and browned, about 5 minutes longer.

Per serving: 268 Calories, 8 g Total Fat, 4 g Saturated Fat, 25 mg Cholesterol, 196 mg Sodium, 34 g Total Carbohydrate, 4 g Dietary Fiber, 16 g Protein, 291 mg Calcium.

POINTS PER SERVING: 5.

Tip: Spray the foil lightly with nonstick cooking spray before covering the lasagna to help keep the cheese from sticking to it.

No time to layer and bake the lasagna? Puree the ratatouille and use as a simple sauce for pasta, or spoon over slices of grilled polenta. Or serve the ratatouille as a side dish, sprinkled with chopped basil and oregano. It makes a tasty omelet filling, or stir it into simmering vegetable stock for a roasted vegetable soup.

Pizza Provençal

Semolina is coarsely ground durum wheat (the type of wheat used to make pasta); it's even higher in protein than bread flour, so it will result in a very dense, chewy crust. If you have a choice, opt for Italian fontina cheese; the French and Danish versions aren't nearly as full-flavored.

MAKES 8 SERVINGS

2 cups all-purpose flour
1⅓ cups semolina flour
1 tablespoon kosher salt, or ½ tablespoon table salt
1 envelope rapid-rise yeast
½ teaspoon sugar
4 plum tomatoes, cut into rounds
1 red onion, thinly sliced
12 kalamata olives, pitted and chopped
¼ cup chopped basil
4 ounces fontina cheese, grated (about ⅔ cup)

1. In a food processor, combine the flours, salt, yeast and sugar. With the machine running, drizzle 1¼ cups hot tap water through the feed tube just until the dough forms a ball.

2. Spray a large ceramic or glass bowl with nonstick cooking spray; place the dough in the bowl. Cover loosely with plastic wrap and let the dough rise in a warm, draft-free place until it doubles in volume and no longer springs back to the touch, about 20 minutes. Meanwhile, preheat the oven to 450° F.

3. Cut the dough in half and place each on a 15" pizza pan. Press the dough with your fingertips to cover the pans completely. Layer the crusts with the tomatoes, onion and olives; scatter with the basil and cheese. Bake until the crusts are golden and the cheese is melted and browned, 15–18 minutes.

Per serving: 278 Calories, 5 g Total Fat, 2 g Saturated Fat, 10 mg Cholesterol, 200 mg Sodium, 48 g Total Carbohydrate, 3 g Dietary Fiber, 10 g Protein, 70 mg Calcium.

POINTS PER SERVING: 5.

Tip: Rapid-rise yeast cuts the time needed for this dough to rise by one-third. If you're planning to buy a pizza pan, choose one with holes, which allow the oven heat to crisp the bottom of the crust.

Gnocchi Marinara

*H*IGH-QUALITY, ALREADY-MADE GNOCCHI is now available in many supermarkets; look for it near the dried pastas. It comes in a variety of flavors and it cooks in 3–4 minutes.

MAKES 4 SERVINGS

1 onion, chopped
2 teaspoons olive oil
3 garlic cloves, peeled
2 tomatoes, peeled, seeded and chopped
¼ cup chopped basil
Pinch crushed red pepper flakes
One 16-ounce package gnocchi, cooked
2 tablespoons grated Parmesan cheese

In a large nonstick skillet, combine the onion and oil. Sauté until the onion is golden, about 5 minutes. Press in the garlic, then add the tomatoes, basil and pepper flakes. Cook until the tomatoes have broken down to form a thick sauce, about 20 minutes. Add the gnocchi; toss to coat. Serve at once, sprinkled with the cheese.

PER SERVING: 252 CALORIES, 17 G TOTAL FAT, 6 G SATURATED FAT, 81 MG CHOLESTEROL, 360 MG SODIUM, 14 G TOTAL CARBOHYDRATE, 1 G DIETARY FIBER, 12 G PROTEIN, 278 MG CALCIUM.

POINTS PER SERVING: 6.

Tip: This is a good, basic tomato sauce that works well with a variety of pastas. Try it with a chunky shape like shells or radiatore, or serve it with polenta.

Baked Eggplant

BROILING THE EGGPLANT achieves a similar taste and texture to the usual, more cumbersome process of dipping slices into a batter, breading and then frying them. It also eliminates the need to salt the eggplant to remove the bitterness.

MAKES 6 SERVINGS

2 medium (1 pound each) eggplants, cut into ½" rounds
3 cups marinara sauce
24 large basil leaves
1¼ cups shredded part-skim mozzarella cheese

1. Preheat the broiler. Put the eggplant in a single layer on a baking sheet and spray with nonstick cooking spray. Broil until well browned, about 4 minutes. Turn the rounds over, spray again, and broil until well browned on the other side, about 4 minutes longer. Remove from the oven and reduce the temperature to 375° F.

2. Spread 1 cup of the marinara sauce in a shallow 11 x 14" baking dish. Add the eggplant rounds, overlapping slightly. Top with the remaining 2 cups sauce, then the basil leaves; sprinkle with the cheese. Bake until the sauce is heated through and the cheese has begun to brown, about 20 minutes. Let stand 10 minutes before cutting.

PER SERVING: 185 CALORIES, 8 G TOTAL FAT, 3 G SATURATED FAT, 14 MG CHOLESTEROL, 901 MG SODIUM, 23 G TOTAL CARBOHYDRATE, 4 G DIETARY FIBER, 9 G PROTEIN, 188 MG CALCIUM.

POINTS PER SERVING: 4.

Tip: To serve this as an appetizer, slice the eggplant lengthwise, top each slice with basil and cheese, roll up and secure with toothpicks before baking.

Fish and Chips

FOR AN AUTHENTIC BRITISH TREAT, serve these with malt vinegar. While the fish and chips bake, mix up a green salad, or serve with Orange and Red Onion Salad (page 155). Ginger Crisp Cookies (page 207) finish the meal.

MAKES 4 SERVINGS

2 large baking potatoes, scrubbed and cut lengthwise into 16 spears each
3 tablespoons Old Bay seasoning
½ cup yellow cornmeal
Four 4-ounce cod fillets

1. Preheat the oven to 425° F. Spray the potatoes with nonstick cooking spray. Place in a sealable plastic bag with 1 tablespoon of the Old Bay seasoning; seal the bag and shake to coat. Transfer to a large baking sheet.

2. In the plastic bag, combine the cornmeal and the remaining 2 tablespoons of Old Bay; shake to mix. Spray the fish fillets with cooking spray and place in the bag; shake to coat. Place in a single layer on the baking sheet with the potatoes. Bake until the fish is golden brown and flakes easily and the potatoes are fork-tender, about 25 minutes.

PER SERVING: 243 CALORIES, 1 G TOTAL FAT, 0 G SATURATED FAT, 49 MG CHOLESTEROL, 1,134 MG SODIUM, 33 G TOTAL CARBOHYDRATE, 3 G DIETARY FIBER, 24 G PROTEIN, 25 MG CALCIUM.

POINTS PER SERVING: 4.

Tip: If you prefer, substitute haddock fillets for the cod. Depending on the size of your baking sheets, you may need to use two. If so, switch the baking sheets' placement about halfway through the cooking time.

Elegant Entrées

Wild Mushroom Risotto with Chicken

CONTRARY TO POPULAR BELIEF, risotto does not have to be stirred constantly, just vigorously with each addition of stock.

MAKES 4 SERVINGS

1 teaspoon olive oil
1½ cups sliced white mushrooms
1½ cups sliced shiitake mushrooms
½ cup stemmed oyster mushrooms
3½ cups low-sodium chicken broth
1 cup Arborio rice
2 tablespoons grated Parmesan cheese
⅛ teaspoon freshly ground pepper
½ pound skinless boneless chicken breast

1. In a large nonstick skillet, heat the oil. Sauté the mushrooms until they have given off their moisture and are soft, about 6 minutes.

2. Meanwhile, in a medium saucepan, bring the broth to a boil. Reduce the heat and simmer. Preheat the broiler.

3. Heat a medium nonstick saucepan over medium-high heat. Add the rice and cook, stirring, until lightly toasted. Reduce the heat to medium. Add 1 cup of the broth; cook, stirring, until the broth is absorbed. Stir in the mushrooms. Continue adding broth, ½ cup at a time, stirring until the broth is

absorbed before adding more, until the rice is tender. The total cooking time should be 25–30 minutes. Stir in the cheese and pepper.

4. Meanwhile, broil the chicken until cooked through and browned, about 2 minutes on each side. Cut into strips. Serve the risotto, topping each portion with strips of chicken.

Per serving: 304 Calories, 5 g Total Fat, 2 g Saturated Fat, 40 mg Cholesterol, 194 mg Sodium, 44 g Total Carbohydrate, 3 g Dietary Fiber, 22 g Protein, 72 mg Calcium.

POINTS PER SERVING: 6.

Tip: Oyster mushrooms do not have to be chopped. When the thick, woody stem is cut off, the mushroom separates into small sections. If you prefer, you can omit the oyster mushrooms and use 2 cups of shiitakes.

Cornish Hens with Apricot Sauce

Serve this with rice pilaf or risotto and a simple vegetable, such as roasted Brussels sprouts or sautéed green beans. For a more traditional and slightly sweeter sauce, use ruby port instead of coffee liqueur. If you're entertaining, leave the birds whole for a more dramatic presentation. Roast whole birds at 350° F for about 1 hour (an instant-read thermometer inserted in the thigh should register 180° F).

MAKES 4 SERVINGS

½ cup orange juice
¼ cup + 2 tablespoons coffee liqueur
¼ cup apricot preserves
2 tablespoons balsamic vinegar
2 tablespoons Dijon mustard
Two 1½-pound Cornish hens, quartered

1. Preheat the oven to 450° F. In a small saucepan, combine the orange juice, liqueur and preserves; bring to a boil. Cook, stirring, until the preserves melt, 1–2 minutes. Reduce the heat and simmer until syrupy, about 4 minutes. Remove from the heat and stir in the vinegar and mustard. Transfer ¼ cup of the sauce to a small bowl.

2. Gently lift the skin from the meat on each hen; brush 1 tablespoon of the sauce from the bowl under the skin of each. Place the hens in a single layer in a roasting pan. Roast until cooked through, about 25 minutes.

3. Just before serving, bring the sauce back to a boil. Place 2 pieces of hen on each of 4 plates; spoon the sauce over each.

Per serving: 296 Calories, 5 g Total Fat, 1 g Saturated Fat, 103 mg Cholesterol, 279 mg Sodium, 30 g Total Carbohydrate, 0 g Dietary Fiber, 24 g Protein, 34 mg Calcium.

POINTS PER SERVING: 6.

Tip: Transferring ¼ cup of the sauce to a bowl before brushing it onto the hens helps to avoid contaminating the rest of the sauce with harmful bacteria.

Paella Valenciana

THIS TRADITIONAL DISH from the Valencia region of Spain can be a real show-stopper when you serve it in the authentic Spanish manner: Bring it to the table in a paella pan, garnished with chopped flat-leaf parsley and lemon wedges. Lacking a paella pan, you can use a skillet, at least 12" but preferably 14–15", with ovenproof handles.

MAKES 8 SERVINGS

3½ cups low-sodium chicken broth
⅛ teaspoon saffron threads
⅛ teaspoon cayenne pepper, or to taste
2 teaspoons olive oil
1 white onion, chopped
2 garlic cloves, chopped
1 pound medium shrimp, peeled and deveined
1 pound skinless boneless chicken breasts, cubed
2 cups Arborio or other short-grained rice
½ cup dry white wine
¼ pound smoked turkey sausage, thinly sliced
1 pound asparagus, steamed and cut into 1" lengths

1. Preheat the oven to 325° F. In a medium saucepan, combine the broth, saffron and cayenne; bring to a boil.

2. Meanwhile, in a very large nonstick skillet or paella pan, heat the oil. Sauté the onion and garlic until they just begin to color, about 2 minutes. Add the shrimp and chicken; sauté until the shrimp turn pink and the chicken begins to brown, about 1 minute. Add the rice and cook, stirring, 1 minute. Add the broth mixture and the wine, then stir in the sausage and asparagus; bring back to a boil. Reduce the heat to medium and cook 5 minutes. Transfer the pan to the oven. Bake until the liquid is absorbed and the rice is tender, about 15 minutes. Serve at once.

PER SERVING: 379 CALORIES, 6 G TOTAL FAT, 2 G SATURATED FAT, 131 MG CHOLESTEROL, 281 MG SODIUM, 45 G TOTAL CARBOHYDRATE, 3 G DIETARY FIBER, 33 G PROTEIN, 66 MG CALCIUM.

POINTS PER SERVING: 7.

Pan-Seared Filets Mignons with Shallot-Cognac Sauce

FILETS MIGNONS ARE STEAKS cut from the tenderloin, so they are lean, tender and virtually fuss-free. Searing is a perfect cooking method for them—it's fast and it seals in the juices—since it lessens the chance of the steaks drying out and becoming tough.

MAKES 4 SERVINGS

1 tablespoon fennel seeds, finely chopped
¾ teaspoon coarsely ground black pepper
½ teaspoon salt
Four 4-ounce filets mignons, about 1" thick, trimmed of all fat
½ teaspoon olive oil
½ cup dry red wine
½ cup beef broth
2 shallots, finely chopped
¼ cup cognac

1. On a sheet of wax paper, combine the fennel, pepper and salt. Coat the steaks on all sides with the fennel mixture.

2. In a medium nonstick skillet, heat the oil. Sauté the steaks over medium-high heat until browned, about 1 minute on each side, then reduce the heat to medium and cook to taste, about 4 minutes on each side for medium-rare. Transfer the steaks to a serving plate.

3. Add the wine, broth and shallots to the skillet; bring to a boil, scraping up the browned bits in the bottom of skillet. Add the cognac; bring to a boil and boil until the pan juices are reduced by half, about 5 minutes. Stir in any juices that have accumulated around the steaks into the shallot sauce. Spoon the sauce over the steaks.

PER SERVING: 269 CALORIES, 9 G TOTAL FAT, 4 G SATURATED FAT, 70 MG CHOLESTEROL, 485 MG SODIUM, 8 G TOTAL CARBOHYDRATE, 1 G DIETARY FIBER, 25 G PROTEIN, 43 MG CALCIUM.

POINTS PER SERVING: 6.

Tip: To keep the fennel seeds from flying all over as you chop them, drizzle them with just a drop or two of olive oil.

Veal Ragout

ALTHOUGH YOU MIGHT WONDER HOW A RAGOUT, which is another name for stew, could be elegant, this flavorsome version certainly fits the bill. Serve it over a hearty pasta like penne or rigatoni or soft polenta, garnished with shavings of Parmigiano-Reggiano cheese, and a red wine like a Chianti or merlot on a winter's night. A salad of mixed baby greens alongside and a dessert like Lemon Curd Tartlets (page 206) or Pineapple and Orange Sorbet (page 197) round out the meal.

MAKES 6 SERVINGS

¾ pound veal top round, trimmed and cut into ¼" cubes
2 teaspoons extra virgin olive oil
1 carrot, minced
1 celery stalk, minced
1 white onion, minced
2 garlic cloves, minced
½ cup dry white wine
One 26-ounce box chopped tomatoes, with their juice
1 bay leaf
¾ teaspoon dried oregano, crumbled
½ teaspoon salt
⅛ teaspoon crushed red pepper flakes

1. In a Dutch oven, combine the veal and olive oil; sauté until the veal is no longer pink, 2–3 minutes. Add the carrot, celery, onion and garlic; sauté until the vegetables are soft, 8–10 minutes.

2. Pour in the wine, increase the heat to high and cook until the wine is reduced to about 2 tablespoons, about 5 minutes. Stir in the tomatoes, bay leaf, oregano, salt and pepper flakes. Reduce the heat and simmer, covered, until the meat is very tender and the sauce is very thick, about 1–1¼ hours. Discard the bay leaf.

PER SERVING: 130 CALORIES, 4 G TOTAL FAT, 1 G SATURATED FAT, 45 MG CHOLESTEROL, 268 MG SODIUM, 8 G TOTAL CARBOHYDRATE, 2 G DIETARY FIBER, 13 G PROTEIN, 31 MG CALCIUM.

POINTS PER SERVING: 3.

Tip: Cook with white wine but serve with red? Yes, indeed: Veal should be cooked with white wine, since red would be too overpowering. But tomato-based stews and ragouts should be served with a medium-bodied red.

Pork Loin and Choucroute

PORK AND SAUERKRAUT are a natural combination that apples only serve to improve. In France, choucroute is traditionally cooked with juniper berries or caraway seeds, onions and plenty of goose fat; this version has only a fraction of the fat. For best flavor, use the sauerkraut found in plastic bags in the supermarket refrigerator section rather than the bottled or canned variety.

MAKES 4 SERVINGS

1 tablespoon Dijon mustard
2 teaspoons thyme leaves
1 teaspoon packed dark brown sugar
1 garlic clove, minced
½ teaspoon salt
½ teaspoon freshly ground pepper
One 1–1¼-pound pork tenderloin
2 ounces smoked turkey sausage, chopped
1 small white onion, minced
1 Granny Smith apple, cored and grated
1 cup apple cider vinegar
1 pound sauerkraut, rinsed and squeezed dry

1. Preheat the oven to 350° F. In a small bowl, mix the mustard, 1 teaspoon of the thyme, the brown sugar, garlic, salt and pepper. Coat the tenderloin with the mixture and place it in a shallow roasting pan. Roast until the pork reaches an internal temperature of 160° F on an instant-read thermometer, about 30 minutes. Transfer to a cutting board and let stand 10 minutes before slicing.

2. Meanwhile, in a medium saucepan, brown the sausage about 5 minutes. Stir in the onion, apple and the remaining teaspoon of thyme; cook, covered, until the onion is softened, about 5 minutes. Add the vinegar and cook until it is reduced by half, about 5 minutes. Stir in the sauerkraut and cook until the liquid is absorbed, about 5 minutes longer.

3. Slice the tenderloin into ½" medallions. Fan the medallions on 4 plates and serve with the sauerkraut.

PER SERVING: 263 CALORIES, 8 G TOTAL FAT, 2 G SATURATED FAT, 102 MG CHOLESTEROL, 1,390 MG SODIUM, 14 G TOTAL CARBOHYDRATE, 5 G DIETARY FIBER, 34 G PROTEIN, 75 MG CALCIUM.

POINTS PER SERVING: 5.

Venison Steaks with Blackberry Sauce

VENISON IS AVAILABLE AT SPECIALTY BUTCHERS and some supermarkets, but you may need to order it in advance. This sauce is also delicious with chicken breasts or, if you're really adventuresome, ostrich steaks.

MAKES 4 SERVINGS

1 teaspoon extra virgin olive oil
1 fennel bulb, thinly sliced
1 small head radicchio, shredded
1 pint blackberries, fresh or frozen
½ cup vegetable broth
2 sprigs thyme
1 tablespoon cornstarch
¼ cup orange juice
Two 6-ounce venison steaks

1. In a large nonstick skillet, heat the oil. Cook the fennel and radicchio over medium-low heat, stirring occasionally, until very soft, about 30 minutes. Meanwhile, preheat the broiler or grill.

2. Reserve 8–12 blackberries; combine the remainder in a small saucepan with the broth and thyme; bring to a boil, then cook until the berries are easily mashed, about 2 minutes. Transfer to a fine-mesh sieve set over a bowl; press the berries with the back of a spoon, taking care to scrape the residue from the outside of the sieve into the bowl. Return the puree to the saucepan.

3. In a small bowl, dissolve the cornstarch in the orange juice. Add to the puree. Cook over medium heat, stirring constantly, until the mixture thickens, bubbles and turns translucent, about 2 minutes.

4. Broil or grill the steaks to the desired doneness, about 1½ minutes on each side for medium-rare. Slice into thin strips.

5. To serve, divide the vegetables among 4 plates; fan the steak slices on top, then drizzle with the sauce. Garnish with the reserved berries.

PER SERVING: 217 CALORIES, 5 G TOTAL FAT, 2 G SATURATED FAT, 48 MG CHOLESTEROL, 225 MG SODIUM, 22 G TOTAL CARBOHYDRATE, 7 G DIETARY FIBER, 23 G PROTEIN, 78 MG CALCIUM.

POINTS PER SERVING: 3.

Roasted Salmon with Fennel and Potatoes

To keep the fennel sweet, take care that it doesn't brown. If it begins to brown, reduce the heat to medium-low.

MAKES 4 SERVINGS

1 pound small red potatoes
4 teaspoons olive oil
1 fennel bulb, very thinly sliced
¼ cup red-wine vinegar
¼ teaspoon salt
⅛ teaspoon freshly ground pepper
Four 7-ounce salmon steaks
2 tablespoons chopped flat-leaf parsley

1. Preheat the oven to 425° F. Put the potatoes in a medium saucepan and add cold water to cover; bring to a boil. Reduce the heat and simmer until tender, about 15 minutes. Drain, rinse briefly under cold running water, then peel and thinly slice.

2. In a medium nonstick skillet over medium heat, heat 1 teaspoon of the oil. Cook the fennel, stirring as needed, until very tender, about 15 minutes; if it begins to brown, reduce the heat. Stir in the potatoes, vinegar, salt, pepper, and the remaining 3 teaspoons of oil; cook until heated through, about 3 minutes.

3. Meanwhile, spray both sides of the salmon steaks with nonstick cooking spray; sprinkle with salt and pepper to taste. Place in a shallow roasting pan and roast until just opaque in the center, 15–20 minutes. Serve the salmon with the fennel and potatoes, sprinkled with the parsley.

Per serving: 379 Calories, 12 g Total Fat, 2 g Saturated Fat, 103 mg Cholesterol, 318 mg Sodium, 25 g Total Carbohydrate, 4 g Dietary Fiber, 43 g Protein, 66 mg Calcium.

POINTS PER SERVING: 8.

Tip: To prepare the fennel, trim off the stalks and feathery ends, cut the white bulb in half lengthwise, slice off the brown root end and thinly slice crosswise using a sturdy, sharp knife or a mandoline.

Paella Valenciana

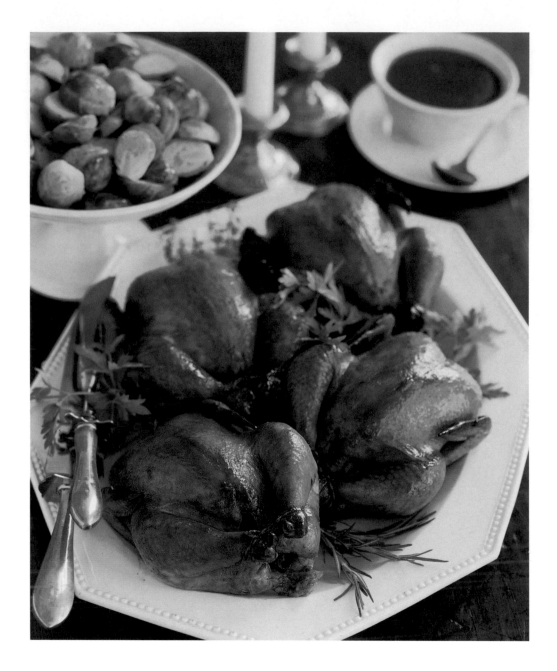

Cornish Hens with Apricot Sauce

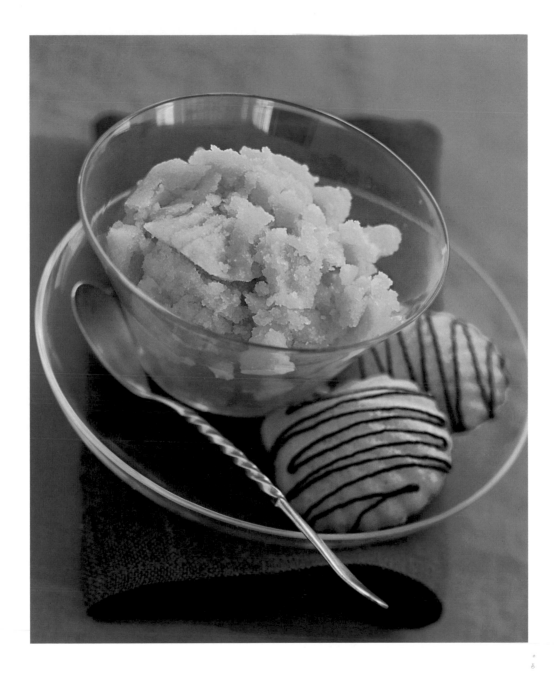

Pineapple and Orange Sorbet and Orange Madeleines

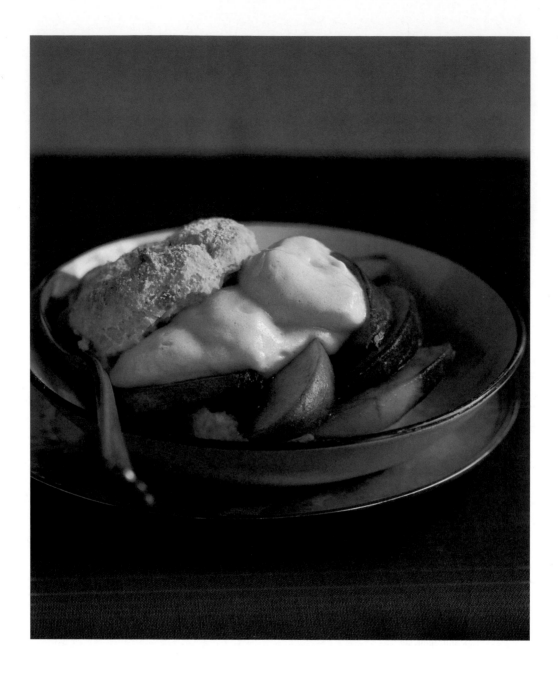

Peaches and Cream Shortcakes

Steamed Sole and Watercress

*B*OILING THE MUSHROOMS SOFTENS THEM, and it imparts a wonderful depth of flavor to the dressing. You could use cod, halibut or red snapper fillets or skate wings in place of the sole.

MAKES 4 SERVINGS

15 small dried shiitake mushrooms, stemmed
2 tablespoons Scotch whiskey
1 tablespoon canola oil
1 tablespoon red-wine vinegar
¼ teaspoon salt
⅛ teaspoon freshly ground pepper
12 very small new red potatoes, halved
Four 4-ounce sole fillets
1 bunch watercress, stemmed
Snipped chives

1. To make the dressing, combine the mushrooms and 1½ cups water in a small saucepan; bring to a boil and boil until softened, about 6 minutes. Remove the mushrooms. Add the Scotch, oil and vinegar to the water; bring back to a boil and boil 1 minute longer. Stir in the salt and pepper, cover and set aside. Thinly slice the mushrooms.

2. Steam the potatoes over boiling water until fork-tender, about 10 minutes. Wrap in foil to keep warm. Steam the fish in a single layer until it turns white and opaque, about 4 minutes.

3. To serve, divide the watercress among 4 plates; top with a fish fillet, then surround with the potatoes and scatter with the mushrooms. Drizzle with the dressing and garnish with chives.

PER SERVING: 281 CALORIES, 5 G TOTAL FAT, 1 G SATURATED FAT, 54 MG CHOLESTEROL, 247 MG SODIUM, 31 G TOTAL CARBOHYDRATE, 3 G DIETARY FIBER, 25 G PROTEIN, 31 MG CALCIUM.

POINTS PER SERVING: 5.

Tip: The easiest way to steam the fish fillets is to arrange them in a single layer on a dinner plate and put the plate into a flat-bottomed steamer basket, such as a bamboo Chinese steamer or the steamer insert of a Dutch oven. Alternatively, improvise a flat-bottomed steamer basket: Rinse out an empty tuna can and remove the bottom; place it in the center of a large saucepan. Add water to come halfway up the can and position the plate with the fish on top.

Salmon Tiles

An Asian green like bok choy would be nice in this, but kale's assertive flavor and brilliant green color are a better foil for salmon. You could also use spinach. Look for the black bean garlic sauce in the Asian section of your supermarket.

MAKES 4 SERVINGS

¼ teaspoon Asian sesame oil
1 bunch kale, cleaned and chopped
1 small red onion, thinly sliced
Four 6-ounce skinless salmon fillets
¾ cup vegetable broth
1 tablespoon black bean garlic sauce
½ tablespoon cornstarch
1 teaspoon grated peeled gingerroot

1. Coat a plate that will fit inside a steamer basket with the sesame oil. Put the kale onto the plate, scatter the onion over the kale and arrange the salmon fillets on top. Place the plate into the basket over boiling water. Steam until the fish is just opaque in the center, 10–12 minutes.

2. Meanwhile, in a small saucepan, mix the broth, black bean garlic sauce, cornstarch and gingerroot; bring to a boil, stirring constantly, then boil until thick and translucent, about 2 minutes.

3. To serve, divide the salmon and kale among 4 plates, scattering the onion over the kale. Drizzle with the sauce.

Per serving: 294 Calories, 8 g Total Fat, 0 g Saturated Fat, 121 mg Cholesterol, 855 mg Sodium, 16 g Total Carbohydrate, 3 g Dietary Fiber, 47 g Protein, 160 mg Calcium.

POINTS PER SERVING: 6.

Tip: If your only steamer basket is the collapsible style with the rod in the middle, see the Tip on page 193 for how to improvise a basket that a plate will fit on.

Sea Bass with Yellow Pepper Sauce

S$_{EA}$ $_{BASS}$, sometimes called black sea bass, is a magnificent fish with a sweet flavor and a flaky texture. It's most often prepared whole, but fillets are becoming more common. Cook it with the skin on (this helps hold the fish together), but remove the skin before eating. Striped bass, halibut, cod or ocean perch fillets can be substituted.

MAKES 4 SERVINGS

Four 7-ounce sea bass fillets
1 yellow bell pepper, roasted*
⅓ cup dry white wine
1 tablespoon fresh lemon juice
2 tablespoons chopped basil
1 teaspoon capers, rinsed and drained
¼ teaspoon salt
⅛ teaspoon freshly ground pepper

1. Preheat the oven to 450° F; spray a large baking dish with nonstick cooking spray. Place the fillets in a single layer in the dish. Roast until the fish is opaque in the center and flakes easily, 10–12 minutes.

2. Meanwhile, in a food processor or blender, puree the roasted pepper, wine and lemon juice. Transfer to a small nonstick skillet and cook, stirring occasionally, until thickened, about 3 minutes. Stir in the basil, capers, salt and pepper. Serve the fish, topped with the sauce.

PER SERVING: 215 CALORIES, 4 G TOTAL FAT, 1 G SATURATED FAT, 81 MG CHOLESTEROL, 308 MG SODIUM, 3 G TOTAL CARBOHYDRATE, 1 G DIETARY FIBER, 37 G PROTEIN, 27 MG CALCIUM.

POINTS PER SERVING: 4.

Tip: Roasted red bell pepper can be substituted for the yellow. One 7-ounce jar of roasted peppers is the equivalent of 1 fresh bell pepper, roasted.

*To roast bell pepper, preheat broiler. Line baking sheet with foil; place pepper on baking sheet. Broil 4–6" from heat, turning frequently with tongs, until skin is lightly charred on all sides, about 10 minutes. Transfer to paper bag; fold bag closed and steam 10 minutes. Peel, seed and devein pepper over a bowl to catch juices.

Fideua

FIDEUA SOMEWHAT RESEMBLES A PAELLA. The key differences: It is made with pasta, traditionally the Spanish noodles called *fideos*, and it is made only with seafood. Traditionally, the shells are left on the shrimp to flavor the stock.

MAKES 8 SERVINGS

¾ pound large shrimp
2 teaspoons olive oil
¾ pound sea scallops
¾ pound halibut steak, cut into 8 chunks
3 cups low-sodium chicken broth
Two 8-ounce bottles clam juice
1 teaspoon paprika
2 garlic cloves, minced
1 pound fideos or bucatini

1. Preheat the oven to 425° F. Under cold running water, slit the shell of each shrimp gently down the back and devein; leave the shells on the shrimp.

2. In a large skillet with an ovenproof handle, heat 1 teaspoon of the oil. Sauté the shrimp until the shells just begin to brown, about 1 minute. Transfer to a plate.

3. Heat the remaining teaspoon of oil. Sauté the scallops and halibut until they just begin to color, about 2 minutes. Stir in the broth, clam juice, paprika and garlic; bring to a boil. Add the fideos to the mixture, pushing them down with a spoon. Bake 10 minutes, then stir to separate the noodles; add the shrimp. Return to the oven and bake until the liquid is absorbed and the pasta is tender, about 10 minutes longer.

PER SERVING: 230 CALORIES, 4 G TOTAL FAT, 1 G SATURATED FAT, 94 MG CHOLESTEROL, 196 MG SODIUM, 18 G TOTAL CARBOHYDRATE, 2 G DIETARY FIBER, 29 G PROTEIN, 66 MG CALCIUM.

POINTS PER SERVING: 5.

Tip: Fideos are available in many supermarkets; they are long strands, but they come in little nests. Bucatini are long pasta with holes running down the center. You could substitute either fettuccine or linguine. If you use bucatini, fettuccine or linguine, break the strands in half before adding them to the broth.

Desserts

Pineapple and Orange Sorbet

*E*VEN IF YOU USUALLY SHUN CANNED FRUIT, you must try this dessert. Canned fruit makes this recipe almost criminally easy, and you'd never guess you're not eating the freshest fruits, laboriously processed. When pureed, the pineapple takes on a pale off-white hue evocative of cream-laden sherbet.

MAKES 8 SERVINGS

One 20-ounce can crushed pineapple in heavy syrup, frozen
One 8-ounce can mandarin oranges in light syrup, frozen
¼ cup packed light brown sugar
¼ cup golden rum

Open the cans on both ends and push the frozen fruit onto a cutting board. Cut into quarters, then transfer to a food processor and pulse about 20 times to break up. Pulse in the brown sugar. With the machine running, drizzle in the rum; process until smooth, about 20 seconds. Spoon the sorbet into parfait glasses.

PER SERVING: 123 CALORIES, 0 G TOTAL FAT, 0 G SATURATED FAT, 0 MG CHOLESTEROL, 5 MG SODIUM, 28 G TOTAL CARBOHYDRATE, 1 G DIETARY FIBER, 0 G PROTEIN, 19 MG CALCIUM.

POINTS PER SERVING: 2.

Tip: It will take the fruit about 8–12 hours to freeze completely. If the frozen fruit does not push out of the can easily, hold the can sideways under hot running water for about 10 seconds, taking care not to moisten the fruit.

Banana Crème Caramel

CARAMEL, BANANA AND RUM combine to make a creamy, superrich dessert with tropical flair. This is the ideal party dish, whether you're hosting or you have to bring a dessert. It's a real show-stopper, and since it needs to chill for several hours, it's a make-ahead (up to a day in advance). The longer it sits, the more the caramel topping will liquefy and take on a saucelike consistency.

MAKES 16 SERVINGS

2 cups mashed ripe bananas (about 5 bananas)
One 14-ounce can fat-free sweetened condensed milk
One 12-ounce can evaporated skimmed milk
1 cup fat-free egg substitute
⅓ cup golden rum
1 egg
½ tablespoon vanilla extract
1 cup sugar

1. Preheat the oven to 325° F.

2. In a large bowl, combine the bananas, condensed milk, evaporated milk, egg substitute, rum, egg and vanilla; whisk until well blended and frothy.

3. In a small heavy-bottomed saucepan, combine the sugar and 3 tablespoons water over high heat. Cook, stirring constantly, until the sugar dissolves, 1–2 minutes. Reduce the heat to medium and cook, swirling the pan occasionally (do not stir), until the mixture has become a very thin liquid and is a deep caramel brown, 7–10 minutes. Pour the caramel syrup into two 4-cup glass bowls or soufflé dishes, swirling to coat the bottoms and partway up the sides. Pour the banana mixture into the bowls.

4. Put the bowls into a large baking dish; add enough hot water to the baking dish to come halfway up the sides of the bowls. Bake until the custards are set and a knife inserted in the center of a custard comes out clean, about 1½ hours. Cool on a rack, then refrigerate, covered, until thoroughly chilled, at least 4 hours.

5. To serve, invert the custards onto platters, letting the caramel syrup pool around the custard. Cut each into 8 servings.

PER SERVING: 219 CALORIES, 1 G TOTAL FAT, 0 G SATURATED FAT, 50 MG CHOLESTEROL, 201 MG SODIUM, 79 G TOTAL CARBOHYDRATE, 1 G DIETARY FIBER, 14 G PROTEIN, 213 MG CALCIUM.

POINTS PER SERVING: 4.

Tip: Sugar syrup can be very temperamental; once the sugar dissolves, take care not to stir the syrup lest it seize up on you. And be *very* careful when pouring the caramel syrup into the bowls. Because it's so sticky, if the syrup gets on your skin it can result in a painful burn.

To cut the baking time by two-thirds, make this in sixteen 6-ounce ramekins instead of two 4-cup bowls. Swirl about ½ tablespoon of the caramel syrup into each ramekin, then put them in the baking dish and fill the dish with hot water. Pour the custard into the ramekins (if you've made the custard in a mixing bowl with a pour spout, this is very easy). These individual custards only need to bake 25–35 minutes.

Chocolate Mousse

Use the best quality chocolate possible. Substitute semisweet or milk chocolate, according to your preference. Serve the mousse on dessert plates or in goblets or other pretty stemmed glasses, garnished with fresh fruit.

MAKES 12 SERVINGS

8 ounces bittersweet chocolate, melted
3 tablespoons orange liqueur
2 tablespoons light corn syrup
¼ cup powdered egg whites
½ cup sugar

1. In a large bowl, mix the chocolate, liqueur and corn syrup. In another large bowl, combine the powdered egg whites and ¾ cup warm water, stirring until the powder dissolves completely, about 2 minutes. With an electric mixer at low speed, beat until foamy; increase the speed to medium and beat until soft peaks form. While mixing, slowly add the sugar. Increase the speed to medium-high and continue beating until stiff, glossy peaks form.

2. With a rubber spatula, stir about one-third of the meringue into the chocolate mixture. Stir well, then fold in another third of the meringue. Gently fold in the remaining meringue until completely blended. Refrigerate the mousse, covered, until firm, at least 3 hours.

Per serving: 150 Calories, 6 g Total Fat, 4 g Saturated Fat, 1 mg Cholesterol, 29 mg Sodium, 21 g Total Carbohydrate, 1 g Dietary Fiber, 3 g Protein, 11 mg Calcium.

POINTS PER SERVING: 3.

Tip: To melt the chocolate, microwave chopped chocolate at 50 percent power for about 4 minutes, stirring every minute. If you microwave it in a large bowl, you'll have one less dish to wash.

Chocolate Bread Pudding

*H*OMEY BREAD PUDDING, all the rage of late, is now being dished up in such new flavor variations as chocolate. If you can't find challah, substitute another egg bread or Vienna bread.

MAKES 12 SERVINGS

⅓ cup boiling water
3 tablespoons unsweetened Dutch processed cocoa powder
1 tablespoon light corn syrup
Two 12-ounce cans evaporated skimmed milk
1 cup packed light brown sugar
½ cup fat-free egg substitute
2 eggs
2 teaspoons vanilla extract
6 cups cubed challah bread (about ½ loaf)

1. In a small bowl, combine the boiling water, cocoa powder and corn syrup. In a large bowl, whisk together the evaporated milk, brown sugar, egg substitute, eggs and vanilla. Whisk in the cocoa mixture, then stir in the bread cubes. Let stand until the bread absorbs some of the liquid and softens slightly, about 30 minutes.

2. Preheat the oven to 350° F. Pour the mixture into a 5 x 9" loaf pan. Place the loaf pan inside a larger baking dish on the middle oven rack. Pour enough hot water into the baking dish to come halfway up the sides of the loaf pan. Bake until the pudding is set and a knife inserted in the center comes out clean, 55–65 minutes. Cool the pudding in the pan on a wire rack. Serve at room temperature or chilled.

PER SERVING: 203 CALORIES, 2 G TOTAL FAT, 1 G SATURATED FAT, 46 MG CHOLESTEROL, 200 MG SODIUM, 35 G TOTAL CARBOHYDRATE, 1 G DIETARY FIBER, 8 G PROTEIN, 44 MG CALCIUM.

POINTS PER SERVING: 4.

New York–Style Strawberry Cheesecake

THIS RECIPE USES NONFAT COOKING SPRAY in lieu of butter to make a graham cracker crust. Be sure to let the cake cool completely in the pan. If you release the springform pan's clamp too soon, the cake may fall.

MAKES 16 SERVINGS

¼ cup fine graham cracker crumbs
Two 8-ounce packages Neufchâtel cheese
Two 8-ounce packages nonfat cream cheese
1 cup sugar
3 tablespoons all-purpose flour
1½ cups fat-free egg substitute
1 tablespoon vanilla extract
1 teaspoon grated lemon zest
3 tablespoons currant jelly, melted
1 quart strawberries, cleaned and hulled

1. Preheat the oven to 325° F; spray the inside of a 9" springform pan with nonstick cooking spray and dust with the graham cracker crumbs.

2. In a large bowl, with an electric mixer at medium speed, beat both kinds of cheese, the sugar and flour until well blended. While mixing, drizzle in the egg substitute. Continue to beat until light and fluffy. Mix in the vanilla and lemon zest. Pour into the pan. Bake until the cake is golden and firm to the touch and a tester inserted into the center comes out clean, about 1 hour. Cool completely in the pan on a wire rack, 2–3 hours, then cover with foil and refrigerate at least 1 hour or until ready to serve.

3. Lightly brush the top of the cake with some of the melted jelly. Place the strawberries on top, hulled-side down, then drizzle with the remainder of the jelly.

PER SERVING: 212 CALORIES, 8 G TOTAL FAT, 5 G SATURATED FAT, 24 MG CHOLESTEROL, 322 MG SODIUM, 25 G TOTAL CARBOHYDRATE, 2 G DIETARY FIBER, 11 G PROTEIN, 95 MG CALCIUM.

POINTS PER SERVING: 5.

Raspberry Napoleons

YOU CAN FINISH THE NAPOLEONS with a dusting of confectioners' sugar, a drizzling of melted semisweet chocolate, or frost them with confectioners' sugar mixed with a little fat-free milk.

MAKES 6 SERVINGS

Two 12 x 17" sheets phyllo dough, at room temperature
2 tablespoons + 2 teaspoons sugar
⅓ cup fat-free egg substitute
⅔ cup fat-free milk
½ tablespoon cornstarch
1 teaspoon vanilla extract
1 pint raspberries, picked over

1. Preheat the oven to 400° F. Place 1 sheet of the phyllo on a work surface and spray with nonstick cooking spray. Dust with 1 teaspoon of the sugar. Place the second sheet on top, spray it, and dust with another teaspoon of the sugar. Cut in half crosswise and position one half on top of the other to form an 8½ x 12" rectangle. Cut into twelve 4¼ x 2" pieces and transfer to a baking sheet. Bake until browned, 4–5 minutes. Cool in the pan on a rack.

2. In a bowl, whisk the egg substitute and the remaining 2 tablespoons of sugar. In a small saucepan, heat the milk over low heat until it begins to steam, 2–3 minutes. While whisking, drizzle the milk into the egg substitute mixture. Pour this mixture into the saucepan and cook over medium-low heat, stirring constantly, just until thick enough to coat the back of a spoon, 8–10 minutes. Dissolve the cornstarch in the vanilla and add it to the milk mixture. Cook, stirring, until the custard is very thick, 5–6 minutes longer.

3. Spread 2 tablespoons of custard on each of 6 phyllo rectangles. Divide the raspberries over the custard, then top each with a second phyllo rectangle.

PER SERVING: 99 CALORIES, 2 G TOTAL FAT, 0 G SATURATED FAT, 1 MG CHOLESTEROL, 95 MG SODIUM, 16 G TOTAL CARBOHYDRATE, 3 G DIETARY FIBER, 5 G PROTEIN, 58 MG CALCIUM.

POINTS PER SERVING: 2.

Tip: For a single large tart, bake the 8½ x 12" layered phyllo rectangle intact, without cutting it into pieces, then thinly spread with the custard and top with 2 pints of raspberries.

Peaches and Cream Shortcakes

SHORTCAKES WERE ORIGINALLY MORE OF A SPONGE CAKE, but buttermilk biscuits or baking powder biscuits are now commonly used. For variety, use 1 pint of blueberries or slice 1 pint of strawberries, or use a mixture of berries, for the peaches.

MAKES 8 SERVINGS

2 cups all-purpose flour
1 tablespoon baking powder
1 tablespoon grated orange zest
1 teaspoon chopped crystallized ginger
¼ teaspoon salt
1 cup low-fat buttermilk
3 peaches, thinly sliced
¼ cup granulated sugar
¾ cup evaporated skimmed milk, chilled
1½ tablespoons confectioners' sugar

1. Preheat the oven to 425° F.

2. In a large bowl, whisk the flour, baking powder, orange zest, ginger and salt. Stir in the buttermilk to form a soft dough. With floured hands, knead the dough into a ball in the bowl, working in any excess flour. Transfer to a lightly floured work surface and pat into a 7 x 8" rectangle about ½" thick. Using a biscuit cutter or a glass, cut out eight 2½" rounds, pushing the dough scraps together for the last rounds, if necessary. Place the rounds on a nonstick baking sheet and bake until lightly golden, about 12 minutes. Cool completely on a wire rack. Meanwhile, combine the peaches and sugar in a bowl; let stand 15–20 minutes.

3. To make the whipped topping, pour the evaporated milk into a chilled bowl. With an electric mixer at high speed, beat until frothy. While mixing, slowly sprinkle with the confectioners' sugar; continue to beat until soft peaks form, about 3–4 minutes.

4. Split the biscuits open. Layer with the peaches, then dollop with the whipped topping.

PER SERVING: 197 CALORIES, 1 G TOTAL FAT, 0 G SATURATED FAT, 3 MG CHOLESTEROL, 219 MG SODIUM, 41 G TOTAL CARBOHYDRATE, 2 G DIETARY FIBER, 6 G PROTEIN, 43 MG CALCIUM.

POINTS PER SERVING: 4.

Tip: Although you can't whip evaporated skimmed milk until it's really firm, it's a great "fake-out" for softly whipped cream. For best results, put the bowl and beaters in the freezer about 20 minutes before beating and make sure the evaporated skimmed milk is very well chilled.

Lemon-Glazed Tea Cake

*I*F YOU GLAZE THIS CAKE WHILE IT'S STILL WARM, all of the lemon sugar syrup will soak into the cake. If you prefer a harder glaze, double the amount of lemon juice and sugar in Step 4; pour half on while the cake is warm and the remainder after both the cake and the syrup have cooled. You can also dust the glazed cake with a bit of confectioners' sugar, if you like.

MAKES 12 SERVINGS

1 cup + 6 tablespoons sugar
1 cup cake flour
1 teaspoon baking powder
¼ teaspoon salt
⅓ cup fat-free egg substitute
2 tablespoons canola oil
1 egg yolk
4 teaspoons grated lemon zest
1 teaspoon vanilla extract
5 egg whites, at room temperature
¼ cup fresh lemon juice

1. Preheat the oven to 350° F; spray a 10" Bundt pan with nonstick cooking spray.

2. Sift ¾ cup of the sugar, the flour, baking powder and salt into a large bowl. Whisk in the egg substitute, oil, egg yolk, lemon zest and vanilla until smoothly blended.

3. In another bowl, with an electric mixer at medium-high speed, beat the egg whites until thick. While mixing, gradually add ¼ cup of the sugar. Beat until stiff, glossy peaks form. With a rubber spatula, fold about one-third of the meringue into the flour mixture. Stir well, then fold in the remainder of the meringue. Pour into the pan. Bake until a tester inserted into the center of the cake comes out clean, about 30 minutes. Cool in the pan on a rack 10 minutes, then unmold the cake onto the rack.

4. In a small saucepan over medium heat, combine the lemon juice and remaining 6 tablespoons of sugar. Cook, stirring constantly, until the sugar dissolves completely, about 2 minutes. Pour over the cake and allow to cool completely before serving.

PER SERVING: 158 CALORIES, 3 G TOTAL FAT, 0 G SATURATED FAT, 18 MG CHOLESTEROL, 104 MG SODIUM, 30 G TOTAL CARBOHYDRATE, 0 G DIETARY FIBER, 3 G PROTEIN, 9 MG CALCIUM.

POINTS PER SERVING: 3.

Tip: When you glaze the cake, place a sheet of foil under the cooling rack to catch the syrup. Pour any syrup that drips onto the foil back over the cake.

Lemon Curd Tartlets

*T*HICK, RICH AND TANGY LEMON CURD makes a wonderful tart filling, or spread it between cake layers—or, for a fast but decadent snack, on graham crackers. Our lightened version provides only 3 **POINTS** per tablespoon!

MAKES 8 SERVINGS

¾ cup sugar
½ cup fat-free egg substitute
⅓ cup + 2 tablespoons fresh lemon juice
4 tablespoons chilled unsalted butter
1 tablespoon cornstarch
1 teaspoon grated lemon zest
8 mini phyllo dough cups, at room temperature

1. In a medium saucepan over medium-low heat, combine the sugar, egg substitute and ⅓ cup of the lemon juice. Cook, stirring constantly, until steaming, about 3 minutes. While stirring, add the butter 1 tablespoon at a time, allowing it to melt completely between additions. Remove from the heat.

2. In a small bowl, dissolve the cornstarch in the remaining 2 tablespoons of lemon juice. Stir into the saucepan along with the lemon zest. Cook over medium heat until the mixture is bubbling and thick enough to coat the back of a spoon, about 10 minutes. Spoon 1 tablespoon of the lemon curd into each of the phyllo shells. Chill 1 hour before serving.

PER SERVING: 175 CALORIES, 4 G TOTAL FAT, 2 G SATURATED FAT, 8 MG CHOLESTEROL, 121 MG SODIUM, 31 G TOTAL CARBOHYDRATE, 0 G DIETARY FIBER, 4 G PROTEIN, 14 MG CALCIUM.

POINTS PER SERVING: 4.

Tip: Allow the curd to cook for the full 10 minutes after adding the cornstarch, even if it appears to be done earlier. Cornstarch needs to cook until bubbling to thicken properly.

Ginger Crisp Cookies

DESPITE THE TABLESPOON OF GROUND GINGER, these crispy cookies actually have a fairly subtle flavor. To boost the spiciness, replace up to 3 tablespoons of the ½ cup granulated sugar used in the cookie dough with dark brown sugar; this will also produce a slightly chewier cookie.

MAKES 24 SERVINGS

1 cup all-purpose flour
1 tablespoon ground ginger
½ teaspoon cinnamon
¼ teaspoon baking soda
¼ teaspoon salt
⅛ teaspoon ground allspice
¾ cup sugar
4 tablespoons unsalted butter, at room temperature
1 egg
2 tablespoons dark molasses

1. Preheat the oven to 350° F. In a medium bowl, whisk the flour, ginger, cinnamon, baking soda, salt and allspice. Reserve ¼ cup of the sugar in a small bowl.

2. In a large bowl, with an electric mixer at medium speed, cream the remaining ½ cup sugar and the butter. Mix in the egg and molasses, continuing to beat until combined. Mix in the dry ingredients. Drop the dough onto baking sheets by the tablespoonful, leaving 2–3" between cookies, making 24 cookies. Spray the bottom of a 2½" glass with nonstick cooking spray. Dip it into the bowl of sugar and flatten a mound of dough. Continue to dip and flatten the remainder of the cookie dough. Bake until the cookies are firm to the touch and lightly colored around the edges, 10–12 minutes. Cool on the baking sheet on a wire rack 10 minutes, then remove the cookies from the baking sheet and cool completely on the rack.

PER SERVING: 68 CALORIES, 2 G TOTAL FAT, 1 G SATURATED FAT, 13 MG CHOLESTEROL, 41 MG SODIUM, 12 G TOTAL CARBOHYDRATE, 0 G DIETARY FIBER, 1 G PROTEIN, 7 MG CALCIUM.

POINTS PER SERVING: 2.

Tip: For a slightly sweeter cookie, roll each tablespoonful of dough in sugar before placing onto the baking sheet; flatten them with a plain glass.

Orange Madeleines

Madeleines are little shell-shaped cakes, crisp around the edge and spongy inside. They are baked in special molds with scallop-shell-shaped indentations; if you prefer, you can bake mini muffins instead.

MAKES 12 SERVINGS

¼ cup fat-free egg substitute
¼ cup + 2 tablespoons confectioners' sugar
2 tablespoons unsalted butter, melted
1 teaspoon orange liqueur
3 tablespoons all-purpose flour
1 teaspoon grated orange zest
1 tablespoon chopped bittersweet chocolate

1. Preheat the oven to 350° F. Spray a 12-shell madeleine mold with nonstick cooking spray.

2. In a large bowl, whisk the egg substitute until frothy. Whisk in the confectioners' sugar, butter and liqueur, then stir in the flour and orange zest. Spoon 1 tablespoon of the batter into each shell of the madeleine mold. Bake until golden brown, 11–12 minutes. Cool in the mold on a wire rack 1 minute, then remove the madeleines from the mold and cool completely on the rack.

3. Put the chocolate into a microwavable bowl. Microwave at 50 percent power about 1½ minutes, stirring every 30 seconds, until melted. Using a small spoon, drizzle over the cooled madeleines.

Per serving: 62 Calories, 2 g Total Fat, 1 g Saturated Fat, 5 mg Cholesterol, 10 mg Sodium, 9 g Total Carbohydrate, 0 g Dietary Fiber, 1 g Protein, 4 mg Calcium.

POINTS PER SERVING: 1.

Chocolate Cherry Biscotti

GLACÉ CHERRIES, sometimes called candied cherries, have been dried and then coated with a sugar syrup. If you prefer, you may substitute an equal amount of dried cherries, raisins or whole almonds for the glacé cherries.

MAKES 30 SERVINGS

1 cup fat-free egg substitute
¼ cup packed dark brown sugar
4 teaspoons vanilla extract
2 cups all-purpose flour
1 cup + 2 tablespoons unsweetened Dutch processed cocoa powder
¾ cup granulated sugar
2 teaspoons baking powder
½ teaspoon salt
1¼ cups glacé cherries

1. Preheat the oven to 350° F. Line a large baking sheet with baker's parchment, nonstick plastic ovenware liner or wax paper.

2. In a small bowl, combine the egg substitute, brown sugar and vanilla; whisk until frothy. In a large bowl, combine the flour, cocoa, granulated sugar, baking powder and salt. Stir in the cherries, then add the egg mixture and stir to form a dough.

3. Transfer the dough to a lightly floured work surface and divide it in half. Transfer the halves to the baking sheet and, with floured hands, form each into a long, thin loaf about ¾" high. Bake until well risen and firm to the touch, 25–35 minutes. Cut the loaves into ¾" slices and stand them upright on the baking sheet. Bake until crisp and dry to the touch, about 20 minutes. Cool the slices on wire racks.

PER SERVING: 82 CALORIES, 1 G TOTAL FAT, 0 G SATURATED FAT, 0 MG CHOLESTEROL, 71 MG SODIUM, 17 G TOTAL CARBOHYDRATE, 2 G DIETARY FIBER, 3 G PROTEIN, 13 MG CALCIUM.

POINTS PER SERVING: 1.

Tip: To gild the lily, make Black and White Dipped Biscotti: Melt 6 ounces white chocolate in a glass measuring cup. Dip half of each biscotti into the white chocolate, set onto wax paper sprayed with nonstick cooking spray and let harden. Then melt 6 ounces semisweet chocolate in a glass measuring cup, dip the other half of each biscotti and let harden on sprayed wax paper. For a less intense but very pretty variation, melt 2 ounces white chocolate and, with a small spoon, drizzle over the cooled biscotti.

Index

Photo Credits

Following page 32

First page: *top*, Lord Lichfield; *middle and bottom*,
Jayne Fincher/Photographers International.
Second page: Private collection of The Duchess of York.
Third page: Courtesy of Weight Watchers.
Fourth page: *top*, Courtesy of Weight Watchers; *bottom*, Brian Iris.

All other photos by Rita Maas